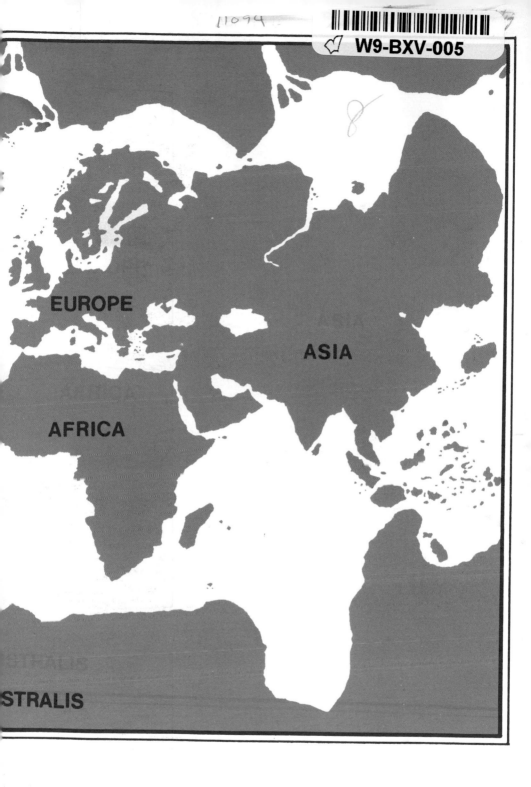

EUROPE

ASIA

AFRICA

STRALIS

WORLD — 1569

Drake, the World and the Golden Hind.

Drake, Captain of the South Seas

by

Grover S. McLeod

Artist: John Anderson

DEDICATION

I do hereby respectfully dedicate this book to Captain Edward L. Beach, USN Ret., Author, Great Submariner and Voyager, being the first submarine captain to sail the world submerged, doing it in the USS Triton SSN 568 (1960).

I do hereby also respectfully dedicate this book to my shipmate Captain Paul C. Stimson, great World War II submarine skipper, being the first submarine Captain to sail around The Horn, doing it in the USS Sea Robin SS 407 (June 1, 1947).

GROVER S. McLEOD

BOOKS BY GROVER S. MCLEOD

The Genealogy of Neil McLeod, Progenitor of a Clan

Sub Sailor

Teodoro

Sketches from the Bar

Stories About Women

Submarine Stories

Civil Actions at Law in Alabama

Equitable Remedies and Extraordinary Writs in Alabama

Trial Practice and Procedure in Alabama

Sub Duty

Civil Actions at Law in Alabama, Second Edition
(with pocket parts)

The Ghost of the Chimera and The Stowaway

Sultan's Gold and Other Fleet-Type Submarine Stories

The Trials of Fat, an Illustrious Member of the Criminal Bar

Worker's Compensation for On-the-Job Injuries in Alabama
(with pocket parts)

Trial Practice and Procedure in Alabama, Second Edition

The Legal Circus

Equitable Remedies and Extraordinary Writs in Alabama,
Second Edition

Drake, Captain of the South Seas

TABLE OF CONTENTS

TABLE OF CONTENTS
(CONTINUED)

ILLUSTRATIONS

PROLOGUE

The Middle Ages had ended and Protestant England was attempting to cast off the shroud of the church of Rome. She was now being led by a young queen who was nimbly seeking her way in a world that was dominated by Spain and Portugal. Even so, it was a time for adventure by sea, which was made much easier because most knowledgeable people now believed that the world was round. But England had only played a minor role in such adventure until a pirate by the name of Francis Drake burst upon the scene—and what a man was he! For he not only was the first sea captain to sail around the world, but in doing so, he returned to England with a shipload of treasure that he had pirated from the Spanish Empire. And Drake, in winning that treasure, experienced many adventures, most of which are worth relating. The circumnavigation alone would have made a great story, but adding to it the story of how Drake won all that treasure makes it an extraordinary one. And with that explanation having been said, the writer is pleased to present to you the full story of Drake's circumnavigation, being possibly the greatest sea voyage ever made.

GROVER S. McLEOD

CHAPTER 1

NOMBRE DIOS

"¿Le gusta, Capitan?" Do you like it? the Cimaron asked the white man standing beside him while he studied his sweat-soaked face, looking for signs. The white man had a youthful but hard face, while his eyes were gray and steeled. He was of middle size but very manly, as he had an athletic body, muscular arms and a thick chest. He wore a red beard, a ragged straw hat, a worn shirt, cutaway trousers and sandals.

Moments before, the white man, Francis Drake, had followed the Cimaron to the top of a tall tree by climbing cleaved steps. He now was standing in the canopy of a Panama jungle, being one hundred fifty feet above the ground. He stood on a clumsy platform that the Cimarons had constructed so that they could view two great bodies of water. And now the Cimaron standing before him was proudly pointing out these bodies of water. Drake looked from his left to his right, seeing on either side of him a great body of water— he now faced the Pacific Ocean. His face became flushed from thinking on this ocean that then was called the South Sea.

Drake was a seaman adventurer who had spent much of his life at sea. He had spent the last few years sailing strange waters, but he had not sailed the South Sea. And so the sight of it had so excited him until he had hardly noticed his surroundings. He had not even taken notice of the beautiful bromeliads, orchids and ferns that profusely grew on the limbs of the adjacent trees. He was even oblivious of a green snake that was staring at him with a frog in its mouth. And the snake knew it, as it bodaciously locked its jaws onto the frog and stared at this man with strawberry red hair and beard.

Strangely, Francis Drake, the pirate, now standing in a rare viewing station of a Panamanian rain forest, only saw the sea.

1

Drake: "I shall sail the South Sea!"

"Me gusta, Diego." I like it, Diego, Francis Drake replied, smiling, thinking, speaking to the youthful black man facing him. Drake spoke in Spanish, a language which he had acquired a speaking acquaintance with during his forays to the Spanish Main. The ebullience in Drake's eyes indicated his pleasure. But it was not the canopy or really the view itself that pleased him, but rather the South Sea and the adventure that it conjured.

"¡Magnifico!" the Cimaron exclaimed. Many months before Drake had captured this black man from a party of Spaniards who had enslaved him. Drake had freed him, then he had made a friend of him. Diego in turn had solidified Drake's relationship with the Cimarons, being mostly a mixed race of Blacks, Spaniards and Indians who lived in the jungles and savannahs of Panama. Their leader was Pedro, a brown-skinned man who was on the ground. Sweat from Diego's body had soaked his thin shirt; his sweat, now thick and oily, was attracting a swarm of gnats. They buzzed him. The heat was irritating the monkeys in an adjacent tree. They pointed their noses at the men using the platform in their tree top. They then opened their mouths and screamed defiance at them for their intrusion.

"What do you think, John?" Drake asked a second white man who had cautiously taken a seat on the tree perch and was apprehensively searching. This was John Oxenham, second in command of Drake's small force that was now on a scouting expedition. Oxenham cautiously looked from one body of water to the other.

"The Caribe—" Oxenham softly exclaimed on studying the azure water of the Caribbean which was on his right.

"Yes," Drake replied. "It is the Caribe," he added, showing his teeth. Drake was not as tall as Oxenham, though he was more stockily built. Drake's face was red and splotched with freckles, being almost the same color as his hair, which was now covered with a straw hat. Sweat also poured from his forehead. The air was humid and smelled of overripe flowers. Drake frowned, continuing to show his teeth; yet his voice bounded with enthusiasm.

"Now, John, turn and face the opposite way!" Drake said on looking toward the Pacific.

"The South Sea!" Oxenham exclaimed with disbelief, using the then accepted name for the Pacific Ocean.

"Right," Drake said, smiling intently, studying the sea. "I shall sail it one day!" Drake confidently said. Then Drake dropped to his knees to a position of prayer, as he was a very religious person, which was most unusual for a pirate. He now was being respectfully watched by the other two men who were crowded onto the rooftop floor. Drake raised his hand above his ear for quiet as if demanding everyone, including the monkeys, the insects and the birds, to cease their noisemaking.

"Dear God, you continue to bless me—and I thank thee for it. I especially thank thee for permitting me to see the South Sea—please show me the way to sail it," he earnestly said, as though it were an absolute must that he do it. "And once I reach it, I shall endeavor to do my best to punish those Spaniards for their transgressions against your word—for I know that they are not true believers, as they are idolaters. Amen."

"And I shall sail with thee," added John Oxenham, who now was resting on a single knee in an attempt to attain a prayerful stance and not fall. "I shall sail it also unless you advise against it!" he solemnly said, making a commitment that would have future importance to him as well as to Drake.

"And you shall go!" Drake said, now staring at the Pacific, as if he were hypnotized by the calm body of water. He broke his stare, stood and said, "Come, we must descend, for we have things to do!"

The three men returned to the ground, where they joined their scouting group which was now within a day's march of Panama, being the Pacific port city for which the treasure ships from Peru delivered their treasure. Drake knew that the rains had ceased and the fevers had subsided—thus, the Peruvian treasure would soon be arriving. It would then be secured to the backs of mules and transported by heavily-guarded caravans across the Isthmus of Panama by way of the Camino Real, being a road paved with stones that crossed the Isthmus to Nombre Dios. On the treasure reaching Nombre Dios, it would then be stored inside the fort and guarded until the Spanish treasure fleet arrived to transport it to Spain. The first caravan from Peru was now expected. Many merchants from Spain and the New World recently had arrived in Nombre Dios and formed a market. Those merchants from Spain had set up booths and tables to display their wares of manufactured goods. Those merchants from the provinces had set up booths and tables to display their wares of cacao beans, vicuna wool, bezoar poisons, pearls, emeralds, gold, silver, hides, indigo and cochineal, being a red dye made from insects. The fair also had its entertainers. Many jugglers and fiddlers were already

4

entertaining for coins. A dozen brightly painted prostitutes had erected flashy tents on a back row—these were elaborate tents that were lined with grayish-red silk and damask, an alluring color to help them entice the merchants, sailors and soldiers inside.

Drake was accompanied by seventeen Englishmen and thirty Cimarons. Most of the Cimarons were a mixture of Indian and Spanish.

Drake had begun his voyage on May 24, 1572. It was on that date that he had sailed from Plymouth, England, with seventy-three men. It was now eight months since he set sail for the Spanish Main. So far the venture had been a costly one. He had lost many men. Some had been killed in battles with the Spaniards, while others had died of fever. Two of those dead had been brothers of Drake.

On Drake's first expedition to the Spanish Main, he had discovered an isolated harbor in the Bay of Darin, being south of Nombre Dios. He had found it to be so safe from discovery that he had made it his operations base, naming it Port Pheasant. On this trip he had left at the hideaway those men who were recuperating from wounds or fevers.

During the beginning of this venture, Drake had devised a plan to attack the fort city of Nombre Dios. This had been a bodacious plan, for Nombre Dios was a city fortress as large as Plymouth. It was here on the Atlantic side of the Isthmus of Panama that the Spaniards stored the treasure that they garnered from Peru until a convoy of ships arrived to transport it to Spain. On Drake learning that its treasury was filled with gold and silver due to a delay in the treasury fleet, he decided to capture the fortress. The Cimarons' leader, Pedro, had previously revealed to Drake the Spanish fortification plans for Nombre Dios. Pedro then had presented Drake with a map that gave him the location of the soldiers' barracks and their large guns. Then on a moonless night in July 1572, Drake led his small army in an attack on Nombre Dios. The attack was successful from the start, for Drake's forces easily got into the fort—and surprisingly the Spaniards panicked as they thought that the attacking force was much larger than it actually was; and so they broke and ran. The fort's treasure seemingly was in Drake's hands. But then the rains came, falling in torrents. Worse, Drake was struck in the leg by a rifle ball, and he began to lose blood. He soon lost consciousness. And on Drake's men learning of his condition, they became so crestfallen that they abandoned the attack, as they were leaderless without Drake. In

5

doing so, Drake lost the chance to capture tons of gold and silver, being the last treasure of the season. Drake was dismayed but not defeated, for on his leg healing, he again began the pursuit of Spanish treasure.

"Sh!" Pedro, the Cimaron leader, whispered. He was standing beside Drake. The two men were in elephant grass up to their shoulders. The grass was sharp and cut when it touched the skin. A snake rustled the grass; it was ignored. The humidity had become oppressive for there was little movement of air. Diego pointed in the direction of Panama, being the city where the Spaniards brought the Peruvian gold. It was just a day's march away. Yet this was the closest that they would get to it. They were waiting for a report from a Cimaron who was on a spying mission. Drake had wanted to learn when the first treasure train would be crossing the isthmus and the number of its guards.

"¿Que?" What? Drake asked. He was inquiring as to the reason for the caution.

"¡Oye!" Listen! Pedro replied, putting his hand to his ear to caution those that had not understood the Spanish word. Their wait would be short, for a few minutes later they were joined by their Cimaron scout, raggedly dressed, who was returning from a visit to the City of Panama.

"Sir! I have much good news," the scout said, speaking to Drake.

"Tell us," Drake said in Spanish.

"Just yesterday I dressed as a slave and I visited the market there—"

"What did you learn?" Pedro, the Cimaron leader, asked.

"The treasurer of Lima is in Panama—he travels to Spain."

"When?"

"Tonight he will travel the Camino Real for Nombre Dios—"

"And will he have treasure?"

"His train will have fourteen mules; eight of these will be carrying gold, silver and jewels."

"That is good news!" Drake excitedly exclaimed.

"And it will be followed by fifty mules which will be carrying provisions—there will be many guards, senor!"

Drake soon thereafter called his men to a conference at a sandy creek bed. He squatted on the ground being watched by forty-seven men. They were a motley crew. More than half were black or brown

6

Cimarons who lived in the jungle savannahs where they grew maize, squash and the like. It was because these Cimarons hated the Spanish with such passion that Drake had been able to use their hatred to entice them to join him in harassing the Spanish. The whites were mainly adventurous young men from Plymouth or its nearby environs. The only uniformity in their dress was raggedness. Most wore sailor pants and sleeveless jackets. Many of the Englishmen wore sandals like the Cimarons. Many carried an extra pair attached to their belts, as healthy feet were important. Some wore bandannas over their hair, while others wore straw hats like their Cimaron allies.

Drake had used his knife to draw a rough map of the Camino Real on the sand bank. This road was the royal highway between the two cities of Panama and Nombre Dios, the first city being on the Pacific and the latter being on the Atlantic, and was as sturdy as those that had been built by the Romans, as its bed was paved with stones.

"We shall attack the mule train on the Camino Real, doing it here," Drake said, pointing. "We will do it before the train reaches Venta Cruces," Drake explained, continuing to point. "Your group," he said to John Oxenham, "will be here; you will attack its rear at this point; however, you will not do so until we attack its head. You will know that we have begun when you hear my whistle!" Drake said, pointing at a wooden whistle which he had tied to a thin strip of leather that hung about his neck.

"I must be two hundred yards ahead!"

"Yes—right here," Drake said, pointing. "It will work, providing no man drinks anything stronger than water from this moment on!" he said, studying his men. Then he placed his hand on his sore leg, which held the rifle ball that he had received at Nombre Dios. He winced slightly, as it still pained him. And he studied his motley crew surrounding him, wondering if one would dare to break the rule. Each carried a sack made of grass or cloth. This sack held extra shot, knives, roasted corn for eating, and in some cases, a bottle of brandy. It also had room enough to hold some captured treasure.

One of the men in the group was Robert Pike, a tall, thin man with a long neck. He wore a long brown beard and unkempt, long hair, which was tied in the back with a piece of leather ribbon. He had a gold ring hanging from the lobe of his left ear. He glanced from Drake to his knapsack, which held his brandy. He did it, knowing that he would have to taste it before battle, as the fear of dying in the jungle was now gnawing at him. A few drinks of brandy would relieve him of that fear.

Forty feet from the group were two dozen women who were talking softly. They were camp followers. All were dressed in ugly sack-like dresses, and each woman carried a sack which held her personal belongings, extra sacks for loot, plus much more corn than that carried by the men. They had started a low burning fire and were preparing a meal of bread made from ground maize; then they would parch some corn to be used as a snack, for a man could eat it while he marched.

"Each will wear a white shirt over his doublet so we can identify each other!" Drake explained, referring to the battle doublets, which were vests of braided steel that many of the men had taken from their knapsacks and were now wearing.

"And the Cimarons?" Oxenham asked.

"Something white—anything white!"

Most of the Cimarons did not have battle doublets like the English; Drake had had these doublets specially made for his men before they had left Plymouth. These vests were of great value for close quarter fighting, as they were ribbed with metal, which in some cases could thwart the slash of a sword.

Darkness soon enveloped the two parties of men who were stationed in the tall grass on either side of the Camino Real. Strange noises emitted from the jungle—crickets, frogs, and katydids noisily sang as if each was vying to make the most racket. Even though many twilight birds were singing their last song, it was not an idyllic setting, for Drake was being savagely attacked by mosquitos even though he had smeared his face and arms with tobacco juice mixed with mud. A leech had attached itself to Drake's left ankle. He pried it loose with his knife, and he flipped it.

"I hear—" a man softly whispered to Drake. He like Drake had heard the sound before. The noise came from the tiny bells that were attached to the necks of mules in a Spanish train. Such a group of animals was called a recua.

"Tinkle—tinkle!" the bells faintly sounded. Drake tightened; he, too, knew that this noise indicated the approach of a Spanish mule train. His biceps tightened and his adrenalin began to flow.

"Sh!" Drake again cautioned. He knew by the sound that the lead mules were about two hundred fifty yards away. This was much too far away for him to begin the attack.

8

"Tinkle—tinkle!" the bells from the nearest mule sounded; they were now a little louder. The lead mule was probably two hundred twenty yards away. The noise excited the men waiting in ambush. It overly excited Robert Pike, lying in the grass just forty feet from Drake. He had drunk his whole bottle of brandy without drinking any water, and he was now drunk, so he had a drunk man's courage. He had foolishly concluded that it was time to attack. He sprang from his supine position and ran toward the approaching caravan. A Cimaron chased after Pike and threw him to the ground. But it was done too late, for both white shirts had been seen by the sharp eyes of a Spaniard on horseback who was an advance scout for the caravan. Earlier, he had been warned that Drake was still on the Spanish Main and that he must be alert for signs.

"Pirates!" he whispered to the soldiers who were leading the caravan.

"¿Donde?" Where? questioned the lead soldier.

"¡Alli—alli!" There—There! the horseman replied, pointing to where he had seen the two men.

The captain of the soldiers guarding the caravan halted the mule train and quickly huddled with the Peruvian treasurer, advising him to pull his main caravan of treasure to the side and wait until morning when additional soldiers would be there to protect him. The treasurer did as he was advised, while a less valuable caravan proceeded for Nombre Dios.

Thus, a pompless caravan approached the pirates, making it obvious to Drake that the treasurer, his family and his mules were not a part of it. Drake let it pass, for he could tell by the number of its guards and its lack of pomp that this caravan did not carry treasure. He wondered whether the treasurer had turned back, or whether he really had left Panama!

Drake returned to Port Pheasant after the botched attack, and most of the Cimarons returned to their village. Now Drake only had fifteen Englishmen who were available to make an attack on a mule train. But Drake was not ready to give up the thought of winning treasure. Even though the number of men at his disposal had been reduced to just a few, Drake committed himself to staying on the Spanish Main until he had obtained some treasure. But that would take manpower. Drake wished for some fearless men. Then his wish came true, for about three days following Easter in the year 1573, Drake met up with a French privateer named Testu, who had a full crew of brave men who were seeking treasure. They thereafter joined Drake's men at Port Pheasant. They spent an evening getting acquainted by feasting and drinking. Once the two leaders had become sufficiently acquainted, Testu made a proposal to Drake:

"Let us join forces and attack a caravan," Testu said. Then he craftily smiled.

"But you have more healthy men than I," Drake said, as though the merger were impossible.

"And so my share would be larger!" Testu said, smiling, showing his gold-capped teeth.

"But I want half!" Drake firmly said, as though he would not compromise.

"Then you furnish twenty men and I shall furnish twenty," Testu thoughtfully said, pondering, as if counting, trying not to reveal his anticipation. He badly wanted Drake's leadership, for he knew of Drake's reputation. Drake was not only fearless, but he was also very clever—then he had a special relationship with the Cimarons.

"Agreed!"

"But the Cimarons do not count!"

"They must!" Drake argued. Five of Drake's men would have to be Cimarons. "My Cimarons will be excellent fighters!"

"Well," Testu said and stared at Drake. Then he nodded his head, thinking, concluding that whatever the cost, Drake was the man that he needed to attack the train. "We will do it."

Five days later two pinnaces delivered the party of forty men to Rio Francisco, being twenty miles from Nombre Dios. Its leader was Drake. His plan was to intercept a valuable mule train which he had learned from Pedro would soon be traveling the Camino Real from Panama to Nombre Dios.

"Will it be carrying treasure?" Drake asked Pedro.

"Much—tons of gold and silver!"

The pirates camped at a site in the jungle near the Camino Real, which was an unlikely site for a pirate attack. Several days later, during the night, while Drake lay in the vine-covered jungle, he heard a faint but familiar sound:

"Tinkle—tinkle!" the mule bells of the King's recua musically sounded. Drake would soon learn that three trains were approaching. One of these was composed of seventy mules, and each of the others was composed of fifty mules. These three trains carried in all twenty-five tons of silver and a considerable amount of gold and jewels. The treasure in these trains at that time was possibly more valuable than that which was held by either the treasurer of France or of England. It certainly was more treasure than Drake and his men could carry without making many trips.

"Move out!" Drake ordered. "We will take our positions over there!" he whispered, and he pointed to a place where the road took a bend. "You, Testu—attack the rear!" Drake whispered. Drake liked to lead the group which attacked first. He had learned that the success of the mission usually depended on how aggressive the first attack was made.

"Aye, Capitan!" Testu softly answered. There was not a tremor in his voice. His hair, though unseen, was long and braided. A red bandanna was tied about his head. Testu was a pirate of some note, as he had most recently bought his release from a French prison. He apprehensively smiled on hearing Drake state that he would lead the first attack. That took courage—enough of it by skilled fighters could overwhelm a superior force.

Twenty minutes later the first mule was at the bend. Drake blew his whistle and the attack began. John Oxenham knew that the Spanish mules were trained to lie on the ground when their reins directed them to do so. He also knew that the other mules would follow the lead mule; and so he ran to the train, took hold of the halter to the first mule, and pulled on it. It immediately lay on the ground. The other mules followed. All were soon lying on the ground. The recuas were now halted. The Spaniards would now have to fight to save their treasure.

"¡Por les Reye!" a Spanish soldier shouted. "For the King!"

"For the Queen!" Drake aggressively replied and charged, forcing the fight. The pirates were excellent in-fighters; most fought without regard for injury or life. Many carried their clumsy hand guns, even though they could only get in the one shot—for loading took time and was difficult to do at night. They fired their guns, dropped them, and then they attacked with brandished swords. They continuously shouted epithets while slashing, making it appear that their number was twice what it was. The attack was so vicious that the mule-handlers immediately fled in the direction of Nombre Dios. Some soldiers followed—others fought, but their fighting was only defensive. Two of Drake's men began to search the bags on the backs of the mules. They were pleased, as some held gold. Others held silver. The majority of Drake's men continued to fight viciously; they pressed the fight and shouted encouragement to each other. Finally, the remainder of the Spanish soldiers panicked and ran toward Nombre Dios. Drake now had full command of the caravan.

"We must hurry—take the gold—some silver. And what silver we cannot carry, bury!" Drake ordered. "Hurry! Pass the word!" he demanded of the men nearest to him.

"¡Capitan, es Testu!" a sweaty French soldier reported to Drake. Urgency was in his voice. To make sure that he was understood, he pointed to his gun and then to his stomach to indicate that Testu had been shot in the stomach. He beckoned for Drake to follow him. Drake trotted after him; just 30 paces away they found the French-man lying on the ground. He had been shot in the stomach by an arquebus loaded with shrapnel. Blood and bowel were flowing from a gaping wound.

"I'm sorry, friend," Drake said on taking a cold, clammy hand of the seriously injured Frenchman. Drake paused, pondering. He knew that he did not have to explain to Testu the law of such forays. Testu had to know that pirates seldom attempted to evacuate the seriously wounded after attacks such as this. And really, what could be done! There was not a surgeon alive who had sufficient skill to save him. "I will do for your men what we promised!" Drake stated, meaning he would honor his agreement to divide the loot.

"Thanks, monsieur!" Testu said. Fear was in his voice; appre-hension was on his face, though Drake felt it more than he saw it.

"Drink this brandy," Drake said, taking a bottle from his knap-sack and handing to him.

"Many thanks," the Frenchman replied. He then nervously uncorked it and drank.

Two hours later a contingency of soldiers from Nombre Dios arrived at the scene. All were angry, for the wounded soldiers on arriving at Nombre Dios had explained to them in some detail about the horrible attack. One of the first soldiers to arrive on the scene of the battle discovered Testu and promptly decapitated him. Minutes later several Spanish soldiers apprehended a drunk Frenchman in the jungle. He had drunk too much wine before the attack, and so he did not have his wits about him when the fighting began. And he had less at the end, as he had kept on drinking; and so he had become lost in the jungle. And when he was discovered, he revealed to the soldiers the location of a part of the silver that Drake and his men had hidden because they had been unable to carry it with them. But he swore that he did not know the whereabouts of the gold—yet the Spaniards should have known that Drake had taken it with him.

Drake and Testu's men had sailed from Port Pheasant to Rio Francisco in pinnaces, being small boats with flat sterns which were sail-rigged. As well, each of these pinnaces carried six oars. But on Drake and his men returning to Rio Francisco, which was miles below the site of the attack, much to their dismay, they discovered that the pinnaces were not there, though Drake had told the sailors to meet them there on April 3. Drake's timing had been correct, for it was now April 3.

"Gone!" shouted Drake, while looking about the dense mangroves that lined the banks, creating an almost impenetrable barrier. There was no mistaking it—this was to have been their meeting place.

"We are lost!" cried Pike, the pirate whose drunkenness had caused the bungling of the attack on the treasurer's treasure train. "The Spaniards have captured the pinnaces!"

"Don't you say lost to me!" Drake said, putting his hand to his scabbard which held his sword while grimacing, doing it as if he would like to put his sword through him. "I'll have no more of your bungling! I'll get you back to the ships!" Drake declared, speaking to all in a voice that expressed his sureness, though his outward appearance differed little from the others. Sweat poured from his forehead and from his thick chest as well, for his doublet was soaking wet. "The pinnaces cannot be far away—if they're lost, there are more at Port Pheasant!"

"They have abandoned us!" Oxenham declared.

"Naye!" Drake declared. And he was correct. Thomas Blackcollar, the expedition's cook, was in charge of the pinnaces because so many of the men were ill from fever. But then he was a very good seaman, as he could box a compass and climb the rigging. He as well was loyal, fearless and a very able sailor. He had sailed the pinnaces to Port Pheasant where he was to wait until the day of return. And he would have been there waiting, but a tropical storm had delayed him.

Yet it was two leagues distance, being twelve miles, to Port Pheasant; and at that moment, this seemed like a thousand miles to the men as they looked out on the river and searched it. For all knew that the Spanish were not far behind them. And worse, they had Spanish gold in their sacks and Spanish blood on their hands.

"I'll get them!" Drake said, meaning that he would locate the pinnaces.

"But how, Captain?" John Oxenham asked. They were near the same age and had the same background, but there was a marked difference between the two, being that intangible that man cannot readily measure. It is especially so in leadership ability. And early in Oxenham's acquaintanceship with Drake, he had recognized his superior ability in leadership. For on Oxenham beginning to sail with Drake, he had never called him anything else but Captain. Drake was his leader—his captain.

"We'll build a raft!" Drake said, appearing to be undaunted at having the Spanish to his rear and having to face the open sea without a boat. "Those men with hatchets—let's use them to cut some trees!"

"Aye!"

"Hurry!"

Drake and Tom Moone, the carpenter, hurriedly built a raft from fallen trees; then they quickly rigged a sail for it from a biscuit sack. Drake, Tom Moone, and two Frenchmen climbed aboard the raft, pushed it out into the water, and commenced to sail and push the raft down the river toward their secret harbor, Port Pheasant, where Drake before leaving on the foray had planted a new garden of corn, peas, squash and melons. He momentarily wondered as to their growth and whether they had been weeded. The raft was not only difficult to sail, but because of its heavy load, its logs quickly took on water; so the men on it were often up to their knees in water. Even so they sailed and rowed the awkward raft for more than six hours in the hot sun. Finally, they were out in the ocean.

"The pinnaces!" Drake exclaimed on seeing in the distant sunny haze the outline of what he envisioned to be pinnaces.

"They could be Spaniards, Cap'n!" Tom Moone said, shielding his eyes with his right hand.

"No, Tom. Those are mine!" Drake surely answered. He was now standing nearly waist deep in water, as the logs forming the raft had become thoroughly waterlogged.

"You're right, Captain!" Moone said. The pinnaces approached; the sailors aboard them warily eyed their captain.

14

"It's the *Bear* and the *Minion!*" Drake said, referring to the names of the pinnaces.

"You're right!"

"It's the Captain!" shouted Thomas Blackcollar, the cook, who was standing on the bow of the lead pinnace. Concern was on Blackcollar's face. And it was rightly there. For why was his captain waist-deep in water with a sack for a sail? Had the mission failed? Had the rest of the men been killed? Would they now have to return to Plymouth after this foray, broke as beggars to be laughed at by the people of the town?

"What kept you?"

"A powerful west wind, Cap'n," Blackcollar anxiously explained.

"Do not look so sad, shipmates!" Drake exclaimed to the men in the pinnaces as they approached. There was a smile on his face as he stood as tall as he could in the water, and he pulled from his shirt a two-pound gold quoit, being a round ingot. He held it up, letting the sun shine on it, which flashed its value as he displayed it. Then he said to them, "Thank God, our voyage is made. We have finally had some luck!"

"Losses?"

"Some!"

"Hurrah for the Captain!" a sailor cried, as he joined Blackcollar in reaching for a sunburned arm of Drake.

"I promised you when you set sail on this voyage that each would return to Plymouth rich!" Drake said, seating himself aboard the pinnace. "And now do you believe me?"

"Aye!"

"Let us find our mates—and count our treasure!"

CHAPTER 2

RETURN TO PLYMOUTH

The sun was almost overhead when Drake's two ships sailed into Plymouth Sound, which was the entrance to Plymouth; it then was a very active port for both commercial and naval ships. However, since it was Sunday morning, there was very little activity in the Sound. The two ships seemingly knew their way, for they sailed directly for Sutton Poole, a tiny man-made harbor that sheltered ships from the wrath of the sea. Those few persons on nearby boats or standing on piers suspiciously eyed the two ships, as both ships apparently were Spanish frigates. All wondered why these Spanish ships were entering Plymouth harbor on a Sunday morning. They continued to stare, little suspecting that the crews of these ships in the main were Devonshire men that had stolen these two ships from the Spaniards. They would also be surprised to learn that seventy-three Devonshire men under the leadership of Francis Drake had sailed from this harbor 442 days earlier in a worm-eaten ship—and now forty of them were returning in two very valuable Spanish ships. The tide was in; thus, the ships sailed directly for dockside being towed by their longboats. When the onlookers on the dock discovered that these men were Plymouth men, many of the crewmen began to shout out their good fortune to those persons standing on the dock. All soon discovered that they knew many of the men.

"We're back from the Spanish Main!" many men shouted.

"And how did you fare?"

"We have gained much treasure—"

"And your losses?" one shouted. And then there was quiet.

"Almost half of our starters—two of the Drakes—"

"Ah!"

17

And while the two crews were securing their ships, a man tip-toed into St. Andrews Church and whispered to a man seated on a back row pew:

"Francis Drake has returned—"

"Blessed be—what is the news?"

"Many of his men are dead—those returning have fortunes in their hands!"

"Rich?"

"Rich as bishops!"

"I must see!"

The news was quickly passed from mouth to ear, and the church echoed from the buzz of the whispers. Then the noise from the word exchanges became so loud that the pastor could not be heard. Before he could begin scolding them, the church had emptied, and all of the churchgoers hurried to dockside. But within an hour of the churchgoers' vacating the church, Drake and those crewmen not guarding their treasure victoriously marched up Woolster Street to that same church, followed by the parishioners. They were led into the church by Francis Drake, who was wearing a showy gold rope chain about his neck from which dangled a large gold medallion. Drake was the first to fall on his knees, and then he cried out so all could hear.

"Thank thee O Lord for thy blessings!"

"Amen! Amen!"

Monetary-wise, the blessings were many. Drake's share of the Spanish loot was such that it made him a very rich man. He purchased a pretentious house on Seven Star Lane, which had three floors and eight fireplaces. And he needed this space, for he now had four servants. One of these was Diego, the Cimaron who had pointed out to Drake the two great bodies of water when he and Oxenham had stood in the tall tree in Panama. The Drakes now had a young boy living with them, being John Drake, an orphan and cousin of Drake. Drake and his wife, Mary Newman Drake, soon became a part of Plymouth's gentry without there being much questioning about his piracy in Panama, as Drake had gained his wealth much like many of the other rich men of Plymouth, though none had been so daring.

Piracy of Spanish ships was generally considered by the people of Plymouth not to be piracy at all; they considered it to be privateering. This was especially so if the ship had some sort of

18

letters from the Queen. But even without letters, the members of the crew were seldom treated as criminals in Plymouth. On the contrary, a ship's captain who took considerable treasure from Spanish ships might be treated with undue respect. And this was just how Francis Drake had been received.

Drake had married Mary Newman in 1569, but from the beginning of his marriage, he had not been able to spend much time with her. Mary was the daughter of Harry Newman, a seaman who Drake had met on a slaving expedition some years before. When they had returned from their voyage, Newman had taken Drake home with him to meet his daughter, Mary. This meeting had led to Mary's marriage with Drake. Thereafter, she had spent much of her time waiting for Drake's ship to return to Plymouth. Being the daughter of a seaman, she should have had some appreciation of the life of a woman married to a seaman. And she did, but she did not like it, for on Drake's purchasing of the house on fashionable Seven Star Lane, she had beseeched him:

"Francis, why do you need to go back to sea? You are now rich!"

"Ah!" he exclaimed, smiling. "It is the salt—I must taste it—must feel the movement of the sea."

"But why, love?"

"Let us walk to the hoe!" he said, taking her by the waist, referring to a grassy plot on a hill that overlooks Plymouth Sound. It is here that one always finds a cool sea breeze even in the heart of the summer. And so they walked arm in arm, passing the castle quadrate, then St. Katherine's Church and on to the battlements. Drake then unbuttoned his jacket so as to allow the wind to blow on his chest and bite him. He liked its feel; exciting memories came to him. He stared at the English Channel, feeling, tasting and seeing the sea. The sight of it intensified his urge to return to it.

"Forget it, love!" she said, sensing his feelings while tightly holding on to his arm. "You do not need any more!"

"I will try," he said, staring at the sea and wondering how he could. His memory of the South Sea still had a strong hold on him.

Drake purchased a coach and two teams of fine horses; he bought expensive furniture and clothing, as he liked to dress in finery. He gave to his church. Then he invested in several trading ventures. But after six months at home, he still had the urge for the sea. It was then that he strolled down Plymouth's busy Looe Street while being admiringly watched. It was not mid-morning, yet Drake was dressed in his finery, having on a purple silk jacket, a white shirt and a stovepipe hat. His shoes were fancy, as they were decorated with silver buckles, while their heels were made of cork. He walked with the roll of a sailor, while his manner was cockish; this made the watchers suspect activity from him, though he had not opened his mouth. Women eyed him and flirtatiously smiled, and loitering men respectfully stepped aside as he approached. Most knew not whether to speak to him or to bow. His name was now known to everyone in Plymouth, as many pamphlets had been written and circulated in Plymouth about his exploits. He as well had become a man of power and mystique. One of the reasons for this aura of mystique was Diego, Drake's black servant who had fought with him in Panama and had returned with him to Plymouth. He was now Drake's body servant and guard, and somewhat like a shadow to Drake; he dressed like him and walked like him. He carried a mahogany cane whose handle had been embossed with a hand-carved devil's head. He was now two steps behind Drake, which was common, as Drake was seldom seen without him. Most of the people in Plymouth had never seen a black man until Diego arrived with Drake. This had created much interest in the thinking of the adventurous boys of Plymouth. Many young men were making plans to sail with Drake on his next voyage; yet Drake was a man without plans.

"Mornin', Cousin John," Drake said, speaking to a man exiting from an office that had a sign painted on its door, "Hawkins & Sons Merchants."

"Mornin', Cousin Francis," the man replied in a curt, polite manner on shaking the hand of Drake. This man was John Hawkins, a taciturn, unsmiling, well-dressed man. He was not as stout as Drake but was of the same height. There was a facial resemblance; the nose of each was similar; each had those gray, discerning eyes. Though it was still early in the day, Hawkins was formally dressed in a black velvet suit with white silk ruff. He wore a black hat with a pheasant's feather on the right side. He was dressed in a genteel manner, but it was in keeping with his office, as he was a member of Parliament from Plymouth. As well, he was a Director of Admiralty.

"What tidings do you bring from London?" Drake asked while smiling.

"War with Ireland—" Hawkins replied, frowning. Those persons close enough to Hawkins to see the lines on his face might have attributed the frown to an old sore that had not healed. Many would have argued that the germ for this sore had come out of the 1568 expedition when the two had participated in a slaving expedition that had ended badly, as a storm had forced them to seek shelter in Mexico. Hawkins had been in command of six ships. He had led them to the island of Juan de Ulua as an emergency measure because his fleet had exhausted their fresh water, and most of the ships had lost their rigging. Even so, Hawkins had taken a risk, as Juan de Ulua was in Mexico and Mexico was Spanish territory. But before Hawkins had done it, he had received a safe refuge guarantee from Don Martin Enriquez, the Viceroy of Mexico. But the guarantee had been a ploy, for once the ships were in this Mexican harbor, they were treacherously attacked by the Spanish, and the English fought back. At the end of this battle, only two of the ships were afloat. One of these was the fifty-ton Judith, which was Drake's first command. Hawkins as well escaped but only after he had had a harrowing sea experience. And for a while, after Hawkins returned to England, he was angry with Drake, but his anger at Drake was more due to his loss of men and ships than Drake's performance. Drake could not have been easily accused of being a coward. Hawkins had to know this. Now any appearance of acrimony between Hawkins and Drake was outward only—for the relationship between the two was really a cordial one. More so, Hawkins had to have had considerable confidence in Drake's ability as a pirate, for he had invested in Drake's last venture. And it had paid well for him.

Hawkins eyed his young cousin, as if studying his foppish clothes; yet it was done in thinking of Drake's skill as a seaman and a fighter, for he was familiar with many of Drake's exploits. Drake now had acquired a name for boldness; many in Plymouth were saying that his name would soon be as well-known as that of Hawkins.

"Trouble in Ireland is not new," Drake said, and he threw out his hand as if to discount the news. "The English have been having trouble in Ireland since there was an England. What can you tell me about the popish lot in London?"

"There is no good news, Francis. Worse, there are now some at court who want your hide!" he said, wrying his mouth, as if doing it to show his reluctance to disclose such news.

"What! I am not that important," Drake said, frowning, shaking his head, as if unwilling to give credence to the thought.

21

"They say that Philip (Philip II, King of Spain) knows you by your name. He wants your head. He claims that you are the leader of the Pirates of Darien."

"What rot!" Drake exclaimed with a proud smirk.

"And the whole court knows about your last adventure at Nombre Dios," Hawkins said while smiling. His eyes were aglow with amusement. "All London talks of it."

"Do they know that on my last voyage to the Spanish Main I also lost two fine brothers?" One had died in battle, while the other had died of fever.

"Naye—they do not care. The Spanish Ambassador has the ear of Burghley," he said, referring to Elizabeth's powerful treasurer. "He wants you arrested, brought to London and tried!" Hawkins said. He was now frowning.

"But the Queen would not do that—I am loyal to her!"

"And I would assume that she does appreciate that, but times have changed. She does not want a war with Philip," Hawkins said, continuing to frown while drawing his cape to his chin, exaggerating the cold. A cold breeze was beginning to chill Sutton's Hole. "I have heard that she will!"

"What do you propose?"

"I suggest that you and I form a venture to help Essex in Ireland. There would be some money in it for both of us. The popish dons are supplying the Irish with provisions. You could capture their ships, and I could find buyers for them as well as their cargos. At the same time, you would be aiding the Queen. We would need to put the frigates back in your hands," Hawkins said, referring to the Spanish frigates that Drake had brought back from Panama. "I have one— Sir Arthur Champernowne has the other. You could possibly use another small one. And I might just persuade the Admiralty to pay some of the cost," Hawkins said, thinking.

"A thought," Drake said, wryly twisting his mouth, showing interest as he pondered the subject, which he obviously was enjoying. For he now had a legitimate reason to return to sea.

"And so it is settled—you will be at sea when the process arrives—you will be in the service of Essex," referring to Walter Devereaux, Earl of Essex. "This also will give you a way to make some important friends at court. Essex can be a valuable ally," he said, adding, "and then those attacks that you made at Nombre Dios will be forgotten by the time that you return."

But Philip II was serious about wanting Drake's head. He had written a threatening letter to Elizabeth, which it was now in her hands. It demanded that Drake be brought to the bar, stating " . . . that this man Drake has to be imprisoned!" Philip had argued that every attack made on a Spanish ship near the Main or on a Spanish caravan while crossing the Isthmus within the last two years had been done by Drake or through his connivance. "Drake is a pirate; he has attacked my ships on the coast of Darien and he has plundered my treasure caravans while crossing the Isthmus. War will ensue unless this man Drake is imprisoned and hanged!" he threatened.

"I follow you, cousin," Drake said on putting his chilled right hand into a pocket. For the first time he had noticed that many persons on the street had stopped and were intently watching the two men, who were being shadowed by the black Diego. The spectators were studying the two men as if their lives might be affected by what the men were discussing.

"How long will it take to acquire those ships?"

"Oh, a few weeks—the *Falcon* is in Sutton's Poole. It will need canvas, rope and victualing—"

"And has the process been issued?" Drake asked, referring to the warrant for his arrest.

"It had not been done on the day that I left London, but I assume that it will happen shortly. It would be wise for you to make yourself scarce until the ships are ready."

"I will use Plymouth men—" Drake said, beginning to ponder on the venture.

"And Portsmouth—its member spoke to me about some men there wanting to sail with you—he has a cousin. May I pass the word to him that there are some berths available?"

"Only eight or ten—the rest must be from Plymouth—Devon way. Show me a Devon sailor and I'll show you a man with salt in his blood!" Drake answered, smiling, grinning at the excitement of the moment.

CHAPTER 3

RATHLIN ISLAND

Drake now had a fleet of three frigates. He took personal command of the *Falcon*, which was the larger of the three ships. Then he raised sufficient men to man each of them. It soon became known to just about everyone in Plymouth that there was now a warrant for Drake's arrest. Some of the recruits were bothered by the talk. They urged Drake to leave immediately. But Drake seemingly was against it. He explained to his recruits that the warrant had not yet been issued, for Hawkins had put a hold on it until Drake sailed for Ireland. Drake further argued that the warrant was just a technicality that a rich man could overcome. Why should he worry when he was one of the richest men in Devonshire? But the warrant did bother Drake somewhat; and so he soon sailed from Plymouth, doing it with the intent to ingratiate himself with the Queen and her aids.

Drake sailed to Portsmouth where he raised eight additional men and boys so as to complete the crews for the three ships, two of which were quite small. Drake thereafter sailed for Dublin. He made an uneventful passage to Ireland and then anchored in Dublin Harbor. He ordered his officers and men to remain aboard ship while he called on Lord Essex, who was the general in charge of the English army in Ireland.

Essex's principal opposition in Ulster was a Scottish chieftain of the Ian Mor clan by the name of Sorley Boy McDonnel. He, along with his four older brothers, now controlled most of Ulster. They had carved out this portion of Ireland as their own, though they had been opposed by the Gaelic lords of Ulster and the best generals that the English could muster. And now Sorley was clearly the leader of Ian Mor, for he had been the one who had kept Essex from stabilizing

Ulster for the English. Essex had taken on the job of subduing Ireland—it had seemed easy enough, for he only had to defeat this minor chief, being the leader of those McDonnels who had been forced out of the Hebrides. But Essex's attempt to subdue Sorley Boy had ended in failure, as Sorley Boy fought only when it pleased him. And once he did fight, he fought furiously. But when he did not want to fight, he faded into the bogs, leaving Essex holding an empty bag. And that was proving to be bankruptcy for the Earl. For he had taken on the job of subduing Ireland based on a contingency, which was the Irish revenue. He was entitled to all the tax revenue that he could squeeze from the Irish, but from this revenue he had to pay all the costs of governing plus the salaries of the soldiers; else he had to pay them out of his own pocketbook.

"Captain, welcome to Ireland!" Essex said, forcing a smile. He had risen to his feet on Drake introducing himself. Walter Devereux, being the Earl of Essex, was dressed in a general's uniform. He was youthful and handsome, though his face was livid from worry.

"I am at your service, Lordship," Drake said and made a deep bow, while his eyes cautiously moved about the room, studying the soldiers in it, wondering whether they would attempt to arrest him, for arrest now was on his mind.

"Thank you!"

"I have three ships with guns—"

"Relax, Captain," Essex said, smiling, taking notice of Drake's tenseness, though as well he was attempting to show his friendship. He, too, needed friends. It was not just the Irish, but it was also this county of Ulster which abounded with crafty Scots. Then he added, "Sorley Boy does not have a navy," and he laughed.

"Oh!" Drake said. His face showed sincere dismay, for he was ready to fight so that he could rid himself of the warrant.

"Have a glass of port!" Essex said, taking a glass container which was filled with port, and he began to pour wine into a glass.

"Thanks very much," Drake replied.

"But we can use you," Essex said, standing, pointing to a map of Northern Ireland which hung from a wall behind him. "You can move my troops—give them some protection. Then you can stop the movement of Scots—they move from Islay to Ulster," he said, pointing. "You can also stop the smugglers!"

"My ships are at your service," Drake said, sipping wine, beginning to relax.

26

"The water off Ireland is treacherous—do you know these waters?"

"No—but I've been to places just as treacherous," Drake answered and smiled, which momentarily caused Essex also to smile.

"I understand," Essex replied. A courier had brought him a letter from Hawkins, who had written to him that Drake was coming, explaining that he was a famous privateer who had made his fortune on the Spanish Main. "The Spanish are supplying the Irish; you will get a chance to stop their ships," he added.

"And—"

"A fifth of what you take goes to the Queen!"

"It is paid to you?"

"Of course," Essex said, smiling, pointing out that in Ireland he was the Regent.

"And," Drake said, "there is a warrant for my arrest."

"I know—and I will straighten it out in due course!" Essex said, and he gave a half smile, while raising an eyelid, which was a warning.

The writer has previously stated that the principle opposition to Essex was a Scottish chief by the name of Sorley Boy McDonnel. His father was Alistair McDonnel, Lord of the Scottish Isles of Kyntyre and Islay. The McDonnels were Highland Scots as well as being Irish Catholics. They were neighbors to the Irish, since only twenty miles of water separated their ancient home from Ulster, making it easy for these Scots to take an interest in the affairs of Northern Ireland when it pleased them. And there were plenty of affairs, for the Irish seemingly were always engaged in war among themselves; more so, the clan Ian Mor now controlled Ulster. Previously, the English had connived to use one Irish chief against the other. The English in 1561 had used Sorley Boy McDonnel to weaken the strength of the O'Neils. The two chieftains of the clans McDonnel and O'Neil had warred until 1567 when Sorley Boy defeated the O'Neils. But then Sorley Boy had refused to submit to the will of the English, though they had instigated the war and had funded him. But by then Sorley Boy had become much stronger. For by then, there were thousands of additional Scots in Ireland. Many of these Scots were Gaeloglass, who were Scottish mercenaries from the Hebrides. These were the fiercest fighters in the islands. Elizabeth feared them worse than the Irish, and with good reason. For centuries they had dominated Ireland, and man-to-man, the English could not stand up to the Gaeloglass, as

Elizabeth: "Get rid of the Scots!"

they were the greatest fighters in Europe. Elizabeth had negotiated without success with Sorley Boy until 1573; then she had sent the Earl of Essex to Ireland to get rid of the surplus Scots, who she considered to be popish rebels. And so Essex had accepted her offer of a contingency. When Essex was readying to sail for Ireland, she had given him the charge: Get rid of the Scots! For she believed that an Ireland without the Scots would be easy for England to rule. Essex had tried to rid Ireland of the Scots, but he had not been successful. Sorley Boy's Scottish Gaeloglass were just too savage of fighters, and worse, they only fought when it suited them. And when they did fight, as a rule, they inflicted heavy casualties on Essex's men.

Drake had been in Ireland for more than a year when in June 1575, he received a message from Essex that would change his life. He was to proceed fifteen to twenty miles northwest of Belfast—he was to go to the small town of Carrickfergus; there his three ships were to take aboard three hundred English soldiers who were commanded by General Norreys. Drake was to take them to nearby Rathlin Island, being a tiny, rocky island which was surrounded by dangerous waters. Drake's three frigates boarded the English soldiers without encountering any problems. The last to board Drake's frigate, the *Falcon*, was the party of General Norreys.

Norreys was accompanied by Essex's secretary, Thomas Doughty, a lawyer-trained aid to Essex, who would share a cabin with Norreys. Their cabin was directly across from the larger cabin of Drake. Doughty was a smooth-talking, handsome young man with an aristocratic manner, who would soon make it known to Drake that he had worked for many men in high places. He had ostensively boarded Drake's *Falcon* to make sure that the Scots on Rathlin Island were taught a lesson; yet his real reason for joining the expedition had been to make the acquaintance of Francis Drake, who he had learned was the famous pirate of the Spanish Main. He knew also that he was rich from the plunder that he had gained on the Spanish Main. He also knew that Drake was a money grubber, for he had learned that even while Drake was serving his penance in Ireland, he had been increasing his wealth by capturing and selling Spanish and Scottish ships. Doughty liked this, as he was avaricious and desirous of accumulating a fortune. Thus, Doughty was a schemer—and so he had made his plans to meet Drake and to get to know him well enough so he could aid him in putting together a privateering venture to the New World. And in doing so, he hoped to make his fortune.

"Captain Drake, I am Thomas Doughty, secretary to Lord Essex," Doughty said, joining Drake on the poop deck. He spoke to Drake in a distinctive Cambridge accent. His words were well-formed, having tone, while Drake's were flat. He then added, "Previously, I was secretary to Sir Francis Walsingham." Drake curiously raised an eyelid, showing interest, as he knew immediately that Doughty's connections had to be first rate. Drake would soon learn that Doughty was a protégé of Sir Christopher Hatton, who was the Queen's favorite and would soon be England's chancellor.

"Welcome aboard!" Drake replied, speaking in his West Anglican accent. A haughty smile was on his face, as if saying that because of his knowledge of the sea, he was the superior of the two. Yet his sureness was cocksure, for his superior manner was feigned. Drake had an inferiority complex when he was about men of education and birth. Doughty's speech and manner made it obvious that he was graced with both. Drake had long before decided that he would have to make up for his shortcomings in education and birth by the accumulation of wealth and feats of besting. And he had made much progress in that direction. Drake's dress indicated that he was a man of means. He was dressed in a brown leather jacket, matching woolen trousers and a wide leather rain hat. Silver bells decorated his sleeves, which merrily jingled when he moved. He as well wore the soft leather shoes of a successful seaman.

"Can you take us to Rathlin Island," Doughty said, speaking for both himself and the General.

"Of course," Drake said. "I know it."

"And reaching it does not present any problems?" Doughty asked. He had been told that the island was surrounded by treacherous shoals.

"Do you wish me to bombard it or land these troops?"

"Land the troops—"

"I can get them in, but there is nothing there," Drake said in an informative way. He had reconnoitered this island within the month, sensing its importance, doing it even though he knew that it was mostly rock—when he last saw it, its only habitation had been a herd of sheep grazing near a castle ruin.

"There is now," Doughty said, grimly smiling. "Sorley Boy has put his women and children there." Truthfully, there were a thousand or more McDonnel women and children now living on the island in caves and lean-to huts. Sorley Boy had put them there for safekeeping, as he intended to lead his army in an engagement with the army of Essex at the Southern Glynnes. But Essex did not intend to use his forces until Norreys' three hundred men had done their dirty work. It had been shortly after Sorley Boy had put them there that an informant by the name of Stevenson had informed Essex that the McDonnel women and children were on the island.

"Keep our army at the Southern Glynnes," Essex said, studying a large map. "And have Norreys give the sword to those on Rathlin!" This order of Essex would be his undoing, while it would be the making of Drake.

"They will not be there for long," Drake said, half grinning, eyeing the non-talking General. Then he looked down below and studied the deck of his ship. The rails were lined with English soldiers. Most had their backs to the poop.

"Do you have any problem helping us do the job?" Doughty asked.

"Are they popish?"

"Yes—and rebels against the Queen!"

"Enough said," Drake replied. He was not only anti-Catholic, but he was strongly partial to the Queen. And more so, Drake wanted the warrant for his arrest and confiscation of his treasure lifted. He was sure that Essex would do it if he participated in crimes against the Scots. Thus, at last he had found the way to end his penance.

Thereafter, Drake busily engaged himself in giving orders to his crew. A tempest had arisen and the *Falcon* was wallowing in troughs. Some soldiers were lying on deck, others were standing on deck retching, as they lacked sea legs. But Drake's mind was busy. He had aboard ship a man who obviously had an entry to court; and he could be his entry—Doughty could even find important backers for him. And thus, the two had much in common. For Doughty little knew it, but Drake seriously wanted to make a venture to the South Sea. He had never forgotten the scene from the tall tree on the Spanish Main. And on Drake pondering it, he knew that this would take a considerable investment and some important backers; it would as well require the Queen's support. For he now realized that he could gain a shipload of treasure from Spain, but then lose it to the Queen unless she were a part of the venture.

31

The following day the weather had abated. Drake stationed himself on the bridge near the two steersmen. The extra steersman was a precautionary measure because of the backlash from the rudder if the seas became very rough. To Drake's right was a youthful sailor, being twelve-year-old John Drake, a cousin to Drake. He was a permanent resident with Drake, as he was an orphan. Then in the rigging and looking down on Drake was Diego, who seemingly always had an eye out for Drake's welfare. He wore a long knife in his belt, and his hand moved toward it when he sensed Drake was in danger. Drake now had Rathlin Island in full view; he conned the *Falcon* to the starboard. His carpenters were on deck busily hammering together pinnaces similar to those small ships that Drake had used in Panama. Drake was cocksure in his sailing of the *Falcon*; she handled well, so he drove her for the rocky shoals that partially protected the island.

"Right rudder!" he ordered. The seamen on deck turned the main sail—it caught the wind. Drake actually wanted to go to port or the left but the rudder handled that way. The *Falcon* quickly heeled. "Steer for that rock!" Drake ordered, pointing to a large rock which ominously faced him. This tiny island was the home for thousands of sea birds. They rose from its crags and screeched at the approaching ships.

"Furl the mizzen sails!"

"Aye, sir!" the master answered. Then sailors began to collapse and roll the sails on the after mast.

"Larboard full rudder!" Drake ordered. The seamen turned the main sail, and the *Falcon* cut to starboard and entered a small cove.

"Aye!"

"Furl them all—drop anchor!"

"Anchor's hooked, Cap'n!" a sailor cried from the bow. The two small ships following the *Falcon* soon anchored alongside her.

"Put the pinnaces over!"

"Aye, Cap'n!"

"Man them, ye men—make your landing!" Drake shouted to the soldiers milling the deck, speaking to them as if he were their general.

Thirty minutes later the pinnaces reached land. The soldiers stepped from the boats to the rocky landings and scurried toward an old abandoned castle. Hundreds of women and children stood outside, anxiously studying the soldiers; then the soldiers began to fire their guns at them. Women and children scampered for caves—some jumped in the water, only to be pursued by soldiers.

"Beastly mess!" said Doughty, who was now standing beside Drake who was intently eyeing the scene as if it were his responsibility.

"Catholics!" Drake exclaimed.

"Supporters of Mary!" Doughty exclaimed, referring to Mary Tudor, Queen of Scotland and France. The reader should not confuse this Mary with Catholic Mary, who reigned over England prior to Elizabeth. Mary Tudor was a cousin of Elizabeth, the present Queen of England.

"And she would deny our Elizabeth the throne!" Drake bitterly retorted.

Mary Queen of Scots, on becoming Queen of France, had done some foolish things. The most foolish one had been her claiming the title of Queen of England, though her bastard cousin had been put on the throne by an act of Parliament. And later when Mary had matured, she had refused to back down on her claim. Thus, the Protestants in England hated her as they dreadfully feared a Catholic's return to the throne.

"These will not get the chance to deny her!"

"I would like to do the same for the lot!" Drake replied without any show of feeling, though women and children were being slaughtered before his eyes. Drake was there of course because he wanted to curry favor with Essex. He also had a deep bitterness toward the Catholics, which he was glad to express. During Catholic Mary's reign, who was Elizabeth's older sister, Drake's father, Edmond, a Protestant minister, had been banned from England because of his beliefs. He had even been prohibited from putting foot on English soil. Thus, for a period of time he had raised his twelve children in the hulk of a ship on the Medway near Chatham Harbor. On Elizabeth coming to power, she had restored Edmond's civil rights to him. She had even seen that he was given a church at Upchurch Kent. Essex had similar feelings for the Catholics, for he had seen Protestants being burned at the stake by gleeful Catholics. But his hatred was not the sole reason for his bestiality toward the Scots—it was his inability to defeat Sorley Boy. And so he had decided to kill Sorley Boy's women and children and break him. Yet the massacre would not bring Sorley Boy to his knees. Instead it would make him more defiant. For just then Sorley Boy was without a boat and helplessly

33

standing on a nearby cliff on the mainland, where he was looking across Murlough Bay, witnessing the massacre of his women and children. He cried and wailed from his inability to release his army so as to put out boats and stop the slaughter. Sorley Boy thereafter would be a terrible enemy of the English.

"Do you plan to make another trip soon to the Spanish Main?" Doughty asked. He was now standing within touching distance of Drake.

"Some day—" Drake replied still intently staring.

"Adventure agrees with you, Captain—" Doughty said, smiling at Drake, showing his admiration.

"Thank you—"

"And if you had the ships and the Queen's backing, where would you sail?" Doughty asked, turning his collar to protect his throat from the chill.

"To the South Sea," Drake said, expanding his chest and standing tall.

"Not Cartagena?" Doughty asked.

"Nay—I have been there—and it was almost mine—"

"Is there more gold to be had in the South Sea?" Doughty eagerly asked.

"Yes. It is a source of the Spaniards' gold and silver. As well, it is a sea that I have not sailed."

"Why not do it then?"

"The time is not right—the Spaniards have too much power at court."

"Times are changing—the Queen could be made amenable—" Doughty said in a conversational voice, as though the slaughter they were witnessing was not real.

"But I don't have an entry. There is a warrant for my arrest," Drake said, testing Doughty so as to see what power, if any, he had.

"If I got you a visit with the Queen—got the ear of those persons close to her—voided the warrant—would you take me with you?"

"Of course—" Drake said, turning so he could look directly into the eyes of Doughty.

"With a general's share?"

"Hmmm—" Drake said. Then he added, "Yes—but shares are paid only if you make it back to England!" Drake warned.

"An equal command?"

"I command!" Drake sternly said. His voice had changed at the thought.

"Captain of a ship?" Doughty asked.

"I would see—when would you begin these efforts?" Drake asked.

"On our return to Dublin," Doughty replied and directed his attention to two startled teenage girls. He momentarily stared at them. They were being chased by two soldiers with bloody swords.

"Ships to starboard, Cap'n!" a sailor cried.

"Aye," Drake said, turning and staring. Then he added, "Hoist the anchor—on the double! Get me sails!"

"What is it, Cap'n?" Doughty asked.

"Scotch galleys!" Drake declared, pointing toward Islay, a small island to his right. There in sight were eleven Scotch galleys, being vessels of war with long decks, one square sail and twenty-four oars. All were loaded with soldiers; some rowed, while others stood, displaying guns and bows, while the galleys rapidly proceeded to Rathlin. Drake knew at a glance that their number was sufficiently large enough to stop the massacre.

"Anchors aweigh, Cap'n!"

"Give me sails—quickly!" Drake ordered.

"Aye, Cap'n," a sailor answered. He and two other sailors were pulling on a block and tackle that was hoisting a huge sail.

"Gunners, man your cannon—bowmen, take your places." He was referring to four men who were holding six-foot-long longbows. Each of their belts held six metal-tipped arrows.

"Aye!"

"Make your shots count, or I shall have your hides!"

It did not take but half an hour before the *Falcon* had the galleys within gun range.

"Left rudder!" The helmsman had to turn his whipstaff left in order to go right. The seamen as well had to turn the yards on the mainmast. "Fire your port guns!"

"Boom! Boom!" the guns noisily sounded.

One galley was hit dead center—it immediately began to sink. Another was hit—it, too, began to sink.

"Fire again!" Drake shouted.

"Boom! Boom! Boom!" Two more galleys were hit. The bowmen fired into the remaining galleys. Many were hit; others jumped into the cold water. Drake continued the attack until all of the boats were sunk.

"Steersmen, bring me back around—take me back to Rathlin Island!"

"Aye!" the principal steersman said in a normal voice, though all on the *Falcon* had heard, as quiet now reigned.

CHAPTER 4

DRAKE'S FIRST MEETING WITH WALSINGHAM

The Rathlin Island mission was a sordid one, one that would forever taint Drake's name while resolving nothing. This was so even though Essex was elated on receiving General Norreys' report, as he was of the opinion that it would end the Scottish occupation of Ulster; however, it did not. Even so, the Rathlin mission was just what Drake needed, for on the *Falcon* returning to Dublin, Doughty met with Essex and gleefully explained to him how the mission had been a success and what an important role Drake had played in it. Then Essex wrote a letter withdrawing the warrants against Drake. And on September 19, 1575, Drake sailed for Plymouth a free man. His first thoughts had been idyllic, for Drake had decided to give up adventure and to enjoy his comfortable home in Plymouth and the riches that he had won at Nombre Dios, which he had added to by the Ireland venture. He had even decided to leave the sea and live the life of a Plymouth gentleman. But that was not to be. He would not be able to do either, as he would soon be challenged by a new venture that would be more to his liking. A month after Drake returned to Plymouth, he received a letter from Sir Francis Walsingham, Secretary of State. Its pertinent part was as follows:

> ... it gives me considerable pleasure to advise you that the Queen desires an audience with you as soon as it is practicable for you to appear ... you will advise me of the time that you can appear at Windsor ... make your arrival date after 5:00 p.m. so as to allow a goodly hour for a dinner visit with myself ...

Drake was elated. An audience with the Queen was more than he had expected. He of course knew that Doughty had influence, but hardly this. Why, Walsingham was Secretary of State! He was almost as powerful as Lord Burghley. Many people thought that he had more power then the Queen. So shortly after Drake received the letter, he and his servant Diego mounted horses and set out for London. Once they were in London, they took a four-wheel coach to Windsor. Drake was dressed in a velvet suit with a matching tall hat. He wore a short sword at his side. The time of his arrival at Windsor Castle was shortly after 5:00 p.m.; Drake stepped from his coach and was immediately confronted by the guards at the gate.

"State your name!"

"Captain Francis Drake—"

"Your business?"

"I am here at the request of Sir Francis Walsingham!" Drake replied in a forceful voice, appearing undaunted by the show of steel from the crossed spears of the two guards that were blocking his entrance into the gray walls of the castle that at that moment was the seat of power of the Queen of England, though it was not permanent since the Queen utilized numerous castles. Each had a particular fascination to her. She spent some time at each—the exception was the Tower of London, where she had been a prisoner during the reign of Mary.

"By whose request?" the guard repeated.

"Secretary Walsingham," Drake said, referring to Secretary of State Walsingham, who was one of the Queen's principal advisor-administrators.

"We shall see," the spokesman said and turned to a nearby page, who was dressed in a scarlet costume. "Take a message to the Honorable Secretary Walsingham! Tell him that Captain Drake is at the gate. He claims that he is here at the Secretary's request."

"Yes, sir!"

"You may stand at ease!" the corporal of the guard said to Drake.

"And your servant?" the guard asked, referring to Diego.

"He will have to wait in the coach," Drake said, meaning he would not accompany him to the meeting.

"There is an inn just across the road, sir," the guard replied in a civil tone while pointing.

"Very good," Drake replied. "Take my servant to the inn," Drake said to the driver, pointing. "I shall join him when I finish my business."

"Aye!"

"Wait for me—I may need you!" Drake said to Diego.

Minutes later the young page returned. Drake was uneasily standing by himself at the gate. The page confidently said to the guards:

"Cap'n Drake is expected. Sir, would you please follow me!" the page said to Drake.

"Thank you," Drake replied and sternly eyed the guards, who ignored his countenance. Then they smartly changed their spears so that they no longer blocked Drake's entrance.

Drake followed the young man down a long candle-lit hall whose walls were decorated with rich tapestries and fine paintings. Drake tried to keep his eyes from them, as he did not wish to be intimidated by the castle's rich furnishings.

"This way, Sir," the youth said and led Drake into an office. Two men were seated at high-topped desks. Each held a quill pen in his hand and was using it to copy a document by candlelight. Both men simultaneously raised their heads, curiously studied Drake, and then returned their eyes to the documents before them, as if they had seen enough of him. But it was only a stance, for they wanted to see more, as they were curiously interested in this visitor—Drake, the pirate! So they surreptitiously raised their eyes and studied Drake who was following the young man. He entered an open door to a side office; then he abruptly stopped.

"Sir," the young man said to a man seated at a desk behind which was a partially opened window. "I am pleased to present Captain Drake."

"Thank you, Richard," the man said and stood. He was of middle height, thin, and had pigeon-like shoulders. He wore a tam on his head, a baggy woolen cardigan, and heavy woolen trousers, as the room was chilly. Cold air was entering it from the partially opened window; yet a fire was burning brightly in a grate. The man had very sharp Norman features which were dramatized by a neatly trimmed, pointy beard. "I am glad to know you, Captain Drake."

"Thank you, sir," Drake replied and courteously bowed to this powerful man who was one of the Queen's Secretaries of State. Walsingham, like Drake, was a Puritan and extremely anti-Catholic, which was based on politics as well as religion. He also had an intense hatred for the Spanish. Such hatred was possibly the mortar that then bound together most of the English.

39

"Be seated, Captain," the Secretary said, smiling, showing stained teeth, while speaking in a very formal manner. "Any good news from Ireland?"

"We did the Rathlin thing—"

"I know—I know. It was a foolish move—not you, not you. You did a good job. But—it should not have been done," the Secretary said while shaking his head and frowning. His grey eyes were hard and decisive. "It is the Irish—and the Scots!"

"It is a quagmire, sir," Drake frankly said, while frowning at the recall of the brutal scene. Drake then looked about the richly decorated office. To the Secretary's right was a silk tapestry that depicted a jousting scene, while to his left was a marble statue of Zeus. The chair on which Drake was seated had armrests with carved dragons on them.

"I know—and Essex?"

"He is well but chaffed," Drake answered, adding, "It is a problem that he is finding difficult to resolve." He could have added that the move was rapidly bankrupting Essex. As the writer has previously stated, Walter Devereaux, Earl of Essex, had foolishly agreed to fund the Queen's army in its attempt to put down the rebellion in Northern Ireland. He had expected to collect sufficient taxes to pay for the cost, but he had soon discovered that the Irish would not be taxed.

"Oh, those popish fools!" the powerful man exclaimed. He then dropped his eyes to a map on his large desk, as if he wished to discuss other subjects. The map poorly depicted the New World. The drawing also inaccurately depicted South America, as it showed it to be too small. The map hardly portrayed it as the continent that we now know it to be. There was a large land appendage to the Magellan Strait entitled "Australius," which was a figment of the cartographer's imagination.

"My sources tell me that you are a seaman and that you enjoy fighting the Spanish. Also, that you even have a score to settle with them," the Secretary said, while half smiling. Walsingham prided himself on having many sources of knowledge. This had come about because of his keen interest in espionage—he had even developed a spy school, teaching his students at his London house. He was so interested in cryptography that he taught a subject on it to his students who thereafter operated throughout Europe. He was actually fanatical about acquiring information—so much so that he often paid for it out of his own pocket. Essex had paraphrased Doughty in his comments about Drake. Doughty had written Walsingham that Drake was not only an excellent seaman, but also a good fighter and one of the most ruthless men that he had known in Ireland. He had stated, "He is loyal to the Queen and could be very useful in undertaking any dangerous sea mission." And Walsingham was searching for such a person.

"Yes, sir!" Drake replied.

"And where do you think he can be hurt?" Walsingham asked, while thoughtfully stroking his beard. He of course meant the Spanish.

"At sea, sir—" Drake quickly replied, knowing that the Spain of Philip II had the most powerful army in Europe. He also knew that the tight-fisted Queen Elizabeth would not fund an army to tackle Philip in Europe. She would not fund a navy either. She would depend on privateers such as Drake and Hawkins to man a private navy for her.

"How at sea?" the Secretary asked, smiling, now keenly studying the stoutly built, ruddy faced man, whose red hair was ruffled, as he had not touched it since he removed his hat.

"Attack his treasure ships! Bankrupt him—it will do it, for he is in constant need of gold and silver to pay his troops!" Drake said, eyeing the Secretary, as if wondering why he had not seen this.

"But they are well-guarded—"

"But they can be attacked by choosing the right men—and the reward would be worth the effort!" Drake answered. The Secretary's countenance and demanding eyes had not intimidated Drake.

"And you know how to steal such treasure?" Walsingham asked, half smiling. Then he had a small fit of coughing, which he relieved by tightly clasping a small bag in his right hand. He was a man troubled with poor health and unable to participate in such adventures, but he had a great admiration for those men with courage enough to do it.

"Well—" Drake replied, unsurely smiling. He was not intimidated by Walsingham, yet he was uneasy with this powerful man, who he knew had so much influence over the Queen, who in turn controlled England, which he believed should be a Protestant England. John Hawkins had warned Drake: "Take care in talking to him, as he has a network of spies who only answer to him." So he was reluctant to speak out. Had not the speech of his father caused him to be exiled to a ship's hulk in the Medway near Chatham dock-yard, England's main naval base? And such as well had caused him to be exiled from the England that he loved. Drake's crimes were many; he had made numerous forays to Africa and the Spanish Main, and during these ventures he had participated in many attacks on Spanish ships, caravans and forts. Why, he had killed for gold! Months before he had participated in a massacre that he knew was a crime against a people, and he was reluctant to discuss the details.

"Speak man—you're amongst friends!"

"How so?"

"I'm a Protestant—I, too, dislike the popish Spanish!"

"And the Queen?"

"Of like mind—but there are other persons around her that do not think of the same mind. There is Burghley—" he whispered, frowning, referring to the powerful Treasurer, with whom at times he would be in accord. There would be other times when they would be in opposing camps. And was that not intrigue enough to make the job interesting?

"He is popish?"

"Naye—he just wants to do business with them—"

"It can't be done!" Drake replied, saying it with a resolve. "They're too greedy. They want it all—the land, the gold, the power—they must be driven from the sea!"

"How can ye?"

"We can attack their treasure ships!"

"And are you prepared to lead such attacks?" the Secretary asked, while intently eyeing Drake.

"With the Queen's blessing," Drake replied, though in truth if the right opportunity had presented itself, he would have returned to the Spanish Main without her blessing.

"You will need ships."

"And investors?"

"I can arrange that—I will draw your documents, obtain money for outfitting the ships—victualing—have papers drawn to outline our relationship—" Walsingham said, standing, limping across to the fireplace. He took a sliver of wood, lit it from the fire in the grate, and in turn he circled the room lighting additional candles. He returned to his desk and then closed the window.

"And the Queen?" Drake asked.

"We shall see her shortly. It is better to talk to her about this after she has dined. But the details of your meeting with me and the Queen must not be divulged to anyone. Else it will be revealed to Burghley. The Queen would want it that way!" he cautiously said while sternly eyeing Drake.

"Of course," Drake replied, assuming by the Secretary's tone of voice that the Secretary believed that such might even be whispered to the Spanish ambassador.

"Here is our dinner," the Secretary said, pointing his head at two waiters entering the room. "I hope that you like roast beef—anyway, I have a bottle of claret for each of us. You will like it. The claret will loosen your tongue so you will confide in us some of your adventures," the enfeebled man said. And he chuckled at the thought, as if considering that information about Drake's adventures would be worth the listening. Then he took a small jar from his desk, took a spoon from the tray, filled it from the jar, and put it in his mouth; he then washed it down with a half-glass of claret.

"It is for my stones!" the Secretary exclaimed, frowning bitterly. "Eat man—make your gullet ready for a talk with the Queen!"

CHAPTER 5

QUEEN ELIZABETH

A page led the two men into a very large state room, which was adjacent to the Queen's living quarters. Elizabeth was seated on a chair, as though she was not expecting company. She held an open book in her hands, while a young girl a dozen feet away was strumming a lute, being a stringed instrument with a large pear-shaped body. The room was ornately finished, as its walls were dressed with a dozen paintings and tapestries with intricate designs. A small chapel was at the rear. Two small Holbeins hung above a bookcase filled with books and manuscripts; it set against the wall near the lutist. The floor was half-carpeted with a large oriental rug woven from silk. A fire brightly burned in the fireplace near the Queen; it was faced with a massive limestone mantlepiece on which was carved a Biblical scene of David and Goliath.

"Yes, Francis," she said, raising her head from her book and acting surprised. She wore a hair piece that was the color of a maple leaf in the fall of the year. Her face was attractively formed; yet it was overly powdered. Her neck was aristocratic and powdered, while her eyes shone with seeming interest in the visitors. Her eyes were focused on Francis Walsingham.

"Your Majesty, I have someone interesting—someone that I would like for you to meet—" Walsingham said, smiling and bowing.

"And who is this gentleman, Francis?" Elizabeth asked, standing, showing her girlish figure. She was tall and slim, with tiny breasts which were almost childlike. Her dress was violet, which contrasted with the color of her hair. She wore a white ruff around her neck which opened so as to permit her to display her immature cleavage. She wore pearls in her hair, around her neck and attached to her ears; as well, she wore rings on two of her fingers that also had pearl settings.

"Well—" Francis Walsingham said, hesitantly answering, while pointing his head and eyes at the lutist, as if he would not speak until she left the room.

"Leslie, you are dismissed. You may go to your room," Elizabeth smartly said to the young musician, while moving her hands as if shooing a chicken. She silently watched the girl walk over to a panel and press it. It opened revealing a secret passageway. She then left the room and closed the panel behind her.

"Your Majesty, this is Captain Francis Drake from Plymouth. He has been with Essex in Ireland. Essex has written a long letter to me explaining what a commendable job he has done for him. He claims that Captain Drake is one of the best seaman that he has ever seen. He says that he is a tremendous fighter—someone who can be useful to you! I thought that you should meet him."

"From Plymouth," she said, smiling to Drake who was withdrawing from a deep bow.

"Yes, Your Majesty."

"Do you know Admiral John Hawkins?" she asked. Hawkins was now Comptroller of the Navy. But it was not a significant job, as the major part of the Navy's work was being done by privateers, such as Drake. This she knew and encouraged when it pleased her, as it did not cost the crown any money. Elizabeth was very frugal with the state's money, which was one of the reasons for her popularity with the public.

"Your Majesty, he is my cousin," Drake proudly said, speaking in his broad West Country accent.

"And have you sailed with Hawkins?"

"Well—"

"Answer me!" she demanded. Her voice now had become school-marmish.

"May I answer without fear?"

"Of course," she replied. "Tell me the truth—I know about his antics. I have even invested in his voyages. Some were profitable!"

"I made the last voyage of Admiral Hawkins, Your Majesty. I commanded the *Judith* at Juan de Ulua."

"And you escaped?" she asked, raising her eyebrows. She was fully aware of the disaster that had happened to Hawkins fleet when it had to make an emergency entry into the Mexican port; for it was then that it had been deceitfully attacked by the Spanish. She as well knew of the role that the *Judith* had played in rescuing some members of the besieged fleet.

"I did—but in a fair fight we would have beat them. We were tricked—ambushed. The Catholics cannot be trusted!"

"I know; I've tried it with Philip," meaning Philip II of Spain. "But it did not work. I have tried to be a friend to him because of the kindness that he rendered me during my sister Mary's reign," she said, speaking openly, referring to the fact that possibly without him, Mary might have had her burned at the stake. Mary had been Elizabeth's older sister who had ruled as Queen during a terrible religious period. She had succeeded her brother, Edward VI, who of course had succeeded their father, Henry VIII. Mary's reign had been a bloody one, as she had ruled as a Catholic; it had not been helped by her marriage to King Philip of Spain, though at times he had befriended Elizabeth. He presently ruled Spain. "I am now ready to try a different tack. Do you have any suggestions?"

"He must be attacked at sea," Drake said, speaking fast in his West Country dialect, which sharply contrasted with Elizabeth's English, which was very proper, as she spoke very distinctly. She was very literate, as she had received one of the finest educations possible in England. She spoke English, French and Spanish; and as well, she read Greek and Latin. She was an avid reader who had made herself familiar with most literature of importance.

"But where?" she demanded to know.

"At the source of his treasure," Drake replied, and he quickly unrolled the map that Walsingham had handed to him. "This is a map of the world as we know it," Drake said, while stretching the map out on a side table. He studied it while looking for bearings.

"The map is correct?" she asked.

"I doubt it," Drake replied, adding, "The world has not been fully explored, nor properly charted. But as I explore it, I shall draw new ones—" he confidently said, as if it were a job that he must do.

"Please do!" Elizabeth cattily said and smiled at Drake's audacity.

"But I am a very good navigator. I may be the best in England!" he confidently said.

"Oh, you are!" she haughtily said, smiling, flashing her eyes in a flirtatious manner. But she did not fully give herself to him, though she did do it to other men to whom she had an attraction. There was

47

an attraction, but she saw that there was something lacking in Drake—it was polish, breeding and schooling. And then she sensed that there was something worse; there was a cruel streak in Drake that she knew would make him a dangerous lover.

"I have spent much of my life on the water. I have wooed it as a man would a pretty woman," Drake explained and half smiled at the comparison.

"Oh," she said, as she had been only half listening. "This is where you privateers have been harassing Philip's caravans," she added, pointing to the Spanish Main.

"Right—and this is where the gold and silver is landed," Drake said, pointing to Panama on the west coast, having the same name as the present state. "It crosses the isthmus by the Camino Real. It arrives here at Nombre Dios," Drake said, pointing to a dot on the Atlantic side that represented the fortress town.

"Cartagena is the fortress for this important area?"

"That is true."

"Attack it—take it and England controls the Main!" Elizabeth said.

"We could not hold it if we took it. Philip presently has too many ships and soldiers. Your Majesty, I have visited Cartagena and captured the Spaniards as they left it, but I could not take the fort. It has too many guns. But you can hurt Philip just as well by stopping his flow of treasure."

"The treasure crosses the isthmus," she said, pointing to the narrow body of land.

"During the dry season only—"

"And they deliver it to Nombre Dios," Walsingham said.

"And is it well-defended?" she asked.

"Yes and no," Drake said, pointing, thinking. "I attacked it from the sea with seventy men—and I took it!"

"Why not take it again?"

"Your Majesty, I had it. I entered it with forty of the seventy men. We had drums beating and trumpets blaring," he said, speaking excitedly. He continued, "We took the castle, even the town. And it is as large as Plymouth. The Spaniards had run into the jungle. I entered the Governor's house—there on the floor was a sight to heal all the aches of a Devonshire man. There were stacks of silver bars seven feet by ten feet by twelve feet high. And you would not believe it, but there was also a cache of gold, just as valuable, which was in the

48

Governor's treasure house near the waterside. But then there came a storm the likes of which I have never seen. It rains dreadfully hard on the Darien coast. It poured rain for thirty minutes. And during this time, we could not leave. I fainted for the lack of blood, as I had a rifle ball in my leg. My boot was filled with blood. My men became so concerned about my welfare that they gathered me in their arms and carried me to a pinnace, though I was gaining my senses. On my doing so, I cursed them—I cried out to them, 'I have brought you to the treasure house of the world, and if you leave without it, you may henceforth blame no one but yourselves!'"

"And did they?" she asked, intently smiling, showing her excitement at the adventure being told by Drake.

"Aye! They took me and abandoned the treasure."

"And why not return and take it again?"

"It seems the logical thing to do. Yet on the other side of the isthmus, there is the South Sea, and it has a great attraction for me. The Cimarons on one occasion took me to a tall tree in the middle of the isthmus, which I climbed. From there not only could I view the South Sea, but at the same time I could see the Caribe. The South Sea is a magnificent body of water—blue as the eyes of a fair woman. I believe that it is in the South Sea where I can put the hurt on the popish dons."

"How?" she curiously asked, being partially spellbound by the adventurous talk of this sailor from Plymouth. She especially enjoyed such talk, since she had spent her life house-bound.

"The Cimarons and captured dons have told me that the Spanish ships, even when loaded with treasure, sail the South Sea without guns. They have also told me that the dons have found a mountain in Peru that is solid silver which they are mining and gradually removing to Spain. Why, they treat the South Sea as their lake, sailing it without fear, doing it because there is no one to harass them."

"But how do you reach the South Sea?"

"By the same route as Magellan," Drake explained, putting his finger on the strait named after him. "If Magellan did it, then I can do it. Surely I am as good a sailor as he—maybe better!"

"I have read of his voyage. It was a very difficult one. The strait is not a traveled lane; it would take good ships, strong hearts and much courage. And then you might fail!" Elizabeth thoughtfully said, while studying the map.

"I have the courage, and I will not fail! On making my passage, I would sail up the coast, searching it for treasure and new lands."

"You would need ships, victuals, and men—"

"And your blessings?"

"That I can give you, but you must not disclose our relationship. It might do England considerable harm," she said, shaking her head, once again speaking in the school-marm voice.

"And as well, I would like secrecy, as I would not want the dons to know of my entering the South Sea until they see me," Drake replied.

"That you will have from the Queen. Of course, we have others in this government who do not see things as I do. Take care with whom you speak concerning our business—that includes my court!"

"That I will do," Drake said.

"And if the dons capture you, you are not to say that you are on a mission for me!" she emphatically said, while thoughtfully fingering her pearl necklace.

"I agree," Drake said, bowing to show that he knew the informal meeting was at an end.

CHAPTER 6

THE INVESTORS

Drake had to meet with Walsingham several more times before he was able to put together the details for the South Sea venture and ready his fleet for sailing from England. These visits were ostensibly made by Drake for business purposes connected with the venture. He came to Walsingham to obtain money to pay suppliers or else he called on the Secretary so as to give him an accounting of his expenditures. Drake looked forward to each visit, as he was eager to establish a closer relationship; however, Walsingham never let Drake get any closer to him than that relationship established on Drake's first visit. Yet on Drake's second visit to see Walsingham, the two men did speak on more friendly terms, though Walsingham kept the meeting on a business basis. The Secretary's office was now at Greenwich Palace, as the Queen was in residence there. Greenwich Palace was located by the tidal waters of the Thames River. It was a long, irregular building crowded with battlements and was the Queen's favorite residence for the summer, possibly because she was able to stand at her bedroom windows and watch the tall ships slip down the Thames on the ebb tide. At this second meeting, Drake, like Walsingham, wore a high-standing collar attached to his doublet, called a ruff. It was held taut by a specially devised drawstring. His doublet had been stylishly filled with bombast, which was a stuffing that made his chest appear larger and his waist much smaller.

"And what progress are you making in preparation for your voyage?" the Secretary asked, as he handed Drake a paper.

"We are doing quite well. The bark *Marigold* has been delivered to me at Plymouth."

"That was provided by Sir Christopher Hatton," the Secretary said in a knowledgeable voice, as if he were pointing out that he had engineered the transfer of this small ship. Hatton was a member of the Queen's privy council, and he subsequently would become Lord Chancellor. He was such an enthusiastic supporter of the venture that he had placed his fifty-ton bark at Drake's disposal.

"We are probably going to need four more ships—Rawls, the ship builder, has agreed to make four pinnaces for us."

"And how will you transport them?" Walsingham curiously asked, while dropping his eyes so as to study a document that a clerk had placed before him. The secretary was not an outdoorsman, and he knew very little about boats, though he did know that the pinnace was a large, double-banked, square-sterned sailing boat. It was principally used as a tender to large ships. He raised his eyebrows as he momentarily thought on the pinnace. He just knew that the pinnaces would take up a lot of deck space on the small ships.

"They come apart and are stowed below deck. They are easily put back together. We will use them for shallow water operations. However, I will keep one tethered to the stern of the lead ship when it is not in use. An expedition of this kind could not be completed without the pinnace," Drake explained and glanced at Walsingham's eyes, hoping to incite a flame. It did not come.

"I see—I have formed an ad hoc stock company for the venture," Walsingham said in a business-like voice. "Here is a list of its investors. The names of the investors must be kept secret. Many of them have important positions with Her Majesty's navy. These names include the Earl of Lincoln, Lord High Admiral of the Navy; Sir William Winter, Surveyor of the Navy; his brother, George Winter, clerk of the Queen's Ships; John Hawkins, your cousin, who will soon be Treasurer of the Navy. They as well include myself, the Earl of Leicester and Sir Christopher Hatton." The latter three were members of the Queen's privy council. "As well, the Queen has invested a thousand crowns. Imagine that!" he said, smiling.

"Well, that is an impressive list. Relay my thanks to each; as well, advise them that I am so confident of the success of the venture that I am investing a thousand pounds of my own money in it." And he placed a small leather bag on Walsingham's desk; it jangled noisily.

"Well, now that is certainly important for the success of the venture," the Secretary said. "And you will be needing money today?"

"Yes, Sir Francis. I will need five hundred pounds. I must make a payment to Hogg for my cannons." Ralph Hogg of Sussex had developed a method of casting iron guns. Drake did not explain that Hogg's cannons would not be placed on his ship, which he planned to name the *Pelican*. His ship would carry eighteen cannons, most of which would be cast of bronze. He had secretly planned a visit to the Spanish Netherlands where he would contract for the casting of the *Pelican*'s guns. Each would carry a plate with Drake's adopted coat of arms, which was a globe and a star. Hogg's cannons would be placed on the *Elizabeth*, which would be commanded by John Wynter. "Then I must begin the purchase of cordage, canvas and the like. As well, I will advance a bit of silver to those experienced men who have previously sailed with me and are committed to the venture. I will give you an itemized list of the cost on my next visit."

"And do you have many good men committed?" Walsingham asked, being curious as to the number.

"Oh, I do have some," Drake replied, adding, "We'll lose some to others. But the best of the lot, John Oxenham, has already put together a crew with ships, and he has sailed for the Spanish Main. Oh, John was a beauty. I could use him on this one. He was game for anything that I suggested," Drake said, smiling at the reminiscence.

"Maybe another one just as good will turn up from this group," the Secretary said, while turning to accept a cup of hot broth from a servant.

"I hope so. Well, anyway, we will have a touch of gentry with us," Drake said, and then he turned to accept his broth.

"Oh!" the Secretary lightly exclaimed, blowing on his broth.

"Yes, Thomas Doughty is joining the venture," Drake said without pointing out the actual role that Doughty had played in putting together the venture.

"Well, well, that is something!" the Secretary said, smiling while thinking about the young lawyer who had served as his secretary as well as the secretary for other senior officers in the cabinet of Elizabeth. "I know him well. He worked for me. He is a bright young lawyer. He has had some good experience. I admire him for going. He surely will have some stories to tell on his return."

"That may be so—" Drake said, thinking, not commenting further. Then he sipped on his broth.

"And the Queen has asked me to convey to you her message that in the event that you are captured or compromised, you are to destroy all official documents. And at all times you are to deny that you are in her service!"

"I understand—"

"Oh, she sends you another message. She asks that you visit with Dr. John Dee, her astrologist. He is at Mortlake south of London—"

"Astrologist?" Drake curiously asked.

"Well, he is a man of many talents. He is also the greatest geographer in all England. He possibly can give you some good advice," the Secretary said, standing. He opened Drake's bag of coins and counted out five hundred pounds of gold coins, which he then pushed across the desk to Drake. "You will need to sign here," he said and put before him a sheet of paper.

"Thank you, sir," Drake replied, standing. He took the coins, and then he shook the Secretary's hand and exited from the office.

"Well, now," Drake said in a surprised voice on seeing Thomas Doughty exit from the office of Lord Burghley, the Queen's Treasurer. Surprise also showed on Doughty's face as Drake approached him.

"Good evening!" Doughty nervously said on nearing Drake.

"And what might you be doing with the Lord Treasurer?" Drake asked. A hardness was in his voice, as if he were demanding that the other man give him good reasons for having visited the Treasurer's office. Doughty had to know that Burghley would be opposed to the expedition; Drake's thoughts were so firmly directed toward the great venture to the South Sea that he had difficulty considering anything else. He as well was very reluctant to discuss the voyage with outsiders. He had not yet fully discussed the voyage with his wife; however, she did know that Drake was planning a future voyage, and she was strongly opposed to it.

"Oh, the Earl sent for me—wants me to work for him," he explained in a casual manner, as if it were a common occurrence for the Lord Treasurer to call on him.

"And what did you reply?" Drake curiously asked.

"I told him that I had other plans."

"Like what?"

"Like practicing as a barrister. I told him that I will be at the middle temple."

"Does he know anything about our venture?"

"Not a word—"

"That is good," Drake said, smiling deceptively, as it was a West Country smile. Doughty should have noted that the face around it was as hard as if it had been exposed to a North Atlantic gale.

"Would you like a pot of ale?" Drake asked as he shouldered his cape.

"Sure," Doughty replied. "There is something that I want to talk to you about."

"What is that?"

"I have nine gentlemen friends that would like to make the voyage with us."

"What have you told them?" Drake curiously asked Doughty, who like Drake wore a ruff. He as well wore a velvet jacket, knee pants, and dark hose with bombast. His shoes were also covered with velvet and were topped with silver buckles.

"Nothing, except that we will sail on a venture, possibly to Egypt. The fact that you are a leader of the expedition is sufficient reason for them to want to come!"

"And when did you say that we would be leaving?"

"I said that it would take a year to put it together."

"And what have you told them that their duties would be?"

"I did not say—"

"But if they sail, it would have to be as seamen!" Drake said, positioning them for the worst, though he knew that he would have to have soldiers as well. And he had to know that the gentlemen venturers would be better qualified at soldiering than serving as seamen.

"Oh!" Doughty said. He knew that none of the nine men had ever done any hard work; most were still in school, such as inns of court where they were studying law. They were poorly equipped to serve as seamen.

"There is no other way that it can be done, which you will soon learn on your own," Drake said. Irritancy was in his voice. A seaman's life was normally very hard—he was expected to stand watch irrespective of the condition of the sea, and then he had to work when not on watch. It would be worse in this expedition, for to begin with, there would not be sufficient bunk space, nor space to stow all personal gear. And worse, there would be very little space to move about, and the ships would require a lot of work. Sails had to be hoisted, furled and repaired in all types of weather. A seaman would need the agility of a monkey and the endurance of a pack horse in order to handle it.

"I will so advise them," Doughty said, though there was a ring of insincerity to his words.

CHAPTER 7

THE QUEEN'S ASTROLOGIST

Drake curiously eyed the man pacing back and forth in front of him. And it was with reason, for his appearance and manners were strange. He had stooped shoulders, a beak-like nose and hawk-like eyes. He wore a long white beard. He looked like a gnome, as he was short and fat, while he was dressed in a clerical cap and a black robe. He had been talking continuously for almost an hour since Drake had arrived. He had randomly dissertated on a myriad of subjects without asking Drake's opinion on a single one, doing it as he paced the room with his outstretched hands, which he expressively used, though walking was not easy, as books, manuscripts and navigational equipment cluttered the floor. Most of the topics that he had discussed were incongruous, for he had spoken on the weather and how it was created by atmosphere, which he had said was the ups and downs of it and on how to make gold from certain chemicals by mixing them with pottery clay. He had even lectured on the right of a king to rule over his kingdom; and then he had related to Drake that the selection of a regent could only be done by an act of God. He then had quickly changed the subject to laws—those laws that must be written and those that do not have to be written. Finally, he had spoken of the difference between poets and rhymers.

The speaker was Dr. John Dee, the controversial astrologist and geographer of Queen Elizabeth. The two men were in Dee's library of 25,000 volumes at Mortlake, which then was the largest library in England. The room would have delighted a bibliophile. Old books and manuscripts were scattered about the floor and on the tables. The walls in the huge room were lined from floor to ceiling with shelves that were filled with books. A collector of curios would also have enjoyed it, as the floor was littered with many interesting objects, such as a toy turtle that walked when Dee touched its nose.

"So my lady has chosen you to prove the existence of the Strait of Anian?" Dee asked, chuckling, momentarily facing Drake, studying him, finally mentioning the subject that had brought Drake to Mortlake. And, as well, he was finally asking Drake a question. Drake's facial expression showed his relief.

"Well," Drake hesitantly said, not knowing how to answer him. He had studied the map on the table before him while Dr. Dee had paced the floor and expounded on subject after subject. Drake was familiar with the place called Anian, which was a name that the cartographers such as Dee had given to an area at the top of the map near what is Northern Canada. Yet they did not have any evidence that such place actually existed.

"And your plans are to enter the Southern Sea, which Magellan has called the Pacific Ocean, doing it by way of the Magellan Strait?" Dee asked, turning back and half facing Drake. Then he skeptically studied Drake, as if he were doubting that he would actually make the trip.

"That is one plan," Drake again answered hesitantly, being reluctant to confide in this strange man. The reader will recall that Drake was so close-mouthed about his plans that he at first had been reluctant to confide in the Queen, and with good reason. For Drake was an unreformed pirate who had a self-taught understanding of matters of state. And so he knew that legitimate acts of war under one regime may easily become crimes under another.

"Enough! Enough! Answer me! My Lords Hatton, Leicester and Walsingham were here less than a month ago," Dee said. Dee removed his cap, exposing his bald head, while fanning himself with the cap. He then shook it at Drake while continuing. "They excitedly confided in me about your plans. Now, speak to me! Tell me, will you go there to explore?"

"Of course," Drake replied. Yet he did not have any fixed plans on finding new lands. His main purpose in making the voyage was to plunder the Spaniards of their gold, silver and jewels. He as well had some minor reasons for setting out on this dangerous venture, none of which would have interested such a learned man. Firstly, he was a man of action who craved adventure, and so he wanted to sail the South Sea. Secondly, he wanted to punish the Spaniards who he intensely hated. But in the main, he was a greedy, avaricious man who wanted gold and silver just like the Spaniards. On his last voyage to Nombre Dios, he had acquired sufficient treasure to make him a rich man for life. Why, he already had a big house, a good wife and several servants! But that had not sufficed. He now had the desire to be rich beyond the dreams of most men, and he believed that his desire could be fulfilled by a voyage to the South Sea.

"Then once you are through the Strait of Magellan, you must sail west. There you will find a new land called "Australias in Cognita." I call it Beach. It is a whole new continent waiting for our colonization."

"How do you know that it exists?" Drake asked, studying the map.

"Exists!" Dee exclaimed while momentarily staring at Drake with bristling eyebrows. "You see it has to exist. For one of the rules of the world is that there has to be as much land south of the equator as north of it. It is the law of balance. If you study this map, you will find that it is top heavy with land," Dee said, pointing to the ill-drawn map of North America. "Thus, there must be vast bodies of land located here," Dee said, pointing to what we now know as the Southern Pacific Ocean, which of course is devoid of a continent. "And once you arrive there, you will find plenty of gold, silver, and jewels, for they are created by the heat of the sun."

"And you are asking me to discover this land and take it for England?" Drake asked, eyeing this man who had questioned him as though he were seeking a reason why he was visiting him. Walsingham had told Drake that Dee's voice was the voice of Elizabeth in such matters. It was done with good reason, for Elizabeth was quite learned in math. Early in her regime, she had begun to seek the advice of Dee in such matters. He had taught navigational math to most of England's navigators. He had calculated a departure table and had designed a compass fly, dividing it into degrees as well as points. In 1550 he had devised the circumpolar chart for the use of the Muscovy Company's navigators in northern waters. And as well, he was England's most prolific writer on the subject.

"Absolutely—it would be the beginning of a British Empire. We could use those persons rotting in prisons to colonize these lands."

"But they would lose England!" Drake argued as though that were the worst punishment that could be rendered an Englishman. This was with reason, for even though his father had been banished from England and had had to raise his family in the hulk of a ship near Chatham navy yard, he had continued to love England—it was a Catholic Queen that he hated, not England. And Drake's ties were just as strong. He could not imagine life without England being a part of it. He had sailed from England on many occasions, but always with the intent of returning.

"Naye, they would be an extension of England. Imagine lands all over the world with happy, intelligent, English-speaking persons. They would produce raw goods. And in turn we would import them, manufacture them into finished goods, and then sell them back to them. All of us would become rich. The gold would solidify the relationship!"

"And what are we going to do about the Spanish?" Drake asked, attempting to return the conversation to present-day problems. He was sure the principal one was Spain, for he was smart enough to know that it had the army and navy to interfere with such settlements.

"Utilize our skills as seamen—drive them from the seas. I understand that you and I are in accord on this subject," Dee said, indicating that he had discussed this subject at his last meeting with members of the privy council.

"We are—and I have been doing my bit in that direction."

"Well, so I hear," Dee said without smiling. Then he crossed over to the map on the table near Drake. He studied it and then he said, "And once you have made your discoveries on Australias, then you must sail north, discovering and plotting new land space. As you go north, sail this way," he said, pointing out directions on the out-of-proportion map. "And on your coming to Anian," he said, pointing to an area near present-day Canada, "you will find a strait similar to that of Magellan. You will utilize it to make your exit. It has to be there because the world is full of balances. I have already remarked about that. So if we have a strait here," he said, pointing to the Magellan Strait, "then we must have another one here," Dee explained, pointing toward the place called Anian. "If there is a tall mountain in the Southern Hemisphere, then there has to be one in the Northern Hemisphere to offset it," he said while superiorly smiling.

"How sure are you that the Strait of Anian exists?" Drake respectfully asked Dee, who was quizzically staring at Drake.

"I am as sure as you are that the Magellan Strait exists," the man confidently replied. He now looked much like a monk, as he had put his hat back on his head. He then removed his hat and rubbed his askew hair. "Its location is fixed; it is governed by the law of proportions!"

"I will seek it," Drake said, nodding his head. His voice was full of confidence.

"And when you do find it, then your name will be with those of Columbus and Magellan. Men will write books about you, for you will have found the shortcut to the East," Dee said, smiling, showing brown teeth.

"And do you have a map for my use?" Drake asked, hoping that it would be the one on the table. It was dated 1569. It had been made by Mercator, a Dutchman, who then was considered to be the best cartographer in the world.

"Oh, this one is yours. It is the most up-to-date."

"Thank you, Doctor," Drake said and respectfully nodded his head.

"It has all of Magellan's discoveries on it—"

"And the strait?"

"It is there—but its fault," he said, referring to the map, "is in the latitudes. Mercator fails to recognize that the earth is a sphere divided by imaginary longitudinal and latitudinal lines. Mercator did not understand that the latitudinal dividers widen as one leaves the poles."

"Are you saying that the earth is a sphere?"

"Yes, that is my opinion."

"And its belly is the equator?"

"Yes, if you sail the equator, you take the long route. And so on your finding the Anian Strait near the North Pole, the distance to the lands of Marco Polo would be narrowed. But back to traversing east to west. You must calculate your movements with the use of a time piece, otherwise you will not know your location for sure," he said, pausing as if counting.

"But time pieces are difficult to maintain, and at sea—"

"I know," Dee thoughtfully said. Then he added, "Could you tell me the date of your birth?"

"Well, it is May 13, 1541."

"May 13, 1541," Dee repeated. Then he stood and crossed the room to a large book lying on a table. He opened it and studied it. "Aries—a ram—a ram," he said, chanting as he crossed to the door. He opened it and went outside to study the heavens. Moments later he returned to the room and sat back down in his chair.

"What is it?" Drake asked on noting that the man's face had turned ashen.

"This conversation has been a waste—the stars tell me that at the time of your birth, a wild ram raced across the heavens—it is still there. This indicates that you are hell-bent—none can advise you!" he said, frowning as though appalled at his discovery.

"I am sorry," Drake said in a concerned voice.

"There is nothing that can be done—it is written and beyond our hands!" Dee said in a voice filled with finality.

"I am sorry," Drake replied again and stood, for he sensed that the meeting was at an end.

"And so am I, but good luck to you. And if you do go north, search for Anian," Dee said, picking up a manuscript and aimlessly turning its pages.

"I will," said Drake, carefully rolling the map and momentarily pondering, as if he, too, saw a wild ram racing across the heavens. He wondered whether that ram could be himself?

CHAPTER 8

THE CREW OF THE *PELICAN*

The tide had flooded Sutton Hole, Plymouth's tiny inner harbor. The *Pelican* had moved alongside the main dock so as to load stores. She would move out a few feet when the tide ebbed, and then she would lay on her side until the next tide entered. She was newly painted. Her masts were fully rigged and ready for sails. A small, ragged line of men was on her deck. All of the men were waiting to see the Captain, who was in his cabin. The *Pelican* was a French ship and was unusually well-made. Drake had purchased it from Sprayberry, a London merchant. But before Drake had taken delivery of the *Pelican*, he had required the merchant to build a cabin where previously there had been an open poop deck. This cabin was now a commodious room, as it had two bunks that could be pulled up when not in use and a table for navigating and dining. Six men could dine there in comfort, but it could accommodate eight if necessary. A dozen men could easily assemble there for a meeting. Each side had four windows. Through its aftermost part there was a door for a small gun that was called a murderer, while above it was a window. Almost to the after part near the small gun protruded the whipstaff, which was a wooden rod that traveled from the deck above to a yoke that was attached to the rudder, which was beneath the water. It was from the poop deck just above Drake's cabin that the helmsman steered the ship by the use of the whipstaff. It was from this deck that the *Pelican* would be conned.

"Tom Moone!" Drake exclaimed, standing, broadly smiling at the man entering the room. The man was not as tall or stout as Drake; he had stooped shoulders and a boyish face, which was marred by several smallpox scars. His brown hair carelessly fell over his eyes. He smiled, displaying two missing front teeth. Genuine surprise was on Drake's face. Drake eyed him, wondering if Moone was to be his John Oxenham.

"Cap'n, I am glad to see you!" Moone answered, and he hurried to Drake and clasped his hand. The two men had made several voyages together. They had even served together on Hawkins' third slaving expedition; Moone had been with Drake in the *Judith* when they escaped from Juan de Ulua. Then Moone had been Drake's carpenter on Drake's last expedition to Nombre Dios. It was he who had helped Drake rig some logs into a sailing vessel at San Fernandez so they could locate the pinnaces.

"What work are you doing, Tom?" Drake asked, smiling, showing genuine fondness for Moone. Drake was dressed in a shirt, pants and calf-length boots.

"Carriages, Cap'n. I am in partnership with my brother-in-law."

"I hope business is good."

"Business is slow—people don't seem to have much confidence in a four-wheel carriage," Moone said in a casual way, as if he were indifferent to the business.

"And would you like to sail with me, Tom?"

"Do you have a carpenter?" Moone asked, speaking in the same indifferent way, as if he were not very interested.

"Yes, but I can make a place for you—"

"I dunno—but then I could use a bit of gold—a man gets greedy after he has had a taste of it—" Moone said while rubbing a silver coin with his right fingers. Yet it was more than that—he missed the adventure, for he was that rare type of man who craved it like a drinking man craves strong drink.

"Well?"

"Where do you sail for?" Moone asked.

"Alexandria," Drake replied, contorting his face so as to form it into the Devon grin, which was commonly done by Devon sailors when they had said something that they did not expect to be believed.

"Do the popish Spaniards have treasure ships there?" Moone asked, forming the same grin, as if sure that Drake would be voyaging for Spanish treasure.

"We will be looking for them—I guarantee ye gold!" Drake said, half frowning, half smiling, again forming his face into the Devon grin. "I would like to have you join up, Tom—" Drake's voice had an

64

unsureness to it, as if he were uneasy that Moone would not sail with him.

"And if there is no gold?"

"You get the wages of the sea—" Drake said, referring to the pittance that by custom was paid to seamen. Moone had the greed of a pirate, so he would not have taken it if it had been offered.

"Ah, that won't buy victuals for the missus!"

"That's the law of the sea," Drake replied.

"I know—and how large is your fleet?"

"I have a fleet of five ships—this is the *Pelican*; it has a one hundred-ton burthen. I am its captain. She has eighteen guns. There is the eighty-ton *Elizabeth*. She is commanded by John Wynter. Do you know him?"

"The Admiral's son—"

"Yes. And there is the *Swan*, which is a fifty-ton store ship. It is commanded by John Chester, the ex-Mayor of London's son. Then I have the *Marigold*, which is a bark merchantman; it is commanded by John Thomas. Lastly, I have a fifteen-ton bark named the *Benedict*. If you sign aboard, then I shall make you its Captain. You will be the messenger for the fleet."

"Well—"

"And the command would give you an extra share in the treasure," Drake quickly added.

"And when do you sail?"

"November 15," Drake replied. Then Drake cleverly smiled and added, "We have many men already signed whom you know—William Hawkins has signed on—"

"One of the Hawkins boys?"

"Son of the Mayor—and there is Richard Minivy -"

"Old Hard Head!"

"Yes—and my brother Tom, my cousin John," Drake said, pointing to a youth standing near the door. "There is Edward Bright—"

"And top men?" Moone asked. He was referring to seamen who could work the topmost sails. This work required extremely good seamen. Moone knew that a long voyage could not be successful without good top men.

"Oh, plenty for the *Pelican*—we have Black Halter, Hood, Hurd, Carden, Bos'n Fowler, Blackcollar—"

"Good men—" Moone said, wavering. "Blackcollar's not a bad cook!" Moone said. Blackcollar had served as cook on Drake's last expedition to Darien; yet he was also a good seaman. He would eventually do much of the baking. Drake had already selected his cook when Blackcollar asked to join the expedition.

"Oh, we have William Horsewill as cook. Remember him?"

"The herb cook," Moone replied, smiling. "No horse on your ship," Moone added. He was speaking of the salted horse meat that was common fare on most ships.

"The best cooks come from Tavistock—"

"They all know how to cook," Moone said, referring to the people of Tavistock, which was a village that was located a few miles north of Plymouth. Horsewill was a good representative of his village, as he was an excellent cook. He was that rare cook that one occasionally found on an English ship. Most cooks were cooks because they had lost an arm or a leg and were no longer able to climb the rigging, so in order for them to go to sea, they took on the job of cook. Most usually just threw horse meat and peas in a pot with water and cooked them as a stew until they were eaten. And most sea captains accepted it as a fact that shipboard cooking had to be bad. The exception was Drake—he liked to be well-fed. Furthermore, he was ahead of the time in his thinking on the role of food, as he was convinced that disease was less of a problem when the men were well-fed. Having the Tavistock cook aboard would make the difference to Moone, for Moone knew that the pudgy Horsewill would set the food standards for the voyage, as he would be taking many different herbs on the voyage which he would use so as to change the taste of meat, fish and soups. He knew that Horsewill would be cooking his mutton with thyme and seaweed—his pease puddings would be extra tasty, as he cooked his puddings with pieces of boiled bacon, mint and honey.

"Diego!" Tom Moone exclaimed, and his face brightened on seeing the black man enter the cabin door. Diego was dressed in a leather jacket, baggy woolen pants and boots that came up to his knees. He had a brown leather throng tied about a long tail of wiry hair which hung down his back. He wore a gold chain about his neck which was attached to a large gold coin. It had been Diego who had talked his chief, Pedro, into furnishing Drake with the critical information as to the fortification of the town of Nombre Dios. And then he had been the one who had enticed Pedro into joining Drake in

66

making the attack. The black man was so happy to see Moone that he gave a loud whoop, then he grabbed the carpenter and embraced him, and, in doing so, raised his feet a foot off the ground.

"You, too, join us?" Diego asked in his halting English.

"If you whisper to me where you sail—"

"Alexandria!" the black man answered, falsely smiling. Then he attempted to contort his face so as to form the Devon grin.

"Ah!"

"True, Moone, true—"

"But where?"

"Follow the Cap'n. He get plenty gold this time!"

"I'll sign, Cap'n," Moone said, smiling.

But at the "Old Ring of Bells," being a popular pub on Wolster Street located near the waterfront, a different form of recruitment was taking place. Doughty and his gentlemen friends had been appearing there nightly to drink ale and wine. It was now half-past eight—a boisterous time for the pub. Huge lanterns were lit—their flames flared each time the street door was opened. Many of these young men had been drinking for hours. Some were droopy from too much drink; others were boisterous and loud. All of the men wore sailor or lumper attire except Doughty. He was not only older, but he was dressed differently. He wore a velvet jacket with a ruff collar, which was loose, as he, too, was almost in his cup. His sleeves were flared from bombast, making his arms appear much larger. A bearded sailor with a flat nose and a scraggy beard leaned over to him, and speaking above the noise, he said in a heavy, West Country accent:

"And by your words, I know ye be sailin' with Francis Drake!"

"That I will," replied Doughty. "Would you like to sail on the expedition with us? We could use another seaman."

"Are you sailing as a seaman?" the sailor curiously asked, smiling through an ugly beard, showing missing teeth, while studying Doughty's ruff and his velvet jacket. It was obvious to a good listener that the speech of Doughty was that of a Cambridge man, which automatically made him a gentleman. And so the inquirer was talking down to Doughty, for a gentleman rarely did a seaman's work. Doughty momentarily paused. The sailor's voice was unduly filled with curiosity. He obviously wanted his question answered first.

"Naye," Doughty replied. "I am a gentleman. I will be going on the expedition as a soldier."

"Drake has hired thee as a soldier!" the sailor exclaimed, momentarily studying the man who had the build of a ballroom dancer. Then he said with a scoff, "Drake does not make a difference between a sailor and a soldier; he expects all of his seamen to be soldiers. Have you seen him fight? He is a lion—a tiger! And he loves a fight! Stand clear of him when he is angry!"

"I have served as a captain in the army, fought in Ireland. I am in charge of the land forces for the expedition!" Doughty surely said, though his speech was slurred from drink.

"Oh, you are," the sailor sarcastically said, sardonically smiling, being intently watched by a smiling, toothless sailor seated beside him. A mug of dark beer was before him. He was obviously enjoying the badgering which was commonplace in the pub.

"And how did Drake come to make you the head of his army?" the sailor sarcastically demanded, as though he did not believe a word of it.

"It is I who got him this commission from the Queen—"

"From the Queen?" the man asked with a sneer, opening his mouth wide and showing ugly teeth. He said it as though it were not possible. And it was done with some truth, for most of the ships sailing from Plymouth did so without commissions.

"Yes—this is a joint expedition."

"Don't tell me that—"

"It is true—"

"Ah—Drake ain't seen the Queen!"

"Yes, he has. I got him a meeting with Queen Elizabeth—and she gave him a commission to make this expedition. We are joint generals—I have the same authority as he."

"Beware that you don't tell him that, or he will have your head!" the sailor said and put his hand to his throat to show a severance. The seaman had an obvious dislike as well as a fear of Drake. Much of it was jealousy. There were many persons in Plymouth who considered Drake to be the total leader—one who could lead but could not stand to have a boss over him. There were others who were so jealous of him that they often spread terrible stories about his abilities or loyalties.

"He knows it—we've talked it out. Without me, he would not have a command!" Doughty said with emphasis.

"And for where do you sail!"

"Alexandria—"

"For what reason?"

"To trade," Doughty replied, smiling.

"Drake trade—that is absurd, mate! He is a pirate—a man for Spanish gold. You're bound for the Spanish Main—" he sneered, showing once more his ugly teeth, and he drank from his tankard, spilling ale down his chin, which he wiped with the back of his hand.

"Have you been there?" Doughty curiously interrupted.

"Yes—" the man thoughtfully said. "I took the fever—got a bullet in me leg, and I came back poorer than I went. Never again, I say!"

"With Drake?"

"Naye, but if I'd gone with him, I would have been better off, as he has luck. It is the devil in him!"

"I'm sorry that you did not."

"Need you be? I say with a motley lot like yours and a leader like Drake, you can expect a peck of trouble," the sailor said. Then he threw back his head and gulped down the remainder of his tankard of ale and patted his stomach to show his pleasure.

"You have to be wrong!"

"More ale!" the sailor shouted above the noise.

"But I'm general of the soldiers," Doughty attempted to explain, becoming vexed at the man for not understanding his position.

"Soldiers for a pirate like Drake?" the sailor asked, as if it were not possible for Drake to use them.

"Yes, that is our agreement. And Drake is to be general of the sailors."

"But with Drake, every soldier will be a sailor—and that leaves you without an army. You will find yourself a Cambridge man at sea with a pirate," he said with a sneer, while wiping his beard with the back of his hand.

"I think that you're wrong—I'm in a different situation—I got him his commission from the Queen."

"What else can you get him?" the man asked with a leer.

"But do you want to sail with us?"

"Naye, I would not want to see it!"

A week later Doughty had his first real confrontation with Drake. It came about soon after a party that John Hawkins gave at his house for the gentlemen, Drake and his captains. John Hawkins was now Treasurer of the Navy, and he would play an important role in the building of the English Navy. His family had been in ships and shipping for years, giving the appearance of wealth. But in truth their fortune had come from slaving expeditions. John Hawkins now had ambitions at court, and he knew of his own knowledge that Doughty had considerable influence with the Queen's ministers. And so he knew that a word from him might secure him the post of Admiral of the Navy. So during the party, he had had a short, whispered conversation with Doughty so as to stay on his good side:

"And how do you like working with Drake?"

"So far, so good—he has some polishing to do—but he will learn—"

"Oh!"

"He does not understand order of command."

"Are you in charge?" Hawkins cagily asked.

"Well, John, the expedition was my idea—I invested my money like you—it was basically my idea," he repeated. "The Queen wanted me to be in charge. She just did not trust Francis."

Hawkins was ordinarily not a bearer of tales; yet he knew something about expeditions. He had made several important slaving expeditions to Africa, bought the slaves and then merchandised them in the West Indies. He had been the leader of an expedition to the West Indies where his fleet had been treacherously attacked by the Spaniards, resulting in the loss of six ships. The *Judith*, commanded by Drake, had been one of two ships to survive the attack. Thus, Hawkins' relationship with Drake was close, though many swore that it was not so. Yet how could it have been otherwise. Hawkins' nephew, William, was sailing as a seaman on the *Pelican*.

And so the very next day, Hawkins conveyed the substance of his conversation with Doughty to Drake, who bristled on being told what Doughty had said.

"He is in charge, eh!" Drake said, frowning, feeling more hurt than ordinary, because the news had been brought by his more accomplished cousin. The news made it appear that the Queen did not think he was qualified to command such an expedition when he knew that he was.

"That is what he said—" Hawkins said, contorting his face into a grin to show that he thought the statement was ridiculous.

The man in charge of storing the fleet was James Lytle, the master of the store ship *Swan*. Lytle was a tall, stoop-shouldered seaman with considerable experience at sea. He was nearly forty years old. He had been a master for fifteen years. Drake had assigned him the job of storing the five ships because he knew that he could do it well. The job was done, but it had been a very difficult one. The hull of each ship was deep, and so goods had been stored on top of goods. This was acceptable so long as the goods were stowed so as to be available when needed. Lytle had stored numerous casks of beer and wine in each ship. Lytle as well had stored much foodstuffs, which included dried beef, pork and fish, rice, cheese, salt, honey and biscuits. Each ship had barrels of turnips and yams; the latter had been introduced by John Hawkins. None of the ships carried the Virginia potato (the Irish potato), as this newly introduced vegetable was not only scarce but expensive. Each ship carried extra woolen and linen clothing for the men. Lytle had put in the holds of each ship shoes, hats, caps, dishes, bowls, tankards, and the like. Each ship had a plentiful supply of wood and coal for its galley stove. Each ship also carried extra sails, rope, pitch, tar and resin. Each had a supply of twine, needles, nets and fish hooks. There were also tools, such as scoops, shovels, mattocks, hatchets, crowbars, nails and spikes, and the tenders carried much more.

The magazine of each ship carried a full supply of handguns, powder and balls, swords, pikes and the like. Each carried at least a dozen longbows; all were more than six feet long. The magazine of each ship also carried hundreds of twenty-eight-inch arrows, each having a metal tip and vanes made of goosefeathers. The *Pelican* and the *Elizabeth* as well carried culverins that fired fifteen-pound shots. All were mounted and ready for firing.

"All ships are stored, victualed and ready for sea," Lytle said, uneasily facing Drake, who was seated at the chart table. Doughty was seated across from him writing a letter.

"Very well," Drake said, raising his eyes. He sternly eyed the sailor.

"Would you like to inspect my work?"

"I already have—"

"Are you satisfied, Cap'n?"

"No, I am not," Drake sternly replied, causing Doughty to start. Doughty's mouth was open, as this exchange had shocked him, for he had previously established a nice relationship with James Lytle, which had given him a chance to watch him work. Even though the only formal education that James Lytle had had was grammar school, still he was considerably educated because of his fondness for books. He was especially fond of poetry, which he sometimes discussed

71

with Doughty. The latter often had joined Lytle at his job of directing seamen in the storing of the hundreds of items necessary for the voyage. He would stand beside him and the two would talk of Greek poets and the Greek wars, and of late they had talked of the Reformation of England, being the rightful place of the Protestant church and the fact that the English language was becoming the language of the court. Drake was familiar with the relationship.

"It is the language of the people!"

"Of England," Doughty corrected him.

"What is wrong?" the sailor asked. Perplexity was on his face. His voice choked as he softly spoke to the man who all Plymouth now referred to as "The Captain." For some it was done out of respect; others did it out of fear.

"You should know—you have been doing this for years."

"What can I do to right my error?"

"Nothing—you are dismissed. I will not take you on this expedition!" Drake firmly said.

"Cap'n—" Doughty interrupted. He, too, like all the other men when he was aboard ship called Drake "Captain." "Tell me what the man has done wrong!"

"He did not do his job!"

"He has done it, too—I say he goes with us!"

"I am the General of this expedition—and he does not sail with us!" Drake emphatically said.

"But we have joint authority, Cap'n!"

"He leaves, else I will have him forcibly ejected from my ships!"

"I am leaving, Cap'n," the bewildered sailor said, while backing toward the door. "I must first get me sea chest and horn," being the cow's horn, in which he kept tallow and needles for sewing sails and lubricating his hands when working.

CHAPTER 9

THE DEPARTURE

Drake's fleet of five ships slowly maneuvered their way out of Sutton Hole amidst great noise, much of it coming from the *Pelican*. As crewmen she carried one trumpeter, sixteen-year-old John Brewer, one drummer, John Drake, and two viol players, a pair of seventeen-year-old boys, John Martyn and Edward Mincy; each of the latter played a six-string instrument that was almost as tall as the player himself. All of the musicians vigorously played their instruments as if their lives depended on it, though at times they could hardly be heard from the noise of the ships' guns being intermittently fired. These guns were in the charge of Gunner Clark, a tall, strongly-built Englishman, who had been a prize recruit of Drake. This was because he had been trained in the Netherlands where he had served with the Spanish army. Many thought that it was the best place to train a gunner, as it not only had superior craftsmen, but the gunners were able to develop their skill in the Lowland wars that were seemingly endless. As well, he understood the usage of the various sizes of gunpowder.

Another prize recruit of Drake's had been Robert Winterly, who would work with Clark, though Winterly was a bowman and one of the best in all of England. He had powerful shoulders and arms, which gave him great leverage, while his accuracy with the bow was uncanny.

The dock and banks of the harbor were lined with people who waved and cheered at the ships being towed by their longboats out of Sutton Poole. There was other noise—the bleating of goats, the cackling of hens, and the grunting of pigs. However, it was barely heard above the noises of farewell. Then as the ships sailed clear of the harbor, most of the spectators ran up the hill to the hoe, being the grass-covered cliff with battlements that was above the Sound. And when the women reached this point, many of them began to cry and wail. Some frantically waved at the ships, for the significance of the ships' leaving had now dawned on them. They knew that the ships would not return for at least eighteen months. Much could happen in such a period. And now they were feeling the time—there would be a year and a half of waiting! But that was not the worst part. Most knew from recalling past expeditions that possibly only one-half of those leaving would return. Which men would not return?

The *Pelican* sailed south along the coast toward Lizard Point being closely followed by the other four ships. Drake paced the poop deck of his tiny ship, which was the deck which served as the roof for his cabin. He wore a leather hat and jacket and his woolen pants. The strong Atlantic wind had stimulated his face, bringing forth its redness. He eyed the men looking down at him from the rigging. Many were idly perched on yards like terns on a seawall.

"Your sail is too tight—loosen it a bit!" Drake shouted up to the men in the high top of the mainmast. "Smartly now!" he added in a warning voice.

"Aye!"

"Bring me five degrees starboard!" he said. But he actually was ordering his helmsman to bring the ship five degrees toward the port side. This was because of the way the rudder was rigged, for the helmsman steered with a whipstaff, being a stick rather than a wheel, and he had to turn his whipstaff to starboard in order to gain left rudder. This was achieved by a fulcrum located deep in the ship. And when he requested more than five degrees rudder, then the boatswain of the watch would have to have seamen turn a yard which moved a sail, as the helmsman could not do it by himself.

"Aye!"

"Helmsman, I want to run clear of the Lizard!" Drake shouted, referring to Lizard Point, being the last point of land that the Englishmen would see on their leaving England.

"When shall we see the Lizard, Cap'n," asked John Drake, who was now a boy of fourteen years. He had lived with Drake since he returned from Nombre Dios in 1573. As well, he had been with Drake during his entire Irish service. He was standing to Drake's right. The young man had a downy face and a body between that of a boy and a man. He had his feet spread wide apart so as to offset the roll of the ship, as he was an experienced seaman.

74

"Noon tomorrow, if we are lucky—"

"Right, sir," John Drake replied in a respectful voice, as the two generally retained a formal relationship between themselves.

"And John," Drake said, speaking to his young cousin, who would be his sideboy and assistant navigator. He was one of fourteen boys included in the crew of the fleet; their ages were from eight to fourteen. Each was serving under a sponsor who was an experienced seaman. Two of the youngest were a pair of eight-year-old boys, Joey Kidd and Willie Fortescue, who were serving as mess cooks to Horsewill the cook. They were so tiny that they were elf-like. Each had long hair and very rosy cheeks. "I shall have the beef pie for my dinner. It is in the basket in my cabin. It is the one that my wife brought me. Take it to Horsewill; ask him to warm it. I will have it with a bottle of claret. Also, tell the viol players that I want music with my dinner—but nothing sad. I want them to play lively tunes. It is sad enough leaving Plymouth!"

"Right, sir!"

The cabin that Drake had had built on the poop deck would enable him to travel in some splendor. His cabin would not only serve as his living quarters, but it would also be the navigational and strategy room for the fleet. It was furnished with stout oak furniture, some of which Drake had had ornately carved with grotesques on the arm rests and backs. He had his own bed and a rug for his floor. He had cabinets which he was using to store his clothing, linens and table silver; he had brought a sufficient supply of clothing so that he could dine in a different costume every evening of one week. As well, he had a box of dress-up costumes to be worn when he wished to do just that. Drake would eat his dinner in style while his trumpeter sounded his horn in order to call all hands to their evening meal of plain fare. Drake would dine in regal splendor, usually with a guest, while the rest would eat from a bowl while seated on the deck. Then Drake's viol players would join him and his guest, and they would play before and during the meal. Drake and his guest would dine on silver, as Drake had a full supply of silver cutlery and plate. Drake could easily afford to voyage in such splendor, as he was now one of the wealthiest men in Plymouth.

On the following morning at seven, the *Pelican* was proceeding as planned, making four knots which had put her almost abreast of the Lizard. Drake walked the short poop deck, eyeing the rocky shore, while sniffing the damp air. He suspiciously smelled it; he cocked his head and noted the calm of the seas and the bag of the sails.

"Hmmm!" he said, shaking his head. A change had come over his countenance.

"It's a great morning, Cap'n," Thomas Doughty said, while climbing a ladder to join Drake who had glanced at the hourglass being turned by the helmsman.

"Hmmm!" Drake said, making a study of the horizon, which was now gray and bedded with clouds that looked like neatly stacked feathers.

"And there is the Lizard," Doughty lightly said, pointing to the jutting land, as if trying to awaken Drake from his study. He added, "It is the last of England."

"Not for long!" Drake tersely said. "John," he said, speaking to Boatswain Fowler who was in the braces looking down at him. "Raise my flag for Tom Moone—get him alongside immediately!"

"Right, Cap'n!" the boatswain replied, and he hoisted to the mainmast a red and blue flag, being the call flag, which was a rudimentary system for signaling. Drake would use this flag and lanterns hanging on the *Pelican*'s stern to communicate with the *Benedict*. The *Benedict* was a thousand yards to the port side of the *Pelican*. Moone saw the call signal; he quickly changed course and brought the *Benedict* within hailing distance of the *Pelican*.

"Tom!" Drake shouted.

"Yes, Cap'n—" Moone said. He was carelessly leaning on the *Benedict*'s tiller, which was traveling parallel to the *Pelican*.

"Pass the word to the fleet—follow me to Falmouth!"

"Sir?" Moone questioned, as though he had misunderstood the message.

"There's a bad storm comin'!"

"I accept that to be true," Moone said, saying it as if it were not what he believed but what he recognized as an order which he must obey.

"Let's seek the shelter of Falmouth!"

"Right, sir!"

"And do not tarry!"

"Cap'n," said a sailor with a solemn face that seemingly had been hardened by the sea. He was ascending from the lower deck accompanied by a young sailor with a trumpet.

"Yes, Preacher—" Drake replied.

76

"I would like permission to call the men together for morning worship—"

"Denied, Preacher!"

"What is the matter, Cap'n?" the preacher asked. Shock showed in his voice and on his face, as if Drake had taken the name of the Lord in vain. The man making the request was Francis Fletcher, preacher for the expedition. He was a tall, lean man with sallow complexion and a hawk-like, unsmiling face. He had thin, tight lips and a nose with a hump on it. He was no stranger to Drake, for he had sailed with him before. During previous voyages, Fletcher had usually called the men together twice a day for church services.

"We must suspend it—we're making for Falmouth—a bad storm is approaching!"

"Why turn back from a storm?" Thomas Doughty asked, standing on the poop deck, studying the horizon, looking intently, but he was unable to see the storm. His voice indicated that he did not believe that a storm was approaching.

"About! About!" Drake shouted. "Can't you see?"

"Where is the wind?" Doughty asked John Fowler, the boatswain, who was an old seaman with wide shoulders and powerful arms. He was toothless, and so his chin at times neared his nose. Fowler was an expert at splicing, seizing, parceling, pointing, worming and serving, all having something to do with a ship's rigging, as he was an expert in the use and repair of ropes. He frowned and studied the horizon.

"It is there," the boatswain said, pointing to the feathers.

"But can you be sure?" Doughty asked.

"The Cap'n knows, and I know it, too," the boatswain said while tugging on a rope. "He has been going to sea since he was a tiny boy, and he knows much of it. And so he knows the sea like a farmer does his land."

When Drake was twelve years old, he had been apprenticed to the owner of a small trading schooner that traded with the cross channel ports of France, the Lowlands and nearby places. Drake had worked for the owner for seven years, not only learning the business of a trader but also learning the coastal waters of the channel ports. Then the owner had died, leaving the schooner to Drake. Drake thereafter operated it, trading along the coast of England, France and the Lowlands as had the deceased master, doing it until he was twenty years of age. And during his tenure on the trading schooner, he had learned much about the sea and especially storms on the English channel. All his senses now told him that a big storm was heading for the channel coast.

Drake's premonition about the storm was correct; his fleet had no sooner entered Falmouth Harbor, than a ferocious storm struck the coast.

"Furl those sails!" Drake shouted. He would attempt to secure the ship. But the wind had become so noisy that Drake's voice was barely audible, and so his shouting had been in vain. It would not have made any difference, for the men in the braces were unable to touch the sails.

"Damn it, bend those sails!" Drake shouted, standing on the deck in front of his cabin. He now was drenched. His red hair was shredded over his face. His shouts, however, were for naught—the winds were now hurricane force of almost one hundred miles an hour. The sails were quickly ripped to shreds, and they angrily flapped in the wind. The *Pelican* was anchored, but her anchor dragged. She rose up and down, and then she wallowed. A great sea, tall as a building, gray as an old snow bank, rolled toward the *Pelican* and then it crashed onto her deck. The deck was under water—it appeared that the ship would not re-emerge—then she arose from the water like a beleaguered whale; however, the emersion had drowned two pigs and dozens of chickens, who had been in their pens.

"Save yourselves, men!" Drake cried.

The *Pelican* rolled so that Diego, the black sailor, who was hanging in the braces, vomited into the wind, which then blew it back into his face. The skin on his face stretched so until his face became quite distorted. Yet he tightly clung to a rope in the braces, being blown about and even at times immersed in the sea.

Wave after wave rolled over the *Pelican*, and she wrestled with the storm by dragging her anchor. It appeared to all that she could not be saved, as she was being steadily blown toward the shore— Drake knew that on striking it she would founder and be torn to pieces. Drake reached an axe that was secured to the mainmast. He took the axe and began to hack at the foot of the mainmast.

"Down from the yards!" Drake cried.

"Give a man a minute!" Diego cried out. He had worked his way to a mainmast yardarm, and he was the furthest man out on this yardarm. He at times was immersed in the water as the *Pelican*

78

drifted across the harbor. The mainmast still carried enough sails to move the ship. The mast had to come down!

"Cut your foot rope—ride it down!" Drake ordered. "Hurry men—hurry!" he shouted. Now he was joined by John Laus, a tall, strong Dutch lad of eighteen. He also had an axe. He, too, knew enough about the sea to know that the mainmast had to be cut. He swung at the mast. "Swing hard, John!" Drake shouted at the young man on the opposite side.

"Comin' down!" Diego shouted, hanging to a rope which swung him to the deck where he landed as a wave rolled over the deck and then threw him against a railing. He grabbed it and desperately clung to it while fear contorted his face.

"Mast aweigh!" Drake shouted as the mast crazily fell across the deck and into the water, taking with it a tangle of ropes, pulleys and the like used for hauling and lowering sails and the securing of the mast.

"We must get over another anchor!" Drake shouted.

"Aye, Cap'n!" replied Fowler.

"Hurry men, hurry!"

"Aye!"

"And close the door!" he shouted to Fowler who was going below decks to get a spare anchor and rope. He was being followed by four seamen. They returned minutes later with an anchor and rope, which they put over the side. It immediately began to slow the drag.

"It's caught, Cap'n!" the boatswain cried.

"I feel it!" Drake shouted, studying the deck, eyeing the water that was cascading over the deck and the mainmast with shredded sails and tangled ropes that were lying across it; amazingly, the mainmast was now acting as a clumsy anchor.

"And we've had the worst!" a water-drenched sailor shouted.

"She's built for our voyage!" Drake shouted back in a schoolboyish voice, referring to the *Pelican*, which was now riding out the worst hurricane that had struck England in the memory of anyone then living. Even so, Drake could not hide his enthusiasm for the *Pelican*, though he had to know that she had much more dangerous sailing to do.

CHAPTER 10

To Mogador

On the storm abating, the crews of the five ships began to rig temporary sails. Once rigged, the five ships then sailed from Falmouth to Plymouth where each crew made the necessary repairs to its ship, which really were not that extensive considering the severity of the storm. Most of the damage was to the ships' masts and rigging. Then on December 13, 1577, Drake's fleet made ready to sail out of Plymouth. After all the visitors had departed and while the sails were being hoisted on each ship, Drake sent his dinghy to the other ships and collected the captains as well as Doughty. Then Drake held a brief meeting with his captains—all were seated at the navigational table in Drake's cabin. Glasses of red wine were before each. Drake not only enjoyed red wine, but he believed that it was good for the blood. He made a fetish of it, usually declaring that the last glass of wine was for his blood.

"Let us drink to a safe voyage!" Drake said, raising his glass of claret to his lips.

"To a safe voyage!" all answered.

"And if my ship gets separated, where shall I proceed?" asked John Thomas, the tall, slender captain of the fifty-ton *Marigold*.

"You will proceed to Alexandria, of course," Drake said as though he should know, and he raised an eyebrow at the question. Then he set his empty glass on the table, saying, "Good sailing!"

"Good sailing!" each said on standing and shaking the hand of the man nearest to him.

Two hours later all the ships were in the English Channel with their sails bagged with wind. Drake donned a new soft leather jacket which was stylishly trimmed with leather balls. He stepped from his cabin to the portico deck, put his weight on the handrail, and climbed onto the poop deck. He faced Thomas Cuttill, the sailing master who was doing the steering, while to his left was Thomas Blackcollar, who was the auxiliary steersman. The reader will note that once the *Pelican* was at sea, she often required two steersmen because of the backlash. Cuttill was a man of thirty-two years. He, like Drake, had been going to sea since he was twelve. He was of middle height and average build. His hair was thin. His face was slightly pocked from smallpox. He was dressed in a canvas jacket that had been tarred at the seams. His right hand was in his right pocket. His left hand tightly clutched the whipstaff. The master's position was a very special one. He had to be a navigator; he as well had to know his ship, for he was in charge of the seamen personnel. And so in most ways he was captain of the ship except that he was not, for there was a ship captain above him who had the last say. And in this case it was Drake. But in many cases, the captain was a soldier who knew very little about the sea. Drake was an exception to the rule. And in subsequent years, he would do much to make it the rule that the captain of an English ship must be a qualified seaman.

"You have a good wind, Tom?"

"Yes, but it's from the southwest."

"Tack so as to keep wind in your sails."

"That I will, Cap'n."

"Tom, now that I command a fleet, I would like for you now to call me General—" Drake said in an authoritarian voice.

"Oh, sorry," Cuttill said, quickly looking away from Drake, as if uneasy at the new relationship, though it was not unusual for captains to assume titles. This was especially so where he commanded more than one ship. Drake eyed his compass and then the sails; all, including the spanker, being a fair weather sail, were bagged with wind.

"Take me southwest—"

"More port rudder?"

"Naye, we steer for Mogador," Drake said, referring to the tiny Moroccan island off the West African coast, saying it as if Cuttill knew it well, while glancing from the sails to the water. And Cuttill did know the island, as it was an accepted water stop for English slavers. Drake was a natural navigator; he quickly studied the cloud formations and the waves, noting the drag of the ship. And then he caught Cuttill's eye. The master knew much about Drake's navigational ability. He knew that Drake could give an accurate estimate of the speed of the *Pelican* by just a glance, while for most navigators it would have been necessary to have tossed a log from the bow that was attached to a rope; then he would have had to measure the time that it took the log to reach the stern by use of a glass of sand. It, of course, measured a half hour, being located near the helmsman. The navigator turned it when it became empty. This then was multiplied in order to make a mile. "Six knots—" Drake said.

"I believe that you're right. Are we sailing past Gibraltar, Cap—General?" the master curiously asked, as he was puzzled as to the change of orders. He had been prepared to sail for Alexander.

"Right. Our next stop is Mogador."

"And the others?" he asked, meaning the other ships, saying it as though he was wondering whether they, too, would be sailing to Mogador.

"All for Mogador—hoist my call flag!"

"Right, General," Cuttill said. Then he shouted to a sailor, "Hoist the call flag for the *Benedict*!" As the writer previously stated, Drake had devised a simple system of signals by the use of the call flag and lanterns; the lanterns were used at night.

Fifteen minutes later the fifteen-ton ship, the *Benedict*, being in truth a pinnace, came within hailing distance of the *Pelican*. She was heavily armed for a pinnace, as she carried three swivel guns, being quick firing mankillers. She also had oars which could be manned when she was becalmed. Tom Moone, her captain, was an excellent choice for her command, as he was not only fearless, but he was also a good seaman. Then as a bonus, he was skillful in the use of tools. He was especially loyal to Drake, not only because of the hometown loyalty, as both were from Tavistock, but because he had great respect for Drake's skill as a seaman.

"Tom!" Drake shouted.

"Aye, Cap'n!" Moone replied, having one hand to an ear and the other on the ship's tiller.

"Inform the other ships that we are sailing for Mogador!"

"Morocco?" Moone asked. He was familiar with it, as he, too, had visited it on a slaving expedition.

"Right!"

"And we're not stopping at Gibraltar?" Moone asked. He knew that Mogador was five hundred miles south of Gibraltar, which of course was the entrance to the Mediterranean. "And we're not sailing for Alexandria?"

"Right," Drake answered without commenting, though hours earlier he had seriously related to his captains that they were bound for Alexandria. "I intend for the fleet to rendezvous at the island of Mogador," Drake said, saying it as though he had not given the earlier order.

"I gotcha, Cap'n," Tom Moone said, smiling, while leaning his body against the tiller, though his left hand was firmly gripping it. "I was suspicious about that Alexandria business," he said to no one in particular and grinning. He put more weight on his tiller and cut to the left. Then he sailed for the *Elizabeth* which was a mile astern of the *Pelican*.

At six in the evening, Master Cuttill rang the ship's bell four times; this was the signal that advised all hands that the second dog watch was taking place. The helmsman was relieved as were the foretop men and the deck men; thus, the watches would change. And since each watch stood four hours on and four hours off, a different watch would always have the midnight-to-four watch. Those men who had been on watch would now be able to descend to the orlop deck, which was also the crew's quarters, where there was the cook's grill and a giant copper pot that hung from chains attached to the grill. The grill easily converted into a stove, where fish and bread could be fried. A hearth was beneath it on which was a fire. Horsewill, the chubby cook with double chins, was beside it, stirring and testing the mixture of meat, peas, turnips, mint and honey. A barrel of dried bread was near it. Beside it were two eight-year-old boys: Willie Fortescue and Joey Kidd. Each wore a stocking cap that hung down to the side and a cotton jacket and short pants that gave each the appearance of an elf. Their faces were smutty, as one of their jobs was to man the fire. Each had long, girlish hair; Willie's hair hung down in ringlets.

"More wood, Joey!" the cook said, speaking to Joey Kidd, who was chubby like the cook. Horsewill would utilize other sailors and soldiers when he needed them in his cooking chores. One of those that he would lean on heavily would be Thomas Blackcollar, who had served as cook on Drake's last voyage to the Spanish Main.

"Aye!"

"Come and get it, mates!" Horsewill said, speaking to the men that were seated on the deck or on a row of swagging hammocks.

84

Now the two boy mess attendants took ladles and began to dole out pease soup to the men leaving their hammocks. Drake had learned of the use of hammocks while serving in the Caribbean. He had had a sailmaker make dozens of them. The hammocks as well could be rigged on deck during warm weather. Some hammocks had two men assigned to them. "No need to rush! There's plenty," Horsewill said. "It is a Tavistock special!"

Minutes later young John Brewer sounded his trumpet. It was loud enough to be heard throughout the fleet. This would become a common ritual, as the bugler would stand on the *Pelican*'s portico deck and sound his horn at the second dog watch change, which was done to inform all hands that Francis Drake, Captain of the *Pelican* and General of the fleet, was being called to dine. Drake stepped to the door and spoke to the trumpeter:

"John, please advise Thomas Doughty that I would like for him to dine with me—"

"Aye, sir," the young man replied, turning and tightly holding his horn. He hurried forward, asking sailors as to the whereabouts of Doughty.

"He's usin' the heads," a sailor explained, informing the trumpeter that Doughty was using the mild weather toilet, being a platform with grates on the lee side of the stern of the ship. Doughty was crouched in a seated position, holding to a rope's end. He had already gotten himself soaked to the skin when a small wave had slapped the *Pelican*.

"Sir!"

"Yes," Doughty replied, raising his hands to protect his face from the tail of a wave. It was in vain, for it soaked him. "Oh, damn!"

"The General wishes for you to dine with him tonight—"

"General?" Doughty curiously asked.

"Yes, the Cap'n—General—" the youth said.

"I will be there as soon as I am decent!"

A quarter hour later, Doughty joined Drake in his cabin. Two candles lit the handsome room. The table was set with silver plate, silver serving bowls and silver knives, forks and spoons. A nosegay of dried flowers in a vase set in the middle of the table. Drake was seated. He was dressed in a velvet jacket with stiff, white ruffs at his neck and wrists. He wore knee-length velvet trousers. Silver buckles were on his shoes. Drake stood and extended his hand toward a chair, indicating for Doughty to take a seat. Drake returned to his seat, which was opposite to Doughty's. Drake's nephew, John Drake, took a place behind Drake's chair. Diego, the Cimaron, entered with a tray and set it on the side table.

"Roast beef—Yorkshire puddin', Cap'n," the black man said, lifting the lid of a silver pot. "Shall I serve you now?"

"Yes," Drake said. "As well, open a bottle of claret."

"That I will," the black man said.

"And music!" Drake ordered. His young page quickly left his position, went to the door and beckoned. Two young men, John Martyn and Edward Mincy, entered the cabin carrying their cumbersomely large viols. They stood to the left of Drake and began to play a very slow tune.

"Play a lively tune!" Drake ordered, waving his hand for them to increase the tempo. The players immediately sped up their playing.

"I'm sorry about arriving wet—I got a good washing at the heads. I do have a change of clothes, but they are in my chest in the orlop deck, and it is covered with stores."

"Your attire is forgiven. I will now ask the blessing," Drake said, looking piously at Doughty. Drake never ate without first asking the Lord to bless the food and the partakers. He began to speak his prayer, while talking as if God were seated at the table with them. He spoke of the vicissitudes of shipboard life, the devilish Spaniards, and he spoke in a strong voice as to his concern for their loved ones back at Plymouth. His voice was strong and filled with complete belief and determination. And in truth this prayer was just a continuation of the church services now being held twice each day on the *Pelican*. Reverend Fletcher had already held the evening service. He had spoken to the crew on the flaming sword that guards the tree of life. "Take up that sword and protect mankind from the heathen!" Fletcher had said.

"I'm glad that you asked me for dinner, Cap'n," Doughty said. "There are some things that I would like to discuss with you."

"I would appreciate it if you would call me General," Drake said, putting bread in his mouth, looking suspiciously at Doughty, while his voice had an obvious chastisement to it.

"And am I to be called General, too?" Doughty seriously asked, while frowning, as if he expected it.

"There would be a conflict!" Drake replied, shaking his head, chewing on a piece of meat.

86

"But why? We have joint commissions!"

"There cannot be a joint command of ships at sea!" Drake said, shaking his head and frowning as if Doughty should have known it.

"But the Queen wanted it that way—"

"My orders provide that I shall be in command, not me, you, and John Wynter!" Drake sharply said. He had heard that there was talk amongst some in high places that there were to be three generals, a title that was interchangeable with that of Admiral; those mentioned were Drake, Doughty, and John Wynter, who was in command of the *Elizabeth*. The latter was included because he had come from a well-placed naval family. Wynter had given much thought to the title that he should have, and he had finally decided to call himself Vice Admiral Wynter. Yet the men were not fully complying with his title, as most still called him captain.

"But I am in command of the ground forces!"

"But while you are at sea, you do not have a command, as there are no ground forces," Drake countered and limply smiled.

"May I share your cabin?" Doughty abruptly asked. And then he looked from bunk to bunk.

"Share!" Drake exclaimed, stopping the breaking of bread, as if he were shocked at the thought.

"Yes, you have an extra bunk. Otherwise, I've got to sleep when I can in a hammock in the stinking orlop. It is infested with bugs and rats. It creaks, groans and stinks!" he said, referring to the crew's quarters which was also the gun deck. It was presently being heated by the cook stove. There were three tiny cabins beneath Drake's cabin. They were occupied by the master, the carpenter and the sailmaker. Beneath them were also three small cabins which were occupied by officers of less stature. Each of course shared his cabin with another officer. Doughty had rigged himself a hammock, but he was sick from the thought of having to use it. And really he had not seriously believed that he would have to sleep for long in a hammock in the orlop deck because he was convinced that with the right approach, Drake would share his cabin with him. And rightly so, for Doughty truly believed that he was a general as well as Drake.

"But how can I?" Drake asked, eating with his fork, flaunting it to Doughty, as if he had to know that the only other forks aboard the *Pelican* were in his cabin. "My cousin, John Drake, is assigned to that bunk. I intend to teach him navigation while he acts as my page. And so he needs to be near me."

"Well—" Doughty said, sipping his claret, pondering, searching for words, but the wine and the intimidating nature of Drake had subdued him. And so just then the right words did not come forth.

The next day, the air was decidedly cold; jackets were needed though the sun was high. When the sun was at its highest peak, sailing master Thomas Cuttill took the ship's astrolabe, which was a primitive sextant. He then used it to ascertain the height of the sun; thereafter, he made a quick mathematical calculation. He then went into Drake's cabin, took a double ruler and drew a line on the Mercator chart, drawing it from Plymouth south, putting an "X" at the end to indicate where he thought the *Pelican* was presently located. But it was nowhere near correct, because the navigator did not know anything about declination, refraction or parallax. More so, the navigator did not have a chronometer so as to figure longitude. However, some few men were able to do it with some proximity. One of these men was Francis Drake, as he was a born deep sea sailor.

"The drift is important in figuring distance travelled," Drake explained to his young cousin.

"How so, General?"

"There is a current in most waters. Each moves at a different speed. The navigator has to learn them; else his plot will be off. I will take the master's line and move it this way," he said, and he drew a line to the left of Cuttill's. "It will put us here. We had a good wind last night and did not need to do too much tacking; thus, the point here is more near the truth."

"You do not need to use the log?" the young boy admiringly asked, referring to the log attached to a knotted rope located on the deck outside the door. Cuttill had thrown it over the side so as to judge the ship's speed when he was making his plot.

"Naye, lad," Drake replied. "Most of my life has been spent on the water, and so I have trained my eye to judge the water, the wind and the like," he said, stroking his beard that now was golden because of the rays of the noonday sun.

"This is the latitude?" the youth asked, pointing a finger from left to right.

"Yes—and this is the longitude," Drake replied, moving his finger up and down on the map. "A good clock is needed to keep up with time, but that we do not have. And, in navigation, it is very important to know so one can plot the location of land, harbors, shoals and the like."

And so the lessons continued. And at times when John Drake was not engaged in learning navigation, he sketched.

"You like it?" John Drake asked. He was drawing a picture of a gull on a page in an empty book.

"And a tern?" Drake asked, requesting him to draw a comparison.

"The tern has different tail feathers," the boy replied, superimposing the tern's over those of the gull. John Drake had always sketched, but his sketches now were getting much better as the subjects were interestingly coming to life.

"John, I would like for you to sketch the discoveries that we make of new animals, peoples, mountains and the like."

"Thanks—"

"And I will sketch, too," Drake said, opening a book of blank paper. He then began to sketch the rolling sea, above which were gulls, doing it almost as well as his young cousin who sketched as if he had had considerable training.

CHAPTER 11

THE CAPTURE OF FREY

On the morning of December 27, 1577, Drake ordered his fleet to anchor in six fathoms of sea-blue water between the island of Mogador and the Moroccan mainland. The air was warm and balmy. Breakfast was still being served. Horsewill and his elfish boy mess cooks, dressed in tiny aprons, were filling eating bowls with oatmeal from a huge pot that set on the stove, which now was on the main deck. Those sailors who had already eaten were at work. Boatswain Fowler and a working party of seamen were holy stoning the decks. Two of these shirtless men hauled buckets of sea water to the deck, which they then splashed onto the wood; others who were stooped on their hands and knees vigorously rubbed it with stones. The work being done by the sailors was in sharp contrast with the effort being expended by those men who called themselves soldiers. They were standing and eating while lining the rails and studying the mainland with anticipation. Many were talking with their buddies about what they would do once they reached it. They seemingly were convinced that Drake would let them disembark and visit Morocco, where they could trade, imbibe spirits, flirt and even establish sexual relationships with the natives. But they should have known that such visits were rare for ship when she was on a mission. This was mainly because the captain had a natural fear that the men would desert the ship once they got ashore. And that was with good reason. For really, if they made a liaison to their liking, what did they have to lose by deserting? Life in a strange port could be an adventure, while shipboard life was hard. Even now, the orlop deck was contaminated by odors and sweat. Also several on-deck fusses were beginning between the scrub-down crews and some of the sailors and soldiers. The principal reason for this was that the scrub-down sailors kept splashing scrub-down water onto the soldiers' hammocks which many of the men had moved from the orlop deck to the main deck.

"Tom," Drake shouted from the poop deck. He was speaking to Tom Moone who was chatting with sailors standing on the bow of the *Benedict*, which was anchored nearby. All five ships had neatly anchored so that they were in a tight cluster.

"Aye, General!"

"I want you to pick up three men from each ship. Then pick up some empty water barrels from each—take them to the beach—find some fresh water and fill 'em."

"Right away?"

"Well, before it gets too hot—you'll need to flush out the barrels—then fill them. Return to the fleet." Potable water now had become important, for water that is placed in wooden casks without doing anything else to it soon turns green from the new life of a low origin that begins to grow in it, and its taste becomes putrid. This was the present state of the fleet's water supply.

"Right, General!"

"You might try the fishing once you get close—"

"We'll do it—"

"The men would like that. John here," Drake said, pointing to John Martyn, a soldier on the *Pelican*, who was standing on the opposite side of Drake with a line in one hand. "He is already fishing. Any luck?" he asked Martyn.

"None here, General."

"I see natives," Drake said, turning to study the beach. "Take some trinkets—attempt to trade with them for green vegetables," Drake said. He was showing concern that the men stayed hearty. He would show more, as he was convinced that plenty of green vegetables, herbs and fresh drinking water would keep the crew from coming down with plagues, fevers and scurvy, which he referred to as the "gum sickness."

"I understand, General."

"Master," Drake said, speaking to Cuttill. "Get me a workin' party of three men. Have them put three empty water barrels on the *Benedict*. Rig your ropes for a barrel drop."

"Aye, General."

"General!" Moone shouted to Drake on the *Benedict* bumping the side of the *Pelican*. He now was pointing at the shore. "There are now a hundred people or more on the beach!"

92

"Right you are—let's hold up the water party until I have a look. Master Cuttill, put over the pinnace." He was referring to one of the prefabricated boats that the carpenters had assembled earlier. The pile of planks that they had set on deck had now become a fully-rigged pinnace, though smaller than most.

"Right—you men there, attach that belt; put it under the pinnace. Hook it! Now, let's haul away!" The sailors had previously rigged a derrick to a heel, which they had attached to the mainmast. A dozen men began to pull on ropes attached to blocks and the pinnace rose from the deck.

"Easy men," Drake cautioned.

"Pull your guy!" Cuttill said, speaking to the three men who had their hands wrapped around a rope that controlled the lateral movement of the derrick. They did so and the single spar turned, lifting the pinnace over the water which lazily lapped against the hull of the *Pelican*.

"Lower her—do it easily—that's it—now secure her—secure your lines—well done!" Cuttill commended.

"Master Cuttill, I want twenty armed men available to sail with me in the pinnace," Drake said.

"Right, General. It will take us an hour to rig her mast, sails and bowsprit," Cuttill said. The latter was a long spar that would project over the bow of the pinnace so that a sail could be attached to it.

"Well, shake a leg. I want to speak with those Moroccans before the water party lands!" Drake said, looking out at Moone who was eyeing him. He had let the *Benedict* drift away from the *Pelican*.

"Aye, sir!"

Then Drake ordered Moone to return the *Benedict* to her anchorage while he and the landing party boarded the pinnace. Once all were aboard, they sailed the pinnace toward the mainland. Drake ordered the sails of the pinnace furled when she was within two hundred feet of the beach; he cautiously studied the beach. It now was crowded with Moroccans. Most shouted and waved their arms in an unfriendly manner at the men in the pinnace.

"Speak to them, John," Drake said to a tall sailor with long hair which was the color of fresh straw. He was standing on the bow near Drake. The man was John Frey, a Devonshire sailor, who the year before had been shipwrecked on a Moroccan beach. He had been the only person saved when his ship foundered. And on Frey reaching the shore, he had walked to the city of Rabat, where he had been well-received. He had been taken in by a leather goods merchant with whom he had lived and worked for four months before being able to board a ship for England. He claimed that during his stay in Rabat he had learned sufficient Arabic in order to make himself understood.

"We are English—we have come to trade!" Frey shouted in Arabic. But he was not fully understood. Then he held up several items of clothing, which created sufficient curiosity in two Moroccans for them to wade out to the pinnace. An English sailor in turn waded ashore, offering himself as surety in order to show the natives that the men in the pinnace did not have any ill will toward them.

"We need fresh fruit, vegetables, chickens—we will trade—" Frey said, speaking slowly and deliberately to the two babbling men who were approaching with outstretched hands. Their manner still indicated that they did not understand. Strangely they climbed onto the pinnace with outstretched hands, as if they were holy beggars.

"You can have this shirt—and you can have this javelin," Drake said on handing an item to each.

Each Moroccan nodded while babbling and bowing his thanks; and they both spoke to Frey while they again humbly bowed. They then descended into the water on the short ladder on the port side of the pinnace. As they walked the shallow water to the beach, the sailor on the beach returned to the pinnace.

"We can trade tomorrow morning, General," Frey said. "They promised to return tomorrow with plenty of items to trade. They said that they would bring plenty of fresh chickens, but they are short of water."

"Short of water—" Drake repeated, thinking. He looked from the crowded shore to the men in the boat. Then he said, "We will return to our ships—we shall wait for morning; then I will see if their word is worth anything!"

The next morning the sun rose early. The water was blue, as if freshly dyed and without a ripple. The sky was very clear with only a few huge puffy clouds. The sailors standing on the deck of the *Pelican* began to point toward the shore, noting the arrival of a caravan of thirty camels which was approaching the creek where the day before Drake had attempted to land. The comments of the men on the deck of the *Pelican* were generally that this appeared to be a good sign.

"General, there is a caravan of camels at yonder creek—each is loaded with goods," John Frey said, speaking up to Drake who was standing on the portico deck near his cabin door while eyeing what appeared to be a peaceful trading group.

"I see it—"

"Early morning is the best time to trade with Moroccans," Frey explained. "They are easily bargained with in the morning."

"But we have not had our morning church services!" Drake argued.

"I know—but morning is the best time to trade with 'em—I would like to be excused—let me take the dinghy, lead a small party with trade goods. I shall bring back some fat chickens for breakfast. And I'll help prepare 'em!"

"You need to exercise caution in your dealings—and you need to trade so that you do not waste our goods," Drake said, letting the thought of fried chicken for breakfast dim his better judgment about permitting the small party to land and trade.

"I promise to do that—"

"Five of you men go with Frey," Drake said, speaking to the men standing on the main deck.

The six men half filled the dinghy with trade items and then they departed, rowing for the creek where the camel caravan was situated. On the dinghy reaching knee-deep water, John Frey jumped into the water and began to wade for shore.

"Paddle your boat for the creek," Frey said, now walking toward some rocks; the caravan was just beyond them. On Frey reaching the rocks, five Moroccans leaped from behind a huge boulder. They quickly grabbed Frey—one placed a knife at his chest while others quickly bound his hands. Then they led him to six tethered horses. Frey was forced to mount one and ride it to the caravan; its members then mounted their camels and horses and hurriedly rode toward the interior. The sailors in the dinghy quickly rowed back to the *Pelican*.

"General," a barefoot sailor named Edward Careless said in an anxious voice, speaking to Drake who was standing on the *Pelican*'s bow. "As we approached the shore, John Frey left the dinghy to direct our approach. And when we neared some large rocks, the Moors leaped from the rocks and attacked Frey; one put a dagger to his heart and forced him onto a horse—"

"Beat the drum for quarters!" Drake declared. "I want thirty armed men in the pinnace and on the *Benedict*—on the double!"

"Right, sir," Cuttill replied.

"Gunner!" Cuttill said, speaking to a tall sailor, Richard Clark. He wore only knee-length pants. He was six feet tall, being the tallest man aboard. He was an experienced gunner, for as previously explained, he had gained much knowledge in the use of guns, having served many years in the Lowlands as an artillerist. Drake had remarked to Hawkins when discussing his gun crew that he thought Clark was the best artillerist in England. This was why he had paid him his salary for over a year while he did not have any duties. Clark was skillful in the use of the gunner's quadrant, level and shot calipers. He also had the knack for sighting a gun so its shot soon was on target. As well, he had worked with some of the best artillerists in England. It was he who had selected the armament for the five ships. Drake considered him to be so valuable that he would not use him in any risky assignments such as this. "Break open your arms chest—we need muskets, pikes, breastplates, longbows—get me Winterly!" He was the expert bowman.

"Aye!"

"You men," he said, pointing to some men on deck. "On the double! Muskets, bows and swords!"

Drake soon thereafter landed his troops on the beach and they marched in pursuit. They soon discovered the Moroccans, who were in a group standing on a hill within speaking distance. Drake called out, beckoning to them, attempting to speak with them. But they refused to join him. They also refused to fight, for as Drake approached them, they retreated on their horses and camels. Drake and his men returned to their ships more perplexed than ever as to why Frey had been kidnapped. It would be the end of the voyage before Drake would learn that Frey had been captured because of mistaken identity. Frey's Moroccan accent had been so poor that this group of Moroccans had become convinced that he was not English, but instead was a member of a Portuguese landing party that had come to give aid to a rival band of Moors. They would subsequently discover their mistake, and they would correct it by letting Frey board a ship for England, while Drake sailed away from Morocco without filling the fleet's water casks.

CHAPTER 12

FIRST PRIZES

Drake became so agitated over the capture of Frey that he decided to depart Mogador. And so shortly after he returned to the *Pelican*, he called a meeting of the captains to explain his reason for changing his plans. Once they were gathered in his cabin and their glasses were filled with their second glass of claret, Drake explained to them that he had decided to depart immediately.

"I've decided that we can't risk the loss of more men—" Drake said, while looking about for someone who thought as he did.

"And we are leaving?" Thomas asked.

"Yes, I cannot risk the loss of any more men," Drake repeated

"But my water is green," Wynter argued in a superior manner. He could be very arrogant, and when he was, his words cut like the swath of a scythe. Drake felt it but did not say anything.

"It is drinkable!" Drake said, being unperturbed by its sight. He knew that green water was still water and that seamen on long voyages often drank much worse.

"Mine stinks!" said John Thomas, captain of the *Marigold*.

"Add some wine; it will not kill you!" Drake declared. Then he added, "We shall sail within the hour for Cape Blanca." Drake was referring to the bulge on the coast of Africa, which is presently called Spanish Sahara. "There we shall find water!" Drake surely said, though he had to know that finding water there would be difficult. The territory was very hot while its coastline seldom received any significant amount of rainfall.

"We must first pass the Canary Islands!" Wynter said, speaking in the same arrogant manner, saying it as a warning. These islands were Spanish. He knew that it was best that they not be seen by the

Spaniards; else their voyage could be thwarted before they got started.

"We will stay close to the coast of Africa—do the dangerous part at night!" Drake said, studying a partial map of the African coast. "I know for sure that there are some wells here," Drake said, pointing, slightly cocking his right ear so as to hear the whispers of his captains. There were only sighs from Wynter.

Two days after the fleet had put some distance between itself and the Canary Islands, Drake called the captains to a second meeting aboard the *Pelican*. The five captains and Thomas Doughty took their seats at Drake's table in his cabin. The captains, with the exception of Wynter, were adjusting to the heat. However, Wynter's nose was covered with a white salve, while he wore on his near-bald head an outlandish wide-brimmed hat that his wife had given him before he departed.

"What is the condition of your men?" Drake asked Wynter. Drake often singled him out, trying to make it appear that he was willing to share some of the leadership of the voyage, though in truth Drake was not willing to share it with him or anyone else.

"Good—I don't have a sick man," he answered, as though they had plenty of water.

"You're lucky," Drake replied. Then he added, "When any of your men do come down with open sores, fevers and the like, you must relieve them of watch standing and give them special treatment."

"What kind of special treatment?" Wynter suspiciously asked. He was aloof from the men, thinking that was how it should be done, following the suggestions of his father and uncle. Really, he was not a seaman, since he had never served in a ship in any capacity except as a captain. Wynter was several inches taller than Drake. He as well was more stoutly built. He had a thick neck, double chins, and a thick chest.

"Relieve them of watch, feed them soups laced with herbs. Doctor their sores with salve!"

"Well," Wynter stated, raising an eyebrow, making a tiny arrogant smile without agreeing.

"How is your ship?" Drake asked, once again speaking to Wynter.

98

"She is taking on about ten to fifteen gallons of water a day, which is no problem—my pumps easily handle it," Wynter explained. "However, our fresh water tastes pretty awful."

"I know, but as I have said, it will not kill you. Have your men mix their ration of wine with it." Each man, according to his importance, was receiving one to two pints of wine and nearly a gallon of watery beer daily, which meant that most kept an alcoholic glow on most of the time, which did much to keep harmony on the ships. "And you, Mr. Mayor?" Drake asked John Chester, captain of the store ship *Swan*. Chester's father had been mayor of London, and because of that he was nicknamed, "Mayor." Drake was seeking a condition report from him.

"Our problems are much like Captain Wynter's. However, we do have plenty of stores available when you need them."

"Thanks, Diego," Drake said on the Cimaron offering him a glass of claret from a tray that held six glasses. Diego was not just a waiter; he was also a seaman/soldier. But he enjoyed acting as Drake's valet, and he had had much experience doing it. He had been serving as Drake's valet since his return from Nombre Dios. Diego, more so, was playing an important role in Drake's life, for Drake liked pomp, ceremony and the appearance of importance. Diego helped in this regard. And at the same time, Diego's presence had done much to add to Drake's mystique. He had become known by some persons in Plymouth as "The Sea Captain with the Black Serving Man." Diego had been the first black man that many people in Plymouth had ever seen. He was then the only black man serving in the *Pelican*. Each of the other officers then took a glass from the tray, while Drake continued to ask them questions as to the fitness of their crews and ships. Then he said to them:

"From this point on down," meaning south, "I want to take prizes—"

"Prizes?" Wynter asked, as if he were unfamiliar with the subject. He would subsequently indicate by conversation and by log that though he was the captain of a privateer, he had a disdain for the subject. Yet his father had been a privateer, though he now was an admiral. And Wynter had to know that, on joining the venture, having Drake as general of the fleet meant that the ships would take prizes.

"Yes, prizes!" Drake said, smiling as though he were ready to reveal something new.

99

"From what nations?" Wynter asked.

"Spanish, Portuguese, African—" Drake said, superiorly smiling, as though not willing to tell all. He was enjoying his present position, for he was making it appear that he had a commission to rob and plunder under the law.

"And by what authority?" Wynter asked, as though wishing to dispute Drake's right to do so. Doubt was in his voice and manner.

"It is here," Drake confidently said, touching his shirt, as if he had a document under his shirt that gave him such authority. This caused a smile of admiration to come to Tom Moone's face. Interesting thoughts flowed through his brain. Francis Drake, the pirate of the Spanish Main, had not changed; he possibly did have some authority from the Queen; but Moone guessed that such authority would be so enlarged by Drake's bodaciousness until it would be sufficient for Drake to do whatever he wanted. For he suspected that Drake's authority was more from his heart, being his feeling of hatred toward the Spanish. Moone welcomed this, as he shared the same feeling.

"And what kind of prizes do you prefer?" Wynter asked.

"Those with gold 'n silver are the best," Drake said, smiling, which drew broad smiles from the others. "But for now, those prizes with fresh water will suffice," Drake said.

"Rob for water?" Wynter asked with disbelief.

"Yes—"

"And where are we bound?" John Thomas, captain of the *Marigold*, asked. Thomas now was wearing a nicely dressed beard. "I am hounded by such questions from my men—they keep asking me the question, Where are we bound? Many are saying that they signed on for Alexandria only!"

"Well now, tell them that we are sailing for Brazil—"

"Why not tell them our plans, General!" Thomas Doughty interrupted, adding, "Can it be so wrong for you, and I to know and the others not?" Doughty asked, turning his head so as to face the seated captains, who nodded their heads in accord. Doughty had attended all of these conferences with the captains where Drake had treated him as if he were a captain, too. But this question had aroused Drake's ire—his face became flushed with anger.

"I will reveal our destination and explain our purpose at the appropriate time!" Drake resolutely said and frowned with contempt at Doughty. At this moment, he became extremely suspicious of

Doughty, for Drake like most great leaders had a suspicious side. So he wondered whether this outburst had come from his lack of understanding as to the seriousness of their undertaking, or from spite because Drake would not make him a general and let him share his cabin. Drake momentarily wondered whether Doughty wished to cause mischief to the expedition. Drake's plans actually were to be kept secret, as they involved matters of state. This was because the five ships were to sail to Brazil; then they were to follow the American coast south to Tierra del Fuego, to pass through the Magellan Strait, and then to sail north and plunder the coast of Peru. Drake knew that at this stage the capture or desertion of a seaman, who thereafter reached the hands of the Spaniards or Portuguese who learned of the plan, would cause the venture to end in disaster. The Spanish would not only attempt to thwart it, but the Englishman involved would most likely be slain or captured. The latter could be more horrible than death.

"But—" said Doughty, indicating that he disagreed.

"Enough!" Drake said, and he placed his hand on his side near where he had his dagger. Diego intently eyed him as if expecting an expression. Then he, too, dropped his hand to his side where he kept a sharp dirk. The moves were noticed by the others.

"I am a general—and I am jointly in command!" Doughty stated in a voice of defiance, as if indicating that he was not going to let the matter rest. And he angrily stared from Drake to his black valet. The other captains anxiously looked from Doughty to Drake, immediately wondering as to how this confrontation would end. All knew that Drake had a temper, and all now knew that Drake was clearly in charge of the venture. Would he consider this to be a usurpation of his authority? And if so, would it cause him to use the dagger that he always carried in his belt? Such would be a tragedy!

"You are not a general, and you will not reveal my plans! Else you will answer to me!" Drake said, his eyes angrily glaring. His voice and eyes made it clear that he did not wish to hear anything further on the subject.

"But—"

"But nothing! And," Drake said, once again addressing his captains in a business-like voice, "we will shortly find ourselves a bay for careening purposes. Once we are there, then I want each of you to have gun drills from seven to ten each morning. I want you to work your men hard. Acquaint them with all the guns, large and small.

The bowmen must practice firing at small targets—use target arrows (arrows with blunt ends)! You will soon be glad that you did, for we will soon need all of them!"

On the fleet reaching the rich fishing grounds of Cape Blanca, where the African fishermen usually made plentiful catches of sea bream and mullet, the ships began to make a serious search for prizes. The men now were dressing for the heat. Most went about shirtless, while they wore cut-away pantaloons. Most were barefoot, and their feet had toughened, since the decks were extremely hot. The sun was close and oven hot—and so the men sweated and they thirstily drank the putrid water whose top was covered with green slime, mixing it with wine and then spitting after quaffing their thirst.

The *Elizabeth* was the first ship to take a prize. Shortly after the fleet arrived at the Blanca fishing grounds, the *Elizabeth* met up with and captured a Portuguese caravel, being a fishing vessel that was long, fairly light, and had a shallow draught. It had a sharp bow and concave water line. It was similar in size to the *Benedict*. Wynter was not happy about capturing a fishing boat, and so he attempted to protect himself from future problems by cautiously writing in his log:

"On this date, the *Elizabeth* captured a Portuguese caravel with half a load of fish. It was done at the order of F. Drake."

Hours later Captain Thomas of the *Marigold* captured a second caravel; then on the following day near noon, Drake captured a third caravel, which was at anchor at Cape Blanca. The air by then had become unbearably hot and lifeless; the decks burned the feet of the shoeless men. This was so even though seamen continually poured buckets of salt water on the deck.

"Tom," Drake said, speaking to Moone who was on the *Benedict*. "Advise Captains Wynter and Thomas that I want a working party put on each of the captured caravels—they will come from the fleet!"

"We already have boarding parties aboard each, General!"

"But the fish?"

"There were only a handful on the first caravel!"

"These two should have fish—I want a working party to fill a barrel with fresh fish for each ship in the fleet. Tell them that they must gut and clean the remainder; salt them; dry them in the sun for our voyage to Brazil," Drake said as though the caravels were laden with fish, while in truth the catch had been sparse. Worse, he would soon discover that the newly-captured caravels had had a poor supply of fresh water.

"Right, sir!"

"And they must follow the *Pelican*!"

"Right, sir!"

"I will be anchoring the *Pelican* in yonder bay," Drake said, pointing. "So inform the captains to follow me—and once we are at anchorage, I want each captain to wash down his ship and trim it," he emphatically said, as though he would not tolerate it otherwise and with reason. For most sea captains did not understand the importance of cleanliness; however, Drake was one of the few who did. He knew that keeping the bilges clean was an important sanitation problem. And their bilges were filthy, for during the cold weather the men had used the bilges as a latrine; as well, the cook had used the bilges as a sink for disposing his dishwater. The stench now was almost unbearable. A trip below decks was a trying experience. Cleaning would be difficult for the seamen. "Two floodings may be necessary!"

"Aye, sir!" Moone said, waving his arms in a salute as the *Benedict* departed from the *Pelican*.

"Master Cuttill," Drake said, speaking to his master who was expectantly waiting for his orders. The two men were standing on the poop deck near the helmsman. They were the same height though Drake was more stockily built. "Set me a course for yonder bay. I wish to anchor there and explore that region. Then you must put together a working party in order to clean the hulls—inside and out. I want those rocks to shine!" He was referring to the rocks in the bilges that were being used as ballast. Many of these were large, weighing nearly seventy-five pounds. "'N get rid of that grass!" he said, referring to the seaweed that was now growing on the hull.

"Right, sir!"

"And Doughty," he said, addressing the tall, slim soldier, lawyer and court intriguer who was standing near the rail watching the *Benedict*. The lawyer smartly turned and faced Drake.

"Yes, General," Doughty replied. He was a handsome man, as he had a well-shaped face and a tall, slender but well-formed body. His appearance at court had been a pleasurable one for the ladies. He had promised his hand in marriage to a few; yet he had not really planned to take the vows with anyone until he was rich. No one now would have believed that he had had such background by judging his present appearance, since it belied it. His hair was long and his beard was sparse. He was dressed only in a pair of sailor's pants, which were knee-length and tight-fitting. He was barefoot.

"I want you to organize the soldiers. You are to take seventy men and teach them the art of close quarter soldiering. You are to drill them for the next few days. I want you to practice the use of swords, pikes, gun-handling and the like. The bowmen need to wax their bows and practice their shooting an hour each day. I plan to be at anchorage for four to five days while we clean and provision our ships. Utilize that time to your best advantage so as to train these men!"

"What about the heat?" Doughty asked. It was unusually hot.

"Work around it," Drake replied.

"Am I to use sailors as soldiers?" Doughty curiously asked. There were only forty soldiers which as well included officers. Doughty had been of the opinion that the men being carried as soldiers would do all the land fighting, while their officers would be the gentlemen soldiers.

"Yes, our sailors need to be trained in soldiering. If you have any problems recruiting, report back to me!"

"But—"

"They must be trained, too!"

Drake was never in one place long during the five days that it took to clean and provision his fleet. He supervised the careening of each ship. Each was towed into very shallow water; then the dirty ballast rocks were removed and cleaned in salt water. The bilges as well were then flushed out with sea water so as to clean the planking. This water then was pumped to sea by hand pumps. Then the *Pelican*'s and *Elizabeth*'s heavy culverins, being deck guns weighing two tons each, were shifted to the side opposite where supporting posts were placed. This was sufficient shifting of weight and formation of an angle of the ship in order to careen her. Sailors then rigged scaffolding so as to clean the side that was out of the water. And by doing such, they ridded that part of the hull of barnacles and grasses. They then sealed that side of the hull with grease and tar. They next did the other side; thereafter, they returned the fixtures to their places. The smaller ships were more easily careened. Then the ships were provisioned from the *Swan* and the *Marigold*.

Drake took a great interest in the careening of the *Pelican*. For when she lay on her port side in shallow water, Drake stood in waist-deep water and admiringly eyed her for the longest time, studying her as if she were a pretty woman. His facial expression as much as said that the *Pelican*'s measurements were ideal for a rugged voyage. Her breadth was twenty-eight feet, while her keel was fifty-seven feet—yet her deck was ninety feet.

"You like the cut of her, General?" Cuttill asked on joining Drake, who was studying the French-built ship.

"Aw, she careens beautifully!" Drake said.

"And she is a great sailor!"

"That she is! I've never sailed in a ship that handles a gale like she!" Drake said, continuing to study the *Pelican*.

CHAPTER 13

CAPE VERDE ISLANDS

It was on January 21, 1578, that Drake's fleet sailed out of the sheltered bay on the sunbaked coast of Africa. The stop had been a useful one, as Drake and his captains had used it to careen and refurbish their ships. Then they had trained their men. The lead ship as always was the *Pelican*. It seemingly was a poor time to leave, as the water was so calm that the *Pelican* barely moved; the ship's topside was stifling hot, while below decks it was worse. All the windows were open in the great cabin, and as well, all had canvas airscoops attached to them so as to intake air. Yet Drake was profusely sweating, even though he was scantily clad, being dressed only in cutaway pants. He was seated at his cabin table studying a partial map of the West African coast that included the Cape Verde Islands. Master Cuttill was seated beside him; he, too, was quietly eyeing the map.

"We will sail southwest for Cape Verde Point," Drake said, speaking to Cuttill, who thoughtfully nodded his head. Drake was pointing to the bulge in the middle of Africa that extends outward into the Atlantic where there are ten volcanic islands known as the Cape Verde Islands. These islands are located 385 miles from the west coast of Africa. "When we get here," Drake said, pointing, "we should have some nice following winds." Drake was speaking from experience, while mulling his route, reflecting on slaving voyages that he had made. Both men viewing the map knew that it was the ingenious Portuguese who had devised a simple route to Brazil that any seaman could follow. They had learned to sail south along the African coast to Cape Verde Point; then they sailed west to the Cape Verde Islands, which because of their number and location were almost impossible to miss. There they took on fresh water. Then they sailed due west to Brazil; and by doing so, they had simplified a complicated way of sailing between the continents. Drake wanted to make sure that he made contact with these islands, as he, too, planned to stop there so as to take on fresh water. And even though he was a skillful navigator, he would utilize the Portuguese method. And so he set sail for Cape Verde Point.

On January 27, 1578, a lookout on the *Pelican* sighted the island of Boa Vista, which was a flat island located near Africa. But Drake ignored it, sailing past it in search of the island of Maio, where he knew from previous visits that his fleet could obtain a nice supply of water. It like the other islands was populated by black slaves who had been brought there by the Portuguese from Africa. Many of these had gained their freedom, and some of these freed slaves held slaves as agents for Portuguese slave traders who called for them when they were needed.

"Tom," Drake said, speaking to Thomas Doughty, being one of several men seated in Drake's cabin. These men included Drake, Cuttill, Thomas Doughty and John Wynter. All were studying a roughly-drawn map of these islands. Wine glasses were before them. A plate of sea biscuits set in the middle of the table. "I want you and John Wynter to take seventy armed men and march on the principle town—it lies about three miles inland—over that hill," he said, pointing to the map before the men. "You will march at night so as to surprise the residents. Once you confront them, you can then bargain with them for water."

"Will they be armed?" Doughty asked.

"Possibly, but I don't want any firing on them unless they fire first. I am sure that they will submit to your numbers! Remember, numbers are important!"

"I see—"

"And John," Drake said, speaking to Wynter who was seated close to him with his head bent, as he was studying the map. "You must take care in landing. The shore is rocky!" He was referring to the volcanic pumice which can be as sharp as glass.

"And you do not think that we can wait until morning?"

"It is like I said earlier—if they see you, they probably will think that you are enemy slavers and that you have come to steal their slaves. And if that happens, they will poison their water and go into hiding until you leave. It is a common practice of theirs."

When the party of soldiers reached the small town in the early morning darkness, they quickly discovered that the town was in ruins. And worse, the wells and springs that would have supplied them with water had been fouled and were not usable. This apparently had been done just days before by a group of enemy slavers. So the group of men was disheartened when they sat to rest and think. And while the men were taking a rest from their long hike, Doughty took Wynter aside and confidently spoke to him:

"It is a long hike for nothing," Doughty said, cautiously eyeing Wynter in the darkness, trying to ascertain his views on Drake. He had concluded that Wynter was not in accord with Drake's policies. And so Doughty wanted Wynter to join with him in a cabal, beginning to think on the venture as though it were some political event that would permit the taking of sides. Doughty was doing it because he was a born conniver. This was possibly because he was a lawyer/politician, as he had worked for several senior cabinet officers. And by the nature of the work, it had entailed political intrigue. The reader will recall that Elizabeth, as well as much of her cabinet, was backing Drake which ostensibly was against her public policy. Truthfully, this venture had been put in motion by Doughty who was a master at court intrigue. He knew how to work a dislike into a repugnance; and he knew how to work one cabinet officer against the other. Thus, he knew well how to use superiors to do his bidding. He knew that he had to find some way to neutralize Drake. Else Doughty had decided that his influence on the venture would be null. So in order to neutralize Drake, Doughty had decided to use his political skills—and they were extraordinary. Had he not directed Essex to exterminate the Scotch women and children just so he could watch this man Drake in action!

"So it is," Wynter replied, whispering.

"His policies have cost me my position with the fleet!" Doughty angrily whispered.

"Let us watch it," Wynter said, as if making a commitment to Doughty, while in truth not doing so as he was by nature a fence straddler.

"And there is no water?" Drake asked, speaking to his younger brother Tom Drake, who was the messenger who had brought him the report that the water on the island had been fouled. Drake fondly eyed his brother, who was ten years younger then he. Tom Drake was built much like Drake but not as heavy. He was a good sailor as he could navigate, while his shipboard skills were first class. He easily accepted orders and obviously was enjoying the venture. The two had had little contact since the voyage began, as Tom Drake had tried to keep as much distance as possible from his older brother so as to prevent talk from the men. He was even sleeping in the *Pelican*'s orlop deck.

"No, General," the younger Drake replied in a respectful voice, as if there were no brotherly tie. He was standing on the main deck of the *Pelican* while leaning on a handrail. Both men were facing the island, studying it, though because of darkness there was not much that they could see.

"Tom, advise Captain Wynter and Doughty to join me on the *Pelican*—have the remainder return to their ships," Drake said.

"I will do that, General," Tom Drake replied, smartly turning toward the ladder. Even though there was a military relationship between the two, it was not hard and fast, and Tom Drake was trying to maintain a rigid one so he could keep aloof from his brother. Even so, his loyalty to Francis Drake was very strong and would grow stronger, as the reader will discover.

"We sail for Santiago," Drake said to John Wynter on the dinghy delivering him to the *Pelican*. He was referring to another Cape Verde Island, which was one of the leeward islands. Wynter followed Drake to the poop deck. Drake pointed at the speck of an island, being about thirty miles from his present position, and he said to Cuttill who was steering, "Keep some distance from the shore; there probably are forts on it!"

"And will we find fresh water there?" Wynter asked.

"No. There is water, but the island is too heavily fortified to land. And the natives hate the English!"

"But why go?" Wynter asked.

"We go there in search of prizes," Drake answered, superiorly smiling as if chiding Wynter for asking. But the smile was more, because he knew that Wynter did not like the idea of prizes.

"But why take them if they don't have value?" Wynter asked. A frown was on his face. He previously had made it clear that he did not like to take prizes. This was especially so of the types of prizes that now were part of the fleet. For the three fishing caravels were trailing the fleet. What good were they? They did not have any valuable cargo. Wynter would write as much in his log. He just did not see the world like Drake, who saw it as a giant aquarium where the big fish ate the little. Nor did he see it as a place where the strong took from the weak so that they could become stronger. On the contrary, he saw it as a place of rules which favored those born to a special class who did not have to take since they already had.

"It is the job of us that are engaged in this venture to do our part in bringing the enemies of the Queen to their knees—and Spain and Portugal are her enemies!" Drake said, trying to explain militarily why he had taken the prizes and why he would take more. He was determined to be diplomatic with Wynter for several reasons: he had family members who had invested heavily in the venture and who as well had considerable influence with the navy. Then they were also close to the Queen.

"And where will we get fresh water?"

"We will have to get it at Brava, a small island west of Togo. The wait will be worth it, for the water there is very sweet," Drake positively said without revealing his fears. He knew that if they did not fill their barrels with water at Brava, the venture would possibly fail since there were no other nearby watering places. Thus, a continuation of the venture could possibly cause many of the men to die of thirst.

"I will return to my ship," Wynter said. Irritancy was in his voice. His eye caught that of Doughty. No words were exchanged between the two, but there seemingly was an accord.

"Don't despair, John!" Drake said in a light voice, as if he were unconcerned at Wynter's likes or dislikes. If he saw the meeting of the eyes, he took no note of it.

"Thanks, General," Wynter replied, stepping into the dinghy that would take him to the *Elizabeth* which was trailing the *Pelican* by some two hundred yards.

"Master Cuttill," Drake said, speaking to the master standing beside him who had his left hand on the whipstaff. "Steer for that island," he said, pointing to Santiago, being an island that was largely inhabited by a mixture of Portuguese and Negroes and their slaves who spoke mostly Crioulo, being a Portuguese dialect. These people, being a mixture of Europe and Africa, were evolving differently. It certainly was not toward Europe, since they had bastardized their learning of Christianity, as they were practicing an Africanized form of this religion.

"I want to coast it," Drake said.

"What's the water like?" Cuttill asked, meaning its depth.

"We will stay out a mile or so—stay clear of the reefs. This as well will keep us out of range of their guns."

Six hours later in the early morning, Drake's fleet was abreast of the island of Santiago. The eight ships slowly cruised it. All hands were on deck and were wide awake. They curiously pointed and quietly conversed. The sight was eerie. For each cape, point or headland had a large cross erected on it, which had painted on it the face of a devil. The sight of these ugly crosses disturbed Drake immensely, as he joined his crew members who were seated on the deck for morning church services. They were singing their first hymn. All had joined hands in Christian solidarity which was their custom.

"Preacher Fletcher," Drake said, speaking to Francis Fletcher the chaplain, who was a tall man with wide shoulders and long arms. He was not handsome, as his nose had a hump on it and the corners of his mouth drooped, while his eyes were slightly crossed. Yet at times they were deeply fixed, as if he were staring in the beyond like a mystic. He was squinting while studying his Bible that he held about six inches from his eyes. "That cross is a mockery to our Lord!" Drake added.

"And to the Christians on this expedition!" Fletcher replied, maintaining a tight mouth, as if reluctant to say more, which was his custom.

"Would you like to destroy it?" Drake asked.

"That I would, and the devils who erected it."

"Well, then," Drake said. "Take the pinnace and a dozen armed men, destroy it and return to the *Pelican*; then deliver us a good sermon!"

"Praise the Lord!" the unsmiling minister said, who then pointed to the sailors and soldiers that he wished to join him in the pinnace which was tied to the stern of the *Pelican*. A half hour later Fletcher and his band of men landed on the shore. There was no opposition, so they quickly scaled the cliffside and tossed the cross into the sea. Then they returned to the *Pelican*. And once Fletcher was aboard the ship and the men were once again seated, he delivered a fiery sermon on how God would cast his wrath on all idolaters.

" . . . They shall be cast into the fires of Hell and burned without pity for their cries . . . "

The *Pelican* sailed by a small town composed of many small houses located on a hillside; the occupants stood by their houses and angrily stared and waved their fists at Drake's crew standing on

112

deck. The English were undaunted at the hostility, for they shouted epithets back at them. Many of the men on the *Pelican* were in full fighting dress. Some of these held cutlasses in their hands, which they waved as if to show their eagerness to land and attack the inhabitants. Gunner Clarke and his gunners mates were in the orlop deck where they were manning the culverins. Those on the port side were charged and ready to fire balls of iron at the town. The townspeople apparently knew this; thus their hatred was being vented only by the waving of their clenched fists. The *Pelican* soon passed the town; then it approached a fort on the side of a hill.

"Boom!" a gun sounded from the fort.

"Shrr-y!" a ball screamed as it raced through the air.

"Splash!" a ball fell a hundred yards from the *Pelican*.

"Master gunner!" Drake shouted to Richard Clark, who was standing on the stairway to the orlop deck. "Give him two rounds—let him know that we are not afraid of him!"

"That I will do!" Clark said. Then he descended the ladder to the orlop deck, carefully holding a lighted linstock, which he then touched to a tiny hole on the top of number six culverin.

"Boom!" the culverin noisily sounded.

"Boom!" a second gun fired and its ball fell on the fort.

"That should quiet him!" Drake said, speaking loud enough for all of the men on deck to hear as he studied the town and then the fort until it had faded out of sight.

"General," Cuttill said. "We are approaching St. James." He was speaking in reference to the island where the capitol of the territory was located.

"Right, there is a block house there—give her a bit of right rudder. We'll keep our distance from it. It may have a more powerful gun!"

"Boom!" a gun sounded from the fort.

"Shrr-y—" the ball whistled as it headed for the *Pelican*.

"Splash!" the ball landed short of the *Pelican*.

"Boom! Boom! Boom! Boom!" the *Pelican* barraged. The *Elizabeth* closed and also barraged the fort.

"Yonder, General!" a lookout shouted, pointing to two ships just outside the harbor. The one nearest to them seemed to be larger than the *Pelican*. Both were trying to reach the sanctity of the harbor and the protection of the guns located on hillsides above it before the fleet reached them.

"Man the pinnace!" Drake shouted.

"Tom! Tom!" Drake shouted to Moone on the *Benedict*. It was within hailing distance.

"Aye, sir!"

"Make ready to board the pinnace—I want you to lead a boarding party to take that ship! Show these men how to board!" Drake said as if they did not know—and he was right. But Moone did, as he had learned it on the Spanish Main.

"I'll do it!"

"Diego, you go—John, you go. Thomas, you go!" Drake forcefully said to his younger brother, Thomas Drake. "And you, John—you go!" He was speaking to John Winterly, the bowman. "Take grappling hooks. Use them immediately—show your knives—move fast—on the double!"

The fast-sailing pinnace quickly reached the *Benedict*, and it took aboard Moone and two of his men who carried longbows. These were very lethal weapons, as they could fire further and were more accurate than any of the handguns. All of the men wore cutlasses. The pinnace was a fast sailer, and so she easily overtook the Portuguese who could not get enough wind in her sails in order to gain the protection of the guns on the hillside.

"Boom!" a gun from the fort fired, but it was in vain. The pinnace was soon onto the largest ship. Its guns were manned; but the gunners panicked and abandoned their guns.

"Hook 'em!" Moone shouted, throwing a grappling hook onto the ship's deck. It caught; then he began to scale its side.

"Up! Up!" the men shouted in unison as they climbed on the lines that were attached to the hooks. Then they landed on the deck to the bewilderment of the crew, who then threw down their small arms and lined themselves up against the deck house.

Moone took charge. He shouted orders, "You, Tom Drake, man the helm! You men, man her yards! Bring her about! You, Tom, take their arms—stack them! You, John, you, you—go below. Check the cargo—quickly!"

"¿Quien es el commandante?" Who is in charge? Moone asked in Spanish, demanding that the captain step forward and identify himself.

"Soy." I am, a bearded man answered. He was a short, thin man with a beard and a dark complexion who appeared to be in his late fifties. "Me llamo Nuno da Silva." My name is Nuno da Silva, the man said, giving his name. It would soon become a common one with the men on the venture, as unknown to them all, da Silva would spend the next year as a prisoner of the Englishmen.

CHAPTER 14

THE MARY

The newly captured vessel was the *Santa Maria*, which was a ninety-ton caravel. She had two forward masts, a lateen-rigged mizzenmast, and a flat stern. Because of her rig, the English would find her a difficult ship to sail. The captured ship was owned by Nuno da Silva, a Portuguese, who a month earlier had sailed from Oporto, Portugal, for Brazil. The caravel was carrying a fairly valuable cargo, as she was loaded with 150 casks of wine, several cases of wool, linen, silk and velvet cloth, and many chests filled with fish hooks, combs, knives and scissors. It also carried a dozen male passengers, who because of their dress appeared to be men of wealth. All were fearfully huddled on the bow.

"Well done, Tom," Drake said on climbing the sea ladder to the *Santa Maria*. Drake was directing his words to Moone, who was standing between Diego and Nuno da Silva, the short, slight-of-build captain, who appeared to be almost frail and out-of-character for a seaman. The Portuguese sadly looked about the deck, obviously depressed on seeing Drake's men scamper about his ship, knowing that they soon would lord over it. Four men were in the rigging making adjustments to sails, as they were turning the *Santa Maria* about. Da Silva slowly put a hand to his beard and gently tugged it, as if to awaken himself from a bad dream. But the events were real, and he now was a ruined man. Not only were his ship and cargo lost, but he as well was a captive of a pirate, and he did not know it yet, but he was the captive of the world's most daring pirate.

"This is the ship's captain," Moone said, pointing at da Silva whose eyes nervously blinked.

"Very well!" Drake replied, eyeing the small man who now was anxiously studying his captor as if wondering what would be his fate. "Diego, does he speak Spanish?"

"Yes, General—"

"Be my interpreter; I do not yet trust my Spanish," Drake said. He had been fairly conversant in Spanish when he left Panama in 1573, but since then, much of it had slipped away because of non-use.

"What is your name?" Diego asked in Spanish.

"Nuno da Silva," the captain replied in very distinct Castillian.

"And who is the owner of this ship?" the Cimaron asked in Spanish.

"Soy." I am, he softly replied. He had a very pallid complexion, as if he were suffering from a serious illness.

"And where were you bound?"

"Brazil," the Portuguese whispered, as if he were too weak to speak any louder. He nervously looked from left to right.

"Have you made the trip before?"

"Many times—" he softly said, while nervously flicking his eyelids.

"May I see your charts and navigational equipment?" Diego asked, repeating what Drake had said to him. Diego had expected the question, as he knew that Drake had an insatiable appetite for navigational charts and instruments. He had previously watched Drake make a careful search of each of the captured fishing boats, searching for navigational aids. He had eagerly taken possession of their hand-drawn maps of the African coast, treating them like they were valuable jewels, rather than poor aids to simple navigation.

"Yes—they are in this cabin," the Portuguese said. Then he turned and led Drake and his party into a neatly arranged cabin where they found on the navigational table a chart of the coast of West Africa which as well included the Cape Verde Islands. It had many neatly-drawn arrows on it, indicating the direction of the winds; dates were beside the arrows. It as well had a course plot to Brazil.

"Very good," Drake commented, smiling on studying the chart.

"Do you have others?" Diego asked.

"Well—yes—in that drawer," da Silva said, and he crossed to the desk and pulled out a wide drawer. It held a dozen charts, which Drake hurriedly studied. He quickly noted that several of these were charts of the Brazilian coast. These had numbers on them which pointed out the depths of the water and their distance from the shore.

"Do you have any special qualifications for commanding a ship?" Drake asked, speaking for Diego to interpret. Drake knew that historically the Portuguese were further ahead of other countries not only in map making but also in practical navigation. This knowledge had enabled them to further their quest for exploration, which in turn had enabled them to find the way to the Spice Islands. Diego repeated the question.

"Yes," da Silva replied. "I am a licensed pilot—" His voice was soft, while his eyes expressed the fear under which he was suffering.

"And?" Drake asked.

"I am a navigator—"

"And?" Drake asked, looking hard at the diminutive Portuguese. Drake's eyes were non-compromising, while his face lacked expression. The only change in his countenance was a nod of understanding. Drake's ear was becoming somewhat tuned to the Spanish.

"A ship's captain—" da Silva finally said.

"Your answers are good," Drake said. "Are you familiar with the coast of Brazil?"

"Not really—" the Portuguese nervously answered while frowning. Da Silva, on seeing the change of expression on Drake's face, now recognized that he had been too truthful with his answers.

"Don't lie to me!" Drake said, sternly eyeing the Portuguese. "Would you like to sail it with me?"

"Do I have a choice?" da Silva asked, frowning, his face contorting as if he would cry.

"No, you do not!" Drake snapped. "But I will do you a favor as I will give your crew and your passengers their freedom. I will let them take my pinnace with sufficient supplies so that they can return to Portugal."

"Then I accept your invitation," the Portuguese pilot said, nervously grinning. Then he closed his eyes and did his beads, silently praying for deliverance from what appeared to be a very bad situation.

"And what is her cargo, Tom?" Drake asked, speaking to Tom Moone, now directing his attention to the ship's goods.

"It is valuable, General, for she is loaded with many items of trade—she as well is carrying one hundred or more casks of wine."

"Well, da Silva, we will take your ship with us. I will need someone to command her. Let's see—oh, yes," he said as if recalling the differences that he had had with Doughty and now had decided to right the relationship. "I will put Tom Doughty in charge. Then I will make Tom her master," referring to his brother. "He can keep an eye on Doughty—keep him out of ship problems," he said, knowing that Doughty had never commanded a ship.

"Tom—Tom!" he said on stepping out of the door. He was speaking to his brother who was just a younger edition of himself. He had red hair and a youthful face, which was sparsely covered with a reddish beard.

"Yes—General," the young man politely replied, trying to stay aloof, attempting as usual to avoid any future problems with fellow crew members who he knew were suspicious of the fact that he was a brother to Francis Drake.

"You stay on the *Santa Maria*—on the *Mary*. Yes, that will be her new name. Doughty will be in command. I will give him a try!"

"Right, General!"

"And Tom," Drake said, speaking to Moone. "Give the *Benedict* to da Silva's crew and passengers—give them a chart, some supplies, some water and send them on their way."

"Right—"

"And the fishing caravels. Dismiss them with this consideration—keep the large bark. It is much stronger than the *Benedict*—swap your gear with her. Put your guns on her. We'll rename her the *Christopher*; then let the three go. I will make an inspection of the *Mary*. Then I shall return to the *Pelican*—I shall set a course to Brava so we can fill our water casks."

It was night when the *Pelican* breasted the island of Fogo, which was near Brava. The name "Fogo," being a Portuguese word for "fire," was a good name for the island. The island was now engulfed with smoke that was belching forth from the island's active volcano; thus, the night appeared much darker than usual.

"Boom!" The volcano uncannily erupted just as the *Pelican* breasted the island; fire spectacularly belched from its center. Then a fiery stream of lava flowed down the mountainsides and into the sea, emitting popping noises, changing the night strangely into day.

"Give her right rudder, Master Cuttill!"

"Right—"

"I don't want to get too near it!"

120

"It's raining rock, General!"

"It's small stuff—it'll wash off—" Drake calmly said while studying the island.

"It's the Lord showing His sovereignty, General," Fletcher said. He had joined Drake on the poop deck and was now standing beside him, which was not uncommon as the preacher roamed the ship at will. Drake earlier had had Fletcher to dinner. He had asked him to join him so the two could have a prayer session. Drake had been particularly interested in thanking the Lord for having delivered the *Mary* to him, for she not only had aboard her much valuable stores, but a careful count had disclosed that she had 150 casks of wine, which if necessity demanded, could be mixed with the water so as to make it palatable. Then the Lord had delivered to him da Silva, the pilot, who he knew would aid him in coasting Brazil. They had thanked God for such deliverance; then the two had prayed long and hard to God that he would fill their casks with sweet water from Brava.

But their prayers would only be partially answered. For on their arriving at the tiny island of Brava, the English found that because of the great depth of the water, they could not anchor their ships. But Drake was determined to fill his barrels with water, and he once again had at his command a small ship, as he had put together another prefabricated pinnace. Drake directed a working party of fourteen men, led by John Wynter, to board the pinnace which was carrying a dozen empty casks. Once they were on the small island, they found a plentiful supply of water, but the shoreline in places was so precipitous that they had a difficult time in filling the casks. Then it was a more difficult task in getting them to the edge of the water. Also, due to the depth of the water, anchorage for the fleet was impossible; thus, it was very difficult for the ships to keep together. John Wynter was standing on the bow of the pinnace when at sundown it returned to the *Pelican*. Drake spoke to him:

"How did you find it, John?" Worry was on Drake's face. The pinnace had sailed for the shore shortly after breakfast. It was now sundown, and this was the first time that the men had returned to the fleet. He knew that they should have already made several trips to the larger ships.

"There is water, General; however, it is very difficult to fill the casks and get 'em down. Miggins had a bad fall," he said, pointing to a seaman with a strapped leg who was seated in the boat. "He may have broken his leg. We need a hand in getting him off."

"Boatswain!" Drake shouted to Boatswain Fowler, who was in charge of the rigging of sail and the like. "Rig a pallet! Fetch that injured man onto the *Pelican*, and I'll doctor him myself!" Drake said. Drake had been carrying an officer on the *Pelican* who had signed on as a medical man, but on leaving England, Drake had discovered that the man's knowledge of medicine was nearly nothing. That very night he would become so irritated with him that he would transfer him to the *Elizabeth*.

"It will only take a few minutes, General!"

"And John," Drake said, speaking to Wynter, who now had joined him on deck. "Did you fill all casks?"

"These twelve are not fully filled. Even so, it took all day!"

"I know—board three on the *Pelican*—three on the *Elizabeth*—two on the *Marigold*—two on the *Mary*—then one each on the *Christopher* and the *Swan*. And then John, take as many casks of wine from the *Mary* and distribute them. We shall mix wine with drinking water, then let us be off for Brazil!"

"Aye, sir!"

The morning after Drake's fleet of six ships sailed west for Brazil, John Brewer, the trumpeter and a crewman from the *Mary*, boarded the *Pelican*. He was nearly sixteen but tall for his age. Drake had developed a fondness for John Brewer because of his industriousness, as he not only did his musical chores, but he also stood regular seaman watches. The young trumpeter entered Drake's cabin where the two Drakes were sketching.

"General," the young man said.

"Yes—how are things on the *Mary*?" Drake asked on raising his head to note who had entered.

"Not good, General," Brewer hesitantly said. Then he quickly added, "Captain Doughty has charged your brother Tom with stealing cargo from the *Mary*!"

"What?"

"He did it this morning!" Brewer said. "He declared that he was goin' to punish him, report him to you. But, General, Tom only got a few things, like the rest of us did. And Captain Doughty has taken many things for himself. He has a large sack full. I thought that you needed to know about that right now!"

"Right you are, John. Take me to the *Mary*!" Drake said, having turned and now standing erect.

"I can do that," the young sailor said on stiffening his back. He was now coxswain of the *Mary*'s dinghy. And during the day the small boat made many trips to other ships, as there was much visiting being done amongst the crews.

In fifteen minutes, the dinghy crossed the placid blue waters to the *Mary*. Drake quickly climbed the ladder to board the ship. Doughty was on deck waiting to greet Drake.

"Mornin', General. I am glad that you are visiting the *Mary*," Doughty said, smiling. "I need to make a report to you on the pilfering of goods from her," Doughty said and withdrew his hand on seeing Drake's unusually red face.

"And I guess that you want to report that it was my brother, Tom!" Drake shouted. His eyes and cheeks were now fiery from rage. He was upset at Doughty for having made accusations directed toward a member of his family, for Drake was sensitive about his family. He had refused to give his brother a position of importance in the fleet because he did not want the criticism that he knew it would bring. This was so even though he knew that the younger Drake was capable of command. And up till then, Drake had made him sail as a seaman, requiring it even though he was very fond of his brother. More so, Drake was very touchy about the low position his family had held during his childhood. The writer has previously mentioned that during the reign of Catholic Mary, Drake's father had been exiled to the River Medway in Kent because of his Protestant views. It was here that he had raised his family of twelve sons in the hulk of an old ship because he could not touch English soil. Francis was the oldest; he had left home at twelve to begin a seaman apprenticeship. But he had remained quite close to his family. For until he was married, each time that he returned from a voyage, he had given most of his wages to his father. And so Drake had taken the attack on his brother as an attack on his family, and Drake's thin skin had caused him to believe that Doughty had done it because of his higher social position.

"Yes, that is true!"

"And do you wish to report that you have been pilfering, too?" Drake stated, putting his hands on his hips, being apprehensively watched by the Portuguese navigator who hardly knew how Drake would handle problems with a member of his crew. He wondered but that he would run his sword through him.

"No, I have not!" Doughty declared.

"Enough! Enough! I will hear no more!" Drake declared. His normally red face was now livid.

"But—but!" Doughty argued. "I was in command," he said, as though that gave him the right to pilfer.

"No more. You are relieved of your command!"

"But, General!"

"Well, now. I will take command of the *Mary*," Drake said, angrily snorting, thinking, still not wishing to make a complete break with the lawyer/soldier, remembering his ties with the influential cabinet members. He paused and then said, "You take command of the *Pelican!*" He said it as if that were punishment, while in truth it was a promotion to captain of the flagship.

"I will take my belongings and report to her promptly."

"But you will not take anything from this vessel," Drake ordered. He was very sensitive about keeping goods together that had been taken from prizes. He knew that otherwise it could easily cause mutinous dissent. So he was determined to distribute it himself at the proper time. Yet the reader will soon discover that the rule did not necessarily apply to Drake.

"But I was given presents by some Portuguese crewmen—"

"They did not have presents to give, for on my taking their ship, their goods belonged to my command!" Drake stated.

"Well—" Doughty replied in a defeated manner while leaving the cabin.

Doughty thereafter boarded the *Pelican*. On his doing so, he quickly made it known to all the officers that he, not Drake, was now the Captain of the *Pelican*. He promptly spoke to Master Cuttill:

"As you know, I am now Captain of the *Pelican*. What do you say to that?" he asked, meaning, "Do you not think that it is better that I am in command?"

"And the General?" Cuttill asked without fully answering Doughty's question. The master had always spoken to Doughty with great respect. This was because he knew of his connection with the Queen, and this was enough in Cuttill's eyes to give Doughty undue respect.

"He now commands the *Mary* so that he can be near his popish friend!" Doughty said. He would later explain to Cuttill that Drake had begun to speak in Spanish with Nuno da Silva while Doughty was leaving the *Mary*.

"Well, I will say to you congratulations! But where will this lead?" Cuttill curiously asked.

"It leaves us bound for the Magellan Strait!" Doughty said, smiling in a deceitful way. Up until then Cuttill had not known where they were going. Doughty then added, "And then we are bound for the South Seas. You need to know that Drake intends to take on all Spanish Peru—" Then he smiled and asked, "Did you not know?"

"Naye—he never said. I had thought that we would coast Brazil and then go up to the Spanish Main."

"It is a dangerous undertaking—it may be a death trap! And Drake appears to be mad—will you promise me your support in case worse goes to worse—"

"Support? What am I to do?" Cuttill curiously asked, frowning to show that he did not like the puzzle of which he was being made a part. Cuttill was an able seaman and a good navigator, but otherwise he was a poorly educated seaman who knew very little of the intrigues that involve men in high places.

"Support me, man. I will do great favors for you. I have the Queen's ear. My master is Sir Christopher Hatton, the Queen's favorite. Why Cuttill, it is I that put together this venture. Did you know that the money for it came from me and my friends? And you have seen how Drake shows his appreciation of my bounty!"

"I did not know that—I promise!" Cuttill weakly replied, being cowed by the fact that he was standing beside a man who was so close to the Queen of England. For he knew that the Queen was the power and might of England. She was in charge of its lawmen, its judges and its admirals. He knew that Drake was a general, but he also knew that that was insignificant in comparison to someone who had the ear of the Queen. For such person in essence was the Queen.

The very next day John Brewer and Diego boarded the *Pelican* in order to borrow Drake's silver plate so it could be used for Drake's evening meal, as he was dissatisfied with the plain plate which had belonged to da Silva. Eating to Drake was the time to show his rank. And rank entailed silver plate.

"And what do you want, snitch!" Doughty asked, speaking to Brewer as the two men approached the captain's cabin.

"The General wants his plate, his silver!" Brewer answered in a haughty voice without showing the slightest fear of Doughty.

"I guess he does," Doughty sarcastically replied, "while his men eat with a spoon and sail knife." Then he quickly said to Cuttill, "Seize his arms, Master Cuttill—I wish to give this imp a few whacks with the back of my sword!"

Cuttill, being larger and stronger than the trumpeter, seized him and held him while Doughty hit Brewer several times across the backside with his sword.

"That will teach you in the future to hold your tongue and not gossip about your superiors!" Doughty declared, frowning at Brewer.

"Unhand me!" Brewer angrily shouted while pulling away from Cuttill, who then released the trumpeter who angrily glared at Doughty.

"And best you not tell this to the General, or the next time you will get the point!" Doughty haughtily said while fingering his sword.

But on the two men climbing to the deck of the *Mary*, John Brewer ignored Doughty's warning and asked Tom Drake to give him an audience with Drake.

"Sir," Brewer said on entering Drake's cabin. "Captain Doughty beat me with the back of his sword," he said. Then he dropped his trousers and showed his backside, which had red marks on it from the sword.

"Why?" Drake demanded. Irritancy was in his voice.

"He said that I was a snitch for you!"

"Oh, he did—" Drake said. His face had become flushed, and his eyes had become intense.

"And General," the trumpeter added, "he has told his men that we are voyaging to the South Seas by way of the Magellan Strait. He has told them that it is a very dangerous strait and that many ships will not make it. He says that once you reach the South Seas, you intend to fight all the Spaniards in Peru. And, sir, a seaman told me that he has told some of the men that you are mad—and I warn you that he may have Cuttill's support!"

"Well, now," Drake said in a soft, strong voice, though his face now had become fiery red. "Is this true, Diego?"

"Yes, General—it is true! We talked to the men on deck and to the line handlers."

"Diego—take the dinghy. Tell Captain Doughty to come to the *Mary* immediately!"

"Aye!"

A half hour later while the men in the *Mary* were having prayer service, the dinghy pulled alongside of her. Doughty was standing in its bow; he eagerly reached for the sea ladder as if he were in a hurry to board the *Mary*. Drake on deck looked down at Diego who had his hand on the tiller; then he quickly eyed Doughty whose hand was on the sea ladder.

"Remove your hand from that ladder, Thomas Doughty! Return to your seat!" Drake said.

"Why can I not come aboard?"

"I intend to send you to another place!"

"Where, sir?"

"To the *Swan*!" Drake sternly replied, referring to the small store ship.

"Why, General?"

"You are to go there as a prisoner—inform the captain of the *Swan* of your status. I will deal with you later!"

"Please, sir!" Doughty begged.

"Enough!" Drake said. Then he turned and spoke to Preacher Fletcher. "Resume church services, Preacher, but let us first hold hands to show God that we are a unified body."

CHAPTER 15

THE PILOT

On Drake boarding the *Mary* and making a cursory examination of Nuno da Silva's charts, he decided that it had been a wise decision on his part to keep the Portuguese. He further concluded that Nuno had to be an exceptional navigator. This was partially because he had noted the numerous pencil notations on da Silva's charts with arrows which pointed out the direction of the winds and of the current. Drake knew that an understanding of the movement of the winds was very important to the captain of a square-rigged ship like the *Pelican*, for it needed a following wind. He also knew that a captain who understood the currents would have better command of his ship. And then one could judge a tradesman by his tools, and Nuno's were much superior to Drake's. For one thing, Drake had found a dress sphere of the world, which was a definite navigational aid. But Drake had not made da Silva his prisoner because he himself was a poor navigator. Drake was just thinking ahead, for he knew that soon they would be sailing in poorly charted waters, and he needed all the expertise that he could garner. A pilot like da Silva might be the edge that could make the voyage a success.

Thus, this was the reason that Drake, on returning to the *Pelican* to assume its captaincy, had brought da Silva with him. For Drake now was convinced that da Silva was an important addition to the expedition, and so he had decided to cultivate him by giving him special treatment. The first gratuity that he gave him was to permit him to sleep in the bunk that John Drake had been using. And thereafter, they spent much of their time together either in Drake's cabin or on the poop deck. They now were in Drake's cabin. Drake was seated at the chart table where he was curiously studying the charts that he had obtained from the *Santa Maria*. Then Drake began to question da Silva in his poor Spanish:

"¿Cuantos dias a Brazil?" How many days to Brazil?

"Sixty-three days from the Cape Verde Islands," da Silva surely answered, as though it took all ships the same amount of time to sail to it.

"And will we have wind?" Drake asked. He was forever interested in the horizontal movement of air.

"It will soon die—" da Silva thoughtfully answered, frowning while stroking his beard, pointing out the fact that they soon would be in the equatorial doldrums, being the area where there was little wind.

"And then?"

"We will survive—" the Portuguese philosophically replied with a shrug of his shoulders. Then he touched his beads and began to pray as he often did when he thought on his plight.

"Oh!"

"And General, your Spanish is not good," da Silva said on finishing his prayer, saying it in a slightly critical voice, speaking like a professor. The Portuguese in many ways was a very formal person, and his manner carried over into his speaking. He never used slang or vulgarity. As well, Drake would soon learn that it irritated da Silva to hear a speaker who could not distinguish between the masculine and the feminine nouns in the Spanish language. And even worse, he knew that Drake did not have the slightest concept of person, for his sentences usually were formed by using the infinitive verb or the present tense.

"I learned it from the Cimaron on the Spanish Main."

"I see," da Silva said. "You had poor teachers—permit me to teach you the language," he politely said, smiling in a solicitous manner, as he made it obvious that he did not wish to get crosswise with Drake.

"Please do," Drake replied, smiling to show his appreciation. For he instinctively knew that on his reaching Peru, it would be very important for him to have a better understanding of the Spanish language since he would be having confrontations with Spaniards. More so, he was aware of his shortcomings in regard to language, for he had had only four years of grammar school, though since then he had added greatly to his school learning. He was a good reader; this was especially so of books that pertained to navigation, ships, the sea and exploration. He had on two different occasions read Piglotta's *Voyage of Magellan*, which was an exaggerated account of Magellan's famous voyage, though Piglotta was one of the few starters who had finished the voyage.

"Pues." Well, Nuno said, speaking in Spanish, as his English was much worse than Drake's Spanish. "We will begin by studying the use of masculine and feminine words."

"La chica. The girl. She is feminine."

"El libro. The book. It is masculine."

Drake repeated the phrases and words while his cousin seated nearby sketched a flying fish as it leapt from the water, soaring through the air in its attempt to elude an attacking bonito. Then John Drake would make a different sketch of the *Pelican*'s deck. Then he would sketch a fish landing near a barefoot, shirtless sailor. And in real life, the sailor pounced on the fish, cleaned it, then presented it to the chubby cook, who without wasting any time quickly put it in a giant cook pan that set on the stove. Horsewill was presently cooking all meals topside. He was cooking fish for just about every meal. Most of the fish were being caught by the fishermen that fished from a small deck beneath the poop deck. He was being assisted by Thomas Blackcollar, who not only liked to eat, but he liked to cook as well. Blackcollar was almost the same height as Horsewill, though he was not nearly as heavy. He had dark hair, bushy eyebrows and very dark brown eyes. He got on well with Horsewill, who was in charge of the cooking, though eventually Blackcollar would do all of the baking. Boatswain Fowler had rigged an awning over the stove to protect it from the afternoon rains. The ships were now in the torrid zone. Wind was scarce, and it would become even more so, for soon the *Pelican* and the other five ships would be becalmed.

"Rain!" cried a sailor from the mainmast.

"Rain, aye!" answered a sailor from the deck, where he and three other sailors had stretched a canvas sail. Then they formed a hollow in it to serve as a catch basin for rain water. The shower soon passed, leaving in the canvas concave many gallons of water. And so Drake's worry about water had almost been for naught, as the fleet was being exposed to a rain cloud every day, which left them with a plentiful supply of water.

While Drake perfected his Spanish, the sailors on deck amused themselves by catching fish with hand-lines or the flying fish with their hands, which regularly sailed through the air and over the gunwales, landing at their feet. They then cleaned them so Horsewill and Blackcollar could cook them. And on the fleet arriving in the doldrums, they soon were followed by several large birds that lazily soared over the ships.

"Are we now near land?" Drake asked Nuno, wondering if they were near an uncharted island.

"No, far from it—those birds are albatross."

"They must sleep at sea!"

"They sleep on the wing while gliding."

"One has landed on the rigging," Drake said, pointing to a large bird which had landed on a rope. The bird was being approached by a sailor with a club in his hand; he obviously intended to use it to kill the bird.

"Stop him!" Nuno exclaimed.

"Why?" Drake questioned, seeing no wrong in killing the bird, as he, too, was a predator who was accustomed to taking from those who were less strong.

"It has the soul of a sailor!" Nuno declared. His face had a troubled appearance, indicating that he was unduly disturbed. Emotion was in his voice.

"Well—" Drake said, wanting to ignore him. But then he reconsidered, remembering that this man was now his teacher, and he did not want to anger him. For he wanted him to continue teaching him. So he hurriedly exited from his cabin and shouted to the sailor:

"Tom! Tom! Stop!"

"Why, General?"

"That bird carries the soul of a sailor who wishes to return to this ship!"

"How do you know?"

"The pilot swears it!"

"Ah!"

"Drop it!"

And the sailor dropped his club.

But the pilot was wise about other things, too. One of these was navigation. Drake now had so much confidence in Nuno's navigational skill that he had given him the job of navigating the *Pelican*.

"Is this Mercator map equal to those of your Portuguese?" Drake asked. He knew that the Portuguese were considered to be the best mapmakers in the world; however, he had been unable to obtain a Portuguese map of the South Atlantic until he boarded the *Santa Maria*.

"Oh, yes—it is as good as there is."

"I have been told the same—"

"Mercator drew his chart so that if we took a pair of scissors and cut it, we could form it into a globe. Then he drew lines on it for longitude. But it does not narrow at the top or the bottom, which it should have done if we are to have a globe. And then he drew these lines for latitude, which we locate by taking sights on the sun or other celestial objects. And so one must study a globe to best understand Mercator's map, for distances from place to place on the seas depend on the curvature of the Earth."

"I know—" Drake unsurely said, while listening intently.

"For instance, the Mercator chart is not a true picture of the world—let me take this ball—but it is not a true example. We Portuguese believe that the world is more like a sphere. Well, anyway, we are en route to the River Plata, and the way to get there is thusly," he said, pointing. "The world differs by location. We are now in the Southern hemisphere."

"And your plots have all been rhumblines?" Drake said, referring to lines that intersect all meridians at the same angle. He was pointing to Nuno's plot that he had drawn on Mercator's map. Drake's fleet had crossed the equator at the same angle since leaving the Verde Islands.

"Yes, that is Mercator's gift to navigation!"

"And this is a curved line?"

"Correct—that is because the Earth is in the shape of a sphere," he correctly explained.

"But it is not necessarily the shortest route?"

"That is why I have plotted you a course by using a series of rhumblines—this course is the shortest route to the River Plata."

"And that will shorten the distance?"

"Yes, that is because we are traveling in a circle, and by doing so, that will shorten the distance," Nuno said, smiling, showing considerable interest in the discussion.

"And where did you learn this?"

"Portugal—it is a navigational secret of ours!" he said, wrying his face as if he wished that he had not revealed it.

"And now I know it!" Drake said, smiling, thinking while closely eyeing his teacher who was not only teaching him Spanish, but confiding in him the secrets of the great Portuguese navigators.

"Why not," Nuno said and indifferently shrugged his shoulders as if his standing as a navigator no longer mattered.

"And when do we reach Brazil?"

"As I said, we reach it on the sixty-third day!"

"And then do we coast it?"

"No, if you will study my charts closely, you will see that the coast is too shallow. We will keep our distance and stay out for seventy-five miles while sailing south to the River Plata."

"Diego! Diego!"

"Yes, General," the black man replied. Expectancy was on his face as he hurriedly entered the cabin.

"Two glasses of claret to celebrate a bit of learning!"

"What have you learned, General?" Diego asked, smiling. He was pleased to see that his master was happy.

"A marvelous thing—"

"What is that, General?" the black man repeated, smiling.

"I have learned how to travel a thousand miles at sea by going eight hundred miles."

"By whose magic, General?"

"That of the pilot!" Drake said, pointing to Nuno while passing to him a glass of claret.

"Gracias!" the pilot politely said. And then he thoughtfully sipped his wine, as if thinking of Portugal and what life could have been had his visit to Cape Verde not coincided with that of Drake's.

"Here's to a long and profitable life at sea!" Drake said, speaking more for himself than for his captive navigator, who sadly smiled.

CHAPTER 16

THE JONAH

Thomas Doughty boarded the tiny provision ship *Swan* as a prisoner, doing it with considerable fanfare. For even though he was not in chains when he climbed the sea ladder, he dramatically made it appear as though he were. For as he was leaving the *Swan*'s sea ladder and stepping onto her deck, he held out his hands and shouted in a maligned voice to its captain, John Chester.

"John, I am now your prisoner!" Doughty said to Chester, a short, slight-of-build man of twenty-eight years. Doughty spoke as though he had been tried, convicted and sentenced, seemingly doing it to divide the men in the fleet. Most already knew of the dissention between Drake and Doughty concerning the *Mary*. The soldiers immediately formed themselves in a group and began to point at Doughty while they anxiously confided with one another.

"For what reason?" Chester curiously asked. Concern was on his face. He heretofore had looked on Doughty with respect, firstly because at one time he had been so close to power. And Chester, being a mayor's son, could readily respect such a person. Then Chester had been convinced that Doughty was a leader of the venture. But he obviously did not speak for his shipmaster, John Saracold, who was standing beside him. Saracold disdainfully frowned at Doughty, while sharply eyeing him. This was primarily because he considered Doughty to be a landsman—he did not like shipboard landsmen. Then he also knew that Doughty was engaged in a row with Drake. And Saracold was a Plymouth man—and on a voyage such as this, that made them kin. On the other hand, there were more than a dozen men aboard the *Swan* who were in a similar status as Doughty. All behaved like passengers; they refused to do sailor work, though the sailors had also trained to be soldiers. And these landsmen were contentious, as they griped and quarreled with the sailors. The sailors were always busy—they were ever examining, tightening, straightening and replacing the standing rigging, which embraced all ropes that supported the masts and sails. This rigging was not only extensive but complex. And the sailors were proud of their knowledge of it. Saracold was a seaman and so he despised the landsmen. Now he had one more landsman. And worse, Doughty was crosswise with Drake, a Devon seaman; and as the writer has previously stated, Saracold was from Plymouth, and Doughty little understood Devon seamen. For at sea they were as clannish as members of a secret society.

"The General has accused me of mutinous behavior and treasonous conduct!" Doughty said, speaking in a loud but childish voice, doing it as if he wanted every man aboard to know of his grievances with Drake.

"Well, I am surprised and bothered to hear it. Irregardless, you will have the freedom of the ship until I hear further from the General," Chester said in a sympathetic voice.

"And this is the thanks I get for putting together this venture," Doughty said, speaking directly to Chester, doing it as though the young captain fully understood the background of the venture. "For it was I who obtained the Queen's permission for the venture; it was I who found the investors. And further, the principal part of the money for this venture came from me," Doughty said, grievously frowning, though in truth the money for the venture had not come from Doughty.

"I am sorry that you two are having your differences. It is not good for the venture!" Chester said, speaking in a low voice without commenting on Doughty's claim. He had noted that the landsmen standing in a group on the bow were intently listening to their conversation. The ship was just too small and too crowded for secrets. Chester's sympathies were with Doughty; yet he did not want to put himself at odds with his master. It was he who was doing the navigating, for in truth, Chester was not a seaman.

"And Drake has not told you where we are bound?" Doughty asked, speaking loudly, showing surprise, as if it were important that all should know.

"Only to the River Plata!" Chester replied, saying it as though that was sufficient. In reality, he had not expected to be told in advance the details of the venture. It just was not the custom. Revealing secrets of a voyage was the prerogative of the general in charge.

"Well, we're sailing from there for the Magellan Strait—but I doubt that this flyboat can make it through such a dangerous strait!" Doughty said, using the term "flyboat" to refer to the type of ship that the *Swan* was. It had a nearly flat bottom and a high stern. Thus, it was not the ideal ship for such a voyage, as it had actually been designed for coastal trade. A man with more experience might not have undertaken such a voyage in a flyboat.

"Well, now, I've found her to be strong and sturdy—and where do we go from there?" Chester curiously asked without revealing in the slightest that he was afraid to take the *Swan* through the strait even though she was a flyboat.

"Up the coast of Peru—that is, those ships which make it through the strait will go up the coast of Peru," Doughty said with a shout, as though he intended for all to know.

"Keep your voice down—and then what?"

"And then we will take on the Spanish fleet—" Doughty said, still speaking loud enough for the soldiers to hear.

"You may have said too much!" Chester warned. His voice now chided Doughty for his use of reckless words. As well, his face now had a sternness to it that seemed to indicate an undue reaction to Doughty's remarks.

"But I have that right. I am a general just like Drake!"

"Enough! Maybe we can talk more at dinner. You can dine in my cabin with me and the master, eh, John!" he said to his master, who was intently eyeing the two. Saracold had not liked what he had heard. One of Saracold's eyes was half-closed from the sun; the other was steeled. His lower lip drooped. Saracold had not spoken since Doughty boarded.

"I will not eat with him; I shall eat with the seamen!" the master declared. Saracold walked into Chester's cabin where he took his metal pewter plate from a shelf; then he took from a drawer a pewter spoon, which he put in his pocket. His sail knife with which he also ate was attached to his belt. He then strode out of the cabin, passing the pair without speaking.

"I will teach you to look at me like that when we return to London!" Doughty said in a hateful voice. His eyes now beaded the master as if he had some strange power.

"You'll hang first!" the master replied on turning. He then frowned at Doughty, as if to show Doughty that he was undaunted at his threat, and he spat at him.

"Chester, he is insubordinate to you! You must do something!" Doughty said, speaking in a chastising voice.

"What can I do?" Chester said. Perplexity was on his face, for he was not ready to cross the master. Then he did not want to lose the goodwill of Doughty.

"Join with me," Doughty said. "Follow my leadership. I will give you all the authority that you need to do your job such as to discipline your master!"

"But why join with you?"

"Drake will have to step down, and I will fill the void!"

"That is dangerous talk!"

"It will soon have to be faced—the gentlemen and the land soldiers will be with me in a showdown!" Doughty declared while Chester thoughtfully eyed him, and then he eyed the landsmen on the bow staring at them.

Thereafter, the fleet of small ships lazily continued to sail for Brazil. And while it was doing so, Doughty had the free rein of the *Swan*. He roamed her decks, cornering sailors or soldiers, haranguing them on their loyalty to Drake, and even whether they would support him in a showdown with Drake. On one such occasion, Doughty strolled to the bow and joined Edward Cliff, a young seaman, who had his face down while he carefully coiled a rope.

"Have you been told that I have the power of the devil?" Doughty asked the young sailor. During the short time that Doughty had been aboard the *Swan*, he had done much to create the belief amongst the poorly educated sailors that because of his superior schooling he had supernatural powers. And this was not difficult to do since the sailors believed that there were persons with such powers. They believed that there were witches and wizards. Each had the power to do supernatural acts, such as fly through the air. This thought was helped by the many sermons by ministers which were directed against such evils. Then all believed that there was a god. And if there were a god, did he not have a counterpart, being the devil?

"That I have, Mr. Doughty," the sailor replied, continuing to coil the rope without looking up to face Doughty, being timid in his presence, as he considered him to be an officer. That in itself was sufficient power to cow a young sailor.

"And would you like to see me use my power?"

"Well, now, I would, providing you did not do something to destroy the *Swan*, sir!" the young sailor fearfully said, raising his head for the first time. His face showed fear, indicating that he did believe that Doughty had magical powers. And there was strong reasoning for such belief. He knew that Doughty had attended Cambridge and had studied law in the Middle Temple; he also knew that he spoke Latin and Greek. A man with such a background had to have great powers. He could even be a wizard. Then he had worked for the Queen's ministers. And now he stood before him threatening to use his great power. And so he was convinced that such persons had to have great powers.

"Abra-babra-cabra-dabra! Devil help me!" Doughty muttered, while studying the rolling waves that were being baked by the midday sun. "Look up and see what the devil has created!" Doughty ordered the sailor, who then again raised and turned his head so that he could see the sea. A small storm, being a williwaw, was crossing the bow. It was twirling spray high in the air, and it continued to gain power as it took in water.

"My Lord, did you do that?" the sailor asked, eyeing the small storm with astonishment while it continued to take on more water and grow.

"Yes. And if I wished, I could create a much larger storm—big enough to sink this fleet!" Doughty confidently said, as though he did have such power.

"But you would not!" the sailor fearfully said.

"I will unless I am returned to my rightful position!" Doughty declared in an angry voice as if he had the power to do it.

The matter bothered the young sailor immensely. So he thought on it and thought on it. And so on the next occasion that he joined the dinghy crew to row over to the *Pelican* in order to supply it with provisions, and on his boarding her, he asked Diego to obtain an audience for him with Drake.

"The General is busy!" Diego replied, guarding the door to Drake's cabin. But the answer was false, for in truth Drake was seated at the cabin table where he was leisurely sketching.

"It is very important, Diego. It concerns Mr. Doughty!"

"Oh, then he will see you—" the black man said before ever speaking to Drake, as he knew that Drake was interested in news of the lawyer-adventurer.

"And General," Cliff said, speaking very rapidly, "he has the power of the devil. I saw him conjure up a storm; he told me that he had the power to call storms. He said that he would demonstrate that power by calling up a small storm. He first spoke in a foreign tongue; then he said, 'I will now show you the power of the devil—look up!' and I did, and there was a small storm!"

"Ah!"

"I swear, General—"

"He is a sorcerer!" Drake declared on hearing the story, saying it as though he knew it to be a fact. Drake, like young Cliff, believed in witches and devils. He as well believed that there were some evil men with the power of the devil, being able to call up winds. That in itself was not evil if the ship was in need of wind; yet it could be so where such power was used to call up storms.

"And he has asked the captain of the *Swan* to join him in taking charge of the fleet!" Cliff hurriedly said.

"What was the response of Mayor Chester?" Drake asked, while steeling his eyes.

"The captain has not committed himself—" Cliff said, blinking his eyes nervously, appearing worried at what he had said. Then he quickly added, "Master Saracold has refused to eat with him!"

"He's a Plymouth man—"

"I felt that you should know this, for I fear for your safety—remember, General, we sailors will support you!"

"Do not worry, and thanks for coming—I will deal with this matter of Doughty at the appropriate time!"

"Thanks, General!"

On the morning of April 5, 1578, Nuno da Silva stepped onto the portico deck of the *Pelican*, smelled the salt air, turned back to Drake and said to him:

"¡Estabamos aqui!" We are here, he said, meaning that they had arrived at the coast of Brazil.

"How can you tell?" Drake asked, also stepping on deck, searching the west for signs of land birds or land itself. He saw nothing and was puzzled.

"I smell it!" the navigator explained on touching his nose. For some uncanny reason Nuno had been able to smell the faint odor of perfume that was emitting from the coast of Brazil.

On the following day, the *Pelican* sighted a faded outline of the Brazilian coast, which was two hundred miles westward, being in the direction that they were sailing.

"We now sail southwest," the navigator said.

"Not coast it?" Drake asked, being accustomed where possible to follow the coast.

"It is too shallow," Nuno surely said, as if there could not be any compromise.

"Tom!" Drake cried out, having stepped to the door. He was attempting to get the attention of Tom Moone on the messenger ship. The reader will recall that Moone's original command, the *Benedict*, had been given to the African fishermen on their being released with the Portuguese who had been captured at St. James, the capitol of the Verde Islands. Moone then had taken command of the strongest fishing bark, which Drake had named the *Christopher*. "Advise each ship that our next rendezvous will be the River Plata!" Drake said it as though it were a bay, while in fact the entrance to the River Plata is more than one hundred miles wide. "Once we are there, we will rest, take on water, scrape the hulls and ready ourselves for the next leg of the expedition."

"Aye! And the coast of Darien is out?" Moone wistfully asked. The money that he had made with Drake on their last venture to the coast had made him eager to return. Yet he now had doubts about their going north along the Brazilian coast, for he had heard of the stories that Doughty was telling. He was confiding in anyone who would listen the secrets of the voyage, telling them that the fleet was sailing for the Strait of Magellan and then to the coast of Peru. He had decided that there had to be some truth to them.

"No, not this time."

"I hope that this voyage means gold?" Moone asked, speaking in a friendly voice.

"More than you can imagine!"

"Tally ho!"

"To the River Plata!" Drake ordered his navigator.

"¡Correcto!" Nuno replied, while studying a chart of the Brazilian coast.

The following day a great storm struck the fleet, and the small ships helplessly tossed about. The *Pelican* rolled and tossed so that it was difficult to stand on her deck without having a hold of something. Drake studied the green seas and fierce winds that lashed against the bare masts, and he shouted to Nuno da Silva:

"It is Tom Doughty. He has conjured up this storm so as to destroy my fleet!" Drake hatefully said while contorting his face so as to indicate that he truly believed Doughty was a sorcerer.

"Naye, General! It has been done by the Indians of Brazil," Nuno said. He, too, believed that certain persons had the ability to conjure up storms. But he was convinced that the persons who had created this one were the Brazilian Indians. "They saw our masts and they concluded that we were Portuguese who they do not like. So they conjured up this storm to drive us away. They have that power. They pray to devils, while tossing sand in the air. General, we must keep the *Pelican* headed out to sea!"

"It is difficult!" Drake shouted. He now had his hand on the whipstaff, though Thomas Hood was standing beside him in case there was a need for a second hand on the whip, as the force of the sea could quickly throw the rudder to the other side. Rain lashed both men in the face.

"Yet we must!"

And the *Pelican* did; however, when the storm cleared, the *Christopher* was missing.

"Moone's ship is missing," Drake said to Nuno after counting the ships. "The *Christopher* is missing!"

"He may have been blown ashore," the pilot answered, shaking his head as though Moone were lost. The storm had been so intense that it easily could have driven a small ship ashore.

"I doubt it," Drake surely said, frowning. "He is a Devon seaman. I would think that he is far out to sea—he is storm wise. He will turn up later—"

On April 14, the five ships of the fleet entered the River Plata, being a great estuary which drains the river systems that we now know as the Parana and the Uruguay. Its entrance is quite large, as it is 140 miles across. Drake followed the southern shoreline of the estuary which was fairly shallow, as its depth in places was only ten feet. They sailed into a small bay.

"Master Cuttill, drop your anchor!"

"Aye, sir!"

142

"Find me six able men to man the dinghy!" Drake said, speaking to Fowler. Many of the men were suffering from scurvy and not able to work. The cold and dampness had greatly aggravated their sore joints.

"Aye, sir!"

"Belay the word!" Drake said, canceling the order to man the dinghy.

The skies were ominous and with good reason. For as they sailed from the estuary and into the partially sheltered bay, they were meeting the first of many storms. The seas soon were tumultuous. The ships were tossed about as though they were canoes, for there were waves taller than the *Pelican*. Drake stood on the wobbly poop deck while counting his ships. He had accounted for all except the *Christopher*.

Soon after the fleet anchored, Cuttill brought good news.

"General!" declared Cuttill, smiling on entering the cabin. "The *Christopher* is here!"

"Well, glory be!" Drake declared, looking outside through a window while holding tightly to a storm rail. "I knew Moone could make it—John!" Yet he had worried, as he was depending more and more on Moone.

"Yes, General?"

"Pass the word to Gunner Clark—fire three volleys from a culverin for the *Christopher*."

"Aye!"

"And ask the preacher to come to my cabin—I want him to lead us in prayer."

"Aye!" he said.

"And ask Diego to step inside—I want each man served a glass of claret."

Seconds later the culverins loudly sounded:

"Boom! Boom! Boom!"

Drake named this bay Joyful Bay so as to commemorate the finding of Moone. But it was not joyful for long. The winds increased and their effect on the shallow water caused the small ships to move about and to drag their anchors. Drake was forced to move his fleet further up the estuary. Soon he had them anchor on the leeward side of a rocky island which acted as a shield against the southern winds, which at times blew with such force that the anchors dragged. Drake used the longboat to make daily trips ashore so as to take part of the

143

men there for recreational visits. Once the men were on land, they walked and stretched their limbs so as to regain their strength. Many played with a pigskin. Others could not because their legs were too swollen, as they were in the early stages of scurvy. Drake was a pragmatist. He ordered the men to kill seals, so as to obtain fresh meat. Horsewill and Blackcollar cooked a portion; then Drake aided them and the boys in the salting down of others so they would be available to be eaten on the trip south. He led a working party that put other seals in a large cook pot and boiled them until they became oil. He, Preacher Fletcher and the ignorant ship's doctor went about the ships with a bucket of oil, pouring a cupful for each man on the sick list; each was forced to drink a portion, then rub his legs and arms with the remainder. And if a man were unable to do the rubbing, then the ship's doctor and Fletcher did it for him.

On April 27, 1578, when all the sailors and men in the fleet had somewhat regained their strength, Drake had Moone notify each ship's captain to meet with him on the *Pelican*. It was now fall in the southern hemisphere. The weather had appreciably changed, becoming much colder and very damp.

"Diego, please serve a glass of claret to each man!" Drake said, shaking as if ridding himself of the chill. He was dressed in a leather jacket, a woolen sweater and a leather hat. A fire was in the grate.

"Aye!"

"How is your crew?" Drake asked Wynter.

"Good—they are strong enough to gripe!"

"And yours," he asked the others.

"Well—"

"Good—"

"Ready—"

"Very well, then we will leave within the hour."

"And where will our next assembly point be?" Wynter asked.

"Here," Drake said, pointing to the map on the table. His finger was pointed at a bay which is located much further south on the Patagonian coast. Drake would later call it Seal Bay.

Shortly after they sailed from the bay, they encountered one storm after another; Doughty was blamed for each. The men on the *Pelican* uniformly cursed him. The first storm was a nasty one which they encountered shortly after they sailed out of the River Plata. When the storm had abated, Drake studied the horizon, and he was able to account for all of the ships except the *Swan*, which was the ship on which Doughty was a prisoner.

"That Doughty has conjured up another bad storm! Find me the *Swan*!" Drake said with a snarl on this face. He had shouted to Master Cuttill as if he intended to discipline the ship.

"She is still not in sight, General!" Cuttill said after making a careful search. Then he returned to the cabin table where Drake, Nuno and John Drake were seated.

"We need the *Swan*!" Drake declared, speaking more to himself than to Cuttill. He knew that without the *Swan*'s stores, it would be difficult for the fleet to complete their voyage. Then he spoke in Spanish to the pilot who was looking over the shoulder of John Drake. The boy was sketching the head of a seal; he now was drawing its whiskers.

"That Doughty has conjured up another storm!" Drake bitterly said, repeating what he had said an hour earlier. His face wore a sour frown.

"And much dissension!" Nuno warned, like he had done an hour before. Unknown to him, he had fallen into a pattern, slowly becoming a part of the venture.

"I will deal with his mutiny at the proper time!" Drake declared, saying it as if he knew that a mutinous crew was worse than a plague.

CHAPTER 17

SEAL BAY

On the morning of April 27, 1578, Drake's fleet sailed out of the Plata estuary and into the Atlantic Ocean on a strong breeze. The slack winds did not tell the full weather story, as it was a poor day for sailing the south Atlantic waters, for a storm appeared imminent. The skies were overcast, while gray clouds restlessly moved about the heavens. At midday the skies became very dark. Winds by then were at gale force. Thunder clapped from the sky, sounding like cannon fire. Lightning flashed. Rain angrily lashed at the ships. The winds increased; the waves rose, and the *Pelican* rolled and wallowed.

"Batten her down!" Drake cried out. He was standing beside Cuttill whose hand tightly clutched the whipstaff. Drake put his hand on it, too, and tightly clasped it. To Drake's right was Nuno, dressed in rain clothes; he stared with wide-opened eyes at the tall waves that were now following them. Their danger now was obvious, as they were rolling toward the *Pelican* like breakers as if they intended to end the voyage. Drake looked out at the dozens of sailors seated on the yards with their feet on a horse rope. All tightly clutched a hand rope as if their lives depended on it—fear was on their faces. Two key boatswains, Fowler and Hood, were seated on the yard for the giant main sail, being astraddle it, barefoot, having their toes tightly clutching the horse, being the foot rope. Drake studied the seas.

"She refuses to answer, General!" Cuttill shouted, as if waiting for a signal, speaking to no one in particular. He was referring to the rudder. Drake knew it, too, as he could see and feel it. The rudder did not have any mechanical device to keep it from moving with the seas. Thus, in rough seas, steering required two men. The seas were

Moone, Horsewill, John Drake, and Fletcher: "On to the South Sea!"

now moving almost as fast as the *Pelican*. This placed the *Pelican* in considerable danger as she could capsize from the following seas.

"Reef your sails!" Drake shouted. He wanted them shortened.

Drake knew that he had to shorten sail because the winds from the storm could cause the *Pelican* to capsize. But then Drake faced a dilemma—too much wind would capsize the *Pelican*, while not enough could cause the following sea to overtake her, roll over her poop deck, and possibly destroy her. This was called pooping. And when she pooped, she most likely would become broadside of the sea. And in such case, she would be in great danger of rolling over.

"Aye!" Fowler shouted. He had seen the danger, but he was waiting for the word. He had swung from a rope to the mizzen yard where he had put his bare toes about a horse; one hand was on the yard and the other on a sail while attempting to shorten it.

"Keep her into the sea!" Drake shouted. "Men from Plymouth, you can do it!" he shouted continually in a voice that now had a cadence to it by which soldiers could have marched. All hands on deck, on the yards and in the braces keenly listened to its tone above the roar of the wind and noise of the sea. A change would have caused them to panic. "Keep her into the sea!"

"She's got a bite!" Cuttill shouted, meaning that the rudder was taking hold and giving the *Pelican* direction.

"I feel it!" Drake cried, hanging onto the whipstaff. Water ran down his hat and onto his face. The *Pelican* dived under a wave which covered the main deck, then she rolled forty-five degrees to port. "That Doughty has brought forth this storm!" Drake cried out, while searching the seas, as if looking for a sea monster that would attack them. The day before, Drake had led a serious discussion on the sighting of sea monsters. He had been of the opinion that they were more apt to appear during a storm. Yet Drake would not get to see a sea monster, nor would he see much other than the waves since they were so high. The deck of the *Pelican* was covered with water. She would have flooded except for the battened hatches; even so, she was taking on water. And four men in her darkened bilges were manning her pumps.

"Clickety-clap!" the pumps sounded while the men noisily puffed.

"¡Es mal!" It is bad! Nuno said, hanging onto a rail, while looking for a break in the seas.

"It is Doughty!" Fowler cried out from a perch on the yard. "I've never seen so many storms!"

"The bastard!" Hood cried while bitterly frowning. He was seated on the opposite end of the yard where Fowler was perched. "The lowdown bastard!"

"The bastard!" Boatswain Hurd shouted, as if Doughty were a traitor who had been convicted. "He wants to sink us!"

"The bloody bastard!" a voice cried out, as if making the charges unanimous. It had to be the work of Doughty, thought all. Had he not conjured up a small storm? Had he not threatened to bring forth storms big enough to destroy the fleet? And had he not claimed to have the power of the devil? Did he not speak Latin and Greek? Was he not a lawyer? Was he not against the General? He next would be bringing forth demons from the depths of the ocean, which the old sailors such as Drake were sure existed. He was even being cursed on the *Swan*. And he was not doing anything to stop the talk by the sailors that he was the wizard who had created the storms.

"She is out of it!" Drake shouted, half smiling, while blowing water from his face. The *Pelican* had righted herself. "Replace that jib!" Drake shouted, pointing out to Fowler that he wanted the seamen to replace the jib sail with a heavier one. It was now the only sail in use.

"She'll make it, General!" Cuttill sympathetically shouted at Drake though he was only feet from him.

"I know—don't let her poop!" Drake cried. He wanted to make sure that the *Pelican* did not get broad side of the sea.

"She's holdin', General!"

"Aye!"

"She can take it, General!" Cuttill said, referring to the *Pelican*. "She sails like a gull." The master's clothes were soaked, while his hair was shredded. And his eyes were beaded as they searched the angry seas, searching for a change or looking for that giant serpent that could be riding a wave.

"Where is my fleet?" Drake cried out, looking about the storm-driven waters. Spray swirled over the tops of the tall waves so that it and the dark clouds interfered with visibility.

"There is the *Elizabeth*," Cuttill said as the skies sufficiently opened so the men on the poop deck could see over the seas. Now all the ships were in sight except the *Swan*.

"Where is the fly boat?" Drake shouted, referring to the store ship *Swan*, which was commanded by Chester.

"I don't see her!" Cuttill said in an apologetic tone of voice while searching the waves.

"Find her!" Drake shouted to the high lookouts who were standing in thimble-like baskets that lurched and bobbed with the seas.

And even though the skies continued to lighten, the storm remained severe and it did not abate until the following morning. Then the rains stopped and the skies partially cleared, but the wind continued to be high. However, the *Pelican* was rolling less, which was permitting Horsewill to light a fire under his cook stove which at times danced about. His boy helpers were now stacking wet wood beside the fire in order to dry. Horsewill had been able to cook a pot of oatmeal for breakfast, which Joey Kidd and Willie Fortescue would soon be ladling into bowls that the sailors were holding out to them. They would eat it with a little honey and water. Horsewill was now attempting to realign the fire on the hearth so he could roast some ducks that were already cooking on the spit. The aroma from the smokestack on deck was beginning to permeate the main deck where sailors clung to yards and riggings. It was a sensitive odor, being one of hope— hope for hot food and hope for relief from the storms.

"There is Moone, General," Cuttill said, pointing. The *Christopher* was just now on a tall wave; Moone was standing bareheaded on the stern of the tiny *Christopher*, dressed in rain clothes; his right hand tightly clutched the *Christopher*'s tiller. He waved at the men on the *Pelican*. They shouted greetings to him, and then he was lost in a tall wave.

The wind now was coming from the southwest; it had the chill of winter to it, and it easily pierced Drake's pants. He motioned to Hood to take his place at the whipstaff. Once it was done, Drake descended to the portico deck. He entered his cabin and took a pair of thick woolen trousers from a closet and put them on. Then he stepped back onto the portico deck. The change of clothing was what he needed, as the trousers immediately relieved the chill. The storm abated and Drake's thoughts turned to land. He directed his thoughts toward finding a sheltered harbor where the ships in his fleet could safely anchor, but finding one that would fit Drake's needs would prove to be difficult.

151

On May 10, 1578, the four ships finally found anchorage in a rocky bay at forty-seven degrees south. Drake on entering it decided to name this bay Hope, which expressed his thinking. On anchoring, he called his four available captains to a meeting on the *Pelican*. Their first discussion involved whether they could utilize the bay.

"This bay will not serve our needs," Drake said, waving his right hand, referring to the bay where all of the ships had presently anchored in a nest. The shelter was poor, as it was partially open to the sea. "We need to explore that inlet over there. It may lead to a suitable anchorage," Drake said, pointing to what appeared to be a bay that had to be entered through a narrow inlet.

"The entrance appears to be guarded by dangerous rocks!" Wynter said, looking out a cloudy window, pointing to the inlet's neck where there were several large rocks. The nearby water was white from three-foot waves striking it.

"I know," Drake said. "But it has to be done!"

"If that be the case," Moone said, "let me do it in the *Christopher*."

"No!" Drake said, as if it were too dangerous for the *Christopher*. "I'll explore it in the dinghy."

"But if a storm comes up?" Moone asked, thoughtfully eyeing Drake. Both knew that the coast was subject to storms, whether Doughty was instigating them or not. And furthermore, they struck without much warning.

"I can manage the dinghy—I have spent much of my life in small boats," Drake explained as if the subject were closed. Drake did not want to use anything larger because of the possibility of striking rocks. And then he thought that the risk should be for himself, since he considered himself to be the better seaman.

Drake and four seamen took the *Elizabeth*'s dinghy and rowed it into the inlet whose shores were lined with huge boulders. They were just inside what appeared to be a sheltered harbor when a tremendous storm blew in from the southwest. But the inlet was not sheltered, for the storm was blowing across it, bringing with it waves that were twenty feet high; they rolled across the inlet and headed directly for the dinghy. Drake tightly clasped the tiller with both hands, knowing that they were in great danger, and he shouted to the four men on the oars:

"We must row back the way that we came!"

"They're too high—the dinghy can't make it, General!"

"Yes, it can—row hard—we must row back into the bay!" Drake said. Drake, being a good seaman, just knew that he would be safer in the open sea than in or near the rocky inlet.

"We can't make it, General!"

"We must get away from those boulders!" Drake shouted. He had lost his hat. His hair was plastered to his forehead. The dinghy was climbing a twenty-foot wave. It reached its top and then it dropped and was back in the bay, but it was being driven toward the rocks near the inlet.

"Row hard!"

"Away!"

And things were not well with the ships that were anchored. They dangerously moved about; and then they were up and down and their anchors began to drag. Thomas, captain of the *Marigold*, was concerned about Drake, and he shouted to John Wynter:

"Someone must rescue the General!"

"We must first ride out the storm!" Wynter replied, thinking first of the safety of his ship.

"But the General will be lost if the ship does not go in after him!" shouted Thomas. He had shown in many ways that he was extremely fond of Drake, as at the captains' meetings he had generally sided with Drake.

"But you, too, could be lost if you go after him!" Wynter shouted into the wind, which was now gale force.

"Eh?" Thomas shouted, as he did not understand the message.

"We're headin' out to sea!" Wynter cried.

"We're goin' after him!" Thomas shouted, having his hands cupped to his mouth.

"Aye!"

An hour later the *Marigold* found the dinghy. All were safe. Drake and the four seamen were soaked to the skin, though they were rowing hard for the open sea. However, they were not making much progress.

"It's a devil of a storm," Drake shouted above the howling wind as he took a hand to be hoisted up to the *Marigold*.

"It is strange country; storm follows storm!" Thomas answered. His pudgy face was now contorted by the rain and the wind, while his wet hands were icy cold from the frigid seas.

"It's Doughty, Doughty! It is the evil of lawyers!" Drake said, ready to bash the lawyers, even tie them to witchcraft at sea. They

153

were fair game for bashing because they were not liked and there was no one there to defend them. Drake then shook his thick red beard that was now partially plastered to his face. He would continue to give his nemesis the full blame for the storm.

"A Doughty storm, I agree!" Thomas said.

"He's a buggar!" a sailor declared.

"A bloody buggar!" said another.

Others muttered like words. All hands on board the *Marigold* were now convinced that the weather which they were experiencing was the product of Doughty's witchcraft. How else could there be so many storms! And unknown to Doughty, what strength he previously had had with the men had departed on their experiencing these storms. And his plan to create the belief that he had the power of a witch had succeeded. Even John Drake had made a sketch of Doughty—it was humorous though serious, for he had drawn a nude devil with short horns, cloven feet, and a short tail. The figure was seated on a yardarm laughing at the *Hind*. And so Doughty had convinced his fellow sailors that he was a wizard. His success would soon work against him!

Drake looked about for the other ships, but by then the *Marigold* was the only ship left at the mouth of the bay. The others had sailed out to sea so as to ride out the storm. And by midday, the *Elizabeth* and the *Christopher* returned. The *Mary* was now missing, while the *Swan* had not been sighted since the storm off the River Plata on April 27, 1578. Drake paced the *Pelican's* poop deck, fussing, for he knew that these two ships had to be found. They carried the bulk of the supplies that were needed for the remainder of the voyage. He did not have to remind Nuno or Cuttill standing nearby that the loss of the two would probably mean the end of the venture; even so, Drake gave orders for the fleet to sail south.

On May 17, 1578, the four ships entered a bay which Drake decided was ideal for their present needs since it was fairly well sheltered from the winds. It offered some change in food, for its shores appeared to be the home of hundreds of seals and thousands of birds. And when the Englishmen landed, they discovered that the birds were so friendly that at times they landed on their shoulders. Some even let the men hold them. There was even a flock of giant birds, being the ostrich-like rhea, which were taller than the mess cooks. A dozen came within rock-throwing distance of the sailors and gaped at them. And so they were easily caught and butchered.

The men soon discovered that the best part to eat was the bird's legs, which were larger than the legs of lamb and were more tasty. Drake ordered his carpenters to begin building temporary shelters on the shore where many of the men would sleep; then he organized a large working party and began to harvest the seals and birds, which were then proportionately stowed in the *Pelican*, the *Elizabeth* and the *Marigold*.

Drake kept the boys busy gathering firewood, as all of the coal had been used. He stationed lookouts on the heads with piles of wood to light in case they sighted a sail. But after the three ships had been two weeks in the harbor, it appeared that their wait was fruitless since neither the *Mary* nor the *Swan* had been sighted.

"One of us has to go to sea and make a good search for the two ships," Drake said to John Wynter. Both were standing on a rocky head, apprehensively glancing from the sea to a dozen men who were playing with a small ball that had been made of tightly wound cloth and bound with a tightly-sewn leather cover. It was the size of a tennis ball. Men were taking turns batting it with a board much like that of a modern cricket bat, while another group of men were playing football, being a rough game that the men fiercely played with a much larger round leather ball covering a pig's bladder that had been filled with air.

"Shall I make the search in the *Elizabeth*?" Wynter asked while studying Drake's resolute upper lip.

"No," Drake finally said. "I'd better go south in the pinnace. I may need to search some shallow bays."

"Good luck!"

Drake's search was immediately successful, for on the very next day a lookout sighted the *Swan*. She was clumsily sailing southward. Drake maneuvered the pinnace until it was within one hundred feet of the *Swan*, and then he spoke to Chester, her captain, who was leaning out with his hand cupped to his ear.

"Glad to find you!"

"Likewise, General!"

"You had problems?" Drake asked.

"Well, yes, General," Chester said. "She leaks and she sails poorly in a storm!" Chester then further explained that the *Swan* was wearing badly and that he was of the opinion that if the *Swan* experienced many more storms, she possibly would come apart.

"Follow me, John!" Drake shouted to John Chester. Thereafter, they entered Seal Bay where the fleet was presently encamped. Seal Bay was the name Drake had given it on his discovery that it had a plentiful supply of seals. "Bring the *Swan* alongside the *Pelican*," Drake said. He then anchored the larger ship offshore near the tent settlement. "I want to transfer your cargo to the *Pelican*!"

"What's the plan?" Chester asked. Expectancy was in his voice. He sensed that Drake was going to make a change.

"It's time to reduce our numbers!" Drake said, speaking over the water. He had decided after listening to Chester's report that the *Swan* could not make it through the strait.

"When do we begin?" Chester asked, sadly frowning and then waving his hand, as though saying, if he must, he must—for he knew that this meant the end of the *Swan*.

"Right away—once you transfer your cargo, I want you to beach the *Swan*. Then remove from her all of her iron and usable gear—stow it on the *Pelican*. We will then break up her hull and use it for firewood."

"Right—and what do you want me to do with Thomas Doughty?" Chester expectantly asked, frowning. He was suspicious of what was going to happen to Doughty, suspecting the worst, though Doughty had not really been a prisoner of Chester, for he had permitted him to have a free rein of the *Swan*. Even so, he had been a problem for Chester, for Doughty's arrest had done much to change him. He had become more belligerent and bellicose. Yet he would have been less so if he had known that the men in the fleet now looked on him with undue suspicion, even considering him to be a wizard with evil powers. Many were ready to divorce themselves from him, as they were blaming him for having conjured up all the storms.

"Oh, I don't know," Drake said, frowning as if thinking. Then he said, "You must work him—work him with the rest."

"I understand," Chester said.

But neither man quite understood how far Doughty's thinking had carried him—for he had mentally detached himself from the fleet, as he not only was sulking, but he had become opposed to its objects. Doughty possibly did not realize how far he had separated himself from Drake and his objects, and then he did not suspect how far the members of the fleet had separated themselves from Doughty. To some it seemed that Doughty was interested in taking command

156

of the fleet by whatever devious means that he could avail himself or else poison the minds of the men as to its objects. Drake had not yet truly faced the issue of Doughty, though he would soon have to do so, as he would soon discover that he had a canker in his midst. For on the *Swan* disembarking her men, Drake observed Doughty confiding with groups of soldiers and even sailors where he belabored them with the problems of the fleet and the dangers of the voyage. One of the points that he skillfully argued to the ignorant soldiers and sailors was that the fleet did not have a second in command, that they would be lost without such command, and that because of his putting together the venture at the start and funding it, he was the rightful person to have such position. And this position was very important to Doughty, as on gaining it, it would be easy then to step into the general's shoes. Finally, on June 1, 1578, when the fleet was ready to sail southward, Doughty brought the issue of his rightful place in the fleet to a head. Drake was standing on the *Pelican*'s poop deck when he was confronted by Doughty, his brother John, and six other soldiers/adventurers. Drake stared at Doughty. His manner was all authority. He outwardly indicated that he was in absolute command. Drake's manner as well showed that he had erected a great barrier between himself and Doughty, for Drake had almost come to a resolve as to what he had to do about the lawyer.

"Why are you here?" Drake sternly asked. He was dressed in his brown leather jacket with bells on the sleeves. He wore a brown leather hat with a ridiculously tall crown. Drake was a faddist about hats, being a quirk of his, as he had a trunk that contained several unique hats.

"I want to know when you are going to appoint a second in command," Doughty stated. His audacious manner was immediately replaced by a show of fear, as he had detected something dangerous in Drake. His voice faltered, as did his face, for on his closely observing Drake's eyes and face, he realized that he had made the wrong move.

"You are my prisoner!" Drake shouted. "And so you do not have the right to such knowledge!"

"But—but -" Doughty stammered.

"Go below to the orlop deck!" Drake ordered, referring to the crew's quarters.

"I will not go down there—I am not one of your seamen, Pirate Drake!" Doughty said, and he looked for support from his friends. They did not give it.

"You must—you are my prisoner!" Drake repeated without his voice faltering in the slightest. He noted that now he was being watched by dozens of men who had been playing ball on the beach.

"I am in the hands of the devil so I shall treat you like him!" Doughty said on regaining much of his confidence and steeling his eyes at Drake.

"Bind him, Master Cuttill! Bind him, I say!" Drake said to the ship's master who was standing near the whipstaff; however, Cuttill ignored Drake's order and stared at the beach as if he had not heard the command. He obviously was siding with Doughty.

"Do it!"

"No!" the master finally said in a hateful voice.

"Diego! Fowler! Bind him to the mast!" Drake said, speaking to the two men who were in the rigging and looking down at the confrontation.

"Aye!" the two men cried as one. And then they quickly ascended ropes to the poop deck. They advanced on Doughty, took hold of his arms, grabbed a rope and quickly tied him to the mainmast.

"Devon dog!" Doughty bitterly exclaimed. Then he shouted so that he could be heard by the dozens of men who were watching, "The Queen will put you in the Tower of London for this!"

"Raise the flag for the *Christopher*!" Drake ordered. And once the *Christopher* was alongside, Drake spoke to Tom Moone, who was standing on his ship's bow with his arms crossed:

"Bring your dinghy to the *Pelican*. I have trouble with the Doughtys. I want you to transfer them onto the *Christopher*. Treat them as if they are dangerous men!"

"Has he done something new?" Moone asked, referring to Thomas Doughty. Moone also believed that Doughty was a conjurer principally because he was a lawyer. His thinking on lawyers was simple. Were lawyers not connivers? And if so, were not all connivers in league with the devil? Weren't their books but guides to transfer the fruits of a working man's labor into a lawyer's pockets?

"This wizard has just now made new threats at me. It is just more of his mutinous behavior. I want his brother to go with him!"

"I understand, General!" Moone said, wiping rain from his face.

"I shall not go on that boat with Tom Moone! He is a pirate like you!" Doughty said, looking about as though he expected help. But the soldier-adventurers had stepped back from Thomas Doughty. Their aloof manner indicated that they were no longer siding with him.

"Boatswain—rig a derrick—rig the tackle necessary to transfer him to the dinghy!"

"I'll do it, General!"

Thereafter, it was obvious that a very severe break had not only taken place between Drake and Doughty, but as well between Drake and his master. It would continue to worsen. For while the *Swan* was being salvaged, Drake and Cuttill worked side by side, but neither spoke to the other. This breach became more evident when the salvaging on the *Swan* was complete; for then it was time to leave Seal Bay. When the last boat was ready to leave the shore, Drake looked out on the ships that were ready to sail south and the dinghy that would take the remaining men to the *Pelican*. Then Drake looked down on Master Cuttill, who sat in dejection on the spine of the *Swan* with his hands cupped around his head:

"Into the boat, Tom; it is time to leave!" Drake politely said.

"I shall stay with the Indians, General," Cuttill said, speaking like a pouting boy. "You have treated General Doughty too harshly for me to continue sailing with you!"

"Nonsense!" Drake said.

"General, you have been too harsh on him!"

"And because of that, you prefer to live with the Indians?" Drake asked while curiously frowning.

Drake was speaking of the Patagonian Indians. He and Cuttill had recently met many of these Indians. They had even visited one of their campsites. The men were tall and very physical, being in truth giants as some were seven feet tall. And though the land was cold and windswept, strangely neither the men nor the women wore any clothes. They apparently got some warmth by painting their bodies with black colors. Oddly, they carried a fur skin which they only used for sitting. There was another strange dress code, as the women shaved their heads with flint, while the men wore their hair long.

"I have decided that these Indians are more civilized than you, General!" Cuttill said, still holding his head in his hands.

"And if you stay, what shall you eat, my hearty master?" Drake sarcastically asked. He was now looking down at his seated master, who had his head bent as if he did not want Drake to see his eyes. Drake's question had been caustically made, for he knew that the Indians ate their food raw; and their meat mainly consisted of sea lion meat that not only had a foul odor to it but even when it was cooked, it was not easily digested.

"I shall be fine!"

"And what shall you wear—what they wear?" Drake asked, referring to the fact that they walked about naked.

"If they can do it, then I can, too!" Cuttill said, speaking in a boyish voice while continuing to stare into the sand which was now being soaked by a hard rain.

"Fire your gun if you change your mind, Master Cuttill," Drake said, referring to the arquebus standing beside Cuttill. Then Drake stepped into the small boat. "We will allow you thirty minutes to change your mind before we sail!"

Cuttill did not answer. Yet there soon was a change in Cuttill's attitude, for on the dinghy reaching the *Pelican*, Drake heard the sound of a gun shot.

"Boom!"

"Go get him, coxswain!" Drake ordered. Then he added, "But take him to the *Marigold*!"

CHAPTER 18

SAN JULIAN BAY

On June 3, 1578, Drake's fleet sailed out of Seal Bay and proceeded to sail southward, keeping the coast in view. The fleet now consisted of four ships: the *Pelican*, the *Elizabeth*, the *Marigold* and the *Christopher*. The *Mary*, under the command of Tom Drake, was still missing, while the *Swan* had been scrapped at Seal Bay. The weather was foreboding; dark clouds raced across the sky. Then on the fleet getting out to sea, a sixty-knot wind blew out of the southwest, bringing with it cold rain that came down in sheets. The *Pelican* rolled and tossed, first in troughs, and next on top of twenty-five-foot waves. Drake's cabin creaked and groaned as if it were going to come apart; the *Pelican* lurched and dipped. A lantern broke loose and noisily crashed into the corner.

"Get that lantern!" Drake shouted, frowning. His face was contorted from irritancy.

"Aye, sir!" John Drake answered, diving for the lantern, catching it, and lifting it from the floor. There was no possibility of fire, as its candle was smudged out.

"It's that Doughty. He has created another storm!" John Drake said, frowning also.

"And a bad storm!" Nuno said, holding to a storm bar.

"A Doughty storm!" Drake declared, holding onto his bunk while steeling his eyes to show his ire. And with his free hand, he nervously stroked his chin whiskers.

The storm continued without letting up until June 12, 1578, when its winds suddenly subsided. But by then the fleet had badly scattered. The *Pelican* had been driven back and forth until it was near Seal Bay, and on the seas subsiding, the *Pelican*, the *Elizabeth*, and the *Marigold* regrouped. Hours later they sighted a fourth ship.

"The *Christopher*!" a lookout on the *Pelican* shouted.

"Where?" Drake cried, stepping outside his cabin and searching the horizon.

"There!" the high lookout answered, pointing to the *Pelican's* port beam. "Her sails are still reefed, General!"

"I see her mast!" Drake said. "Now I see her," he added.

"Aye!"

"Raise my call flag!" Drake said to Thomas Hood, who was now steering. Hood was now the *Pelican's* master, as he had relieved Cuttill of his job. Hood had been a boatswain's mate before he had become master. Drake had chosen Hood over several others because of his solid navigational background. This group had included Boatswain Blackcollar, who was now doing a good job as a baker, though in truth he was a boatswain. But then Hood had served as master on coasters before he had signed on with the *Pelican*. The reader will recall that on most ships, the master did the navigation. Thus, this prerequisite had eliminated many men that otherwise were very good seamen. Some men such as Fowler just would not learn navigation, though he knew landmarks. He could navigate so long as he was near enough to the coast for him to find a land bearing. Drake eyed the *Christopher*, which was approaching, saying to his master, "Thomas, as soon as possible we must transfer the *Christopher's* gear, stores and crew to the *Pelican*!"

"Aye!"

"Are you all right, Tom?" Drake shouted to Tom Moone who was leaning on the tiller which was used for steering the ship. The *Christopher* was low in the water; thus, it did not have any need of a whipstaff. The reader will recall that the *Pelican* had a high stern; thus, its tiller was in a bottom hold; it had a gooseneck that was attached to a fulcrum. This was attached to the whipstaff that extended through storage rooms and cabins, including Drake's cabin, and to the poop deck. This whipstaff then was used to steer the ship.

"A bit daft from the roll; otherwise, we are all right, General," Moone replied and tiredly grinned, being watched by a line of men manning the rails on the *Pelican*. Many shouted jests at Moone and his crew. He was greatly admired by the men on the *Pelican*. All of the sailors were of the opinion that he was an extraordinary seaman—and they showed their admiration by jesting at him and his crew. It was done for good reason—his ship was so tiny in comparison to the *Pelican*. It rolled, pitched and tossed, doing wild gyrations in storms; even so, Moone always seemed to have it under control.

"Good—follow me!"

"General, I am sorry that we became separated!" Moone shouted, saying it in an apologetic voice. "It was a bad storm!"

"It was a Doughty storm," Drake explained, and Moone nodded. Then Drake added, "Once we are in this nearby bay, I want you to transfer your gear, stores and supplies to the *Pelican*; then we'll take aboard your crew. Follow me into this bay!" Drake said, while pointing.

"What about the *Christopher*?"

"We'll set her adrift —"

"And the Doughtys?"

"We will transfer them to the *Elizabeth*—let's begin to transfer as soon as we anchor," Drake said, as he suspected that the bay would be a poor shelter from the harsh wind which intermittently blew. When it forcibly blew, it would rock the ships of the fleet like shells. "This may be far enough—drop anchor!" Drake ordered once they were inside the bay.

The *Elizabeth* anchored outboard of the *Pelican*; then the boatswain removed the Doughtys onto the *Elizabeth*. Drake then boarded the *Elizabeth*. Wynter called the men to quarters; the sailors and soldiers formed into three disorganized rows. Then Drake stood on the poop deck and addressed the men who were assembled on the lower main deck:

"I regret that I have had to deliver to you these two men. This is especially so because they have turned out to be so bad. But I had to do it for the safety of the fleet. I guess you know that they want to take command of this fleet even though they do not know anything about the sea or ships. But I will say this for them—they are smart, for they can read Latin and Greek. And they have used their book knowledge to conjure up these terrible storms which we have just experienced. Thus, the suffering that we have just gone through was caused by lawyer Doughty. As well, both Doughtys have done much to create dissension in the fleet so as to harm our venture. This they have done by speaking Latin and Greek and other tongues of sorcery so as to call up harmful winds. So I am ordering you men not to let them speak any language in your presence except English. Now, I must have your support. We are on a great voyage—not only of discovery but of acquisition. For I believe that this voyage will garner

163

us much treasure. And if we do gain the riches that I suspect we will, then each of you shall return to England rich as nobles. And in such case, I promise you that none of you will ever have to sail the ocean again unless you wish it!"

"Cheers!" the men cried as one.

Thereafter, Moone and his sailors quickly stripped the *Christopher* of her gear and provisions, though the seas had dangerously risen, for the winds from the southwest at times were blowing across the bay so furiously that Moone had to disengage from the *Pelican*. Once the stripping was done, Moone set the *Christopher* adrift as a derelict and boarded the dinghy so as to board the *Pelican*.

On June 14, 1578, there were three ships of the fleet in Seal Harbor: the *Pelican*, the *Elizabeth* and the *Marigold*. They slowly sailed south for the Strait of Magellan in search of the *Mary*. On sailing from Seal Harbor, Drake was of the opinion that the *Mary* had passed them and was sailing south. But after two days of sailing, Drake changed his opinion, and he called for a conference of the captains. Each was soon comfortably situated in Drake's cabin with a glass of claret in his hand while warming his backside to a great fire.

"It has been a month since we last saw the *Mary*!" Drake said, shaking his head in wonderment. Yet he did not appear to be in a fearful mood.

"Do you think that she is safe?" Wynter asked Drake on finishing his glass and motioning to Diego to give him a refill from the jug that set on the floor. The wine decanter had been safely stowed for its own protection.

"Yes, Tom is a good seaman; it is just that his ship does not sail well," Drake replied. "She is hardheaded like most Portuguese!" he said, snorting and smiling at Nuno, who in turn smiled though he had not understood Drake's remarks. But if Nuno had, he could have explained to the men seated at the table that possibly Tom Drake and his men did not know how to sail a carrack, which was a problem because of its high fore and aftercastles. Then it had too much girth. It was even more of a problem to sail when it was sailing near the wind.

"Does Tom know how to traverse the strait?" Thomas asked.

"Yes—before we last parted I made a copy of Magellan's map, which I gave to Tom."

"It may be difficult for the *Mary* to make the strait if the sea is rough and the wind is high," Thomas answered, thinking of the problems that Tom Drake was encountering in sailing the carrack. His manner exuded confidence, indicating that he, too, thought that Tom Drake's *Mary* would soon appear. It was not unusual for ships in a fleet to get separated. This would be more so where one was a carrack that the men aboard her were not accustomed to sailing.

"I doubt that she has got this far," Wynter thoughtfully said while rubbing his backside. "Let us sail north and make a sweep. And in doing so, I think that we will find her. Then let's transfer her provisions to the ships of line and salvage her!" Wynter said and confidently nodded his head toward Drake.

"Let us drink another glass of claret to good luck!" Drake said, nodding to Diego.

"To luck!" Drake said.

"Here, here!" Wynter said.

On June 18, 1578, when the fleet was near the 49th parallel, a lookout on the *Pelican* happily shouted: "The *Mary*—the *Mary*!"

"The *Mary*!" the men shouted throughout the ship. They lined the rails to eye the Portuguese.

Drake thereafter sailed the *Pelican* within hailing distance of the Portuguese. He studied her and noted that she seemed to be in good shape, though she was plodding south at less than two knots. Then when he was within hailing distance, he spoke across to his brother:

"Tom, good to see you!"

"And here, too!"

"How does she sail, Tom?"

"Poorly, brother," Tom Drake spoke out in an apologetic voice, shaking his head. "She is difficult to sail when traveling into the wind. For she is too high out of the water with too much girth, and she is leaking badly. We must man the pumps most of the time."

"And your crew?"

"All are well!" he said, smiling. "That is, in spite of their looks."

"Can she make it through the Magellan Strait?" Drake asked.

"I doubt that she could if we had to face a very bad storm!"

"Then we shall sail for Julian Bay; it is a safe harbor and located just a few leagues from here. You must stay close to the *Pelican*. Once we are there, we will transfer your cargo and crew to the *Pelican*; then we shall salvage the *Mary* for her firewood."

"Aye!"

Nuno da Silva was standing on the poop deck; he was warmly dressed in a woolen cap, a sweater and a leather jacket. He turned and stared at Drake. His ears had perked up on hearing the name of this bay, for the name "Julian Bay" had conjured up some ominous images.

"Port San Julian!" Nuno exclaimed, looking into the distance. He vividly recalled that it was here in 1520 that his fellow countryman, Magellan, had wintered. It was also here that Magellan had used strong measures to resolve the dissension amongst his captains which had become so bad that it had ended in mutinous conduct. Nuno knew that Drake had serious dissension amongst his men, which Nuno believed was threatening to get worse. In 1520 Magellan had handled his dissent by hanging and gibbeting the instigators. Nuno, while staring from Drake to the blue-green sea, wondered how Drake would handle his dissenters.

Julian Bay is entered by a narrow bottleneck on the northeast shore, which then opens out to a protecting bay, making it an ideal place for Drake's fleet to spend the winter. Drake led his fleet of four ships into the harbor; then the ships anchored near a sandy island, which was a short distance from the mainland. Shortly thereafter Drake took the pinnace and led a party of ten men to the mainland so as to make an inspection. His party was greeted by hundreds of screeching geese, ducks and crested grebes. The latter bird is much like the loon. Many of the mother grebes were out for frolics, as they were teaching their young to dive. The mothers did this by allowing two or three of the tiny birds to lie on their backs; then the mothers would dive and surface, watching the floundering young birds learning to swim. But Drake's thoughts were presently on something other than this aspect of learning in the life of the grebe. Drake stopped, and then he spoke to Preacher Fletcher and Tom Moone:

"I believe that this is the place where Magellan wintered!"

"How can you tell, General?" Fletcher asked.

"That apparently is the gibbet that he used to display the carcasses of two of his mutinous captains," Drake said, pointing to an upright piece of a spruce mast with an attached arm that obviously had been carved by man. And it was actually the gibbet that Magellan had utilized to bring order out of chaos. Magellan had had three of his captains mutiny in this harbor. He effectively took care of one captain, Luis de Mendoza, by having him assassinated; he had had a second, Captain Gaspar de Quesada, beheaded. Magellan then had the bodies of these two men quartered and displayed on this gibbet. He had left a third captain and a priest to the mercy of the

Indians, whose mercy could not have been much, for they hated Magellan because he had manacled two Indians in an attempt to kidnap them and to take them back to Spain to exhibit—these two had escaped, killing one of Magellan's soldiers.

"Yes, General. I believe that you are right," said Fletcher, tapping the gibbet with his sword.

"And if you dig at the foot there, you will find their bones," Drake said, using his foot to rake the surface beneath the gibbet. "There!" he said, reaching for what appeared to be a humerus bone.

"May God bless their souls!" Fletcher exclaimed.

"But they were mutineers, Preacher!" Drake contemptuously exclaimed, as if questioning the authority of a fleet leader damned their souls forever.

"But their souls?" the preacher asked.

"They are now with the devil!" Drake replied in a surly voice, as if they could not be anywhere else.

"Amen!" Fletcher softly stated, looking about the strange shore, eyeing the woods. Many trees grew in thickets; others were leaning near the ground. Then there was a huge mound onto which the members of the party walked.

"It's kelp!" Drake exclaimed, kicking at the debris which had piled onto the water and the shore.

"There are treetops beneath it!" Moone declared in a show of amazement.

"It is a strange land," Drake said as he looked about the huge bay and studied its busy waters, which were being blown willy-nilly by the southwest winds which seemingly irritated the petrels flying above it, causing them to make half-starved quacking noises while in truth they were well fed.

"We will winter in this bay!" Drake firmly said as if he had just decided to do it.

Drake and his party then returned to the apparent security of the ships. They now knew that hundreds of Indians were on the mainland, as they had sighted dozens of them, though they had kept in the distance. The Indians had refused to come close though the Englishmen had offered them trinkets. Drake was undaunted in his thinking that with time he would be able to establish a relationship with the Indians.

The next day Drake returned to the shore with a small hunting party, which included Thomas Drake, John Thomas, Captain of the

Marigold, bowman Robert Winterly, Thomas Oliver, a gunner's mate from the *Pelican*, John Brewer, the trumpeter, and Thomas Hood. Their plan was to cross a mile of wooded mainland to a small lake where they planned to hunt the crested grebe, which is a form of a duck. All were armed, though most carried only their swords and shields. Their most effective weaponry, the longbow, was being carried by Robert Winterly, the expert longbowman, while Thomas Oliver carried a fowling gun. Shortly after the hunting party arrived on the mainland, they met up with three nude Indians—two giant men and a boy; the men were at least seven feet tall and well-proportioned. All had curious designs painted on their nude bodies. The men carried bows and arrows. Their bows were different from the bow carried by Winterly, as the bows of the giants were much smaller, while the bow of Winterly was the deadly longbow. The Englishmen smiled in a friendly way at the Patagonian Indians; then they offered them some trinkets. The Indians surprisingly approached the Englishmen—then they eagerly accepted the gifts while childishly babbling.

"They apparently want to be friends," Drake confidently declared. He foolishly believed that he could establish friendly relations with any people who were less civilized. For whenever he was questioned about his beliefs on primitive people, he would relate the success that he had had with the Cimarons in Panama, though he did not relate that the Cimarons had had serious grievances with the Spanish and needed allies.

"They like my longbow," Winterly said and smiled.

One giant touched the well-waxed bow, while jabbering in a strange tongue to the other, who frowned as if disbelieving its effectiveness. These Indians were unusual in the way they handled their nudeness, as they stood before Drake's party nude and not shaking, as if oblivious to the cold, for it was now winter; yet the English were dressed for it, as they wore sweaters and jackets. Yet these giants did enjoy a fire. They made it from a tinder, which was a filmy web of the puff ball or down from a bird's nest. They kept this tinder in the bladder of a seal and ignited it by striking iron stones above it. They liked a fire so well that they maintained constant fires in their primitive wigwams; they even kept fires in their canoes when they were in use. They built their fires on heaps of sand or moist turf in the center of the canoe, and then if they were forced to camp, they had fire for the night. Drake and the men would soon see these fires when they

168

entered the strait; and it was from seeing such fires that the principal island, Tierra del Fuego, had derived its name, being the "Land of Fire."

"Keep your piece charged," Drake said, speaking to Oliver, the gunner's mate, who was armed with a fowling gun. It was called a "Guter," having been designed by Guter of Nuremburg, and had been made of well-tempered steel and fired a scattering of hail shot. Its weakness was in the firing of it, for flint had to spark and ignite the gunpowder. It would do it so long as it was dry. But it had begun to rain, and unknown to Oliver the powder had become damp.

"I will show them what they will have to contend with if they want trouble," Winterly proudly said. He was the best bowman in the fleet. He held a longbow that had been made of yew, which gave the bow great bending strength. It had been especially made for Winterly and presented to him by Drake, who had recruited him because of his great marksmanship. He took from his belt an arrow with a metal tip point and goosefeather vanes. He put the arrow to his bow, pulled the string, stretching the bow, and fired it. The arrow hurtled through the air more than two hundred yards; it was an excellent shot, for it struck the tree for which it was intended.

"Chohm—ah!" the Patagonians loudly said in awe.

"Beat that!" Winterly exclaimed, pointing to their bows.

"Ugh!" the larger and stronger of the two men grunted a reply. Then he took an arrow and he fired it from his bow, but it only traveled half the distance.

"Hahruph!" the Patagonian doing the firing exclaimed in a loud, gruff voice, showing his disappointment. He then was joined by two older, giant-like Patagonians who had emerged from the woods. Both had long, shaggy hair that came down to their shoulders. They conferred, while watching Winterly ready his bow for a second shot. The Indians seemingly had concluded that the white men had superior weaponry; and so the mood of the moment had changed, for the Indians strangely began to study the white men. This possibly was because the older Patagonians had been told of the white man Magellan's attempt to kidnap some members of their tribe. Then maybe they had recognized the white man's superiority and had advised the younger members to attack the white men when they were able to do so. And so the Indians began to eye the bowman strangely.

"Ca-thop!" The string to Winterly's bow broke.

169

"Damn!" Winterly exclaimed, and he quickly took a new linen string from his jacket pocket. He was astounded to see that one end did not have a bowyer's knot, which is a loop that attaches the bow string to the bow. It would take minutes to plait the knot. Then Winterly noticed the faces of the Indians, and there was hatred! He panicked.

"On guard!" Drake shouted, for he, too, had noticed a change in the face of a Patagonian. But he was too late, for the Indian quickly fired an arrow at Winterly, which struck him in the chest. Oliver raised the clumsy fowling piece to his shoulder and took aim, but it would not fire, for his touch hole had allowed dampness from the rain to enter it.

"It refuses to fire, General!" the gunner's mate shouted.

"Oh!" Drake exclaimed on seeing a second Indian aiming an arrow at Oliver. The Indian fired—the arrow struck Oliver in the chest, piercing his heart.

"Duck and weave, men!" Drake shouted to the other men as they began to move. "Now form—those with shields in front—take their arrows! After them!" he cried, urging the others to press the fight, while proceeding toward the Indians who were retreating. "Collect those arrows!" he shouted. His plan was for those men with shields to press the fight and force the Indians to fire their arrows. They then would collect the arrows of the Indians as they were fired; thus, when they had fired them all, they would be weaponless. The Englishmen could then attack the Indians with their swords.

"I shall handle this bugger!" Drake exclaimed on seeing that now only one of the Indian bowmen had an arrow. Drake quickly took up the fowling piece from the side of the dead Oliver. He hurriedly primed it and fired it at the giant with the single arrow, who was the one who had instigated the fight. It struck him in the stomach and disemboweled him. The rest ran as if they had had enough of Drake.

"Hurry!" Drake exclaimed. "Let's get Winterly back to the *Pelican!*"

"What about the gunner?" Tom Drake asked, referring to Oliver who had been shot through the heart.

"He is dead—hurry!"

The men quickly carried the injured bowman back to the *Pelican*, but it was in vain, for he died two days later. And on the evening of the fight when Drake returned for the body of Oliver, he discovered that it had been disgraced by the Indians, for they had thrust an arrow through his right eye. As well, they had curiously removed a shoe, a sock, and Oliver's cap. Drake was appalled; he would soon vent his ire!

CHAPTER 19

THE FUNERAL ORATION BY DRAKE

It was another blustery day; the clouds wildly moved about the sky. Near the ground the wind blew so hard that walking was extremely difficult. This was especially so for the members of the funeral cortege that were winding their way to a hillock where a sailor working party had previously dug a single grave. Each body lay in a coffin that the fleet's carpenters had made from planks taken from the deck of the *Mary*. The cortège was led by John Drake, the drummer, who somberly beat his drum, followed by the trumpeter and the viol players; all mournfully played a funeral dirge. The musicians were followed by: twenty sailors and soldiers carrying muskets and longbows, who were the honor guard; the two coffins, each being carried by six men, who had to lean into the wind in order to keep from falling; the captains and the ships' masters; Preacher Fletcher and Drake, who walked side by side, each carrying a Bible; the fifty or more remaining seamen and soldiers, all of whom were armed; and finally by the boys, with Willie Fortescue and Joey Kidd, the two boy mess cooks, bringing up the rear. Each boy wore a black ribbon around his left sleeve and carried a basket of green leaves that would be given to the mourners to place on the grave.

"Praise the Lord for His blessings!" Preacher Fletcher solemnly declared when the coffins had been lowered into the single grave. "And we ask the Lord to take unto him the souls of our departed shipmates . . . "

When Fletcher had finished his sermon, Drake, with Bible in hand, addressed the assembly of sailors and soldiers:

"I have been on many ventures on which I have lost good men. The loss of each has pained me dreadfully. On my last venture to Nombre Dios, I lost two of my brothers. You can imagine my sadness, for I loved them dearly. It was also on that venture that I climbed a tall tree, where I viewed the South Sea. I saw a vision of two seas that I will never forget, and I became so enthralled with the South Sea that I swore that I would sail it one day. And I still intend to do it—but back to that enigma, death—it is a part of war. I am hardened to war, and I dare say that it has been my life since I first joined my kinsman, John Hawkins, in an expedition to Africa and the New World. My first experience of great loss was in Mexico, when the Spaniards by trickery cost our expedition four ships and many men. It was there that I discovered how deceitful the Spanish could be, and it was then that I dedicated my life to warring with Spain, whether it be official or unofficial. You know, of course, that the Spaniards and the Portuguese with the help of the Pope divided the New World between themselves. But it was not done by God's authority, for how could it be? England is Christian. God is with England. God would not deny the English a share in the New World," he said, looking about at the faces that were intently eyeing him, as if looking for disagreement. Then Drake looked up at the sky as if he now would speak to God—and he began by pointing an index finger at the blustery heavens: "The denial was done by a clandestine covenant between Spain, Portugal and the Pope. It was done to keep you, me and England from our rightful share of the wealth of the New World. I have said this to you so as to explain to you that we are on an official mission for Queen Elizabeth, as I am serving under orders on behalf of England. My orders are here," he said, touching his doublet, being watched admiringly by the sailors from Devon, who were extremely proud of Drake. He was one of them—and they believed that they were the best sailors of England. They now were convinced that Drake was the best of all of them. How else could he have obtained a commission from the Queen! "And so these two men, Winterly and Oliver, were killed in the line of duty on behalf of the Queen of England. I cannot stand before you and say that the total cause of their deaths were those simple Indians. For they were just instruments for a soothsayer, conjurer and magician, who ever since this fleet left England has done everything possible to hinder its progress. You know as well as I that he has conjured up a hundred storms to impede our progress. He has instigated the soldiers in this fleet not to work with the sailors. He has encouraged sailors and soldiers to rise up in mutiny against my leadership, which is an attack against the Queen and England. And further, it is my opinion

174

that before he sailed on this venture, he informed Lord Burghley, the Treasurer of England, who is sympathetic with the Spaniards of our venture. And if that be the case, then when we reach the coast of Peru, we may be greeted by dozens of Spanish war ships. Our surprise will not only have been lost, but we will face Spanish imprisonment or death. Now the next days will be trying days, for we must pass through the Magellan Strait. We must draw together as Englishmen—I will not allow any more soldiers to refuse to do seamen work. Those that refuse will be put on half rations, and they will not share in the spoils of the coast of Peru, for that is where we are bound. That was the reason for my secrecy. I promise that if you obey my orders, you will share in gold beyond your dreams. Now as for that nemesis, Thomas Doughty. I charge that he is the one who is responsible for the deaths of these two men. And for doing such and for a hundred other reasons, I am charging him with treason against the Queen of England and mutiny in her ships. I do hereby order each of you who has information concerning Doughty to write it out and sign it before a captain. And as soon as that is done, we shall try Thomas Doughty on the same shore where Magellan disposed of his would-be mutineers."

"Amen!" Preacher Fletcher cried, shaking his head with closed eyes while his face was contorted as if he were in great agony.

Many of the men standing straight began to breathe heavily, as they had been stirred by Drake's speech.

"Now, attention all hands—men," Drake said, speaking to the honor guard, "fire your muskets!"

"Boom! Boom! Boom! . . . "

"Now each man in turn shall empty a shovel of dirt on our departed shipmates!" Drake exclaimed, wiping rain from his face, momentarily eyeing a flock of geese crossing the bay as if ready to challenge it for interrupting this solemn moment.

"Quarack! Quarack!" the geese mournfully cried.

Drake took a shovel and cast the first dirt onto the coffins. Then he handed the shovel to Preacher Fletcher, who cast the second.

CHAPTER 20

THE TRIAL OF DOUGHTY

Shortly after the funeral of Winterly and Oliver, Drake ordered Thomas Marks, the *Pelican*'s carpenter, to take planks from the *Mary* and construct a court to be used for the trial of Doughty. He ordered Marks to erect a judicial bench for Drake, a dock for the prisoner Doughty, and a dias for the prosecutor. On June 30, 1578, Drake ordered all hands from the fleet to assemble on the mainland at the place of the court, which was near the site of the gibbet where Magellan had exhibited the bodies of the mutineers; all were to attend the trial of Doughty. They then numbered 160 men and boys.

Drake sat on the judicial bench with his arms on the bench while looking down on Doughty, who was standing on the dock. John Thomas, Captain of the *Marigold*, who was the prosecutor, was standing opposite to Doughty. Thomas held in his hands a roll of affidavits which would make up Drake's case against Doughty. The court had two masters at arms, Thomas Hood and John Saracold, the master of the *Swan*. One stood on either side of Doughty.

"Thomas Doughty," Drake said in a loud, authoritarian voice that rang with sarcasm. He wore a strange witch-like hat with a pointed crown and a rain cape about his shoulders, as it was raining intermittently. "I am here today to preside over your trial whereby you are charged with treasonous and mutinous conduct."

"And would you name the law that gives you such authority?" Doughty asked in a disdainful voice, as if discounting the power of the court, and more so, as if he expected the men watching to deliver him from its clutches, not realizing that most of the men now truly believed that he was the wizard who had conjured up most of the storms they had experienced. But then Doughty was thinking like a lawyer, little realizing that Drake had little respect for the law unless he was benefitted by it. And so Doughty, having been trained as a lawyer, knew that there was no law under the English common law that would condone such a trial.

"Law? Do you now speak to me of English law when we are in the wilds of Patagonia?" Drake asked, and he waved his hand as if to scoff at the idea.

"But I am an Englishman. I am entitled to a charge based on a law; else you will have to answer to Elizabeth and her ministers when you return to England!" Doughty vowed, saying it in a haughty voice, as if Drake had to honor it. Yet he knew that the English legal system was a puzzle that Drake could not have understood, composed largely of some statutes, many judicial decisions and a caste system based on birth. Very little of it was definite.

"But I have the authority of the Queen!" Drake answered.

"Show me that authority!" Doughty demanded, as if he were sure that Drake did not have it. Good lawyers lean heavily on authority.

"I will show you nothing, Thomas Doughty. Since you have not shown this fleet any authority to your claim to leadership, you do not deserve a showing. You started out in Ireland being a friend, and I was your friend, but you lost my friendship when you began a course of mutinous conduct designed to take command of this fleet!"

"But you do not have any authority over a general in charge of troops!" Doughty cagily argued, looking about at the men who formed a circle about the proceedings which many were intently studying. Doughty had raised an important issue. Up to this point in history, it was generally considered that the general in charge of troops aboard a ship had superior authority to that of the ship's captain.

"Under English law and in English ships, no soldier can have a superior command to the ship's commander!" Drake declared. He said it as if that were a fact. It was not—but it would become such. For on this voyage being completed and its precedents having been digested, such would establish with the English navy the principal that the captain of an English ship would be in charge of all persons on that ship while at sea.

"And by what law!" Doughty demanded to know.

"By the natural law of the sea!" Drake sharply answered, as if such existed.

"There is no such law, you pirate!" Doughty shouted and lunged for Drake. He was quickly grabbed by the two masters of arms; each tightly took hold of an arm. John Saracold looked at Doughty with suspicious contempt.

"Tie his arms behind him!" Drake declared.

"Aye!"

Once Doughty had been securely bound, Drake said to the men assembled, "We will now empanel a jury of forty men selected from the sailors and gentlemen to hear the charges. When your name is called, you will assemble to my right," Drake said, pointing to an open space that had been reserved for the jurors. "Captain Wynter, will you read the names of the jurors!"

John Wynter stepped forward, ignoring Doughty's eyes which sought his. Then he commenced to read the names of the most senior men:

"Edward Bright . . . Vice Admiral John Wynter, who will be foreman of the jury!"

"And do you object to these members?" Drake asked Doughty after Wynter had read the list of names.

"Many are good men; some are bad!" Doughty answered. And he scoffed at the idea of Drake trying him with such a jury. "It's a wag tail jury!"

"But you shall have the benefit of those who are good, providing, Thomas Doughty, that you are innocent," Drake said, looking about, searching faces. Then he said to Captain John Thomas:

"Captain Thomas, Mr. Prosecutor, read the evidence that we have against Mr. Doughty!"

Thomas unrolled the sheath of papers in his hands, and a boy from the *Marigold* stepped forth and stood at the side of Thomas, who then read the first affidavit, being signed by Edward Bright, the ship's carpenter of the *Pelican*:

" . . . and Doughty said to me in General Drake's garden in Plymouth that the Queen's counsel could be corrupted with money; even the Queen would sell her office for money . . . that Lord Burghley had a copy of the planned voyage to the South Seas." All knew or had been told that Burghley was opposed to any voyage that would give offense to Spain. And so the reading of this statement caused much whispering amongst the jurors and spectators, whose attention was so intently directed at the proceedings that they took little heed of the cold rain that was now pelting the assembly.

179

"He cannot have said that!" Drake declared, as if it were too heinous a thing to do. He was further emphasizing that such act could possibly ruin the voyage, for it could mean that when they reached Peru, they would find themselves trapped by a powerful Spanish fleet.

"But I did. I gave it to him!" Doughty angrily declared, contorting his face impishly, as though the giving was no great offense.

"My shipmates," Drake said, "Doughty has confessed the crime by declaring that the giving was no great offense. Do you recall my telling you that the Queen told me that under no circumstances was Lord Burghley to know of the venture? And because of such offense, we may find ourselves greeted by Spanish men of war when we arrive in Peru!"

"Let me live and meet those charges in England!" Doughty begged, his face becoming fearful, suddenly becoming convinced that he had erred in his admission. Drake met his request with mockery.

"Naye, you shall have these charges addressed by this jury of forty men on this day and at this blustery bay!"

And Drake properly described the bay. Storm clouds raced about the sky; the rain had stopped and now snow flurries were falling. Drake's witch-like hat with a black ribbon about it was now blanketed with snow. Directly behind Doughty there was a dwarf deciduous birch tree; snow now blanketed the red and yellow leaves clinging to it, as if fighting for life, much like Doughty was now doing. Beneath it was a tuca-tuca, a burrowing creature which looks much like a guinea pig; it stopped and momentarily listened, as if attempting to eavesdrop on the proceedings. A pair of rheas stood on a hillock, momentarily looked out on the assemblage. They then became fearful, flapping their tiny wings and racing away.

"But why forty and not twelve?" Doughty asked, questioning the makeup of the jury. As a lawyer, he knew full well that the common law of England had evolved a jury system of twelve men; yet the great legal minds could not say for sure why twelve and not some other number. Yet Drake was submitting the factual issue of guilty or not to a jury of forty men, as he had decided that the size of it would lend more credence to his acts.

"More for your betterment, Thomas Doughty—more to judge your crimes!"

Thomas continued to read affidavits until he had read twenty-nine, each of which had been signed by a member of the venture. They included charges such as:

" . . . he asked others to join in overthrowing the fleet . . . "

" . . . he claimed to have higher friends in court than Drake . . . "

" . . . Drake could not do anything without his assent . . . "

" . . . that because of his position he could not be ordered to do any manual labor . . . "

" . . . the sailors who knew Drake were lying knaves . . . "

" . . . he made threats as to what he would do to those who opposed him or his faction on returning to England . . . "

" . . . he claimed that he had laid with the General's wife . . . "

"And now, Captain Thomas, will you give these affidavits to Captain Wynter, foreman of the trial jury."

While Thomas was presenting the documents to Wynter, Drake added, "You and your jury members may study these to see if they truly match the reading of the same."

"General, I am a lawyer, and as such I object to a trial in this fashion," said Leonard Vickery, a lawyer and soldier who had joined the venture because of considerable persuasion by Doughty. He as well was a member of the jury. But he had split with Doughty, for he, too, had filed an affidavit against him.

"I do not have any need of advice from you crafty lawyers, nor do I have any need of your law. I will personally answer to my Queen for what I do today!" Drake declared, adding, "There has been enough of you lawyers and your splitting of hairs; none of you has understood that we are on a voyage of war. The war is undeclared, but it is a war nevertheless. We are on State business that could lead to killing on both sides. On such occasions, the niceties of English law do not exist, and you should have known before you left England that the power of discipline aboard ship rests with the senior officer of the fleet. And that person is me!"

"But do we have to vote on life or death?" Vickery asked. His voice and face showed that he did not want to make such a decision. Doughty was an old friend; they had studied cases and pondered the reasons for judges' rulings while they were students at the Middle Temple. Yet eventually Vickery would have to do just that, for Drake was determined to resolve the matter of Doughty on this day.

"No, Mr. Vickery. That is not the issue that you must decide," Drake deceitfully answered. His eyes were intense while his voice was calm and positive, indicating that he was definitely in charge of the trial.

"Now," said Drake, removing himself from his high chair, "the company will adjourn to the water's edge. The Doughtys," meaning John and Thomas, "shall remain here with the masters of arms!"

"But it is raining—and I cannot wipe my face!" Doughty cried out, reminding Drake that he was still bound. The snow had ceased. It now was raining heavily. The snow was being washed from the trees.

"John," Drake said to John Doughty. "Wipe your brother's face!"

"Aye," the younger of the brothers replied. And he took a rag from his pocket and gently wiped the face of Thomas Doughty.

Once the men were assembled at the edge of the water, they stood or sat on tough, coarse grass or wet pebbles. Then Drake adjusted his peaked hat which had become askew, and he addressed the men:

"I have here my commission from the Queen," Drake said, holding forth a leather tube which held a number of papers. He withdrew them from the tube and began to examine and thumb through them. After he had casually examined them, he spoke again to the assembled men:

"I have numerous papers here that outline my position as General of this venture. I even have a paper from the Queen where she invested 1,000 crowns in the venture," he said, holding up a paper. "Does that not show who is the head of the venture?" he asked, holding forth the same paper, offering it for examination. But his face had challenge on it, as if daring a question to be asked or someone to request an inspection. No one did.

"I even have a letter from Sir Christopher Hatton, asking me to accept as crew members Captain John Thomas and John Brewer. You, Captain Thomas—you, John Brewer—you know to whom you were told to report!"

"Right, General—"

"To you, General—and no one else!" Brewer shouted. He was a very enthusiastic supporter of Drake. He had signed on as a boy; yet he was now standing seaman watches. Contrariwise, he was also considered to be an officer, as he was the ship's trumpeter. He shared a tiny cabin with Fowler, the boatswain.

"Now, what documents has Doughty offered you for your inspection?" Drake asked, again holding forth his papers, pointing out that this was the original point of conflict between the two. And truthfully, Doughty had not mentioned a single paper to show that he was to be a general in the venture.

"And now," Drake said, beginning to argue to the jury, which would be contrary to developing English procedure at law, as Doughty was not only absent, but Drake was closeted with the jury where he was acting as prosecutor as well as judge. And his argument would be very persuasive. "The sea is a terrible place for dissension. The life of a seaman is hard at its best. And it is so easy to turn sailor against sailor and then against their officers. In such case, the sailor can kill his officer, and then how would the sailor find his way back to England? Thus, the sailor has to be governed by a different code!"

"Amen!" cried Preacher Fletcher, for he had been going to sea for many years. Yet he did not know anything about navigation. Finding one's way from place to place by the study of stars was still a great mystery to him.

"I want you members of this voyage to consider your position. It is you that will decide whether we cravenly return to England to be laughed at by all Englishmen, or else go forward and navigate that great strait named after Magellan; then sail north and plunder the Spanish of the gold and silver which they have taken from the Indians. If you follow the course that I set, you will not only become rich, but you will win yourself a place in English history. Do you want to do that?" Drake asked.

"Yes!" the sailors enthusiastically shouted. Yet many of the soldiers were silent.

"Then I am prepared to lead you to riches and glory, providing you vote death for Thomas Doughty! I will not accept less! Those of you who wish death for Doughty, hold up your hand!" Drake demanded. Everyone now had been in the wet Patagonian air for two hours. The rain had ceased, and once again it was snowing. Drake's injured leg that had the lead ball in it was paining him. The pain showed on his face.

A majority of the jury held up their hands to show their accord with Drake.

"And those of you who are opposed to his death, raise your hands," Drake said. There was a snarl in his voice as if he would take offense with those who raised their hands. None did. But many studied their hands, as if wondering why they did not react.

"Then death shall be the desert of Thomas Doughty!" Drake declared. He dropped his eyes and watched his hands, which were now rolling up his documents so as insert them in his leather holding tube, which also was notice to the jury that the trial was at an end.

CHAPTER 21

THE EXECUTION OF DOUGHTY

Drake limped back to his place on the dias, where he took his seat. Thomas Doughty expectantly stared at Drake, who was fidgeting with his leather tube. Doughty's eyes were intense as he leaned forward, studying Drake as if looking for signs. Then Drake stared back at Doughty, noting that his arms had been freed as he had ordered minutes before, and he said to him:

"Thomas Doughty, the jury has voted to give you death. Do you have anything that you wish to say?" Drake asked. His voice now had a sense of finality to it, as though he were glad that it was done.

"Yes—yes," he stammered. His face was now ashen. Tears were in his eyes. "I must say something—it is about my heart. It is so rancored by the result that I am at a loss for words—this is because I know that you have trifled with the jury," Doughty replied, sniffing. "And I cannot forgive you for that!"

"Naye, I have not trifled with the jury."

"But you took the jury to the water's edge, spoke to them without my presence. That is mischief which spoils the trial, Pirate Drake!"

"And to whom do you appeal?" Drake declared, half smiling, noting the impracticality of appealing to some other body. Then he added, "It is your conduct that has trifled with this venture. And so you have asked for what you got! That being so, I am now prepared to give you some choices. You may be executed on this site; else you may be set ashore on this mainland to live with the Indians."

"Well, General," Doughty said. "If it has come to that point, then I beg that you carry me to Peru. There you may set me ashore!"

185

"I cannot grant you that request," Drake replied, smiling, looking more witch-like than ever. "Your presence would destroy the venture!"

"I could carry him in the *Elizabeth*! General, I promise you that your life will be safe!" Wynter said to Drake in an argumentative voice. This was the first time that Wynter had spoken on Doughty's behalf, though the reader will recall that Wynter had made somewhat of a commitment to Doughty when they were on patrol on Maio Island in the Verdes.

"Well," Drake said, thinking. "If we do that, then we will need to nail shut all the hatches and return to England. Do you want that?" Drake asked the jurors, placing the possible destruction of the venture on Wynter.

"No!" the jury chorused before Wynter had even opened his mouth to answer.

"What is your pleasure for Doughty?" Drake asked the jurors.

"Death!" many voices answered. Their tone of voice was sharp and final, as though they wanted to be rid of him. Their voices had rung out as one, as if they were convinced that he were a hex that should be destroyed.

"You have forty-eight hours to prepare yourself for death, Thomas Doughty!" Drake declared, sardonically smiling. "Would you like to choose the manner of your execution?" he asked as if he were extending a boon to him.

"I would like a gentleman's death!" Doughty said, stating in essence that he did not wish to be hung like a thief.

"Then you shall lose your head at noon on the day after tomorrow," Drake decreed, rapping on the table, signifying to all that the proceeding was at an end. The reader will soon see that Drake handled Doughty much more severely than John Hawkins did Edward Dudley, who was the general in charge of Hawkins' soldiers during Hawkins' third slaving voyage. It was on this voyage that Drake had commanded the *Judith*, for in the early part of the voyage, Dudley in a fit of rage attacked Hawkins with his sword and had to be subdued. Thereafter, Hawkins' officers and men cried for Dudley's head. Hawkins tried Dudley for mutiny, convicted him, and gave him a sentence of death. Then Hawkins elected to execute Dudley himself. He put his loaded and primed arquebus to Dudley's head, saying:

"Are you prepared to meet your God?"

"I am—"

"Then—"

"I am ready—" Dudley said in a fearful voice, expecting to lose his head.

"Out of the kindness of my heart, I do hereby pardon you, Edward Dudley!" Hawkins said, which surprised everyone present.

Thereafter, Hawkins was more respected than ever by his officers and men. Yet the two men differed, for Drake was a leader who sought obedience rather than love.

So on July 2, 1578, at 11:00 a.m., while four men were digging Doughty's grave, Drake, Fletcher, Doughty and many members of the fleet assembled near a newly-constructed altar at the site of the trial that had been held two days previously. Drake, Fletcher and Doughty slowly walked to a hillock where a board from the *Mary* lay on the wet ground. A cross was before it. The three men kneeled onto the board.

"Would you like to confess your sins, Thomas Doughty?" Fletcher asked, being unmoved by the new tempest that was brewing in the bay. The fleet now encountered a multitude of daily storms; many of these were so severe that they were interfering with the readying of the ships and their provisioning. And strangely, no one had mentioned Doughty's name in connection with their creation.

"I have none to ask for forgiveness!"

"And you say that the jury of your peers was wrong?"

"It was a jury of Drake, the Pirate!" Doughty calmly replied, though Drake was kneeling on one side while Fletcher was on the other.

"And you have no repentance?" Drake asked, turning his head so as to face Doughty. They were now only inches apart.

"My only regret is that I introduced you," meaning Drake, "to the lords and the Queen who approved this venture!"

"A tart tongue he still has!" Drake cried, turning so as to speak to the audience while still kneeling. "Thomas Doughty, even though you are not showing the proper remorse for your crimes, I shall dine with you," Drake said, standing, pointing to a nearby table with benches. Stewed goose, other food and bread set on the table. All of the food, with the exception of the bread, had been prepared by Horsewill the cook. Boatswain Blackcollar had baked the bread in an

Pacific Ocean

Atlantic Ocean

SAN JULIAN BAY

CAPE HORN

"Death is the lot of all traitors!"

improvised oven. The two tiny mess cooks stood behind the table. Each held a ladle in a hand.

"If it will ease your contrite heart, then I shall dine with you," Doughty said in a haughty voice while being watched by two lines of sailors and another line of soldiers, who held in their hands bill cutlasses and staves, which greatly added to the macabre scene of the impending execution. The two men sat down at the table and picked at their food which the tiny mess cooks had served, while chatting, each making snide remarks to the other. They finished, stood and turned. Drake took Doughty by the arm, and they walked a hundred feet inland away from the execution site, where above them hundreds of birds, being a mixed flock of pelicans, skuas and cormarants, soared over the execution site while shrieking their displeasure of the scene. Then Drake said to Doughty:

"Thomas, I hope that when you reach God's throne, that you will not bear our Lord any ill tidings of me!" Drake said in a warning voice, as if his power were so strong that it extended to the afterworld.

"Why should I not, Francis? It is you who has usurped me and then you will have taken my head!"

"But we are of different schools—I am a seaman—I am a man with blood on my hands. You are a lawyer who thrives on quarrels, which you magnify so as to suit the owner's pocketbooks. Such is a bad mixture for ships at sea. And Thomas, you picked the wrong venture—you should never have made your moves—you misjudged the likes of me!"

"But why could you not have shared your power?"

"There was no necessity, Thomas. The power was already given," Drake said, meaning that he had it all by exercising it. He further meant that by being general of the fleet, he had absolute power over the men serving in the fleet. Drake then turned and beckoned to the line of soldiers, who approached the pair, fell in beside them and walked with them to the execution site, where a block of wood rested on a six-by-six piece of flooring that had been taken from the *Mary*.

"And it is you, Ned, who will take my head!" Doughty declared on seeing Ned Bright standing by the execution block. Bright, a *Pelican* carpenter, had given a very important affidavit against Doughty. He now had the duty of removing Doughty's head.

"It is not for me, but for my wife!" Bright declared, glancing at the ax blade which was razor sharp. There was ill feeling of long standing between the two; it had begun at Plymouth when Doughty had related on many occasions to sailors how when he was at Cambridge he had known Bright's wife. He had stated to them that she was a trollop who had bedded with many of the students including himself.

"And would you like to say a final prayer before you meet your God?" Drake asked.

"Yes," Doughty declared, kneeling in the position where he would lose his head. Then he began, "Dear God, I would like to ask you to bless the Queen in her governing of England. Dear God, also please bless this venture and the future efforts of Francis Drake, though he will have taken my head. And dear God, I pray to you that you will take the hatred from the heart of Francis Drake so that he will not harm any man who has heretofore shown any kindness to me."

"Not if he is a traitor!" Drake interjected.

"Forgive Hugh Smith!" Doughty cried out from his kneeling position. "He has not conspired against thee."

"I will forgive him," Drake declared. "Though I was prepared to cut off his ears!" Drake said, half frowning.

"Ned, do your duty!" Doughty declared, resting his chin on the block and stretching his neck.

"Ready?" Bright asked.

"Careful with your arm, Ned, as I have a short neck!" Doughty warned while tightening the nape of his neck.

"Crack!" the ax fell, severing Doughty's head from his body. It rolled to the wet ground, leaving a trail of blood behind it.

Drake reached down to the severed head, took it by the hair and hoisted it out so that all could see. It was a ghastly, macabre sight that many would not forget, as blood was streaming from it. Drake looked at the open, glassy eyes staring at him. Then he exclaimed:

"Death is the lot of all traitors!"

CHAPTER 22

RELIEVING THE COMMANDS

Julian Bay was now in the midst of winter; six inches of snow lay on the ground, which only partially emphasized the cold, since its frigidity was greatly worsened by the southwest wind which fiercely blew most of the time, sometimes exceeding fifty knots. It easily pierced the clothing of the sailors now careening the hull of the *Elizabeth*. During high tides, she had been maneuvered close to the beach; she had been greatly helped by a sixteen-foot tide variation. Then during the low tides, she had been partially pulled onto the beach. Her crew then had removed her ballast of rocks that were located in the bottom of the ship, which were slimy and vermin-ridden, as the men had been using her bilges as a latrine. Then her crew had shifted the cumbersome deck guns so that they were on the larboard side. She now lay on the larboard side supported by props which had left the starboard side exposed.

A long beard of grass grew from her side. Beneath it was a covering of small shellfish, called barnacles. A dozen men with small spades attached to long wooden handles scraped at the wooden hull. Marks, the *Pelican*'s carpenter, and Williams, the *Elizabeth*'s carpenter, were following behind them, checking the wooden planking for damage from sea worms. And when they found damage, they removed the worm-eaten planking and replaced it.

Fifty feet from the carpenter and the cooper were six soldiers in a circle tossing and catching a ball being thrown from one man to another. A sailor chopped at the grass and crustacean growth; he knocked loose a clump as large as a nosegay. Then he picked it up and threw it at the nearest soldier; it hit him in the face.

"What 'ave you done to me!" the soldier declared, wiping his face with a canvas sleeve. Most of these soldiers called themselves gentlemen; this was because of their superior education. Some had attended Oxford, Cambridge or one of the Inns of Court where law was taught. All refused to do sailor work, which was basically all of the work that was to be done.

"That's for not working!" the sailor declared in an arrogant voice.

"I'll fix you!" the soldier-gentleman said and proceeded on a run toward the careened ship.

"Come if you may!" the sailor declared, brandishing his spade; then he was joined by the other sailors. The attacking soldier was joined by the other soldiers. All crossed from the land to the *Elizabeth*. A sailor standing on scaffolding whacked the foremost soldier with the handle of his spade. He fell into the icy water.

"Stop! Stop!" Wynter shouted, rushing from a tent. He was followed by Drake who silently watched the wet soldier slowly walk from the water, while the other soldiers shouted epithets at the sailors on the hull. Drake had hoped that the execution of Doughty would resolve the problems amongst the crew. He had warned the men what he would do if he had further problems between sailors and soldiers. But that had not sufficed, for shortly after Drake gave his warning, Ned Bright had made an unprovoked attack on John Doughty by hitting him in the face with a carpenter's ruler, leaving an ugly gash. Drake had not disciplined Bright; he knew that many men did not like it, saying to one another that he was administering one-sided justice. Because of this, a seaman named Cook had refused to confess to Preacher Fletcher. Drake had attempted to discipline him by putting him ashore in close arrest for two weeks. Drake knew that the dissension amongst the crew had worsened. He suspected that Julian Bay was having much to do with it. Its bleakness, coldness, dampness and isolation were enough to keep a person depressed. And the interior was then so heavy with snow that snowshoes were necessary in order to pursue game. The men were no longer able to slay the tuca-tuca, the guinea pig-like animals which earlier had made themselves available. And there was no other game unless they traveled further inland. And so Drake knew that everything told him that he needed to leave this bay of blood. But when? It was now mid-winter in the southern hemisphere—he knew also that they should stay at Julian Bay for another two or three more months, for he knew that the weather would be worse in the strait. But he also knew that if he did not leave soon, the men would shortly be at each other's throats.

So on August 11, 1578, Drake called a meeting of all the men. They met under the great tent, being a common room where Horsewill fed the men. Drake was flanked by his two captains, Vice Admiral Wynter and Captain John Thomas. Preacher Fletcher was before him, leading the group in a psalm. The church services were important to Drake, they were a frequent activity for the men in the fleet. Attendance was required for Sunday service; it was also required for special service. This was one of those.

"Shall I deliver the sermon?" Fletcher asked Drake on the singers concluding the hymn. He was positive that the meeting called was for the purpose of worship.

"No, Preacher, I will give the sermon today," Drake said on stepping forward so that he was now standing beside the preacher.

"As you like, General," Fletcher said, stepping aside as Drake raised his chin and looked out on the audience which actually occupied three sides.

"Are all the men present?" Drake asked.

"Yes, General—" a voice cried out.

"Yes, General—" another said.

"Well, then, let us group ourselves into ship companies. Those of you from the *Pelican*, sit here facing me. Those of you from the *Elizabeth*, move to my right, and those from the *Marigold*, sit on my left," Drake said, his voice hardly rising above the noise of the men moving from place to place. Once the men and boys were seated according to ships, Drake continued, "Shipmates, we are still in Julian Bay, and the snow still lies on the ground. The ground has changed very little since we landed here two months ago, and the same is true of your hearts. I was of the opinion that once we executed Thomas Doughty, it would eliminate all the dissension and mutinous behavior amongst the fleet. Yet it continues even though each of you ought to know that such is bad for the venture. We are deep in the heart of enemy territory where you could not find a friend unless he is amongst ourselves. And you sailors and soldiers continue to fuss about whether a soldier should put his hands to a rope or join in scraping a hull. That will end on my giving you some choices. There probably are some of you who want to return home to England without completing this venture. Well, I can spare the *Marigold*; so if you have the proper leadership to sail her, then I will make her available for those wishing to leave. But you will have to leave immediately, for if you tarry and later cross my path, I will sink you like an enemy. Who of you would like to leave this venture and return to England?" Drake asked.

None answered!

"Well, then, who wants to sail with me?"

"We do!" all shouted.

"Do you come of your own free will?"

"We do!" they shouted.

"And at whose hands do you look for your wages?"

"Yours," they answered.

"Will you accept wages or my pleasure?" Drake asked, meaning wages or a share of the plunder.

"Your pleasure!" they shouted in return.

"Well, then, if we gain nothing in Peru, I will still pay your wages when we return to England even if I have to sell all my possessions. And if I were to die before you return, then I assure you that the Queen will pay your wages."

"Hurrah!" they enthusiastically shouted.

"And now," Drake said, turning to Vice Admiral Wynter, "Admiral—I relieve you of your command!"

"What?" Wynter asked, and because of the shock he was momentarily unable to say anything more. He had commanded the *Elizabeth* from the beginning of the venture. He sincerely believed that there was no one else on the venture better qualified to command the *Elizabeth*. Why, command was a family tradition, as his father and uncle had commanded ships!

"And you, John Thomas, I relieve you of your captainship of the *Marigold*!"

"Sir?" Thomas asked. Shock covered his face. He seemed reluctant to say more. Drake did not explain his reasons, and Thomas wondered what there was to Drake's madness.

"And you, Thomas Hood, I relieve you of your mastership of the *Pelican*." Drake had replaced Cuttill with Hood when Cuttill had sided with Thomas Doughty.

"I thought, General," the master said; he was seated on the front row facing Drake. "I thought that you liked my work—"

"Are you saying that I do not have the power to relieve you?"

"No, sir—"

"And you, Will Markham of the *Elizabeth*, and Nicholas Anthony of the *Marigold*," he continued, "I discharge you of your offices of master. And now," Drake said, studying his audience as if he were going to dismiss them, too, adding, "is there anyone here who believes that I do not have the authority to dismiss these captains and masters?" he asked and quietly studied his audience as if looking for that person to challenge his authority. No one did. All looked at him with puzzled faces. "And that being the case, then I have the authority as well to restore each of you to the offices which moments ago I took from you. And so each of you is now vested with such office. But you will notice how fragile such office is, for it is held at my pleasure!"

"And now," Drake continued, "this brings me to the relationship of the soldiers and the sailors; the *Elizabeth*'s bottom must be cleaned and doctored. I want all the soldiers to join the *Elizabeth*'s sailors assigned to that task and give it a good cleaning and doctoring." It was doctored by the sailors painting the clean hull with a mixture of tallow, soap, fish oil and tar. "Is there any of you who objects to cleaning the hull?" Drake asked, having his hands on his hips and a sneer on his face, as if daring someone to defy him.

And there was silence!

"Then I do not ever again want to see soldiers playing ball while sailors are engaged in a work detail like that. Is that clear?"

"Yes!"

"Very well then. Once the *Elizabeth*'s bottom has been cleaned and doctored, and all the stores from the *Mary* have been stored on the three ships, the fleet will sail for the Magellan Strait!" Drake said. He knew that he should spend two or three more months in Julian Bay, but he also knew that the voyage could be thwarted by waiting until spring, as by then the crews could be in complete disarray.

"Hurrah!" the men cried out, smiling, beginning to converse with their neighbors, showing their eagerness to leave this dreary, desolate bay, which many were calling the "Island of Blood." Yet they could not have imagined the suffering that they would sustain before reaching the South Sea.

CHAPTER 23

THE MAGELLAN STRAIT

Drake's small fleet sailed from Julian Bay on August 17, 1578, proceeding south though it was the middle of winter in the southern hemisphere. Three days later they were at the imposing entrance to the Magellan Strait. Tall, snow-capped mountains towered over the turning point, which was Cape Virgin Mary, a mass of steep grey cliffs spotted with black. White spray spouted at the heel of these cliffs. The sky was a soft baby blue, while there were bags of white clouds above the strait. The wind was lacking in force, which made it appear to Drake that passage through the strait would be easy. His right hand rested on the whipstaff out of habit, though the steersmen were Moone and Hurd. But the appearance of the strait was deceptive, as suddenly huge black clouds began to roll in from the southwest and the wind accelerated to fifty knots. These troll-like clouds seemingly had come out to greet the *Pelican* on its arrival at the Virgins, which was the entrance to the strait.

"Steer west!" Drake said to Tom Moone, who was now standing near him. Moone was intensely staring at the strait as if searching it for traps, while his hands tightly gripped the whipstaff with which he was steering the ship. Thomas Hurd, the second steersman, was standing on the other side. Hurd also stared directly ahead.

"Aye—and these are the Virgins?" Moone asked, tensely smiling, his eyes roving, as if he were unable to believe his eyes.

"Yes, and we're doing seven knots!" Drake declared, as if amazed at the speed. This was a lot of speed for the *Pelican*, as she was built more for endurance. She could take the rough seas; then she could easily be careened. A short time later Drake stepped out from the steersman's protective alcove, pointed and said, "There is the white sand hill!" He was pointing to the slope of a mountain on the starboard side of the *Pelican*. "Three leagues from here we shall see on the larboard side three mountains of sand which look like islands but are not. There you will see the mouth of the strait," Drake said. He was recalling comments by Pigafetta who was the chronicler of the Magellan voyage. They were not always to be followed, since he at times had given an exaggerated account of the voyage.

"Aye!"

"Call the men to quarters!" Drake said to his master, Thomas Hood, who was standing beneath him on the main deck. The master was staring at the Virgins with fascination. Hood was standing beside John Brewer, who had his trumpet in his hand. "Sound your trumpet, John—call all hands to quarters!"

"Aye!" the trumpeter replied, and then he loudly sounded his horn, bringing sailors from below decks. All were expecting the call, as each held a cup in his hand while putting on a heavy jacket. It as well was heard on the other two ships, for men began to assemble on their decks.

"¡Mucho frio!" exclaimed Nuno da Silva. He had left Drake's cabin, and he was now standing beside Drake on the poop deck. He did not need to point out to Drake that it was very cold. The wind force had dropped to twenty-five knots, which was to their advantage, though the air had become extremely frigid.

"A taste of the future?" Drake replied, rubbing his hands, but his thoughts were on problems of the moment. "Try the lead line!" he shouted above the wind to two sailors who were standing on the bow.

"No bottom, General!" a sailor shouted on letting out the full length of his line.

"No bottom, no anchorage!" Drake exclaimed, frowning. He had planned on anchoring at the entrance to the strait and then conducting a ceremony. But he now knew that anchoring would be out of the question.

"Attention all hands!" Drake shouted above the wind. All had been forewarned about the icy cold wind and the wet. Most had made themselves canvas jackets and lined them with lambskin or a padding of straw. They had then sealed the seams with tar. The seamen's jackets could not be too cumbersome; else they would interfere with work on the yards and in the shrouds and braces. Too much interference would be courting disaster.

"We are now about to enter the Magellan Strait. All ships lower your top sails!" Drake shouted above the wind. The *Pelican* lowered her top sails, and Brewer sounded his trumpet. Then the other ships also lowered their topsails. Drake was standing on the poop deck and facing the men crowded on the main deck. He then said to them, "This is a great occasion for England, for we are the first English ships to enter the Magellan Strait—and so we have lowered our top-sails in honor of our Queen. Will you charge all cups, Boatswain," Drake said, speaking to Fowler. Horsewill and his two boy appren-tices, Willie and Joey, were helping him fill the extended cups from two open casks of wine. Each of the boys wore a baggy woolen cap and a long coat, and they busily moved about the deck filling cups with wine.

"They're charged, General!"

"Let us drink to England!"

"Aye, England!" the men shouted, and then they drank.

"Let us drink to the Queen!"

"To the Queen!" they said as one. And they drank.

"And to our patron, Sir Christopher Hatton!"

"To Sir Christopher Hatton!" they shouted. Then they drank again.

"And in his honor, I do hereby change the name of this ship to that of the *Golden Hind*!" Drake said. He was doing this because the *Golden Hind*, which was a red female deer, was a part of the crest of the Hattons, and Hatton was possibly the closest person to Queen Elizabeth. This was a well-thought-out political move on Drake's be-half, for Doughty had been the protégé of Sir Richard Hatton. Drake hoped that this move would allay Hatton's wrath against him for having executed Doughty.

"Roll 'em!" Drake shouted to John Drake, the drummer, who was standing at attention. John took his sticks and rapidly beat on his side drum so as to produce a rhythmic rolling effect which was so effectively done that it caused many of the men to stiffen their backs.

"Break the bottle!" Drake shouted to his master, Thomas Hood, who was standing near the bowsprit with a bottle of wine in his hand. He broke it the first time that he swung it. Wine splattered on his legs.

"Hurrah!" the men shouted, cheering Drake and the name change.

"May the *Golden Hind* not only enrich his name but increase his purse!" Drake exclaimed and lifted his cup of wine to his lips. The wine had warmed his insides and charged his mind with romantic thoughts.

"Hurrah!" the men on deck shouted again, and they wiped cold spray from their faces. Then many of them for the second time extended their cups to the two boys to refill them from the wine cask on deck, and they drank again to the name change. "On to the South Sea!" Drake loudly shouted, smiling, attempting to make his voice rise above the winds which now had become gale force.

"To the South Sea!" the men cried. Buoyancy was in their voices as if the worst were in the past. Many warmly slapped the backs of persons nearest to them.

Then Drake returned to his warm cabin, where there was a wood fire burning in the grate. The cabin was soon filled with wet sailors. There was Drake, Tom Drake, Tom Moone, Thomas Hood, Nuno, Preacher Fletcher and young John Drake.

"The strait is deep!" Drake said in Spanish to Nuno da Silva while warming his backside and removing his jacket.

"The lack of anchorage bothered Magellan," Nuno replied, studying a sketch being drawn by young John Drake onto a sketch pad. He had captured the rugged splendor of the entrance to this great strait. He was presently filling in the background, which was unusually forlorn with dangerous overlay. This was because of the darkened sky and brooding clouds that aimlessly moved. The sky had further darkened; huge dark clouds busily moved about the strait. Rain lashed at the fleet. The sailors in the foretop squatted in their perches and attempted to warm themselves by huddling together, while the top fretfully moved back and forth as if it would dislodge itself.

"Magellan passed through it in the summer!" Drake said. "But Englishmen—"

"But it is still winter—and we are not through!" Nuno cautiously warned.

"We must anchor," Drake declared, leaning over John Drake's sketch and then pencilling in a flock of flying pelicans. He often pencilled in objects so as to compliment the younger man's sketches. The strait most of the time has flocks of pelicans flying over it, as if they are its guardians. "Unless we can use our anchor, we will not make any progress—may not get through it!" Drake said, still sketching, knowing that Magellan had traversed the 360-mile strait in the summer of 1520. Even so, he had had a difficult time. This was because in places the strait has tides of sixty feet, and it has tide rips of up to thirteen knots in its narrowest channels. The southwest winds from Antarctica can create terrible water currents. The strait has mists and fogs and unpredictable winds that can easily wreck a sailing ship. It took Magellan thirty-seven days to traverse the strait, and then he exited with only three of the five ships with which he began the voyage. Magellan learned to his sorrow after entering the strait that its winds are interminable, for a ship can gain twenty miles in the morning and lose it back in the afternoon.

"Let's try the north shore line," Nuno said.

"Islands ahead!" John Drake said on raising his head and studying the distant horizon through a window in the cabin. The strait passes through a maze of islands that from the beginning have confounded ships' captains who have traversed it. This is because if a ship makes the wrong turn, it can be lost for days. But these first islands would not cause any serious problem, as they were in the middle of the strait.

"Maybe we can harvest some seals and birds or pick some herbs, providing the weather changes," Drake said, being ever-concerned about the health of the men. As the writer has previously stated, Drake did not know the scientific cause of scurvy, but he did know that its symptoms did not occur when the men had fresh vegetables, fruit or even fresh meat to eat. And he also knew that herbs served as a good substitute for fresh fruits and vegetables.

On the following morning the fleet approached three islands. Drake drew abreast of a small island, and then the sun strangely blazed from the sky and the wind abated sufficiently so that the longboat could be manned and a landing made. All of the islands were barren of trees, though each was covered with grass and herbs. Each as well was home to a colony of penguins, who were black with white spots on their necks and stomachs. When approached, they either ran into the water or scampered into their holes, the roofs of which were like small bridges. This was because each hole had an entrance and an exit. The sailors landed and began to slaughter the birds. They easily slew a thousand or more of these flightless birds. The men would soon discover that when penguin meat was cooked, it tasted much like that of a wild goose.

201

When the men had boarded these birds, Drake ordered the ship's master to up anchor, and they set sail again. It was just as well, for the weather had suddenly changed; the winds had begun to blow fiercely. Rain fell in torrents; then it changed to sleet. And then a second wind began to blow from the southwest, which was parallel with the first. The two created a tornado effect on the water which troughed and went in two directions. On either side were tall mountains that were covered with snow and ice; then the forward motion of the *Golden Hind* dropped to practically zero.

"She ceases to make any headway, General!" Hurd, the senior helmsman, shouted.

"Come about—take me to that cove!" Drake shouted, pointing, then fretfully rubbing his red hands, knowing that he could readily be blown back to his starting point unless he was able to anchor the *Golden Hind* in some sort of shelter. He also knew that it was dangerous to turn his side to the wind. But now the *Hind* was underway for the cove, doing it with short sail.

"Reef that bonnet!" Drake shouted. The small sail at the bowsprit was the only sail in use. Even so, with it reefed, the *Hind* still caught enough wind to give it some mobility.

"Aye!" voices shouted.

"Take me to that point!" Drake shouted, pointing to the north shore. "I want to anchor!"

"Aye!"

"Pilot, we must anchor!" Drake exclaimed to Nuno, now looking out the cabin door, saying it as if Nuno did not know it.

"Keep your bow pointed for shore!" Nuno cried now, looking out a cabin window to the sea, which was an angry devil. The winds were so fierce that once again they had created a trough in the water, and seemingly each side was moving a different way.

"Try your lead line!" Drake shouted to two sailors on the bow who had tied themselves to a railing with a piece of rope. One sailor tossed a line with weighted end. He let it run and then cried out:

"We've got bottom at nine fathoms, General!"

"Drop your anchor!" Drake ordered. Then he added, "Drop a second anchor!"

"Aye!"

"And where is the *Elizabeth*?"

"There!" Nuno answered, pointing to the stern.

"And the *Marigold*?"

202

"There! There!"

"Anchor's holdin'!"

"We'll hold our gain!" Drake exclaimed, shaking rain from his face. His words indicated that he thought the ships would not lose the miles that they had gained earlier.

Drake soon discovered that these islands were inhabited because at night he could see fires; and as well, during the day, he had seen smoke rising from them. On the morning after the *Golden Hind* had traversed half of the strait and passed through dozens of storms, managing to keep much of its gain by being able to anchor, Drake met some Tierra del Fuego Indians for the first time.

"They are harmless, General," John Brewer explained, smiling, pointing down to a male and a female Indian and two small Indian children. One sucked a flabby breast. These Indians were much smaller than the Patagonian giants who previously had been so hostile to the Englishmen. All were seated in a canoe that had been made of stitched bark; it had been put together so well that there was no sign of a leak. And strangely, there was a pile of sand in the middle of the canoe; and in the middle of that there was a smoldering fire. All four Indians were naked; yet they were robust and appeared healthy enough. Contrariwise, the sailors on deck were bundled up so as to keep out the chill. The bodies of the Indians had been painted with circles, inside of which someone had crudely drawn birds and seals. The male smiled at the men on deck, displaying a set of yellow teeth, while his gums were pink, being a sure sign of good health.

"Come here!" Drake firmly said to John Brewer.

"Sir, what have I done?" the trumpeter curiously asked, suspecting that Drake was angry at him.

"Open your mouth!" Drake ordered the trumpeter, and when he did, Drake used his finger to examine his gums and teeth. The gums were grayish and puffy, while his teeth were long, as if ready to shed. "You need some herbs!" Drake exclaimed. Then he looked across the deck for a receptive face, and on catching the eye of Fowler, the boatswain, he said to him:

"Bos'n, show the Indians a hatchet. Offer it to them in exchange for some edible grass!"

"Aye, General!" Fowler replied. He, too, knew the importance of herbs and grass, mainly because of the emphasis put on it by Drake. The men at times in the seamen's quarters called Drake "General Grass." And when there was something strange in the soup, the cook would say, "It is the grass that the General ordered!" The men in their searching had found a handful of antiscorbutic grass on Penguin Island which Drake knew would fight scurvy. Horsewill had cooked it in penguin stew. But it had not been enough to have much effect on the men.

"Ah!"

The sailor attempted to transmit his message by putting his hand to his mouth. The Indians partially understood, as they offered Fowler a piece of a freshly killed seal.

"No, no!" Drake exclaimed. "John, take the dinghy. Encourage the Indians to go ashore; follow them. Find out what herbs that they are eating. Bring some of them back to the *Hind*!"

The Indians were finally able to understand what Fowler wanted, and they rowed for the shore, motioning for Fowler to follow. They pulled their canoe up on the shore which was lined with trees whose bows were heavily weighted with snow.

"Kowwhi!" Shelter, the Indian said, pointing from his canoe to the snow-covered branches. Then he reached beneath a branch and pulled out a clump of olive-green plants, which were as healthy as if they had come out of a green house. This was due to the fact that there was a tremendous difference between the temperature of the mountain heights and that of the shoreline. From the crest of the stupendous mountains, there were swirling mists, while their flanks were massed with snow and glaciers. And from the cliffs, bitter cold winds blew down and hit the water with a spinning motion that created deep hollows and huge waves; yet on the slopes near the water's edge, the water was temperate as if it were in perpetual summer. It was here that the herbs of mint, thyme and marjoram grew, which were healing plants. As well, at the same place, there also grew a plentiful supply of the antiscorbutic plant *apium antarcticum*, of which the men had collected a handful on Penguin Island.

"Mint!" Fowler declared on putting it to his nose. "And tons of it!" he exclaimed. "Edible grass, too!" he added, laughing on pulling up a clump of anti-scurvy grass. He, like most other sailors, knew the plant by sight. They would subsequently discover that it seemingly grew just about everywhere in the southern hemisphere. They also would learn that eating it gave almost immediate relief to joint pains that sometimes hurt like a toothache.

Two hours later John Fowler and his two-man crew returned to the *Golden Hind*; Drake was on deck to greet them.

"How did you do?" he asked.

"Great," Fowler declared, brightly smiling, though speaking like an old man, as he was toothless; he pointed to the shore. "Those snow-covered trees lining the shore act as a shelter for a green garden of mints and grasses. And further up that river I found wild celery. There are many large trees; some are almost as thick as the *Golden Hind*. There is a plentiful supply of birds. General, I saw wild parrots, geese and the like."

"Well, now, I will have to investigate your discovery," Drake said, his voice like his face revealing his elation. Minutes later he would take a boat ashore to investigate. He would be so impressed with the large deciduous beech trees, the *nothofaugus antarctica*, which reach a height of one hundred feet and have a girth of twenty feet, that he would cut one down and tow a portion to the *Golden Hind* and board it for ballast.

"Master," Drake said, speaking to Master Hood. "Have some men pass down baskets to the men in the dinghy and take aboard their fresh herbs. You, Francis," he said, speaking to Preacher Fletcher, who was also acting as the ship's physician. "Feed the herbs first to the men with aching limbs—they must eat them raw. Then have the cook make a soup—mix plenty of herbs and grass in it. You, John, make another trip—we hardly know where we will be tomorrow!"

"Aye!"

"We should be out of the strait in a day or two. And I want a healthy crew when we sail north for gold and silver!"

CHAPTER 24

CAPE HORN

On September 6, 1578, Drake's fleet arrived at Cape Dessado, being the rocky western exit of the Magellan Strait; Drake's fleet now was ready to enter the South Sea, which Magellan had named the Pacific Ocean because of its apparent calmness. Cape Dessado is a pile of rocks located on the westernmost headland of Desolation Island; it is the southernmost island on the western end of the strait. Drake had made record time in crossing the strait, for it had only taken his fleet 16 days to traverse it. And so he was rightly elated. He eyed Nuno, who was seated at the cabin table studying a chart of the strait. The space beneath the strait was shown as solid land, being what the cartographer called "Terra Australias," which appeared to form a continent in the Pacific Ocean. The two had made many additions and corrections to the map of the strait. They had used the letter "A" to note on their map the good anchorage sites that they had discovered. It had become an interesting chart, as John Drake had covered its borders with numerous sketches of Fuegian Indians, seals, penguins and stormy waters; he had even made one small sketch of Fowler with an armload of herbs.

"Nuno," Drake said, speaking in Spanish. There was so much triumph in his voice that John Drake raised his head from his sketching. "It is now the day of the English sailor. Oh, it has to be. Why, you will have to agree that the English are better sailors. Well, it took Magellan six weeks to cross it; and he did it in the summer. And those few who tried it after him took much longer. And each lost ships in doing it," Drake argued, saying what all knew. Traversing the strait was extremely difficult in the awkward sailing ships. The builders had not yet learned how to build and rig ships so they could properly capture the wind. The Spaniards had made three attempts; all had met with some form of disaster.

"It was smartly done," Nuno replied, smiling. "You certainly are through the strait—well almost anyway. The headland is just here—" he said. He raised his eyes and looked out of a cabin window on the port side. "Just yonder, oh, that sky looks ominous!" Nuno said, pointing out that the sky had become almost dark. John Drake had detected this earlier, and so he was lighting the candles in the two cabin lamps.

"I know," Drake said, wanting to ignore the warning. Then he crossed the room, opened the cabin door, and shouted, "Preacher, preacher!"

"Yes, General," Fletcher replied. He was standing on the main deck with a group of sailors. All were anxiously eyeing the darkening skies and the rising seas that had white tongues which anxiously lashed out as if searching for a victim. He turned and approached the ladder to the portico deck for Drake's cabin. Fletcher had long hair, which was greased and tied in the back by a throng. The top of his head was covered with a woolen cap which he had knitted. He was dressed in a canvas jacket and canvas pants. He did not wear any gloves as he did not want any covering to interfere with his feel of the rope. It was bitterly cold. He landed on the General's portico deck, cupped his hands and blew on them; then he entered Drake's cabin which was warm, as a wood fire was burning in the grate. He turned his backside to the fire.

"Do you have your marker?"

"Yes—" the preacher replied, while frowning. Before Fletcher had left England, he had acquired tools so he could make markers and letter them for such occasions. It had been Drake's plan to place a marker on the point of Cape Dessado in order to indicate the date that the fleet traversed the strait.

"And is the longboat ready?"

"Yes, General, but the winds are rising; the seas are heavy!" he said, turning sideways and showing the hump on his nose. He need not have said it. Rain was coming down in sheets; and the *Hind* was riding the waves like a bucking horse. Drake had to know that it would be dangerous to put out to sea in the longboat.

"Stand by anyway!" Drake snapped. He shrugged his shoulders; then he stepped to the cabin door and looked out at the seas which now were more than 12 feet high. He eyed the head of the island, seeing rocks protruding from the seas. Their sight brought him to his senses.

"Let's steer a northwest course for Peru!" Drake said. His charts showed that the west coast of South America extended westward twice as far as it actually does (see Mercator Map inside book cover). "What's your latitude, Nuno?"

"Fifty-two."

"Once we are out of this blow—" Drake said and stopped as if thinking.

"Boom!" A wave as tall as the *Hind's* main mast hit the *Golden Hind*. And its forward motion stopped, then its bow rose up and climbed the wave.

"Master Hood," Drake shouted. "Secure the ship for rough seas! Douse the fires below decks! John, douse the grate fire!" Fire was a continuing fear of Drake's. "Man the pumps!" he ordered while watching tons of angry water roam the deck. The hand pumps would have to be manned continuously because a portion of the water that was pouring over the decks was going down the half-open hatches. Even fish were going down them. The seamen earlier had tightened their sails; then minutes before they had furled them. A half-dozen men were on deck in waist deep water. All clung to ropes so as to keep from being washed away. None were in the rigging.

"Where is the *Elizabeth*?"

"I see her mast, General—and the *Marigold*, too!" John Drake said.

"Put over a sea anchor!" Drake said to Hood. "Put over two!"

"How so?"

"Put over two of the heaviest ropes we have!" Drake said. He was hoping to tie two long ropes to the stern so as to create some stabilizing effect for the ship to keep it from wallowing in the heavy seas.

And soon it was midday, but the clouds were so low and the air so thick from spray that it was dark as night, and it continued that way for days. And Drake was unable to do anything to stop the *Golden Hind* from being pushed southeast by the terrible winds from the northwest. Then for three weeks this weather continued without relief. The *Hind* creaked and groaned, and its beams wrenched as though they would part. Then she was periodically struck by heavy waves that at times were so severe that it appeared they would split the *Hind* into parts. Waves periodically rolled over her deck, spilling water onto the orlop deck, which often immersed it in water. This low-ceiling room was practically in the dark during this period because the men were so fearful of fire. And those who could get into their hammocks got little relief because they were made dizzy by the rocking motion of the ship. And sleeping often did not come because their clothes were always wet. The only food that they had was hard biscuits dipped in wine.

And the winds continued to blow without stopping, doing it with almost hurricane force. The *Golden Hind* helplessly wallowed in the heavy seas, while being driven further southeast; even so, Drake still demanded that the seamen stand watches. They stood on deck, soaked to the skin, hanging onto ropes to keep from being washed over the side. Other watchstanders manned pumps so as to rid the *Hind* of water that came from the open decks and through cracks that could not be sealed. The pumps were such hard work that the watch was being relieved on the half hour. The atmosphere was eery as it was pitch black except for a single burning candle in a lantern. And so the pumps monotonously clanged day and night:

"Click, clack; click, clack!"

"Oh, the sea!" Mincy, the viol player, now a pumper, cried.

"It is a devil!" his buddy answered.

The *Hind* was emitting weird noises. There were the creaking noises, for the joints creaked when the ship rolled, and it appeared that the *Hind* was going to come apart. Then there was the sluicing noise of the water in the bilges. The yards and masts shuddered and bent. And above this noise, there were human sounds:

"Do you hear our boy weep?" Mincy said, looking up at the dark overhead, but continuing to pump. He could hear a boy weeping. There were six of these boys on the *Hind*. The boy crying was a favorite, being Willie Fortescue, a nine-year-old, who was one of two boys apprenticed to Horsewill. Drake had not taken any boys on the venture who were under 12 years old unless they were accompanied by an older brother or cousin. Willie's older brother was able seaman George Fortescue, who had asked Drake to let Willie go to sea on the *Hind*, explaining that his mother was a drunkard and was neglecting Willie. But George did not have much caring to do, as Willie handled himself like a little man. He put in a full day every day of work with the cook. Then when the weather permitted, he attended two hours of grammar school with Preacher Fletcher.

"It is his ear, Minch—"

"Maybe the preacher can give him some herbs!"

"He would not cry but for the ear!"

"He needs a bunk," Mincy said, referring to the fact that the boys had to sleep on the floor in the food room.

"He sleeps with George," the other replied, referring to the fact that Willie was now sleeping with George in his hammock.

And thus it continued until September 28, 1578. For it was during the first morning watch on that day that Tom Brewer shouted to Preacher Fletcher:

"Preacher!"

"Aye!" the preacher shouted in reply. Both men were securely tied to rigging.

"The *Marigold*!" he shouted. The small ship had been trailing the *Golden Hind* by 200 yards. "She's gone over!" he exclaimed, pointing. "Hear them!"

"Help, help!" came the mournful cries of men who were now in the freezing water. But no help could be offered, for a small boat could not have been lowered. And the seamen in it could not have survived if a boat had been lowered.

"It's the Lord's revenge on Edward Bright!" the preacher cried. Anguish was on his face, while his eyes were glassy, as they fearfully searched the angry seas. He was recalling that on the morning the three ships sailed from Julian Bay, Drake had surprisingly rewarded Bright for having been his point man; for Bright not only had given damaging testimony against Doughty, but he had welded the ax which had severed Doughty's head. And so before the *Marigold* left Julian Bay, Drake had rewarded Bright by putting him aboard the *Marigold* as its master. Fletcher had backed Drake in the trial, but he now was wet, tired and afraid of the sea, and so he now regretted it—he felt remorse for the conviction and the execution of Doughty. And he blamed the conviction on Bright. But Fletcher should have known Drake better than that; for he would have had it without the testimony of Bright. For he was convinced that Doughty was interfering with his command; and Drake just was not going to permit that. The trial also gave Drake an excuse to have an execution; and thus, he had an example which could be used to intimidate the men. He knew that his motley crew of seamen and gentlemen adventurers that called themselves soldiers were not working together. Many did not fully recognize him as their leader. He was convinced that they had to recognize him as their leader—in order to complete the mission.

And in order to get that, he had to intimidate them. He had attempted to do this by executing Doughty.

"But why the others!" the preacher exclaimed, crying out to Drake's cabin on the poop deck. "They were good men!" he shouted into the strong wind and heavy seas, as though he knew that Bright was not a good man.

"General!" John Brewer exclaimed to Drake, who was lying in his bunk. He had lashed a rope across it to keep himself in it. "The *Marigold* is lost!"

"How?" Drake asked, untying the rope. He then quickly stood. He awkwardly put on his foul weather clothing and stumbled to the door and opened it. He searched the seas but did not see any sign of the *Marigold* or its crew members.

"It went bottom up?" Drake asked, while searching. He knew that the *Golden Hind* regularly rolled 45 degrees and on occasions a bit more. But apparently the *Marigold* was not as rugged as the *Hind* or was it luck—irrespective, she had made a bad roll and then she had not righted herself.

"She is gone!"

"The *Elizabeth*?" Drake asked.

"She still follows!"

"Twenty-eight men!" Drake said and shook his head. He was referring to the number of men and boys that had been aboard the *Marigold*. Once again he wondered whether he should not have wintered at Julian Bay. Then he quickly thought on the reasons why he had sailed in the winter, as if seeking argument to support his reasoning in departing when he did. His thoughts quickly returned to the remaining two ships and their crews. What could he do to save them? His exuberance was at an end; yet his determination was strong as ever. "Let's be tough—this storm has got to end!" Drake shouted to the men on deck.

"All my clothes—my hammock—are soaked, General!" Thomas Brewer shouted. There, of course, were two Brewers serving on the *Hind*: Tom and John, who was the bugler.

"That will not kill you!"

"I don't feel good! I ache!"

"Be tough! The Indians don't wear clothes!" Drake shouted.

"I'm not an Indian!" Brewer replied in a whining voice.

"What I'm trying to tell you is that being wet won't kill you!" Drake shouted. Water was running down his face. His red hair was plastered to his forehead. Then he turned away from Brewer who was securely tied to a shroud, having cold water pour over him. Drake opened the door to his cabin, saying to the men inside as he entered:

"The *Marigold* is lost—went bottom up!"

"Why?" Tom Moone asked, looking perplexed.

"The sea, the sea!" Drake replied.

"Thomas is gone!" Master Hood sadly declared. John Thomas was a favorite of the men as well as Drake. He had been a steady leader amongst the men. He as well had been a staunch follower of Drake. Doughty might have succeeded in overthrowing Drake had it not been for Thomas. But the men were suffering too much from the sea and the cold to mourn for long the loss of the *Marigold*.

The next day was better as the storm abated leaving a thick fog; and the *Hind* apparently was very close to the shore, for the seamen on deck could hear water washing on shore. The fog slightly opened and Drake conned the *Golden Hind* into a bay, but he had trouble in finding anchorage as the water was too deep. Finally he did; however, as soon as the *Hind* was anchored, the storm resumed its fury and Drake had to slip his anchor and depart. The *Elizabeth* no longer was following. Drake did not suspect it, but Wynter had lost interest in the venture. And so he was conning the *Elizabeth* back to the strait; she would traverse it to the eastern entrance and then she would sail out into the Atlantic; then Wynter would give orders to sail for England. Wynter would later report to the Admiralty that firstly, he had turned back because he had concluded that the *Hind* was lost; and then secondly, he had not completed the venture because his men just did not want any more of it. And thirdly, how could he do it if the men would not follow?

And the *Golden Hind* was again caught up in the storm; it furiously beat at the tiny ship, refusing to let her sail north; and so she was driven south until she was at 54.5 degrees. There the storm abated sufficiently for Drake to thread the *Hind* through a myriad of islands—some large—some tiny—others being just protruding rocks, as he searched for Wynter. The *Hind* was in dire need of water, but Drake decided that the shores of the islands were too dangerous for the *Golden Hind* to move in close enough to anchor. And so on October 13, 1578, he picked an eight-man crew for the longboat.

"Carder," he said to a tow-headed seaman from Cornwall. "You are to take the longboat and land on that island, fill these barrels with water," Drake said, pointing. "Then make a search for herbs."

"Do I need a compass or extra food?"

"No. I do not want you to be gone more than four hours," Drake said. "We will keep you in sight," Drake added, as though it were possible. And worse, the longboat departed without a lantern keg, being a small keg that held a lantern, candles, flint, steel, and hard bread, which formed a part of the boat's emergency equipment.

But 30 minutes after the longboat departed, a storm arose which was so severe that the *Hind* was not able to reach the longboat and thereafter Drake would not be able to find it; it would stay lost though the *Hind* diligently hunted for it. And the men in the longboat would suffer horribly since they not only did not have any shelter, but they did not have a compass or food. And though the open boat sought the *Hind* and it sought Carder and his crew, neither would find the other. Those men with Carder in the open boat would experience the most terrible open boat journey of all time. All would be lost but Carder—and his experiences would be almost unbelievable. He would become a prisoner of the Indians and then of the Portuguese. His experiences would be so arduous that it would take him nine years to get himself back to England; his adventures would be so epic that on his return he would be given an audience with the Queen.

On October 23, 1578, the storm abated sufficiently for Drake to make a landing on a small island where his landing party found some herbs, which included the penny royal, being a sweet-smelling mint, which was growing in clumps as large as half a barrel. But they had only half loaded their boat when the master aboard the *Hind* cried out:

"Storm! Storm!"

"To the boat, men!" Drake shouted. "Hurry, hurry!" The wind had risen and the waves were ten feet high.

"Row hard!" Drake shouted from the coxswain seat. "Hoist the anchor!" Drake shouted to the men on the *Hind*.

"Come aboard, General!"

"You'll lose that anchor!"

"Better that than you, General!" Hood replied. Drake was interested in saving the anchor, while the master had wider concerns. He was worried that if it were hoisted, the *Hind* would part from the boat—and the parting could cause the loss of Drake.

But Drake's conjecture was correct; the *Hind* not only lost her anchor, but her cable as well. For she finally had to cut and run. But they did save their General. However, it appeared that the *Hind* would be lost, for the storm took hold of the *Hind* and whirled it aimlessly about and drove her further south. The seas tossed her bow in the air, moving her sideways then back, much like a wild horse with its first rider. Even so, Drake ordered Horsewill to light his fire in the hearth in the crew's quarters and cook the mint that they had scavenged; this was so that all hands could drink its juice, for many were suffering from terribly sore gums and limbs, which to Drake were obvious signs of scurvy. And then on October 24, 1578, the seas calmed and an island appeared on the *Hind*'s port bow, while on her starboard there was a great expanse of ocean that strangely stretched as far as one could see. The island was a crusty one, as it had a tall peak that was covered with snow; its shores were rocky, while the seas beat against them. To the south were open seas which were only broken by a giant iceberg which was lazily floating along. Drake and his men were the first white men to see this island, being the last of the islands of a chain south of the Magellan Strait. This island would later be called Cape Horn, being named by a Dutchman, naming it after his home town.

"John," Drake said to Brewer, the trumpeter. "Sound quarters!"

"Aye!"

"Master Hood, hoist sail! I want to make a landing on that island," Drake ordered.

"Aye, sir!" the master replied. And then the seamen in the rigging began to move line. One swung lose from the main mast, and unbeknownst to John Brewer, it moved directly for him. And it hit him on the side of his head. And as he was awkwardly standing on a brace, the rope knocked him into the icy water.

"Man overboard!"

"Rope! Rope! The trumpeter is in the water!"

A half-dozen ropes were tossed to him. All missed; then Brewer bobbed up and down in the cold water, fighting for his life, as he was a poor swimmer. His head rose above the water and he shouted to Fletcher:

"Preacher, I'm drowning—throw me a rope!"

"Amen, brother," Fletcher replied. He threw Brewer a rope, and it hit him on an outstretched arm where the others had missed. The trumpeter took a firm hold of it. And the men quickly pulled him onto the deck.

"This is an act of God; and so you are now a child of God!" Fletcher exclaimed. Then he took his Bible from his jacket and held it in one hand, while putting the other on top of Brewer's head while asking, "Do you believe in him?"

"I do—"

"Then you are saved from your sins!"

"It is an omen!" Drake declared, standing beside the two men. "The Lord is with us!"

And thereafter, Drake led an expedition to the island which he would call the Uttermost Island. For to Drake it was the last island in this chain of islands which Drake would give its location to be 56 degrees south, while Nuno would give its location to be 57 degrees south; yet its actual location was 55 degrees, 55 minutes, 40 seconds. And when Drake did reach it, he knew that it was the last island in the chain; this was because of the great expanse of water to its southward side. Drake was in a very weakened condition when he stepped ashore; for his legs wobbled so that he fell. He had the appearance of an old man. His hands shook. His face was gaunt as his eyes were surrounded by deep, dark sockets. His red beard was long and streaked with grey. Even so, he drew himself erect, for he knew that it was an important moment in the voyage. And once they had reached a high place, Drake turned and said to Fletcher:

"Preacher, will you give thanks?"

"That I will gladly do, General," Fletcher said. Then he began his thanks:

"Dear God, bless us poor, tired seamen who stand before you on this island of cold land facing a colder sea. Forgive the souls now with you from the *Marigold*; forgive them of their sins; they were mere mortals. Many of their sins were not of their own doing. And dear God, we do not question your reasons for bringing us to this place. Possibly you brought us here for the purpose of showing us Englishmen something of great significance. For you know and I know that the body of water there is not Terra Australia Incognita, but is water, water, being a passage; and we have discovered it through our General Drake who did it for our great Queen Elizabeth . . ."

And thereafter, Drake spoke to the men in the same vein though his remarks were more pointed:

"They are wrong! They are liars, and they cheat!" Drake dramatically cried out as though he had lost his mind. This caused the sailors surrounding him with their heads bent in prayer to open their eyes and look upward. Was the General mad? All knew that if Drake were mad, they would never make it back to England. All now recognized Drake as being a great seaman; and they looked to him for deliverance from the bottom of the world where they had been driven by the seemingly never-ending storm. All the crew members were still wet and cold. A fire had been lit in the *Hind* only once since they had left the strait, and that was to make mint tea. Their daily food had been a hard biscuit mixed with wine and water. Many were suffering from scurvy. How much more could they take? And yet the sun suddenly burst forth. It was done like it was an omen!

"Dear God, men like Dee, Mercator, the map makers, the philosophers, who sit in the comfort of their chairs and write and draw, have taken us to be fools! If you were to look at the map of Mercator," he said, speaking as though all knew what he knew, though most had not been near his chart table for most stayed clear of power. "You would see what I have seen hundreds of times. That map has the Strait of Magellan attached to a continent called Terra Australia Incognita. And if we were to believe Mercator's map, we should be on top of a land mass. But we are not; and so they are wrong, wrong! Their talk and writing of the necessity of a balance of land is rot! And so I say dear God, you have brought us here to have us demonstrate to the world that the Magellan Strait is the Spanish way to the South Sea, while the English way is through that passage," he said, pointing without raising his head. "And now, dear God, you have blessed us by delivering us from a great storm. Will you further bless us by delivering unto us those eight crew men who sailed in the longboat. Amen."

"Amen!" the sailors chorused and opened their eyes and looked about on the water. Several saw a speck on the horizon.

"It's the longboat!"

"No, it's an Indian canoe!"

"I could cry!" Drake moaned.

"And I!" said the preacher.

"Let us explore this uttermost island!" Drake said. And the men slowly went about the island, searching for food. They were soon feasting on the land; for they found many tiny shellfish, being tiny mollusks and crustaceans. They also found many sweet barberries, which resemble grapes though they have more seeds and which grow on thorny bushes. They ate them until their faces were purple from the juice. Drake gained strength from feasting; and he slowly climbed the tallest peak on Cape Horn, being followed by a dozen men. All were forced to walk deliberately. Yet it was a walk of conquest. All knew that they had done something that no other white men had done. And when Drake reached the point which juts out over the ocean, he said to Fletcher, "Preacher, do you have your plaque?"

"Yes, General," he said, mounting it on the peak.

"And what does it say?"

"Elizabeth, Queen of England, October 24, 1578!"

"And now," Drake said, "you Hood, you Diego, take my feet. I want to lean over this cliff."

"Careful, my General," Diego cautioned, as he took firm hold of a leg. And then while the sailors held his feet, Drake stretched his arms over the water. And as soon as he had been withdrawn from the precipitous peak, he said to Fletcher, who he knew was keeping a diary, "You may now record that I have been further south than any living white person!"

"And I saw it!" Fletcher declared.

"And I do hereby name these islands 'Elizabethtides'!" Drake declared, though the name would not last. Even so this island would become the most famous of them all, and it would be called Cape Horn.

CHAPTER 25

THE ISLE OF LA MOCHA

Drake noted that the weather was continuing to clear, so he reluctantly gave orders to Hood to sail north, though he did not immediately set sail for Peru. This was because he intended to make a good search for the eight-man crew of the longboat, as he was convinced that it was in the vicinity; on the other hand, he had decided that the *Elizabeth* had already set sail for Peru. He had not considered the possibility that she had set sail for England. How could he? Why, the *Elizabeth* had plenty of food, ammunition, cordage, sails and the like; then the adventure was just beginning! Why, they had not yet taken any treasure!

"What are our chances of finding them?" Hood asked, speaking to Drake, while studying his face for signs. Hood returned his eyes to the bow, and he began once more to search the horizon. It was a gray day. For the sky was so overcast that it appeared to be twilight, though it was morning.

"They're slim. But we must continue to search," Drake said, eyeing a small island which now was off the starboard bow. Hundreds of birds were soaring above it, as if waiting for a place to land.

"Tom, ask Horsewill to join us on the poop deck," Drake said to his master.

"Aye!"

"Cookie!" Drake said, speaking to Horsewill, who had joined them on the poop deck. He tightly held a large spoon in his right hand, as if he were frightened someone was going to take it. He had been stirring a pot of stew that he was making from penguin meat, leeks, onions and peas.

"Is the fire lit under your stove?" Drake asked the pudgy cook, whose face formed into a query. Drake had to know that it was lit.

For if he had glanced at the orlop chimney, he could have seen the smoke emitting from it.

"Aye, General! I'll have goose stew in a moment," Horsewill said. He called all the birds "goose"; and he cooked all birds that were brought to him, doing it irrespective of their toughness, trying to make them edible by the use of herbs and lengthy cooking.

"I will wait for eggs—I want you to boil me a half-dozen eggs."

"But we have none—" the cook suspiciously answered.

"But in an hour or so you will have plenty," Drake said, half smiling while studying the birds that were soaring above the island.

"Oh," said Horsewill, seeing the birds. "And if that be the case, then I will heat a pot of water," he said, grinning as he, too, momentarily studied the birds. Then he added, "I'll ask Bo's'n Blackcollar to give me a hand. He may be willing to fry a batch!"

And within an hour Drake led a shore party onto the island. Drake had been correct in suspecting that the ground would be covered with birds. There were so many birds on the ground that it was difficult to walk without stepping on birds or eggs. These birds included gulls, geese, shags and penguins. Drake's party went right to work. And an hour or so after landing, Drake and his landing party had harvested thousands of eggs as well as hundreds of birds. These birds and eggs were a nice addition to Horsewill's larder. They added to the cook's work—the stove was small, so the cooking was limited to Horsewill and Blackcollar. And they were kept busy. Raw eggs were for the asking, while the cooks fried and boiled eggs. They even made an omelet of penguin stew, eggs and mint.

The weather continued to clear as the *Hind* neared the western entrance to the Magellan Strait. Drake now was seated at the navigational table. He was carefully studying his Mercator map while thinking. Was the map correct? Drake knew that the map had been wrong about Terra Australia Incognita. Even so, did he have the right to question it about South America? And so he decided not to do it. Yet he would soon learn that that part of the map which depicted South America was incorrect, as it was way out of proportion. Mercator had not had the advantage of the Spanish maps; thus, he had the continent of South America as being much wider than it is, and he had placed it too far to the west.

"We will have to steer a northwesterly course," Drake said, speaking to Nuno who was seated near Drake. He, too, was studying the map.

"A course like this?" Nuno asked, using his ruler to draw a proposed course which would take them northwest. He, too, had not seen any Spanish maps of the coast of Chili.

"I agree. And then we should sight land in a few days," Drake said.

"What about Peter, General?" John Drake asked. He was referring to Peter Carder and the other men who had become lost.

"Hope for the best!" Drake solemnly said. His tone of voice made it obvious that he had decided to abandon the search.

But Drake's prophecy about sighting land proved to be wrong. For though the *Hind* sailed northwesterly for 12 days, she did not sight land. And worse, none of her lookouts had been able to sight any land signs. Drake discussed this with Hood:

"Tom, we should have sighted land."

"I agree—"

"I want the lookouts to report to me any signs of land birds such as terns, noddies or frigate birds," Drake said. Drake knew that the first two birds have a short range of flight; he as well knew that the frigate bird did not fly too far from the shore because it does not land on water; thus the sighting of any one of these birds would signify to Drake that they were near land.

"I shall advise all, General."

And thereafter, Drake would ask his lookouts again and again whether there were any signs of land.

"Up there!"

"Here, aye!"

"Any sightings of land birds?"

"No, General."

"Any land clouds?"

"None, General!" the lookout replied. The seamen like Drake were wise as to land clouds. For they knew that the color of land clouds was different from those of sea clouds, as they were brighter, and from a distance they appeared to form a V-shape over the land. This is especially so if the land is over the horizon.

"That map has to be wrong!" Drake said to Nuno on entering his cabin and going directly to the map on the table and beginning to study the bulging map of South America. "We are now at 44 degrees latitude!"

"I agree with you, for if it were correct, we would have sighted land," Nuno said on studying the plot which had been drawn on the map so as to touch land.

"I thought that we had learned that the map makers are not to be trusted!" Drake said, shaking his head, while eyeing the map. He wryed his face, made sucking noises with his lips, and then he added as a matter of explanation, "The Spanish might have given false information to the mapmakers in order to hinder persons like us who have passed through the strait from finding their coast!"

"But you know it is there!" Nuno said, meaning Peru. Nuno was speaking almost as if he were a regular member of the venture.

"Aye, I know it is there," Drake said, smiling. He could have added that he had plundered enough gold and silver from the Spanish Main, which he knew came from South America, so as to know for sure that it did exist. "We will now steer to the northeast. By doing that, we are bound to sight the coast."

And as the *Golden Hind* sailed northeast, the days grew warmer. The deck of the small ship was now crowded with men who were attempting to appear busy. All had shed their heavy jackets. The gunners were oiling their guns and sharpening pikes and swords. The bowmen waxed their bows. The seamen were removing the chafing gear and mended it wherever the ropes had come in contact with the standing rigging. Others picked oakum, which would be used for caulking the hull. Still others sat on the fo'c'sle with Fowler, the boatswain, plaiting ropes so as to make interesting handles for their sea chests and hammocks. Some would even cover stanchions with Turk's heads and the like. And Drake permitted the sick to play games such as backgammon with stones and dice.

There were 80 men and six boys presently aboard the *Hind*. The boys were of various sizes; all were larger and older than Willie Fortescue and Joey Kidd, who were the smallest boys aboard the *Hind*. These two had to attend grammar school, which was a daily school that was taught by Preacher Fletcher. They were presently learning to read English. Fletcher was teaching English by the use of a horn book, which was a primer that was framed in wood and covered with a transparent horn. It included the alphabet in small letters and capitals with a combination of the five vowels. The boys were doing so well that they had begun to read the Bible.

Many of the men were sick; all were thin and gaunt. But the cooking of Horsewill was changing that. His oven and cook pot were now turning out plenty of healthy foods. He was being assisted by Blackcollar. The two of them were now serving raw birds' eggs and boiled birds' eggs, doing it without limitation, while Preacher Fletcher went about the sick, forcing them to eat eggs, drink mint tea, and rub their limbs with warm seal oil. And once the sick were able to eat, Fletcher forced them to eat bountiful helpings of stewed and baked goose. And so most of their scurvy complaints were disappearing. Meeks, the sailmaker, and his helpers had made a new set of sails for the *Hind*, and the seamen were beginning to rig them into place while singing an improvised sea chantey.

Hey ho, hey ho,
It's off to Peru we go!

And the creaking *Hind* came alive from the voices of the singing crewmen. This was especially so when they sang the chorus.

We've come to Peru for gold—gold!
Hey ho, we've come for gold—gold!

This singing created a feeling of exhilaration amongst the crew. The strong laughed as they worked, as if sure that the bad times were in the past. And really, how could man suffer more? For had they not been through one of the worst storms known to seamen? And they had survived it, while the *Marigold* crew had not. And do not great experiences at sea make a strong crew?

And soon the *Hind* took on the appearance of normalcy. But as always, time had caused her water to sour. And the men were having to doctor it with strong portions of wine. And so Drake began to look seriously for land. Then on November 25, 1578, a top lookout sighted what appeared to be land.

"Land ho!"

"Where?" Drake shouted.

"Port bow!"

"It's a river!" Drake subsequently said, eyeing the coast referring to the indentation. This could be the place that they needed to anchor, being a place where they could pitch tents on the beach and careen the *Hind* so as to clean her hull. And so he ordered a boat put over the side. He took 10 men and reconnoitered it. But he soon discovered that there was no fresh water near the shore. And the sea water near the land was so deep that it made careening impracticable. Thus, he returned to the *Hind*, ordered her sails hoisted and they sailed north coasting the land, searching for a site that would make a good anchorage. And on the *Hind* reaching 37 degrees south, a top lookout sighted the island of La Mocha, being a sizeable island having a background of the picturesque snow-capped Andes mountains. And so Drake cautiously brought the *Hind* to within a thousand yards of shore and anchored.

Drake studied the island and noted that there were dozens of natives walking on the beach. He decided that, in order to ascertain if the natives were friendly or not, he needed to land and survey the island. Once this was done, he would decide if it were a place where the crew could fill their barrels with fresh water, and then repair and clean the *Hind*. He turned and spoke to Master Hood, who also was intently eyeing the island:

"Thomas, I would like to visit the island, establish a workable relationship with the natives and do some trading with them for water, fresh meat and vegetables. I also would like to find a good spot to careen the *Hind*, so we can do our cleaning and make our needed repairs. I will need a crew of 12 men who will be diplomatic and not create any ill will. But at the same time I will need 12 men who will fight if we have trouble!"

"Well, General, you would want me then!" Hood said, smiling, showing snaggle teeth; yet he was otherwise a fine specimen of manhood, as he was tall with wide shoulders and muscular arms. Hood was ship tired. And so he was eager to leave it for a few hours.

"Right, and—"

"Don't worry I will have the rest of the men in the boat in a quarter hour!"

On Drake and his crew of picked men landing on shore, they were met by a group of what appeared to be friendly Indians who seemingly were unarmed; however, they were unable to communicate as neither could speak the other's language. These Indians had a copper brown complexion, while their features were quite refined. Diego attempted to communicate with the Indians in Spanish:

"¡Agua! ¡Agua! ¡Necesitamos agua!" he repeatedly said, trying to explain to them in Spanish that they were in need of water. He had inadvertently done this out of habit, though Drake had cautioned the men that they were to speak to the Indians only in English, as he was of the opinion that the Spanish had abused these Indians. And he was correct; they were what was left of a nation of Indians that had lived on the mainland; the great majority of these Indians previously had been enslaved by the Spanish and forced to work in the mines. Most of those that had escaped had sought refuge on this island.

And so the Indians were suspicious of the English, thinking that they were Spanish. They thereafter practiced a deceit on Drake for they gave the appearance to him that they were receptive to Drake's entourage while they were not. They readily bartered for the hatchets, knives and brightly colored ribbons that Drake offered to them. They in turn exchanged their live sheep, chickens, maze and white potatoes, which was not yet common to England. But when Drake asked for barrels of fresh water, the Indians replied to him by sign language that he was to return the next day to a nearby creek where they would fill his barrels with water.

And on the next morning the crewmen of the *Hind* eagerly studied the shore. More men wanted to join the party than there were places. This was because all had been told that the party of Indians had included many pretty Indian women and that they had looked at the seamen with favor. The boat was quickly loaded with four barrels and a happy landing party, which consisted of Drake and his 12 men. Drake had been so impressed with the friendliness of the Indians that he had dropped all pretenses of suspicion of them. Before boarding the small boat, Drake explained his plans to the men:

"We will only take our short swords which we must keep in our scabbards—"

"And do we have enough trading goods?" Hood asked, while not mentioning Drake's failure to order bowmen or heavy artillery.

"They are already in the boat," Drake said. "There are probably not enough, but we can return," he added.

"Do we take our shields?" Hood asked, referring to the small shields that the men often wore when they were going ashore in unfamiliar places. These could be used to protect them from arrows or tossed rocks.

"Yes, bring your shields; but keep them attached to your arm. I think that these Indians are friendly; so I don't want to do anything that would destroy our present good relationship. We'll row toward that creek," Drake said on getting in the boat and taking the coxswain's position. The creek was where the Indians had pointed out that they would meet and supply them with water.

"There, see," Drake said, pointing toward a reed-lined creek. He could see Indians at the far end, and they beckoned to Drake to bring his boat to what appeared to be a good landing site. The boat touched land and Tom Brewer and Tom Hood jumped out, stepped onto the sandy shore, took the painter rope, and began to pull the boat onto shore. Then as if startled, they dropped the rope; however, an Indian quickly picked it up and pulled hard on it. The other Indians quickly encircled Tom Brewer and Hood, and they bound the hands of the Englishmen before they could draw their swords. And then they hurriedly pulled them out of the reach of the men in the boat.

"Trap!" Drake shouted.

"A-whish!" A hundred arrows were simultaneously fired at the men in the boat. These came from a hundred Indians who had raised up from their hiding places in the reeds. And they quickly reloaded their bows.

"Oh!" cried Drake and raised his left hand to his left cheek; he had been struck beneath the left eye by a silver-tipped arrow. He attempted to remove it; but it was too deeply imbedded so it hung from his face. Then he was hit in the head by a second arrow; this one so addled him that he was incapable of reasoning. And the group was in desperate need of leadership, for the Indians on the beach were pulling on the painter so as to pull the boat ashore and capture the men. John Brewer, the young trumpeter, took the lead, doing it even though he had a half dozen arrows protruding from him; for he quickly withdrew his sword and hacked the line being pulled on by the Indians. It severed!

"Pull those oars!" John Brewer shouted to John Mariner and Gregory Raymont who were less injured then the others; they quickly took up their oars and desperately rowed though the Indians contin-ued to shoot their arrows into the boat. It was soon out of their range. Yet the Indians had inflicted serious injury on the men in the boat. Drake had been wounded twice. He had a messy head injury; then he had the eye injury where the arrow was so deeply imbedded that he had been unable to withdraw it. And on the boat approaching the *Hind*, all the men and boys were on deck, having been aroused by the cries and wails that were coming from the boat.

"Oh!" they cried.

"Oh! Oh!" they screamed.

"Brothers, what ails you?" Preacher Fletcher shouted from the poop deck. His face had turned white on seeing that the walls of the boat were laced with protruding arrows, while many of its crew were slumped over one another. Some of them had arrows protruding from their throats, chests and backs.

"Ambush!" John Brewer shouted, crying unashamedly.

"Jesus help us!" Fletcher cried out in sympathy.

"Preacher, we are hurt; some are dying!" Brewer cried out. Tears were streaming down his cheeks.

"My God!" Tom Moone shouted on seeing the blood gushing from the wounds of the men in the boat. One man who was seated in a slumped position had a dozen arrows protruding from him.

"Don't cry! Don't worry!" the preacher shouted. "We'll get ye aboard—get ye well!" But it would not be so for Diego, Drake's faithful black man, as he would no longer shadow Drake. For he was dead when they lifted him from the boat. Great Neil, the Dane, who was a senior gunner, would soon die. He had received 21 arrow wounds.

"Wine! Wine!" cried Drake on two men lifting him onto the deck. He was so weak from loss of blood that he could barely stand. Yet his senses were returning. "Tom," he said to Tom Moone. "Take the boat, a dozen armed men; take your arquebuses—rescue Hood and Tom Brewer. They are prisoners of the Indians!"

"Right, General—you men there, on the double, get some hand guns. I will need 12 of you to rescue Hood and Tom Brewer!"

"And Preacher," said Drake after gulping down a cup of wine. "Take my knife, remove this arrow," he ordered, referring to the silver arrowhead that was still deeply imbedded beneath his left eye.

"My hand shakes," Fletcher replied, explaining his reluctance; and then he added, "I must go with Moone, rescue the men on the beach!"

"Nuno," Drake said in Spanish. "Take my knife, remove this arrowhead!"

"General, please, I am no surgeon. My hand would shake," Nuno said. Perplexity was on his face. He was fearful of Drake. There was so much determination in his voice. And he wanted to help. Yet he was no surgeon!

"Then give me my mirror!" Drake shouted. "Quickly!" he said, gulping wine from a newly-filled cup. "I must doctor the men!" he added. He knew that he did not have a surgeon on the *Hind*. The fleet's poorly-trained surgeon was aboard the *Elizabeth*, and she had parted the coast, leaving Drake to fulfill the venture. And the *Hind*'s acting physician was the preacher. And he had left with Moone.

"Here, General," said John Drake, the page. And he handed Drake a mirror. Then he refilled his glass with more wine.

Drake took his sheath knife, sharpened it on a honing stone; then he inserted the knife in the glass of wine. He then drank the remainder in a gulp. Then he probed the arrowhead, grimacing while he did it. Finally, he cut his cheek so the arrow could exit.

"John!" Drake said to his cousin. "Remove it—I am too weak!"

"Yes, sir," the youth said. Then he took hold of the arrow and he screwed out the arrow head. And then Drake's bleeding head fell onto his chest. John Drake raised Drake's head and put a piece of cloth to the wound so as to stop the bleeding. Drake regained his strength sufficiently so as to help bandage his head and cheek; then he said to John Drake:

"I want those men with wounds to come to my cabin—the worst first. I will remove the arrows, cleanse and dress the wounds!"

"Are you able, Sir?"

"I soon will be—bring Diego first!"

"But Diego is dead!"

"Why?"

"I know not why, sir!"

"Who else?"

"The gunner's mate, Great Neil, is dead!"

"Dead! Are there more?"

"That's all—"

"Enough—hurry John, bring me the wounded!" Drake said, as though he could not tolerate being told of another death.

On Tom Moone and his crew of armed men nearing the landing place on the creek, all were surprised to see that the landing site was now being guarded by thousands of Indians. All were armed with bows, spears, pikes and shields. Many of their weapons were decorated with silver which sparkled in the sunlight.

"Look, Preacher!" Moone shouted, pointing.

"Cannibals!" Fletcher declared on studying what was a gory sight.

Hood and Brewer were on the ground. Their feet and hands were tied. Dozens of Indians were dancing near them, while their leaders were standing over the two men. They held long knives in their hands. And then they were bestially carving up the still-alive captives. One sliced flesh from Hood's chest and flipped it to a dancing Indian, who chewed on it and then threw it at the screaming sailor.

"God help me!"

"Save me, General!" Brewer cried. "He's cuttin' off my nose!" he screamed as the blood blinded him.

"We're here!" Moone shouted. Yet they would not be of any assistance. They had to stay out of arrow range, and because of the numbers, Moone dared not order the boat to go any closer. But he wished he could do something, so out of frustration he said to the armed men:

"Fire at them!"

"Boom!" they fired as one.

"Reload and fire!" Moone ordered, even though he knew that it was not having any effect, as there was too much distance between them. Then the arquebus was actually a primitive weapon. It was loaded by tamping powder into its barrel, then shot was loaded and then more powder; pebbles and the like were tamped into it; then wadding was tamped into the barrel; one man usually held the barrel or it was rested on a metal rod. The weapon holder then struck a flint or passed fire to the touch hole so as to ignite the powder. Its accuracy was very poor. Much depended on the loading.

"Boom!" Two men actually fired again. But the firing was a waste, for the Indians, on seeing the men raise their guns to fire, dropped flat on the ground, and the shot harmlessly passed over them. And then the Indians resumed their cannibalistic rite of cutting the flesh from the two sailors and throwing it in the air, which they would then catch and eat.

"We cannot save them; and they could not live if we did!" Moone said while staring at the cannibals. Then he added, "But we can punish them. Let's return to the *Hind*—request the use of the deck guns!"

"Aye!"

And on Tom Moone returning to the *Hind*, he hurriedly entered Drake's cabin; he was surprised to find Drake on his feet. He appeared tired and exhausted; yet he was performing surgery on John Brewer, the trumpeter, who had received 12 arrow wounds; many were still imbedded in his body. Each appeared to be made of different material, as the Indians used a variety of arrowheads. Some were tipped with iron; others were tipped with bone, silver or stone.

"General," Moone said on entering Drake's cabin. "I'm glad that you are on your feet, but I am sorry that we were unable to rescue Hood and Brewer!"

"Not able!" Drake angrily said on quickly turning his head, causing his wound to reopen. Blood ran down his cheek.

"No, there must have been two thousand savages on the beach—we did not dare get within range of their arrows. I would like to request permission to bring up the great guns, mount them, move in close, and let them have it!"

"No!" declared Drake.

"But, General, they are cutting 'em up, eatin' 'em alive! You would not believe it!"

"But it would be wrong to do it!" Drake said while steeling his face; yet tears were in his eyes.

"Wrong?" Moone asked. His tone of voice showed his lack of understanding of Drake's answer. His first loyalty was to his ship and that included shipmates. That meant fighting for them. He had climbed the rigging with both men. Each was a first-class sailor. Neither cold nor wet had deterred either from carrying his load.

"I know how you feel, Tom. But they thought we were Spaniards!" Drake explained while staring out a window at the beach.

"But they've cannibalized two of our men, killed two, wounded you!" Moone replied. His voice was hard and uncompromising. His eyes were steeled while his face was tight and determined.

"But it would not serve our purpose; other Englishmen will come this way after us—they may need their help. And if we turn the culverins on them, our countrymen would never be able to make a friend of them. We'll save the culverins for use on the Spaniards!"

CHAPTER 26

A MOUNTAIN OF SILVER

The *Hind* was now a quiet ship—even the tiny mess cooks hardly spoke when they stoked Horsewill's fire—they were too glum. The four deaths had been to them like losing four brothers. The gloom continued because so many crewmen were ill from arrow wounds. One of the sickest was Drake. He was at times so feverish that he did not understand the reports that he received from Moone, who was acting as master. The reader will recall that Tom Hood had been killed at La Mocha. It was now November 30, 1578. The *Hind* was coasting in a northerly direction.

"Land ho!" a top lookout shouted.

"What, aye!" Moone replied.

"Yonder!" The lookout pointed to a bay that Moone would subsequently learn was Quintero. Moone stood on the portico deck outside Drake's cabin and carefully studied the bay until the *Hind* had reached a point so that she could make a cut and enter it. Then Moone entered Drake's cabin. Drake was lying on his bunk. He held a water-soaked rag to his cheek, which was red from fever. The wound on the top of his head was healing; however, the wound beneath his left eye had worsened. It was now infected and emitting a foul odor. Drake half awoke from a fitful sleep on hearing Moone's voice. His mind at first had interpreted it as a voice of Panama!

"John, what did you say?" He thought that the voice was that of John Oxenham.

"General," Moone said, "we have sighted what appears to be a nice bay off the starboard bow. I would like permission to take the *Hind* into it; then I would like to take a boat, survey it for fresh water, fruit and herbs. The sick can use them."

231

"Oh," Drake said, half opening his eyes. His mind had begun to clear from a deep stupor. And then his vision cleared, and he was able to see and study his master's pocked face, which was made more interesting by his snaggle smile. When Moone was a boy, he had had smallpox. It had left his face pocked with scars that were in the shape of tiny moon-like craters. Drake was not put back in the slightest by Moone's ugly countenance. He saw in him a brotherly at arms beauty that can only be appreciated by men who have gone to war and suffered together from its depredations. Why, he was the ideal soldier! He was absolutely loyal, while he was manly—as well, his fears were minimal. "Yes," Drake said on waking. "But be careful—and make friends with the Indians. They probably have some good herbal remedies!"

Moone anchored the *Hind* in 20 feet of water; then he and ten armed men took the longboat and rowed for shore. Drake fortunately had made use of the *Mary*'s longboat on salvaging her; thus, the *Golden Hind* had had two longboats when she traversed the Magellan Strait. And so, the *Hind* had not been made boatless when Carder and the other seven men became lost. The shore appeared to be devoid of Indians. However, near the shore there was an Indian who was seated in a strange reed boat that was tub-like, where he was fishing with a pole. Moone steered his boat toward the Indian.

"¡Hola!" Hello! Moone greeted the Indian. "Soy inglesia—no espanol." I am English; I am not Spanish, Moone said, attempting to make it clear that the men were not Spanish.

"¡Hola!" the Indian replied and extended both hands in an empty gesture as if trying to show that that was the extent of his knowledge of Spanish. Then he pointed toward the shore and began to row for it.

"Tenemos muchos navigantes enfermos," Moone said, following the Indian, pointing to the *Hind*, and using sign language to inform the Indian that there were many men on the *Hind* who were ill. "Our men were ambushed by Indians," he said in Spanish, as he landed the long boat and stepped ashore. He held in his hands an arquebus. The Indian had already landed his strange boat and was standing on the beach. He was unarmed and obviously afraid of Moone, as it showed on his face.

The Indian nervously walked away from the Englishman and toward a wooded area. Then he stopped and turned back toward Moone. He frowned and once again he used his hands to indicate that he did not understand. Then he pointed so as to indicate to Moone that he had to leave but that he would return to this site. And then he proceeded to walk toward a clearing that was in the midst of a wooded area. And about 20 minutes later the Indian returned with another Indian who seemed to be in his middle years. He had a light copper-colored complexion which was very sallow. He had a round face, small, animated eyes, a handsome mouth, and even white teeth. He was dressed in a cotton white gown that came to his knees. He wore over his shoulders a woolen pancho. He as well wore sandals. His braided hair was snow white, while the first Indian had braided hair that was black as ebony. The Indian with the white hair eyed the white men with apprehension.

"Jefe!" Chief! said the Indian as a matter of introduction. The chief warily approached the white men.

"Mi nombre es Felipe." My name is Felipe, the chief said. He spoke excellent Spanish.

"Somos ingleses." We are English, Moone said, adding in Spanish, "We are not Spanish. We are English. We want peace with the Indians. We have many sick men on our ship," he said, pointing. "Five days before in the south, our men were ambushed by Indians— they were shot by arrows. Some have wounds that are infected. We need medicine, fresh vegetables, fruit and water. Can you help?"

"Well," the chief answered in Spanish, pondering, as if studying his options. And truly he was being torn. For one part of him was telling himself to flee from these white men, while the other was saying to him to help them as he was a herb doctor. "Our supply of fruit and vegetables is not good, and this is not a good watering place. But I know of a herb that may help. Wait!" he said, and then he walked back the way that he had come. He had made his choice.

Moone and his crew sat or stood on the shore in a state of readiness. Bowmen stood with their bows and arrows ready to be fired in seconds. Their arquebuses were loaded and setting in readiness in the boat near four seated men with oars in their hands. But their apprehension was unnecessary, for an hour after Felipe departed, he returned alone, carrying an armload of what appeared to be weeds.

"You must shred the flower onto a poultice," Felipe said, speaking in Spanish, referring to the strange, moldy spores on the end of each plant. Then he added, "Then you must place them on the wound. I assure you that it will clean the wound of rot!"

233

"Could you come to our ship?" Moone humbly asked. He motioned for the men with him to be at ease, and then he asked, "I would like for you to meet and doctor our captain. He is an interesting man. We will pay you—we will give you many presents."

"Well," the chief hesitantly said; then he beckoned to the Indian to whom Moone had first spoken. He was standing alone near the clearing as if he were too frightened of the white men to come any nearer. The chief walked over to him, and they began to whisper. They seriously conversed for five minutes, then the chief returned to Moone and calmly said to him, "I will go with you."

And on the longboat reaching the *Hind*, Moone escorted Felipe to Drake's cabin. Drake was still lying on his back, being half asleep. He was holding a wet rag to his injured cheek; it was fiery red from infection.

"General," Moone softly said on entering and turning, while extending an open hand of introduction. "This is Chief Felipe. He speaks Spanish. I met him on the beach. He agreed to come aboard with his herbs and doctor you; he says that they will help you if they are properly used in a poultice."

"Thank you, Chief," Drake said in Spanish while rising so that he rested on his elbow; then he raised himself so that he was in a sitting position. "Would you like something to eat or drink?"

"No," the chief replied and crossed over to Drake and lifted the rag resting on Drake's face. "Es malo." It is bad, he said, frowning.

"I will need a clean cloth on which to put the herbs—"

"You wish to cook them?" Moone asked, pointing to the door. The herbs were in a pile on the poop deck.

"No—get me a clean cloth and I will show you how to use them," Felipe surely said, as though the preparation were very important.

And on receiving the clean cloth, Felipe soaked it in a pan of water. Then he took one of the long, leggy plants, and he held it out so Drake could examine it. It was unusual in many ways. Its flowery end had thousands of tiny, sporey, mold-like flowers. Felipe utilized his fingers and gently removed the moldy spores onto the cloth; then he carefully laid it on Drake's cheek. "Don't move, General!"

"I understand—" Drake replied in a submissive voice.

"The others?" Moone asked, referring to the other injured crew members.

"Take me to them; I will then show you how to treat them."

234

An hour later Felipe returned to Drake's cabin. He eyed Drake and then he lifted the poultice from Drake's face.

"Do you have to leave?" Drake asked the chief.

"Well, not really," Felipe said, gently putting the rag back on Drake's face. He had answered as though time were unimportant. The rag now was covered with thousands of the moldy spores, being the fruit of a herb that Drake had never seen. Yet it had tremendous medicinal power as it was the herb *penicillium*.

"Do you know this coast?" Drake asked.

"Oh, yes—" Felipe answered, looking deeply into Drake's gray eyes, which were carefully studying the Indian as if he wanted to know more about him. Drake had decided that Felipe was much younger than his gray hair would indicate.

Felipe took Drake's left arm and held it while counting Drake's pulse.

"It is fast!"

"Probably," Drake said, not knowing how to answer this herb doctor. "And do you know where we can get fresh water and fruit?"

"Oh, yes—but not here. Fruit and water are scarce!"

"And could you show such a place to my men?"

"I could—but?"

"I would reward you."

"It would take many days!" Felipe replied and shook his head.

And so the Indian chief remained at Drake's bedside, being a very dutiful nurse to Drake, which was in keeping with his training as he was a machis, being a herb doctor. He slept on a pallet beside Drake's bunk, and during the night, he changed the poultice several times so that the rag stayed filled with fresh moldy spores from the *penicillium* plants, and he dutifully counted Drake's pulse from time to time. And on the next morning when the sun had begun to beam through a window, Drake awoke. He opened his eyes to see his Indian nurse standing near him.

"¿Como esta usted?" How are you? the chief asked in a soft voice.

"Muy bien." Very good, Drake truthfully replied. And it was with reason, for it was the first time in days that he had been free of fever.

"You will now get well," Felipe confidently said. "The fruit of the herb has already drawn out most of the sickness in your face," he said while touching Drake's face. "Now," he said to John Drake, who

235

also had slept on the floor. "The General needs a good breakfast so that he can get himself strong. Please get it for him," he politely said.

"We're under way!" Drake said, feeling the rock of the ship and hearing the flap, flap movement of sails. And so he knew that the ship had raised its anchor and was sailing north. "And you are going to find us fresh water?"

"Yes, I will guide you."

"Where are your people?" Drake asked.

"All are gone, dead—or enslaved at Potosi!" he said and sadly shook his head.

"Potosi!" Drake repeated. The name had a mysterious connotation to it. On the Spanish Main, he had heard the Cimarons speak of Potosi. They had related to him that the Spanish silver came from a mine in Peru named Potosi. But they could not tell him the exact location of the mine. And this was with reason, for they did not know, not many Cimarons did, as the Spanish were very secretive as to the sources of their riches.

"And why have you come here?" Felipe asked.

"Fight the Spaniards," Drake wryly said, adding "We have come to take from them their ill-gotten gold and silver!"

"Are the English crazy for gold?"

"Well, not really—" Drake softly said, wrying his face, trying not to show his avarice.

"The Spaniards are crazy for gold and silver; and they have much. They have much more silver. Potosi is a mountain of silver!"

"A mountain of silver?" Drake exclaimed, and he shook his head in awe. Drake was seated on his bed and leaning against the cabin bulkhead. He was looking directly at Felipe, but he could also look through the window at the stern and see the sea.

"Yes. It was in 1545 that a Quechua Indian in the high mountains discovered a mountain of silver. But he did not get to keep it, for the Spaniards soon thereafter took it from him; and they built a city at the foot of it, which they named Potosi," he said. "It is a high city," he added, referring to the fact that it was located at 14,000 feet above sea level, and the altitude had created numerous problems, for the air was very thin due to its lack of oxygen.

"Is it far?" Drake asked.

"It is in the mountains," Felipe said, pointing to Drake's right, being the starboard side. "If you were to look outside this cabin, you could see the mountains. They are there. It is a difficult place to live for a low-lander like me, as I am Maupuche," he repeated, referring to a tribe of people that were a part of the Araucanian nation who then inhabited the coastal lands from 36.44 to 39.50 south latitude. "The Spaniards say that the city of Potosi is located at 14,000 feet, while the mountain of silver near it is 3,000 feet above Potosi."

"A mountain of silver!" Drake said again in a show of disbelief. And he eagerly licked his dry lips which had become chapped from the fever.

"Yes, it holds inside it millions of tons of silver; the Spaniards say that its ore is almost pure silver."

"And how did you and your people end up being enslaved and working in the mines?" Drake asked. His face was less lined, indicating that he was enjoying the conversation.

"Six years ago a dozen Spanish soldiers on horseback came in a fury to our village. The noise from their trumpeters and drummers terrified us, for we are a peaceful people. They carried banners of Spain and the church, which waved above their spiked helmets. And they were flanked by many ferocious hunting dogs which would have eaten us alive except chains kept them from doing it. The soldiers ordered me and my people to be prepared to leave within an hour."

"And how many were there of you?"

"We were 126 men, women and children. We were Maupuche. We lived near the sea. We spoke the Araucanian language," he said, again repeating his race of people, as he was obviously quite proud of it. "We were marched up the mountain to the city of Potosi, which is a pretty city located on the mountainside. I had never seen anything like it. Beside it, there is the mountain of silver which is shaped like a pyramid. We were first assigned to mud huts at the foot of the mountain. There were no beds—we slept on the floor. The altitude bothered all of us very much. It made me dizzy; my stomach hurt; I had poor balance. The very next day we were ordered outside where there was a large pot in which mutton stew was cooking. Each of us was ordered to eat a bowl of it. Many were too ill; then each of us was given a handful of coca leaves, which we were told to chew. I readily chewed it, as I had been told that it has marvelous effects on the body. I sat near my wife and children on a rock; all of us chewed coca leaves while enjoying the heat of the sun which was taking away the chill, as it is quite cold in the morning at Potosi. After we had chewed coca for an hour, our guards ordered us to march for the mountain of silver, which as I have said before, is shaped like a pyramid. And it appeared to be just a short distance away, but actually it is several miles. On walking, I felt much better, but I was still dizzy. Then we had to climb the mountain. We passed many holes in the side of the mountain, which are called shafts. These are used to enter the mine and extract the silver. The mine has many tunnels in it; these take one to the heart of the mountain. And from the heart, there are many tunnels that go up and down. One can easily get himself lost."

"Excuse me, Chief, but John has my breakfast," Drake said, taking a wooden tray which held a bowl of cooked prunes that had been sprinkled with sugar, a bowl of steamed rice and two hoe cakes topped with marmalade that had been cooked by Blackcollar. The tray also held Drake's monogrammed cup which had been filled with red wine.

"Eat, eat. It will give you strength!" Felipe said.

"But continue with your story."

"Well, near the top of the mountain, we were led to a hole that went into the side of the mountain. It had a dozen mud huts on the outside of it. These would be the homes for those of us that lived. A guard said to us:

"'One woman will remain at these houses. She will keep the children under six years of age; the rest of you will receive more coca leaves, which you may chew for 30 minutes; then you must enter the mine and work. This is your Minka!' he said, referring to the Inca custom of Minka, where an Inca had to work for his land. But we were not Incas. As I have said, we were Maupuches, being flat-landers.

"'Will we be paid?' I asked.

"'Yes—each adult will be paid according to the amount of ore extracted—each child will receive one half of what an adult would receive!'

"'When will we be paid?'

"'At the end of six months, when your contract is up!' he said. Yet I learned that that was a lie, for we were slaves.

"General, when we were kidnapped to work in the mines, I was married to a strong, healthy woman; yet she was pregnant and we had three children: 7, 9, and 12 years of age. All of us worked in the mines from about seven in the morning until seven or eight at night. And during this time, we never ate any food."

238

"Why?" Drake asked. He was now seated on his bunk eating. Tom Moone and Reverend Fletcher were standing near the door. Nuno was seated at the chart table beside John Drake, who was sketching a picture of the mine. All were intently listening to the chief.

"The coca leaf is a magical plant. It kills the desire for food; then the inside of the mine smells so strongly of chemicals that it causes the food to lose its taste."

"And your family?" Drake asked. His face had curiosity to it, indicating that he was touched by the story.

"Two weeks after we entered the mine, my wife gave early delivery of our fourth child. Three days later she and the baby died. We buried them in mine waste outside the mine. And within two months of her death, all of my boys were dead, as they seemingly had lost interest in living. And as well, over half of the other members of our village were dead. This had some effect on the guards, for they changed our work week to one week in the mine and one week outside the mine. While we were outside the mine, we worked with a hammer, breaking the ore. And it was there that I learned Spanish from my Spanish guard. And after I became knowledgeable in Spanish, I was assigned as a boss to a shift of workers in the Ingenerous, which is located at the foot of the mountain. It is there that the ore is crushed, separated and washed with quick silver. It forces the silver to the bottom. And later I was transferred to the mint—"

"Mint?" Drake asked, showing his surprise that a mint would be located in such a difficult-to-reach city.

"Yes, because Potosi produces the majority of Spain's silver, it has the royal mint. I was told by the Spanish soldiers that King Philip uses these coins to pay his soldiers that are stationed in Europe. We had great wooden machines in the mint that were turned by mules. We took many of the silver bars, flattened them into strips, then we stamped coins from them. We shipped these coins to Spain in heavy metal boxes with many locks on them. All of the bars of silver are supposed to go through the mint so as to be counted. And when this is done, the King takes one-fifth of the silver; thus, many miners secretly try to avoid the mint. I became friendly with a Quecha woman who worked for the Santandia family; she told me that the Santandias smuggled a considerable amount of silver down the mountain and to the coast. This family, like all other rich miners, has its own portrait painter. He is a Spaniard who lives in a hacienda near theirs, which is very large and richly ornamented. The Christian churches also have many gorgeous paintings that have been painted by these artists. The Spaniards say that Potosi is the richest city in this world."

"And you escaped?" Drake asked.

"Yes, it seems that it would be easy to do, but it is not, for there are many soldiers at Potosi; and they keep a watch on the steep passes, which one must use to come and go to Potosi; and you might want to know why the miners can smuggle silver to the coast and an Indian not escape. Well, the miners ship their private silver to the coast without being molested, because they have the help of the soldiers. And the soldiers have the help of those huge dogs to search out and find escaping Indians. And when the soldiers capture an Indian who has escaped, they give him 50 lashes with a black whip; then they return him to the mine, never to leave again. I did not want to do that, as it would have been a quick death. Anyway, most miners die early from a cough caused by the dust."

"But you did escape?"

"Yes, but I did it in Arica. I did it after I was transferred to a job on the silver caravan that travels from Potosi to Arica, which is in the north—it is on the coast. Once we descended the mountains, I escaped, found a seaman with a small boat, sailing to Valparaso. And I paid him to smuggle me to Valparaso. It would have been very difficult to have done it by land because the land for some way south of Arica is desert."

"Now I see," Drake said, indicating that he had an understanding of the silver movement.

"You know of these caravans, General?" Felipe asked, wondering how much Drake knew about it.

"No, but I know of others," Drake said, wryly smiling as if recalling the caravans that traveled from Panama City to Nombre Dios, which he and his men had attacked.

"Well—"

"How much silver did your caravan bring to Arica?"

"Maybe 100,000 coins and tons of silver that were in bars. But each caravan is different. Many have less."

"And was it well-guarded?"

"Yes—there were many soldiers—do you wish to take their silver?" Felipe asked and expectantly raised his brown eyebrows while awaiting Drake's answer.

"Yes. We wish to punish the Spaniards by taking from them their silver and gold which they have gained by such cruel methods."

"I can help you, General!" Felipe said, nodding and bitterly frowning.

CHAPTER 27

THE *LA CAPITAINE*

On December 1, 1578, being the day after Drake had had the lengthy conversation with the Indian Chief Felipe, he reversed the *Hind*'s course and he gave orders to sail her south for Valparaso. Felipe had sworn to Drake that if he did, he not only would find fresh water and fruit, but he would also find a large ship which would be carrying much treasure.

"Este barco es muy grande." This ship is very large, Felipe had surely said, frowning and gesticulating with his hands, attempting to dramatize its importance. "You will be pleased!"

"Are you sure that it will be there?" Drake asked. He did not fully believe Felipe; as really, he did not fully trust anyone, though he knew that so far the Indian chief had been truthful, especially as to his medical care, for the poultice with which he had doctored him had done wonders in healing his wounds.

"Yes—the places where it stops are well-known to all—the ship is the *La Capitaine*. And I am sure that we are going to find her in or near Valparaso. This ship was once the flagship of Pedro Gamboa, the explorer. It is said that this ship was with the Spaniard Gamboa when he discovered a group of islands in the South Sea, which he named The Solomons. But it is now a trading ship. And because of that it most likely will have aboard it a considerable amount of gold being shipped from the mines of Valdavia."

"Will it have soldiers on it?" Drake curiously asked, thinking. Drake did not intend to risk his men unduly at this stage of the venture, as he could not afford to lose many more men. He suspected that in time he would possibly lose one-tenth of his crew due to the vicissitudes of the voyage. However, the loss of more would destroy his fighting ability unless he found the *Elizabeth*.

"No—its crew will be small."

"Would you like to lead the attack, Tom?" Drake asked his master, Tom Moone, who was leaning on the chart table; the muscles in his arms had tightened at the question, wondering. Moone knew that it was the kind of assault in which Drake normally excelled. Drake had proven to him on many occasions that he enjoyed hand-to-hand combat. However, he knew that Drake could not presently lead it. For even though his wounds were healing, he was still too weak to do any climbing or fierce fighting. And so Moone smiled and nodded his head. "We will search the bays," Drake said, pointing. "But I suspect that we are going to find her in Valparaso."

"Yes, General, I'll do it—do we need to mount the culverins?" Moone asked. He was referring to the great guns that were in the holds and presently being used as ballast. They fired a 15-pound shot. Many rounds of shot had been stowed in racks near where the guns were normally positioned. Some were made of stone; others were made of iron.

"No," Drake replied. "We will approach her at night. We'll anchor near her, then we will use the longboat to pull alongside her—use maybe 15 men, quickly board her—and take her. We will thereafter use her as a store ship," Drake said. Then he quickly added, "We'll put some of the men on her," saying it as though he already had her in hand. "This will give us more room."

"And when do you think that we will meet her?" Moone asked, rubbing his fingers in anticipation.

"Tomorrow—the day after—we will attack shortly after sundown on the day that we meet," Drake said. He was now studying a poorly drawn map of the coast of Chile. This map had been drawn by Drake from information furnished by Felipe.

"Right," Moone said. "I will put together a crew of soldiers—I shall begin training them right away."

And shortly after Moone had this conversation with Drake, he mustered most of the crew on the forward deck. He exempted from the call the master gunner, the carpenter, the cook, the sailmaker, the boatswain, and the cooper, as he considered these men, most of whom were artisans, to be too valuable to take part in such a boarding. He had just informed the assembled men that in a day or two he expected the Golden Hind to meet a valuable ship.

"And when we do meet her she most likely will be anchored; she will make a good prize, as we think that she has aboard her some

244

valuable cargo as well as treasure. Who of you would like to board her with me?" he asked, lisping his words, while smiling and displaying his vacant teeth.

"Me!" all shouted. Those doing the shouting also included several boys. One of these was nine-year-old Willie Fortescue, who was the smallest person aboard, being still a boy, though he had strong arms and a developing chest. He was standing beside Joey Kidd, who was now an inch taller than Willie. Each was dressed in ragged short pants and a sleeveless shirt. They were standing on the first row.

"Not you boys!" Moone said, waving his hand in their direction.

"Rats!" Willie said, frowning while turning to leave. Dejection was on his face. He was growing strong, as he spent much of his free time climbing in the rigging. He was adventurous and fearless, for he often played hide-and-seek with the other boys below deck, hiding in the rat-ridden holds that were deep in the ship.

"Bully for you men!" Moone replied to the enthusiastic men who had shouted their approval. Their faces were now beaming from the thought of the attack. Most now saw this assault as an opportunity to break the monotony of the voyage. Many had joined the venture with the hope that they could do some fighting with the Spanish—their experience so far had been adventurous but they had not yet been able to do any fighting with the Spanish. Now they would have the chance. There could even be gold. "Well, we'll need 15 or 20 of you to capture the cross back," Moone said, using the English colloquialism for the Spaniard. Moone was notoriously anti-Catholic. "Those of you who were wounded at La Moocha will step over to my right," he said, pointing.

"Why?" John Brewer asked, speaking in an offended voice, holding his hand to his leg as he limped to join seven other men.

"You're crook!" Moone said, meaning still not well. "Don't worry—you'll have plenty of chances to fight, as this is a long coast. And the General plans to use you all."

"That's better," a wounded sailor said, frowning to show his displeasure.

"I will need 15 men from you men who are left. Which of you want to go?" he asked, indicating that he wished for a show of hands. All raised a hand.

"I will make my decision later as to who goes," Moone said, adding, "but bully for you," Moone added, grinning, then he contorted his face into the Devon grin. He removed it and then he added, "Firstly, I will explain to you what I expect from men on a boarding party. We normally board from the bow or the stern by the use of our grappling hooks; but because those men on this ship will think that we are friends, we will board differently; so a part will go up the ladder. You will not show your weapons until we board. And once we are alongside, you then must move swiftly. Those of you not going up the sea ladder with me will cast your grappling hooks upon deck and hand over hand, up you will go! You must move. And you must not lose your weapons—have your knife in your mouth. Look fierce and be fierce. Be ready to attack!" he said, lisping his words because of his missing teeth.

"Do we kill first?"

"Well—follow me, listen for my whistle—I will blow it if they surrender. Otherwise, use your weapons—take the ship. We have learned that if you move fast without hesitating, the crew is more apt to surrender. Understand?"

"Aye!"

"No killing after they surrender!" Moone warned. "But do not let anyone escape. They could alarm the people in the nearby town which we will want to search. There could be treasure there!"

The *Hind* sailed south, making searches of each bay because Felipe had informed Drake that the *Spaniard* likewise stopped in many of the bays. And these searches were taking more time than Drake had anticipated. So finally, on December 5, the *Hind* entered Valparaso harbor. Its principal town, Valparaso, was small, being situated on a broad bay. Those ships that anchored in the bay had a fairly good shelter from southerly and westerly winds, but they were open to those winds from the north. Felipe had assured Drake that the town did not have much of a defense.

"Ship!" shouted the lookout from the top of the mainmast.

"That is the *La Capitaine*, General!" Felipe said. He was standing to himself on the poop deck, pointing to a ship that was anchored near the shore. It appeared to be slightly larger than the *Golden Hind*.

"Bring her in slowly, Master Moone," Drake said, standing on the poop deck near Moone, who had his left hand on the whip staff, while his right hand was presently turning the half-hour sand glass. "I want to anchor near her, but not do it until nightfall. And Tom," Drake added. "No men are to be on deck but the top men and the handlers," Drake said. He did not want to alarm the sailors on the *La*

Capitaine by pointing out to them the number of men that the *Hind* was carrying. Numbers could give her away. But the *Hind's* lines would not give her away—for her gun ports were closed so that she had the appearance of a merchantman. There was nothing on her exterior to indicate that she was a man of war. For her deck guns were down below deck being used as ballast.

And so it was dusty dark when the *Hind* came within 100 yards of the Spanish ship and anchored.

"Boom! Boom! Boom!" arose a rhythmic noise from the *La Capitaine*.

"Drums!" exclaimed Drake. "But it does not sound like a call to arms," he added, after he carefully listened.

"It is the cajun," Felipe explained. "The *La Capitaine* has some African Negroes in her crew. One is beating on the bottom of a drawer from a cabinet. It is a friendly call to feast and drink wine. See the fire?" he said, pointing to the ship. "They probably have killed a sheep and are roasting it. I would think that they have a cask of red wine for your men," he said, smiling, showing his pleasure at the thought of the expected attack. And Felipe was correct. There was a cask of wine near the fire and ready to be opened.

"And we will enjoy it once the ship is ours," Drake said, while thoughtfully smiling. "Tom," he said, speaking to the man standing near him. A comparison between the two is interesting. Drake was short to middle height; yet Moone was two inches shorter. But height was not a consideration—each was a fierce fighter. Moone was muscular, as was Drake. And so one would compliment the other in a fight. But Moone had one advantage over Drake, as he was a carpenter, being very clever with tools. For he could make weapons work when they had failed. Then Drake said, "Are your men ready?"

"Yes, General—" Moone replied. He was very well armed. He wore a short sword and a long knife; a pistol was in his belt; he carried a small shield that was made of metal.

"How many men do you intend to use?"

"Eighteen, plus myself—"

"That is too many—the number could arouse suspicion!"

"But so many wanted to go—and it is dark. They will not know our number until we are aboard."

"Very well—limit your conversation to Spanish!" Drake said, adding, in a solemn voice, "Let us bow our heads for prayer. "Dear God, we now begin a mission against the evil Spaniards—we do this in hopes that we will stop their wanton ways and their false worship of idols. Bless these men and guide them in the task they have before them on this night. Amen!"

"Board your boat—and good luck!"

The *La Capitaine* like Felipe had explained was known to every Indian on the coast; it was not just because of her history of exploration, or because she was a stately appearing ship, though she now had dropped down in the world. It was because she was a coastal freighter. Many of the people on the coast of Chile depended on her for mail and shipping. Sometimes they sailed on her as passengers. She was as large as the *Golden Hind*, though she carried a much smaller crew, being eight Spaniards and three Negroes. One of the latter was rhythmically beating a cajun, being the bottom of a drawer. The crew was expecting visitors. A fire burning in a tub on the deck had burned down to hot coals; a sheep had been put on a spit that hung over it; and it was roasting and emitting an aromatic odor of cooking meat.

"¡Hola!" a Spaniard shouted from the deck.

"¡Hola!" Moone replied from the boat as he tied it to the sea ladder.

"Crack! Crack!" sharply sounded grappling hooks as they hooked to the gunwales of the ship. A keen listener could have detected the sound of feet against the hull as climbers ascended the ropes.

"¿Que es eso?" What is that? a Spaniard asked. The speaker was Hernando Lamero, the master. He had just tapped the butt of wine that set near the fire; then he had tasted it and found it to be satisfactory. And he was now crossing the deck to greet what he thought were fellow Spaniards, who possibly had news of Spain and would relate stories to him while all ate roast mutton and drank red wine, which any good Spaniard could appreciate as it was the color of a valuable ruby while its taste was fit for a monk.

"¡Abajo perros!" Down dogs! Moone shouted. "¡A prisa! ¡A prisa!" Hurry! Hurry! he demanded.

"English!" Lamero shouted. Then he crumpled to the floor and cowered, as the English sailors swarmed onto the deck with drawn swords, arquebuses and bows in hand. Many had small knives between their teeth.

"Stop that man!" a sailor shouted in English.

248

A sailor was running the length of the ship toward the stern. And before anyone could fire, he dived into the water and frantically swam for the shore.

"Shall we go after him, Tom?" a sailor shouted.

"Not yet!" Moone replied. "Let's put these men in a cargo hold. Then we will get him!"

"¡Abajo!" Down! Moone continued to shout, as he directed the herding of the remaining ten men to a cargo hold. When Moone had locked the *La Capitaine* crew in the small compartment, he climbed back to the main deck; then he took an ember from the fire and waved it in the air so as to indicate to Drake that the ship was secure.

"You, you," Moone said, pointing to a dozen men. "Join me in the longboat; we need to capture that sailor before he alarms the town. Here is the General!" he exclaimed, pointing to the dinghy that was approaching the captured ship.

"Is the ship secure?" Drake asked on the dinghy bumping the longboat.

"The ship is secure—it had an eleven-man crew; ten are locked in the forward hold—the eleventh man jumped into the water. We're going to get him!" Moone explained.

"Have you made any sort of search of the ship?" Drake asked as the longboat was pulling away.

"No—"

"I will make the search," Drake said, stepping from the dinghy and onto the sea ladder.

"There is a sheep on the spit which smells good. General, save us a side!" Moone said as the longboat pulled away from the ship; then he ordered his men, "Row hard, men!"

But Moone would not be able to overtake the seaman who had dived in the water. For he was an extraordinary swimmer; he swam so hard that he reached the shore ahead of the longboat.

"¡Piratas! ¡Inglesia Piratas!" Pirates! English pirates! the swimmer shouted on landing, then while running from house to house. "Hide your valuable things; then run for the hills!" he shouted again and again while momentarily turning to stare at the saucer-like harbor, searching it for the boat that he knew was now looking for him.

"¡Alli!" There! he shouted, pointing to the wake of the longboat that now was aimed for the tiny village. "¡Prisa! ¡Prisa!" Hurry! Hurry!

And since many of the villagers were dealers in smuggled gold and silver, they usually kept large amounts of it in their houses. This occasion was no exception. They as well kept themselves in a state of readiness so they could readily evacuate it. They quickly threw their gold and silver in sacks and ran for the precipitous hills that rose from the shore. And so when Moone's boat touched land, he discovered that there was no one in the village. Moone ordered a house search, but found nothing of value; then he came to a large warehouse which was locked. He broke the lock with his hatchet.

"The lantern!" he said, speaking to Preacher Fletcher, who was acting as his aid while carrying the lantern. And he did it well, as he never left his side. "Hold it high, Preacher!"

"Wine, Tom," the preacher said. There were hundreds of clay jugs, which from first look appeared to be wine jugs.

"Flour, salt pork," Preacher Fletcher said, pointing out items that were part of the stores. "And we can use them."

"We will stay here. Guard it for the night," Moone said. "In the morning we will help ourselves to these stores in order to re-victual the *Hind*." Moone then ordered four of the men to return to the *La Capitaine*. "Report to the General that the village is deserted. We have captured a warehouse that is filled with provisions. We will stay here and guard it until morning—ask him for part of the mutton. Tell him that we have plenty of wine!"

Drake made a peremptory search of the Spanish ship. He quickly discovered that she was carrying a cargo of timber and Chilean wine. But that did not satisfy him, as he was mainly interested in gold and silver. For he was as just as avaricious as the Spanish in his craving for gold and silver.

"Bring me the master!" Drake ordered a nearby sailor. Minutes later Hernando Lamero was standing before Drake. He had a swarthy complexion; his hair was in his face. His cheeks were puffy—a scowl was on his face. Dried blood as well was on his face. He hatefully stared at Drake.

"¿Donde esta su oro y plata?" Where is your gold and silver? Drake asked.

"¡No tengo!" I have none! he answered. And he hatefully glared at Drake.

"¡Sus orejas entonces!" Your ears then! Drake shouted, removing his knife from its scabbard and waving it in a threatening manner

250

at the master's ears as if he intended to remove them. The knife gave the appearance that it was sharp and had been often used.

"¡En mi cuarto!" In my cabin! he exclaimed, confessing that he had treasure.

"¡Vamos!" Let's go! Drake ordered, jabbing at the master with his knife. And the master led Drake to his cabin where he pointed to three strong boxes that Drake quickly opened; each was filled with very valuable Valdavian gold.

"¿Donde esta las otras cajas?" Where are the other boxes? Drake asked.

"¡Yo no se!" I don't know! the master answered. His eyes looked furtively from left to right, as if expecting someone to enter and help him.

"There is more!" Drake said, speaking to a sailor near him. "Search the ship for the rest of the gold. Return the master to the hold," Drake ordered.

And on Drake's men making a thorough search of the ship, one man discovered a fourth chest of gold that had been hidden in a below-deck compartment.

"General, we found this chest of gold; it had been concealed in a barrel of meal," explained William Hawkins to Drake, who was now occupying the master's cabin. He was seated at the navigator's table studying a stack of gold bars.

"And this cross," said Minivy, a fore top sailor. He held in his hands a cross of gold that was a foot long; it had attached to it a beautiful gold casting of Jesus, who was holding his hand over his heart.

"And it is gold!" Drake exclaimed, smiling after he had examined it. Then he said to the men standing before him, "This is the beginning of our harvest!"

"General," a sailor said on entering the Captain's cabin. "Moone asked me to report to you that the swimmer got to the village before us, and he warned the people there. All fled. We have not found any gold or silver. But we did find a warehouse that is filled with goods."

"No gold!" Drake exclaimed with dismay, and he bitterly frowned.

"Sorry, General. Moone also asked for some of the sheep cooking on the spit. He has wine!"

"Take half of it; report to Moone that I will join him in the morning; then we can make a better search."

"Aye!"

And on the following morning, Drake awoke, got out of the master's bed; then he made a search of the master's cabin for navigation charts and equipment. He found a coastal chart of Peru, that was being used by the *La Capitaine*; he studied it, noting that it had much more detail on it than that on his poorly-drawn map; then he examined the navigator's astrolabe, three blank parchments of charts for plotting, and a book on navigation by Pedro Medina. He then put all of these in a bag; then he ordered his brother, Tom Drake, to take this bag and the bags of gold to the *Golden Hind*. He ordered him to place the navigation instruments in his cabin, then put the gold in a secure room deep in the hold. He ordered him to lock it and on his return to bring the key to him. Subsequently, Tom Drake returned with the key to the *Hind*'s treasury hold and presented it to Drake. Drake tied a string to it and put it about his neck; then he said to his younger brother:

"Release the prisoners and feed them!"

"In manacles?" Tom Drake asked. He had brought aboard leg irons and handcuffs.

"No, and bring the master to me."

"Aye!"

On the master being brought to the Captain's cabin, Drake attempted to interrogate him:

"Where did your gold come from?"

"I don't know!" the master said, frowning. His face was bloated which added to his appearance of insolence.

"Are there soldiers stationed in Valdavia?"

"I don't know—"

"Feed him and then lock him up!" Drake ordered in a stern voice. "I'll talk to him later," Drake said, as if he knew that the confinement would suffice in order for him to get the answers to his questions.

"You," he said to a tall Spanish sailor with a dark beard, wearing an open shirt that exposed his thick hairy chest. He was standing near the master.

"Sh!"

"What is your name?" Drake asked in Spanish.

"John Greco," the man answered.

"What is your nationality?" Drake asked on detecting an accent that was non-Spanish.

"Greek."

"And what is your job on the *La Capitaine*?"

"Boatswain, sir."

"And do you know navigation?"

"Yes—"

"Do you know the coast of Peru?"

"Oh, yes—" he answered, speaking with a tremor to his voice.

"You will sail with us—be my pilot—I will pay you. The others will leave—be put ashore at sundown," Drake said. Then Drake spoke to Tom Drake. "See that all but him are put ashore," Drake said, pointing with his thumb.

"Yes, sir," Tom Drake replied.

And once Drake had had his breakfast, he boarded the dinghy which took him ashore where he joined Moone, who was in the process of inventorying the goods in the warehouse.

"We have plenty of victuals, General," Moone proudly said, pointing to the piles of stores in the warehouse. A smaller pile was near the front door. These would go on the longboat. "We have made a search of everything but the church," Moone said, stepping outside, being followed by Drake. Once the English were outside, Moone pointed to a small church at the foot of the mountainside. These mountains banked against a picturesque portion of the harbor so as to make a crescent of it. The crevices of its wall were laced with cactus and interesting ferns.

"Well, let's search it!" Drake said and proceeded toward it. Drake had a smirk on his face when he entered the tiny Catholic church. For Drake's thinking was like Moone's in his hatred for the church, as he hated it more than the Spanish government.

"I would have done it, but I knew that you would want to do it," Moone said, grinning, meaning make a search of the church; he was of the opinion that Drake would get some pleasure from it.

And on entering the church, Drake irreverently approached the altar; he studied it, eyed two cruets of silver, being vessels used to hold wine during communion; he took both, put them under his left arm; then he took a silver chalice from the altar, being a cup for taking communion, and he handed the three to Preacher Fletcher, saying:

"Take these cruets, this chalice, and take that altar cloth, he said, pointing. "They now belong to the *Hind*—use them at your next communion."

"They will add to the service, General!" Fletcher answered in a pious voice, while gingerly accepting the gifts as though he was ready to place a great value to them.

"Tom, begin to load what we need to victual the ship."

"Aye, General. Did you find any treasure?" Moone asked.

"Yes, we've got a good start—but we've got a big room to fill!" Drake added, as if doing it now would be routine work.

CHAPTER 28

LA HERRADURA

December 8, 1578, was a beautiful summer day for the *Golden Hind*, as the morning sun was bright and warm, while the sky was a soft blue and cloudless. It as well was an excellent day for sailing, for a northwest breeze gently filled the *Hind*'s sails as she hoisted her anchor. The *Hind* then sailed from Valparaso. She was accompanied by the *La Capitaine*, the historic Spanish ship which was now under the command of Tom Moone, who had a crew of 24 men and two boys—not that all of them were needed. The excess had been put there so as to give more space to the men on the *Hind*. The *La Capitaine* was trailed by her longboat, which was much larger than the *Hind*'s. Drake had decided to use it as a pinnace to make shallow water searches.

When the trumpeter sounded the call for breakfast, Drake was foppishly dressed in a burgundy hat, a pair of gold-colored pants and a white shirt with ruffs. The reader now knows that dress was an eccentricity of Drake's, as where possible, he liked to dress for his meals. The two viol players stood outside Drake's cabin door on the portico deck, holding their cumbersome viols, playing a sweet-sounding English reel. Two soldiers stood guard duty on the main deck. Each wore a sword. Both stood militarily like professional soldiers. Drake's breakfast guests were Nuno da Silva, Felipe, the Indian chief, John Greco, the boatswain from the *La Capitaine*, and Thomas Hurd, Drake's new master. Once again Drake had selected a boatswain—one who had a good understanding of navigation; thus, Drake had chosen Hurd over some of the others who Drake felt did not understand the planetary system as well as Hurd.

The breakfast would be a good one since Horsewill and Blackcollar now had a fresh supply of foodstuffs at their disposal,

Drake and Willie Fortescue dress up.

including many barrels of wheat flour. Earlier Blackcollar had made a dough from flour, water, salt and several tablespoons of molasses, so as to provide fermentation. He had kneaded the dough twice, then he had shaped it into loaves, which he now was baking in the temporary oven.

"Please have a glass of wine," Drake said to his guests. The reader must also know by now that wine was a pleasure in which Drake indulged himself. And the *Hind* now had a plentiful supply, being mostly Chilean white wine, which Drake had boarded with less than full interest since he was partial to the red wine.

"Thanks, General," Greco replied, accepting a glass of Chilean white wine that had come from the Spanish warehouse in Valparaso. Then Greco asked in a friendly manner, as though Drake were his guest and he not a prisoner, "How long do you expect to be on this coast?" His words were said in a friendly way, as if he were wishing to know the time that he must spend on the *Hind* so that he could calculate the delay in his plans.

"I shall stay on this coast until my ship is filled with treasure!" Drake quickly replied, which brought forth chuckles from his new master. Then Drake's eyes steeled at the thought, as if he were judging the value of a ship filled with gold and silver. But who could place a value on such?

"This is a long coast," Greco answered in an inoffensive voice, while half smiling. He had a manner to him that was strangely more diplomat than sailor. He eyed Drake's silly dress, but he did not indicate in the slightest that he was offended by it.

"And the worst part is over," Drake said. He was referring to the strait. Then on Drake seeing the waiters enter the room with food, he said, "Well, we are in luck. We have food! Take your seats!" Then Drake eyed with satisfaction the freshly baked bread, butter, marmalade, stewed prunes, oatmeal, rashers of bacon and fresh-cooked mutton.

"It is fit for a king!" Nuno said in a jovial voice, though he usually spoke in a voice that indicated non-interest. "Bread!" he exclaimed.

"Even a queen!" Drake said, smiling mischievously. Then he quickly added, "I do hereby propose a toast to my partner, the Queen of England!"

"Partner?" Greco curiously asked. Yet he raised his glass to his lips and drank after repeating, "To the Queen!"

"Yes," Drake said, wryly smiling and licking his lips. "She is my partner in this venture!" he said in a boastful way, which complimented his earlier remarks which he had said in a most reckless manner.

"And does she consider England to be at war with Spain?" Greco asked in a curious tone of voice which sounded more conversational than inquisitive. Greco was a native of Greece; yet he had been serving in Spanish ships for more than 10 years. And from the beginning of his service, he had been impressed with the Spaniards' organizational ability. It was true not only of military matters but also of business affairs. He had been more impressed when he had learned that they were so good at it that they could extract tons of gold and silver from lands that were thousands of miles from Spain, doing it with just a handful of Spaniards. And then he was more impressed when he learned that most of this treasure eventually found its way to the King and his rich subjects in Seville without the loss of a significant amount. And so Greco was greatly impressed with Spain's riches, while he considered England to be a poor nation. And how could it be otherwise? England was just an island nation, while Spain was an empire which not only encompassed most of the Iberian Peninsula but a good portion of the New World. Greco also had had a first-hand experience with England for once he had sailed to London, which on reflecting, he had to conclude was a sturdy city; yet he was not ready to compare England with Spain. London was England, which placed on it narrow boundaries, while Spain was made up of much of the civilized world. And so he considered England to be a third-rate power in its relationships with Spain. Thus he wondered at the audacity of this Englishman. He had to be a braggart! How dare him to claim that England's Queen was a party to his acts of piracy? And how could she be? And if she were a party and ready to fight a war with Spain, then she would be a fool! It must be as he had heard, the English were just a race of pirates! And a race of pirates was no match for Spain! Why, it had a great navy!

"War or no," Drake replied in an indifferent voice, while heaping food on his plate, saying it as if war with Spain was of little concern to him. But what he was saying was of the greatest importance to future relationships between the two countries; for what Drake was saying to his captives would be documented and later put in the hands of Philip II and his inquisitors; and even Drake's statements would subsequently be used as proposals for war.

"Well," Greco replied in a voice that indicated he did not wish to give offense, "such are the matters of kings and queens."

"I have papers!" Drake quickly retorted, his face flushing as if he would prove to him that the Queen was his partner in his plundering expedition.

"And I have hunger," the prisoner lightly replied, indicating that such matters were beyond his interest. But they were. For he would later give a statement to the Spanish authorities where he would state that Drake had informed him that the Queen of England was an investor in his piracy venture against the Spaniards in Peru. And he would also state that Drake had shown him papers to that effect. Greco's statement would have considerable effect on subsequent historical events.

"Silence for the blessing!" Drake exclaimed. Then on there being silence Drake prayed in a pious voice:

"Dear God, bless this ship, its crew, and lead us in our mission against the Spanish idolaters," Drake said. Then he paused as if wondering and finally added, "And furthermore, bless Queen Elizabeth, my partner, in her leading our country to great endeavors. Amen!"

That day the *Hind* entered Quintero Bay. This was the same bay that on November 30 the *Hind* had visited and taken aboard Felipe, the Indian chief, who thereafter had taken the oily seeds from the herb, *penicillium*, and used them to cure Drake and his injured men. On their arrival in the bay, Felipe said his farewells to the *Hind* crew who were lining the rails; then he joined Drake in the longboat. Then the rowers took up their oars. Felipe quietly stood beside Drake who was manning the tiller. Felipe was still dressed in his long, white dress with a pancho over his shoulders. On the longboat touching bottom, Felipe lifted his dress and stepped into the water and waded ashore. Drake followed after him.

"I hope that your people are well—" Drake said, faltering as if he were at a loss for words.

"My people are—" Felipe said, pausing, raising a hand at the film over his eyes. Then he said, "Gone!"

"Farewell, dear friend," Drake said and took the hand of the Indian.

"My blessings to you," Felipe replied.

"And I give you this token," Drake said, presenting to the Indian a small cloth bag.

259

"Gold!" the Indian said in a disdainful voice on opening it. Then he added, "I could not take it."

"It is yours—"

"Gold is an evil!" Felipe exclaimed. His face had become contorted, while his eyes had traveled into the distant past as if he were seeing the slavery that he had experienced at Potosi.

"Use it for some good," Drake urged.

"Good? I see hateful Spanish dogs in it!"

"Well," Drake said, accepting the return of the bag. "Give me a warm embrace," he declared. Then he clasped Felipe, who now had tears in his eyes. The chief turned and slowly walked toward the woods, while Drake turned and crossed the sandy beach to the boat. And as soon as Drake was aboard, he said to the rowers in a purposeful voice:

"Shove off—man your oars—take me to the *Hind*!"

Felipe turned back and then waved to the longboat. Then once again he turned and slowly walked toward the snow-capped mountains without turning back again.

Drake cautiously sailed north, searching every bay, looking for a watering place. But the search appeared to be fruitless until on December 18, 1579, when a topmast lookout sighted a bay, being La Herradura; and on Drake observing it and conversing about it with Greco, he became convinced that it was a likely site for water. He even conjectured that it might be a place where he could refit the *Hind*, whose bottom he knew was long overdue for a cleaning. That very morning, Marks, the carpenter, had informed Drake that foot-long worms were growing to the *Hind*'s hull. And they would grow much faster when they reached the tropics. And thus, Drake took the *Hind* within 300 yards of shore and anchored her in 30 feet of water.

"Richard," Drake said to Richard Minivy, a boatswain's mate. "Put together a landing party of a dozen men. Land and search for water. You will need some water barrels. Once you fill the barrels with water, then you will need to scout the vicinity for a place where we can careen the *Hind*."

"Do we take guns, General?"

"Yes, but don't molest the Indians!"

"Aye—"

And thereafter, Drake returned to his cabin, where he joined his cousin John who was sketching the coast; he had begun by penciling a background of the snow-capped Andean mountains. He now was penciling the trees that extended to the water's edge.

"We need to sketch this bay," Drake said, adding "Let's draw it on the edge of this map." All of the maps that they had utilized now had sketches on the borders.

"Yes, sir," John Drake said. He was now 15 years of age. He had come to live with Francis when he was 10 years of age doing it on the death of his father. The reader will recall that John Drake while a boy had served in Ireland with Francis Drake. John now was growing into a man. He, too, was short, but developing strong arms and torso. He had learned much about navigation; he could use the astrolabe to figure the *Hind*'s latitude. He often stood watches at the whipstaff. He as well stood regular lookout watches in the crow's nest; he usually reached his post by climbing the bowlines, doing it with the ease of a monkey. Most of the time his feet were in mid-air.

Near midday, Drake was aroused from his work trance by the shouts of a lookout who had been stationed in the crow's nest.

"Spaniards! Spaniards!"

"What the—" exclaimed Drake as he rushed to the portico deck, where he joined Preacher Fletcher and Thomas Blackcollar; both were staring at the shore. The 14-man landing party was in complete disarray; all were in the water and being chased by 100 men on horseback. And twice that many naked Indians ran behind the mounted men.

"Spaniards!" Blackcollar said.

"If they can only make it to that rock!" Drake exclaimed, sizing up the problem and pointing to a large rock in the water that was exposed during low tide such as then. It would give the men sufficient coverage so as to temporarily protect themselves until help could be brought to bear.

"Aye!"

"Thomas, get a dozen men! Man the *La Capitaine*'s longboat—go and get them!"

"Aye!"

And the members of the landing party did as Drake had hoped; they ran into the water, waded to the rock, and took up positions behind it, while the Spaniards stopped on the beach and conferred as to the good defensive position of the English.

"What is Richard doing?" Drake asked on seeing Minivy, the leader of the party, step out from the rock. He put his arquebus in firing position and fired.

261

"Bang!" he fired. The distance was great and the ball missed.

And then Minivy did a foolish thing, for instead of returning to shelter behind the rock, he remained in the open. He drew his sword and waved it at the Spaniards as if he did not have any fear of them and was going to use it to attack them, which was a streak of hard-headedness that at times weakened his fighting ability, as he was fearless.

"Get back, you fool!" Drake shouted. But it was too late. The Spaniards fired. A ball struck Richard Minivy in the head, and he dropped dead in the water. Minutes later the boat arrived at the rock and took away the eleven men. And while the boat was returning to the *Hind*, the Indians ran into the water, took hold of Minivy's body, and dragged it ashore. Then two Spaniards pounced on it. One had a hatchet, which he used to sever the head and then the right hand. The other Spaniard took his knife and ripped open the sailor's chest, and he cut out Minivy's heart. Then he waved it in the air, as though signalling victory.

"Swine!" Drake exclaimed on seeing the Indians firing arrows into the decapitated body.

"Shall we blast them?" Thomas Hurd asked, now standing beside Drake. He was referring to the guns deep in the hold that were still being used as ballast. Hurd, of course, had become the *Hind*'s new master on Moone taking command of the *La Capitaine*. He had dark hair, a swarthy complexion, bulky biceps and wide shoulders. He was fearless and easily aroused.

"No—it is done!" Drake replied, meaning that Minivy was dead and there was not anything that they could do for him.

"But—"

"I know how you feel, Tom. But as soon as we can, we shall land and bury Minivy. Then we shall search for a safe place to careen. On finding it, I swear to you that I shall put in place those big guns, and with God's will, this will not happen again!"

"Amen, General!"

CHAPTER 29

REST AND REFIT AT BAHIA SALUDA BAY

On December 22, 1578, Drake took the *La Capitaine*'s longboat and reconnoitered a small, isolated bay, which the Spaniards had previously named Bahia Saluda. Then he landed and made a search of the shore for several miles each way. Drake was pleased at his findings. The bay appeared to be an ideal place to refit. He found a sandy beach, while a hundred yards inland there were patches of woods leading to a small freshwater lake. When Drake did not discover any inhabitants nearby, he decided that it was just the place that he needed so as to careen the *Hind* and rest her crew. He ordered the *Golden Hind* and the *La Capitaine* to be anchored near the shore in fourteen feet of water. It was now summer; the sun warmly touched the water, creating a beautiful green; it was such a tranquil color that it touched the shirtless men strolling the decks of the two ships, causing many to forget about the recent death of Minivy. They became boyishly happy—one sailor pushed another, who intentionally fell into the water, which was cool but tolerable. He shouted for others to join. A dozen men were soon in the water swimming, diving and splashing as if they were on a holiday.

But Drake was all business, for he called a meeting in his cabin with some of his principal officers. Those present were Thomas Moone, captain of the *La Capitaine*, Thomas Drake, captain of the soldiers, Thomas Hurd, Master of the *Hind*, Clark, master gunner, Thomas Marks, carpenter, John Fowler, boatswain, Thomas Meeks, sailmaker, and Francis Fletcher, preacher, school teacher and health officer. Horsewill, the cook, was also present, and Nuno da Silva, though he would not participate in the proceedings.

Drake was seated on a chair at the head of the table. This table was permanently attached to the floor, while the eight chairs were not, so that in rough weather the chairs could be attached to hooks that were fixed to the after larboard bulkhead, on which there was also a book rack, though it held less than a dozen books. Several of these were psalm books. There was a Bible and Fox's *Martyrs*. The latter book held many additional looseleaf illustrations of Catholic outrages that the Drakes had drawn and added to the book. There were also numerous sheets of unbound paper containing Drake's notes about his pilotage and discoveries. Next to this rack was a shelf that held an hourglass, an arbalest, and an astrolabe, which was used to ascertain the latitude. A compass was located near the door to the portico deck. Drake spoke to his officers: "Men, this is an important stop, for this will be our last chance to make repairs until we harvest this coast of our share of Spanish treasure. Christmas is just three days hence, and we want to celebrate it properly. Preacher, I want a good Protestant service for this holy day."

"I look forward to doing it, General," Fletcher said, solemnly nodding so as to indicate that he understood the importance of the service. The preacher was dressed in a rust-colored sleeveless doublet, leaving his arms bare. They were hairy, strong and muscular. He wore cotton knee pants and was barefoot. His hair was long and tied in the back by a leather throng. He wore a scraggly beard. His face was long and haggard; it did not evidence any animation.

"Horse," Drake said, speaking to Horsewill, the cook. He sometimes called him "Horse," and other times he called him "Cookie." "I want a good Christmas dinner, a Tavistock dinner with all the trimmings for the men."

"You will have it, General!"

"Christmas at Tavistock!"

"Aye, I wish it were so!"

"With herbs!" Moone said, laughing. He liked Horsewill's cooking, though he often teased him about it, arguing with him that he could not cook without herbs. Yet he knew that the herbs were important, as they not only made Horsewill's food more palatable, but they helped ward off scurvy.

"Ha! Ha!" the men laughed.

"The men stay healthy!" Horsewill replied, blushing and grinning. He understood the importance of his herbs, and he was an activist in their behalf. For every time that a shore party left the *Hind*, Horsewill attempted to speak with its leaders about herbs.

"Bring back some herbs—some fresh thyme or sage would be nice. Goose is not good without herbs!"

"And I want good meals during our refit!" said Drake.

"And if you supply me with fish, Blackcollar and I will cook fish every day. I would like some thyme with which to cook them—it may be dried!" Horsewill testily said, as though it otherwise would not be fit to eat. He was sensitive about his cooking.

"Boatswain, assign two good fishermen to a fish detail," Drake said.

"Aye—"

"And, General, I'm letting Bo's'n Blackcollar do all the baking—he is a natural baker. And so, unless I am further needed, I will return to my stove," Horsewill said. "There is no telling what mischief those boys will be into should I stay longer." He was referring to Willie Fortescue and Joey Kidd whose job it was to keep the fire, stir the pot and add water when it was needed. They were not permitted to add herbs, though the cook was permitting them to turn hoecakes.

"How is their schooling coming?" Drake asked Horsewill.

"Well, General, you would need to ask the preacher," the cook answered.

"How is it?" Drake asked turning to Fletcher.

"Very well, General," Fletcher solemnly said. "Both know the alphabet—they can read English. And they know Latin when they see it."

"Good—"

"We have been reading Bucolica—"

"And do they like it?" Drake asked, smiling.

"No, General," Fletcher answered, smiling at the thought of the pastoral poem that was commonly read by grammar school children.

"I don't blame them. And Tom," Drake said, speaking to his brother, Tom Drake, who he had made captain of the soldiers. However, Drake or Tom Moone would lead most of the subsequent forays. "How many men do we have who are available for fighting and boarding ships?"

"Five of our best men are still suffering from injuries that they received at La Mocha; they are still too sick to fight. Then you cannot count on the boys, though they do plenty of fighting with each other. Nor would you want to use the crafts," he said, referring to men like the carpenter, the ship's cook, the cooper, the sailmaker and the master gunner. "I would say that we have fifty men available to do close fighting."

"Well, then, all hands shall rest until the day after Christmas; then we will begin to work."

"Thomas," Drake said, speaking to Thomas Marks, the carpenter. Marks was a thickly built man with a beak nose and stooped shoulders. Drake eyed him admiringly. This was because he knew that Marks had the magical ability to transform a shapeless piece of wood into something useful, and to Drake that was art.

"Aye, General."

"I want the last pinnace that we have stowed on the deck of the *Hind* to be put together. Then I want you and the master gunner to install a murderer on its bow," he said, referring to the falconet. "It is just like that one," Drake said, pointing toward the after end of the cabin at a gun which had been cast by Huggett of Uckfield. It had a four-foot barrel, weighed about 250 pounds, and fired a quarter-pound shot. The cabin's after window could be removed and the murderer fired from it. "I want it put on the bow of the pinnace so we can repel the kind of attacks which we have recently experienced."

"We will do it."

"Once you put the pinnace together, I will use it to sail south and make a good search for the *Elizabeth*. She must have had some type of trouble," Drake said, still not suspecting that the *Elizabeth* had abandoned the venture.

"And the *Hind*?" Hurd asked.

"I want you to get her as close to shore as possible. Then you must shift your big guns so as careen her. Insert props beneath the hull; rig scaffolding so the men can work. Clean her bottom good! Then, Thomas," he said, speaking to Marks, the carpenter, "you and your men must replace the bad wood; calk her; then doctor her hull with hot pitch, tallow and brimstone. Once you have done that, then gunner, I want you to put the culverins in place," he said, referring to the large guns that weighed almost two tons each and fired a five-inch ball that weighed fifteen pounds. Four of these cannon had Drake's coat-of-arms engraved on them. Drake now was speaking to Gunner Clark, the Lowlands-trained gunner: "Gunner, you will put in place some grape shot, chain shots, cross-bar shots—you will need to have powder ready. You will need to search and find hay for your packing; stow it in a barrel near each gun; you will put in place your tools for firing," Drake said, continuing to speak to Clark, who nodded his head in agreement. He knew that these tools should include a quadrant, a level and a shot calibrater.

"Aye, General," the gunner replied. A serious smile was on his face. He liked his guns and so he had been miffed when they were taken apart and stowed to be used as ballast. Now he was pleased that he could get them out of the bottom of the ship. He would clean and grease them—he would pet them; he would polish the brass pieces and oil the trunions and truck carriages; then he would drill his gun crews so they could load, train and fire the big guns in fast time.

"Then you will train your gun crews. Each man must understand the firing mechanism, the use of gunpowder, and the importance of a glowing fire, which must be protected at all times," Drake said, tightening his biceps at the thought of using the guns. Drake was dressed in a sleeveless doublet and knee-length cotton pants. He was barefoot. Drake did a lot of talking about fire. He knew that it could be as dangerous as the sea. But the fire was necessary to ignite the powder, which was done through a touch hole. "You must teach them the importance of the firing vent!" Drake added.

"I will do it as soon as they are in place, General!" the gunner said. The reader will note the respect that each man now gave Drake. It was not so much from fear as respect for his ability. All now were convinced that he was a great leader.

"And the soldiers?" Tom Drake asked, referring to the men who would board ships or make landings. Their number included the available sailors and those men who had signed on as gentlemen/soldiers.

"Tom Moone will help you to organize these men into four squads of twelve men each. Appoint a leader for each squad. Make sure that all know well how to use the arquebus, the long bow, the sword and the like. Then you will need to train them in the art of grappling; practice on the *La Capitaine*. Each man must have a rope with a grappling hook. Practice using the longboat; practice rowing quietly, but hurriedly. Tie the longboat to the *La Capitaine*'s bow or stern, grapple her and then climb to her deck. But do not ignore your sea ladders. Demand that your soldiers board fiercely. Remember, a quick surrender through surprise is a dozen times better than a victory that has to be won by the use of the culverins. This is especially so if we have to lose a number of men!"

267

"I understand!" Tom Drake said, nodding.

"I as well, General!" Moone replied, grinning at the thought of the assaults. For he was like Drake in that he thrilled at the expectancy of hand-to-hand combat.

"And Nuno," Drake said in Spanish. "I would like for you to continue to tutor our men in Spanish. It is a dangerous for a good man to be on this coast and not know some Spanish! I will demand that they meet with you in classes!"

Nuno nodded without showing any interest; yet he did have more interest than he showed, as he had become an admirer of this bold Englishman, who seemingly met every problem with whatever was necessary in order to overcome it; and his talents seemingly did not have any bounds. And he was made more interesting by his seeming disdain for all authority except his own. For he had summarily executed his patron and partner; and he now was apparently masquerading under the guise that he was representing the Queen of England in acts of piracy. Or was it a guise? If it were not a guise, he suspected that if Drake did not lose his head to the Spanish, he would lose it to the Queen of England when he returned. Otherwise, he was laying the bricks for war between Spain and England. For he had to know that Spain would document his acts of piracy and present them to Philip, who would use them to challenge Elizabeth. And some acts they were! He had never seen such boldness; yet this was barely the beginning of Drake's quest for Spanish treasure, which seemingly had a great importance to him. Yet he also sought revenge from the Spaniards; and this revenge seemed at times to envelop him. He wondered but whether the Spaniards' treachery at San Juan de Ulua, being the Mexican battle where Hawkins had lost most of his fleet, was only an excuse for Drake to cover his greed for gold and silver.

"And once we have refitted and rested, we will sail north to harvest treasure, for I am convinced that we have a right to a portion of the idolaters' treasure. Are we not loyal children of God? And being such, are we not entitled to a tiny portion of that which God has put out for all of his children, and the Spaniards have taken more than their share? God recognizes that we are entitled to a share because we are true worshippers of God! All of you know that we worship God, and that we do not worship rags, bones, saints and painted idols," Drake argued.

"Amen, General!" Fletcher cried out, as though Drake's words had struck a cord.

"And now let us do it!"

"Amen!" all said.

CHAPTER 30

THE NORTH COAST HARVEST

Drake and his crew camped at Bahia Saluda for four weeks. During this period, they divided their time between work and play. And during the entire period, discipline was excellent. This possibly was because the men had come to feel that they were a part of a special crew that was on a great mission, and they wanted to make it work. Drake had promised them riches—and they already had boarded much. There obviously would be more! Thus, they were enthusiastically obeying Drake's orders. This included the orders left by Drake on his sailing away in the pinnace to search for the *Elizabeth*. He had instructed Hurd to make the men careen the *Hind*, clean her hull and doctor it. The sailors and soldiers had done this even though Drake was away in the newly-built pinnace searching the coast for the *Elizabeth*. He of course did not find her, as unknown to Drake, Wynter had elected to abort the venture and take the *Elizabeth* back to England. The reader shall see that in Wynter doing it, he had lessened Drake's ability to make a frontal attack on the Spaniards.

The pinnace was now much better equipped to defend her crew against attacks, as she carried on her bow a small bronze deck gun, being a falconet that could fire a shot of grape, which was a cluster of iron balls that were clamped together; these balls, on coming apart, could easily devastate a group of attackers when they were within close range.

Drake returned, inspected the *Hind*, then on January 19, 1579, he and his tiny fleet sailed north. The fleet was now composed of the *Golden Hind*, the *La Capitaine*, its longboat, and the newly-built pinnace with the gun on its bow, which was called *The Murderer* by the men who sailed her. Shortly after the fleet got under way, Drake spoke to Tom Moone on the *La Capitaine* and asked him to report to

271

the *Hind*. He was to bring Tom Drake and the four squad leaders with him. And once they were assembled in Drake's cabin and had before them glasses filled with white wine, Drake spoke to them in a voice filled with revelation:

"Each of you should know by now that gold and silver are more important to the Spaniard than land, cattle or crops; and since there is a plentiful supply of these minerals in the mountains, then it stands to reason that most of the Spaniards that we will meet in this part of the world will have some of it on their person or in their houses."

"You mean that we are to rob just any Spaniard?" Moone asked, grinning, as if seeing a comical side to it. He had been prepared to rob towns and ships, but not individuals.

"Yes—the reason each of us is here is because of the gold and silver," Drake seriously said, as though he had not been instructed to seek out new lands for English settlers.

"And so—"

"I am saying that every Spaniard is a suspect for treasure. Didn't they rob that Indian who found the mountain of silver?" Drake said with a scoff. "When one crosses your path, you must search him! You may be surprised at what you find!"

"Then we must use the pinnace so we can stay close to shore—spot the Spaniards and then quickly search them before they can avoid us," Moone said, as he now understood Drake's thinking.

"Right—but, of course, I expect that we will also find some large prizes."

"I understand," Tom Drake said, agreeing, which was not unusual, as he seldom disagreed with the plans of his older brother. All of the Drakes who had sailed with the older Francis had likewise followed his orders, which possibly then was an important trait of the English in general, which made them more suitable for the building of a strong central government.

"I agree, also" Moone said, grinning, licking his lower lip. "It'll give us a chance to walk the land," Moone added, pondering the seaman's natural wish to feel and touch land. His thinking, as well, was usually in accord with Drake's. Their backgrounds were similar. Each had come from a poor, Protestant family in the Tavistock Crowndale area of Devon; each blamed the poverty of his family on the Catholics and the Pope in Rome. Each had had a grammar school education. Moone, like Drake, had first gone to sea when he was 12 years old; he had served many years on the decks of coasters; on one of these he had been apprenticed to the carpenter. He had liked it so well that he had worked hard at it and became a skilled craftsman in the use of wood; and thereafter, usually when he went to sea, he spent much of his time working with wood. This continued until he joined up with Drake on a venture to the Spanish Main. Then Drake had discovered that Moone was not only a skilled carpenter but that he had an understanding of navigation. He knew about the stars and their location. He also understood the noon sun and its relationship to present location. This was why Drake had chosen him as his alternate. Even so, Moone was still more interested in mechanical tools than navigation equipment. And the reader will soon see the differences in the two men. For while Drake would always inspect the navigation equipment of a captured ship, Moone would inspect its carpentry and mechanical tools, garnering whatever he liked unto himself. He would share these tools with Thomas Marks, the *Hind*'s carpenter. Shortly after Drake had made Moone captain of the *La Capitaine*, Moone had returned to it and inventoried its woodworking tools. He and Marks thereafter had conducted a more detailed inventory of its nails, clinches, rooves, spikes, plates, rudder irons and pump nails, which each knew would be important when needed.

And thereafter, Drake's small fleet sailed slowly up the coast in search of prizes. Drake's method of operation was for the pinnace to sail close to shore. The men in it made frequent landings; sometimes its captain was Drake; other times it was Moone. Each was always accompanied by one of the well-armed 12-man squads. When Moone was operating the pinnace, Tom Drake was captain of the *La Capitaine*. The men in the shore search parties often traded hatchets, knives and trinkets to the Indians for foodstuff and tobacco, which grew wild though the Indians cured it by drying it in shelters. They carefully avoided those Indians who gave any indication that they might be unfriendly.

"There!" whispered Moone, signing for quiet, pointing to a sleeping Spaniard, who suspiciously lay on top of his saddle bags near a path which they had been following. The location was idyllic for a nap since the man was sleeping near a mountain rivulet, which was flowing to the sea. A clump of poplars was at the sleeper's left, while on his right was a grassy plain. Four hobbled llamas grazed nearby. Beyond them there was as gliding condor, which was circling the carcass of a llama.

"He either has gold or silver!" whispered John Brewer, who had regained his health. And he had protested to Drake so often until Drake had made him a member of a 12-man squad. Brewer was pointing out to Moone that the sleeping Spaniard had to be protecting treasure since he was sleeping on uncomfortable saddlebags.

"Careful!" Moone replied, as he softly approached the sleeping man. Moone held his pistol in his right hand; it was cocked and primed. He held a short sword in his left hand.

"¡Hola!" Moone said in greeting the awakening Spaniard. The Spaniard quickly raised his hat from his face; surprise was on it, as he stared up at the Englishmen who now had surrounded him. All wore helmets and breast plates, and all were heavily armed. "I shall have those!" Moone said, reaching for the saddlebags.

"No! No!" the Spaniard exclaimed with dismay, as if knowing that he was going to lose his fortune. And he was correct, for Moone quickly grabbed his saddlebags.

"Silver!" Moone exclaimed on opening a bag. Then he emptied the contents onto the ground, and there lay 13 heavy bars of silver. Moone then instructed Brewer to take them to Drake, who was aboard the *Hind*. And Drake, on taking possession of them, happily stowed them in the *Hind*'s treasure room.

And the very next day, Drake led a party ashore, landing on the north bank of the Pisagua River. This landing site was also idyllic. The soil was extremely fertile and the vegetation was very luxuriant and vigorous. Near the edge of the water was a field of wild wheat, which was mixed with lupins, mustard and fennel. And shortly after the party began their trek inland, they heard the tinkle of bells. Drake's Panama experience told him that the sound was a recua. In this case it was a pack of work llamas, each having a small Spanish bell attached to its neck. The recua was meeting Drake's party. The noise from the bells grew louder, which was part of their design. For the sound of the bells was not only to entertain the animals, but also to alert others of their presence.

"Down!" Drake exclaimed, ordering his men to lie down in the grass. "What a strange animal!" Drake whispered on seeing the first llama. It, like the other llamas, appeared to be a cross between a sheep and a deer; each carried on its back a pair of suspicious-looking saddlebags. The animals were accompanied by a Spaniard and an Indian boy. As well, there was a beautiful male thrush seated on a limb of a willow tree. It was black except for a yellow spot under each wing. It opened its mouth and sang while hopping from limb to limb, as if doing it to warn the approaching Spaniard. However, the Spaniard leading the recua did not take notice of the warning.

"¡Pare!" Stop! Drake ordered on quickly stepping out into the path of the Spaniard, having his arquebus leveled at the man's chest. This was a deadly weapon, though it was heavy and not very accurate. It as well required fire to ignite the powder. Flint could be used, but the powder had to be very dry. It was also tiresome to load and burdensome to carry. Drake also was encumbered with a flask of coarse powder, a flask of fine powder for priming, and a bag of bullets, and since he did not trust his flint, he held a lighted rope in one hand. A second man held the rest for the musket. Once the musket was fired, then both men would quickly withdraw their swords and fight their opponent hand to hand.

"¡No entendo!" I do not understand! the Spaniard exclaimed.

"You will!" Drake answered.

"Silver, General!" a sailor exclaimed on opening a saddlebag. It held 50 pounds of refined silver. The other bag held a like amount. The llama train carried a total of 800 pounds of silver.

"¡Inglesas!" English! the Spaniard exclaimed. Surprise was on his face; this was partially because he had always been told that Peru-Chile was safe from the English, but that was not so as they were here! And his face suddenly showed absolute fear.

"And now, your silver is English silver!" Drake replied in Spanish.

"No! No!" the Spaniard cried. Hurt was on his face as he said, "It is my life savings!"

"You took it from the Indians and now we take it from you!" Drake replied.

On many of these forays, Drake also took captives. This was especially so of any man who appeared to be knowledgeable. And in such case, Drake would handcuff his prisoner; then he would take him aboard the *Hind*, where at his leisure, he would interrogate him as to the location of silver trains, the movement of ships, the location of harbors, and the Spanish military strength. And he would even inquire of him as to the latest gossip. He kept some as prisoners only for hours, while he kept others for days. None of Drake's officers seemed to understand Drake's reasoning why he kept some prisoners and let others go. Most of these detained prisoners stayed on the *La Capitaine* under guard while Drake searched the coast.

"What is your name?" Drake asked a new captive.

"Pedro Huntez," the man answered. He was of medium height and build and was plainly dressed, wearing white cotton pants and a white collarless shirt. He wore sandals with thick soles and a wide-brimmed straw hat. He furtively looked at Drake, who wore a steel helmet and breast plate on which there was engraved across its ridge Drake's crest, being a globe with the North Star. Huntez was surrounded by a dozen heavily armed men. All appeared to be very intense, for they were breathing heavily and anxiously looking from left to right.

"And what is your business?"

"Merchant—"

"Trading in what?"

"I take hardware goods to Potosi to sell," he said, pointing to a dozen llamas that were loaded with bags of goods. "They hold my wares."

"Where is your silver?"

"I have none left," he replied, making a futile gesture with his hand as would a Spaniard. His eyes nervously blinked. His face was now mottled from nervous loss of blood.

"Where is your home?" Drake asked, detecting something irregular about the man.

"I am English!" the man reluctantly confessed, now speaking in English. He apparently had heard a soldier speak English words; then he had noted that the faces of the pirates were non-Spanish. But Drake ignored the confession, as if he did not believe him.

"Come with us!" Drake ordered and pointed in the direction of the pinnace with which he intended to use to transport him to the *Hind*.

"Please, sir, I am English. I am from Southampton," he confessed. Tears were in his eyes.

"And how did you get to the Spanish Main?" Drake curiously asked in English, pondering, as if he did not believe that it was possible for an Englishman to trade in Peru. It was done with reason, for he had heard that the Spaniards would not let an Englishman visit the Spanish Main, much less trade at the rich Peruvian silver mine. And it seemed obvious that he was going in that direction.

"I have worked for many years for a Spanish trading company in Seville; many people there now believe that I am Spanish—and thus, I have stretched my connections. And so I came here because I felt that I could make my fortune trading at the mine!"

"Do you think like a Spaniard?"

"Oh, no," he quickly said, as if he clearly understood Drake's thoughts.

"Do you worship idols?"

"No! I am a Protestant at heart."

"But—"

"Please, sir, if you take me away, I shall lose my fortune. It is all that I have, sir," he said, pointing to the heavily laden llamas being guarded by six Indians. "I am your countryman—if you like, I will give you some news of other countrymen in Peru."

"What news?" Drake sharply demanded, as if his patience were thin; yet he thrived on gossip. Thus, the man's question had struck an accord. Drake especially longed to hear news of Europe, and this was especially so of the *Elizabeth*, as he was not ready to believe that Wynter had deserted him. Drake had gained much interesting knowledge by questioning other prisoners; he had learned of the deaths of the kings of Portugal, Fez and Morocco, who had been killed in one battle, being the Battle of Three Kings. He as well had learned of the deaths of the King of France and the Pope. And on Drake learning of the death of the Pope, he had informed Preacher Fletcher, who thereafter had preached to the men on the abomination of the Pope and how he must account to God for his devilish delusions and damnable actions.

"Are you Drake, the Dragon?" Pedro asked. Drake would later learn that Pedro's name was actually Peter Hunt. The name "Dragon" had been given Drake by the Spaniards on the Spanish Main. Drake's name was so well-known on the Spanish Main that many mothers used it to discipline their children, saying to them, "If you don't go to bed, I shall give you to Drake, the Dragon!"

"Yes, I am he," Drake answered, looking sternly at the Englishman, as if he were not willing to make any concessions to him.

"I am fresh from Lima," the man said, explaining. "When I was there, it was street news that one of your lieutenants had been captured in Panama and brought to Lima to be tried by the Inquisition."

"Who is he?" Drake asked, his face changing color.

"A man named Oxenham," the merchant said.

"John!" Drake exclaimed, and his face turned ashen, as his mind thought on the handsome young man who had been his boon companion in Panama.

"Were there others?"

"Yes, the Butler brothers and a man named Xerses." He would later learn that Xerses was Thomas Sherwell. "It is said that all have admitted that they once sailed with the pirate, Francis Drake. Señor, your name is spoken with much fear on this coast!" he said, intently staring without taking his eyes from Drake.

"How did it happen?"

"It is said that Oxenham captured a ship with much gold and silver; he then took it to an island near Panama. He was subsequently caught in the jungles of Panama. Many of his men were killed. He and those other persons that I have named have been brought to the central jail in Lima!"

"Jailed in Lima!"

"Yes, and now, sir, I beg you—let me go. I swear that I will not reveal your whereabouts!"

"Go!" Drake exclaimed, pointing to the trail. "John Oxenham is in prison!" Drake again said, thinking. Then he turned and strode down the path that led to the pinnace.

On Drake returning to the *Golden Hind*, he was in a dark mood. Oxenham was not just a friend but also a mate for whom a man like Drake would have laid down his life. Drake, on boarding the *Hind*, sent for Tom Moone, who joined him, Preacher Fletcher and Master Hurd on the poop deck. Hurd was steering, holding the whipstaff in his left hand. All four had participated in ventures to the Spanish Main. All, of course, knew Oxenham and the Butler brothers.

"I have just learned that John Oxenham was captured in Panama. Some of the others that were captured were the Butlers and a man named Xerses. I do not recall Xerses, but he has said that he sailed with me, so he must have given a fictitious name. All are in prison in Lima—they are awaiting a sentence from the Inquisition court. I suspect that they were brought to Lima in order for the Spaniards to get information from them. On that having been done, they probably will hang them."

"A prayer for their souls, General?" Fletcher asked.

"Yes, but later—"

"John Oxenham in prison!" Moone exclaimed, recalling Oxenham, who was so dashingly handsome and so filled with bravado that some Spanish women fell in love with him while he was robbing them of their treasure. And then he recalled Anna, a beautiful Spanish Negress with caramel skin, who doted on him. She was his mistress and slave. She followed him through the jungle carrying his extra goods. She was the prettiest one of all the camp followers—and loyal. Yet he was not satisfied with her, for he loved many.

"What do you plan to do?" Moone asked, suspecting that Drake had a plan.

"Get them out!" Drake quickly answered.

"How?"

"I don't quite know," Drake cautiously replied, adding, "Let us continue with our harvest, and I will be thinking on it—now, let us bow our heads and pray for them," Drake declared. "Preacher, please lead us!" Drake said to Fletcher whose eyes were looking off into the far distance.

"Dear God, we have friends in a Lima prison—they, too, are friends of yours. The idolaters have imprisoned them. We ask for you to show us a way to release them. And in the meantime give them aid and succor—for we know that they are troubled."

"Amen!"

CHAPTER 31

THE *NUESTRA HIJA*

Drake's fleet continued to sail northward, though their progress was slow, since they were searching each bay for ships or caravans. Even so, on February 6, 1579, they were sufficiently north so that they lay off the harbor of Arica, being the official embarkation point for much of the Potosi silver. Drake had hoped to find a treasure ship in this port. He presently stood on the poop deck, having John Greco on his left, while Nuno da Silva was on his right.

"The town is located in a desert," Greco explained to Drake while pointing toward the shore. He was referring to Arica. "See that mountain," he said, pointing to a tall mountain that was to the right of a small town. The mountain was shaped like a huge loaf of bread. "That is El Morro. The Indians call it "The Mountain of Despair." Many Indians have jumped from it rather than be forced to work in the mines. It, too, is desert. Yet there are fertile valleys beyond the town and toward those snow-capped mountains," he said, pointing to the left of the mountain.

"And what is that?" Drake asked, pointing to what appeared to be a small island near the seashore. Swarms of birds rose from it, flying about and then diving into the water for fish. Gulls, terns, petrels, skuas and pelicans flew like a fleet over the water, breaking away by squadrons to dive for fish. The waters offshore were an Eden for seabirds, as the Arctic current flowing there is an endless source of food.

"It is an island manned by soldiers. It has a cave in it that has an iron gate at its entrance. Sometimes the Spaniards keep their silver and gold here while waiting to ship it."

"How many soldiers guard it?"

"Not many, maybe none," Greco replied, expecting further questions. But there would not be any, as Drake was not interested in the tiny fort; he just did not know enough about it. He had decided long before that where possible he would avoid frontal attacks on targets guarded by soldiers. It was not that he lacked the courage to do it; it was because he did not want to risk the loss of men without knowing beforehand whether the value of the treasure warranted the risk. But this fear would not deter him from attacking the ships in the harbor.

"And those two ships?" Drake asked, pointing to two ships anchored in the harbor. They were four miles from the *Hind*. The *Hind* was carrying all of her sails, though she was not making much speed; this was because she was towing dozens of empty wine jars so as to slow her speed. The sun had set; yet there was still an hour of daylight remaining.

"Those ships would be merchant men," Greco said, referring to the two ships. "They might even be carrying silver," Greco said. Then he explained, "The bullion ship is much larger—the silver that those two would be carrying would be private shipments to be used to pay for cargo."

"Hoist the flag for Moone!" Drake said, speaking to the boatswain on the main deck. A sailor crossed the deck and hoisted the red and blue call flag. It furled out from a rope on a yardarm. Minutes later Moone brought the pinnace within speaking distance. It had only taken a few minutes. For once the fleet had begun to approach Arica, Drake had ordered Moone to cease cruising the coastline and join the *Hind*. Drake now said to him:

"Tom, when it gets dark, we must load two boarding parties in the pinnace. You will take charge of one; I will take the other; we will board those two ships!"

"Who will board the first ship?" Moone cockily asked. He was seated on a gunwale with bare feet in the water while eating a piece of fried fish.

"I will board the first one!" Drake said, showing his teeth, using the Spanish Main facial expression to indicate that he was eager to board. "And once my crew is on the deck of the first, then you sail to the second—then take it!"

"Right!" Moone said. Then he also showed his teeth by giving a snaggled grin. And then he tossed a fish bone in the water and wiped his lips with a bare arm.

The English ships approached to within a respectable distance of the two anchored merchant ships; and then the *Hind* dropped anchor. Thereafter the *La Capitaine* dropped anchor.

"Boom! Boom!" sounded two sets of drums.

"Las cajunes!" Greco exclaimed, smiling knowingly. Then he nodded his head while smiling, indicating that he knew that the crews were inviting the new sailors to feast and drink wine; the party would be aboard the nearest ship, which already had a fire going in a tub on its main deck. However, these Spaniards hardly suspected it, but they were flies that soon would be caught in Drake's web.

"¡Me llamo Nicolias Jorje!" My name is Nicolias Jorje! said a short man with a black beard, as he attempted to greet Drake. Jorje was the captain of this ship which was owned by Felipe Corco.

"¡Abajo perro!" Down dog! Drake exclaimed on taking hold of the deck rail. Then he pointed his short sword at the throat of the captain. "¡Abajo! ¡Abajo!" Down! Down! Drake ordered. His voice had an urgency to it that demanded immediate compliance. The captain trembled.

The deck of the ship now became a bedlam of noise; for Drake was joined by a dozen armed men who seconds before had hooked their grapples to the gunwales of the ship; then they had scaled the side; all had reached the deck seconds after Drake.

"¡Quedo!" Quiet! Drake ordered.

"¡Abajo! ¡Abajo!" Down! Down! the soldiers shouted, pressing swords at the befuddled sailors.

And while Moone and his men were capturing the second ship, Drake ordered the newly-captured ship's crew of ten men to be locked in the hold of the ship. The captain was to remain on deck.

"¿Que es el nombre esta barco?" What is the name of this ship? Drake demanded to know.

"De Felipe Corco!" This was the name of the owner, which was commonly given. Yet its name was *Santa Louisa*.

"¿El otra?" The other ship? Drake asked in understandable Spanish.

"De Jorje Diaz!" This, too, was the name of its owner. Its name was the *Nueva Sevilla*.

"¿Donde esta su plata o oro?" Where is your silver—your gold? Drake demanded of the captain, who Drake would later learn was Flemish.

"¡No tengo!" I do not have any! he replied and held up his hands to indicate that he regretted it.

"Search his ship, Tom!" Drake said to his brother who was the squad leader. "Use these keys," Drake said on removing them from the man's thick, belted waist. The keys were large and noisily jingled.

And while Tom Drake conducted his search, Drake interrogated the terrified captain as to the recent movement of ships that were carrying silver.

"Where is the treasure ship?" Drake asked.

"I know not—"

"How much silver did it carry?"

"I know not!"

"You lie. I will hang you by your thumbs unless you tell me the truth!" Drake shouted.

"No, please!"

"Get me a rope!" Drake said to a soldier, who nodded his head and then hurriedly stepped across the deck and retrieved his grappling rope. Drake removed the hook, then put the rope around the neck of the captain and knotted it. The knotted rope against the captain's throat had an immediate effect on him. For he became eager to talk.

"The treasure ship of Bernal Bueno." This was the *Nuestra Hija*. "It sailed four days ago for Arequipa—" he eagerly said, confessing that the treasure ship was four days north of Drake's fleet.

"How much treasure did it carry?"

"It carried much silver—it took many boats and many trips to load it. The silver was in bars; it had been wrapped in canvas, numbered and stamped. It was lifted from the small boats by a derrick to the deck of the ship; then it was stowed in a hold in the ship, being watched and counted by a silver master, who then locked the compartment by sealing its hold with planking," he said while nervously smiling.

"General," interrupted Tom Drake on entering the Captain's cabin. "I have found fifty-seven bars of silver."

"Good—how much does each bar weigh?"

"About twenty pounds."

"Where was it?" Drake asked. He was now examining the ship's chart; it had many notations on it that had been made in Spanish. All pertained to the coast from Panama City to Valparaso. It was apparent by the happy expression on Drake's face that these notations would be invaluable to him. And rightly so, since they pointed out the movement of the winds, the depths of the water and the movement of the currents.

"It was in a hold with other cargo," Tom Drake explained. "She is loaded with much valuable cargo."

"Take the silver to the *Hind*—"

"Shall we keep the ship?"

"Yes, until we inventory it."

"Take him below with the others!" Drake said, pointing to the captain.

"Right."

And just then Moone entered the cabin. "General, the ship," Moone said, pointing at the *Nueva Sevilla*, "is in our hands. It apparently does not have any treasure. Its only worthwhile cargo is its wine—it has 300 jars."

"Any red?"

"Yes—much."

"That is worth something—let's transfer it to the *Hind*."

"What shall we do with the ships?" Moone asked, referring to the two newly captured ships.

"On our making a good search of them, we'll abandon them!"

"How about those fishing boats?" Moone asked, pointing to a nest of small boats.

"Yes, take them—search them—better still," Drake said, "on taking them, put some of the Spanish prisoners on them so they can get ashore."

This would be a foolish move, for on the Spanish being put in the fishing boats, three of them would elect to sail to Chule-Arequipa to warn the treasure ship that Drake was on his way to capture it.

"And the *La Capitaine*?" Moone asked, referring to the store ship that had been captured at Valparaso.

"We must abandon her—transfer your gear. It is time to leave her!"

And pandemonium soon reigned in Arica harbor. For the sailors in handling the wine were soon sampling it; and that led to drinking it. And by midnight, when most of the wine had been transferred to the *Hind*, the harbor became alight from a fire on the *Nueva Sevilla*. This fire was caused by a drunken sailor from the *Hind* dropping a lighted lantern in a box of wax; it quickly ignited and the ship was soon ablaze. Fire is a devil for ships at sea. And the sailors soon

285

were forced to abandon it. And it soon burned down to the edge of the water; however, there were no casualties. But the noise of drunken laughter, screeching viols and blaring trumpets was heard from the other ships until the early hours of the morning.

Drake imbibed little; his mind was too full of thoughts of the treasure ship, which was four days ahead of him sailing for Arequipa. Even so, he was convinced that he soon would capture it. He knew that the treasure from such a ship could fill the *Hind*'s holds. And then he would be as rich as a mogul. Why, he would buy himself a thousand-acre estate—maybe ten-thousand-acre estate. It would have a castle on it where he would live like a lord! And the thought of it so excited him that he was unable to sleep. He thought of the worst—what if some of the freed sailors had elected to sail to Chule (Arequipa's port) and warn the bullion ship! They surely would have had a good start on him. But how could he get enough of the drunken sailors on their feet in order to man the pinnace? But he had to do it! And so at the crack of dawn after a sleepless night, Drake arose and dressed. And he shouted, "Hurd—Hurd—on your feet!"

"Oh, leave me be!"

"On your feet, man!"

"My head," Hurd cried. He had been sleeping under a blanket on deck, which was blanketed with drunken sailors.

"Hurd, get me a crew for the pinnace! I must sail!" Drake repeated. Urgency was in his voice. Hurd slowly got to his feet; then he began to shake sailors.

"I must have 14 men for the pinnace—so up with you! It's the General needing you for the pinnace. Damn you, it's treasure, you fools—up! Up!" Hurd continued to shout and shake sleeping sailors until he had 14 men on their feet. They in turn filled the pinnace with sufficient water, food and wine for several days. They also placed in it guns, swords and equipment for boarding. Drake then boarded the pinnace while giving orders to Hurd.

"Master Hurd," Drake said on looking up at the poop deck of the *Hind*. "We shall sail directly for Chule," Drake said, watching his square-rigged sails bag the wind. Chule was the port used by nearby Arequipa, being a fairly large city located in the mountains. "I hope to overtake the bullion ship *Nuestra Hija*," Drake explained, referring to the ship of Bernal Bueno that had sailed with five hundred bars of silver.

"Aye, General. And good luck to you!"

Yet unbeknownst to Drake, the bullion ship had become a much richer prize, for on her arriving in Chule, she had taken aboard an additional five hundred wedges of gold; each of these weighed twenty pounds. But Drake would not get to touch them.

For even though Drake had good winds and sailed hard, he would still arrive two hours late. For two hours before the pinnace reached Chule, the fishing boat manned by the three sailors sailed into the harbor. These three sailors, who had been prisoners on the *Hind*, arrived, anxiously shouting to sailors on the *Nuestra Hija*.

"English pirates are coming! Remove your silver!" they cried. Distress was in their voices.

"That is impossible!" the master replied. He was standing on the main deck with his hands on his hips. Perplexity was on his face. He had always been told that the South Sea was safe from pirates. He nervously looked about for a sail. Just an hour earlier the crew had boarded the 500 wedges of gold being shipped for Peru. The silver master was now below deck supervising the sealing of the hold by nailing planks over it.

"Yes, we are positive—"

"We were prisoners of theirs—hurry!" another voice shouted. It was positive and demanding.

"Inform the silver smith—ask him to open the hold. We must remove the treasure—take it ashore and bury it!" the master ordered.

"Aye!"

"Boatswain—take a boat ashore. Inform the townspeople of our plight. Ask them to help—get every available bomboat—we will need them to help remove the silver and gold!"

"Aye!"

And the boatswain hurriedly landed on shore. The boatswain then told a crowd of people that had assembled on the shore that the English pirate Drake was sailing to the town to take the treasure.

"Would you help?" he asked.

"¡Si, senor!" Yes, sir!

"Hurry!"

"¿Que es?" What is it? a woman asked on joining the noisy group. She was a large, bosomy woman with rosy cheeks. She arrived wiping flour onto her apron, as she was the village baker. She had heard the shouting in the harbor and had stopped her breadmaking so as to inquire as to the cries.

"Pirates!" the boatswain replied. "We must unload the treasure and bury it!"

"I will help!" she shouted. Then she ran up the street, wobbling like a ship out of control, going from house to house shouting, "¡Piratas! ¡Piratas! Help us bury the treasure!"

And the houses emptied. And within an hour and a half of the warning, the sailors had removed all the gold and silver from the ship and rowed it to shore; then within 30 minutes of that, the women had carried it to the hills where they had buried it. One hour later the pinnace with Drake aboard sailed into the harbor. It sailed directly for the *Nuestra Hija*. Drake quickly boarded it.

"Where is your treasure?" Drake asked. He held a pistol in each hand.

"It is ashore," the master answered.

"Where?"

"None of us knows; the women have buried it!" he truthfully said.

On Drake going ashore, he was met by a dozen women who defiantly stood with their hands on their hips, chanting at him:

"Pirate, pirate, you are two hours late for the treasure!"

"¡Di mi!" Tell me where! Drake demanded. "Or I will cut out your tongues!"

"You may cut out our tongues, but we will not tell," shouted a large woman, who was the breadmaker. She had a scowl on her face; she put her hands on her hips and defiantly spat at the feet of Drake as if she were ready to fight him with her bare hands. "Baha!"

An hour later, Drake, who was more tired than ever, departed Chule without the tiniest bit of treasure.

CHAPTER 32

THE CAPTURE AND IMPRISONMENT OF JOHN OXENHAM

The reader will recall that in the first chapter of this book the writer explained how John Oxenham had accompanied Francis Drake on his 1572 expedition to the Spanish Main. He also explained that the two men were pirates. The reader will also recall that on the two young pirates seeing the South Sea, they had become so excited that they boyishly had taken an oath to sail it. But Drake's wish to sail the South Sea had been thwarted by certain events. For on his return to Plymouth, he was told by his cousin, John Hawkins, that warrants would soon be issued for his arrest for having made attacks against the city of Nombre Dios and the Spanish treasure caravans. Hawkins had suggested to Drake a way out of his problem. He explained to Drake that he could assemble a fleet of ships, sail to Ireland and offer the ships to Essex, who was engaged in a war with the Scottish chieftain, Sorley Boy. Drake accepted the suggestion, for it not only offered a practical solution to his problem, but it also offered adventure. Drake then acquired a fleet of frigates, two of which Drake had captured at Panama, and he sailed to Ireland and offered his services to Essex. The offer was accepted; and Drake spent the next two years in Ireland where he gained many new friends in high places.

John Oxenham was not known to the Spanish; thus, he had not had a price put on his head. And so he had not had to do any service in Ireland. And since he was still keenly interested in sailing the South Sea, in 1575 he began to put together a venture to Nombre Dios, though not in the old fashion, as he planned to cross the Isthmus of Panama, fell trees, build ships, and then sail the South Sea. And by the time that he was ready to sail, he appeared ready for command. He could navigate; and he had the experience of several successful ventures to the Spanish Main. He was known to be fearless—why, he had been second in command to Francis Drake! He therefore easily obtained sufficient investors for the venture; then he fitted out a ship of 140 tons; he assembled a small crew of men and sailed for the Spanish Main. He sailed directly to Point Pheasant, Drake's secret hideaway, and then made contact with the Cimarons. The men were still friendly, though many of the women were not; this included Donna, the caramel-colored ex-mistress of Oxenham. She refused to meet with him, since she was angry at him for having abandoned her in 1573. Oxenham made contact with the Cimaron leader, Pedro, who warmly received him, as he still considered him to be his friend since they had a mutual enemy, being the Spanish.

"What are the possibilities of obtaining treasure?" Oxenham asked. They sat on a log seat outside of the house which Drake had built. Each held a pipe in his hand. Each at the same time put his pipe in his mouth and thoughtfully puffed. Oxenham had been wisely cautious, as he had not immediately revealed his plans to the Cimaron leader.

"Not good," replied Pedro, chief of the Cimarons. He was a tall, well-built brown man with a scraggly beard. He was dressed in a sleeveless shirt, pants and sandals. He carried a machete which was tied to a rope belt. The brown man held a twig in his right hand, which he at times chewed, while he thought. His manner indicated that he was comfortable in the presence of Oxenham.

"Why?" Oxenham asked.

"It is no longer possible to attack the caravans," Pedro explained, speaking pidgin English, which is not easily translated, and so the writer will not attempt to set it down on paper.

"Why?" asked Oxenham.

"Each caravan has 200 to 300 soldiers guarding it." That was five times the number of soldiers that the Spaniards had used in 1573.

"Really!" Oxenham exclaimed. "What about the fort of Nombre Dios?"

"It, too, is well-guarded—and soon the Spaniards will move their treasure to Porto Bello."

"And the South Sea?"

"It may be your best bet; for my friends tell me that it is a Spanish lake—they say that the Spanish ships sail it without soldiers or guns."

"Would you go there with us—help us?" Oxenham asked. This of course was where he wished to go.

"Well—"

"We could leave part of our men here to protect our ship; then we could cross the isthmus, and once we reach the South Sea, we could build ourselves a pinnace. Then we could do much plundering, which would hurt the Spanish very much."

"I will help you on one condition," Pedro replied.

"What is that?"

"That you agree to give me and my people all of the Spanish prisoners," Pedro said, looking directly into Oxenham's eyes, asking for a serious commitment. The Cimarons' hatred for the Spaniards had worsened. This was because they knew that more and more Negroes were arriving in Darien as slaves; they then were being marched across the isthmus in chains and then they were being taken by ship to Lima to work in the silver and gold mines of Peru.

"Well—"

"But you can have all the gold and silver!" Pedro quickly explained, as if to say that the scales were very much in favor of the English. And really, why should Oxenham care what happened to the Spaniards!

"It is a deal," Oxenham replied; and he shook the extended hand of the Cimaron chief, while smiling at the thought of how cheaply he had bargained for the Cimaron's labor, doing it without realizing that the bargain he had struck would result in his death.

Oxenham and Pedro agreed to use twenty Englishmen and forty Cimarons in crossing the isthmus, which is that narrow strip of land of mostly jungle that separates the Atlantic and Pacific Oceans. But before they departed, they built three sleds so as to haul the necessary implements and tools for building, fitting and arming the pinnace. They loaded the sleds with sails, a barrel of tar, axes, saws, hammers, nails and other carpenter tools; they also loaded two small demi-culverins on the sleds, which they intended to mount on the pinnace. These sled loads of items made the crossing an arduous trip, for the adventurers could not use the Spanish Camino Real, being a narrow thoroughfare that was paved with stones. So they had to build roads through the swamps and mountains; then they had to pull and push the sleds. It was made more difficult because they had to hack and slash their way through much of this, as it was virgin jungle. Flies, mosquitoes and leaches attacked them—birds screamed warnings at them:

"Aback! Aback!"

The sweat-soaked adventurers finally arrived on the Pacific Coast without having been detected. Oxenham immediately put some of the men to work felling trees; he put others to work sawing logs into boards. Six weeks later, after much hard work, they had built a usable pinnace; they launched it, fitted it with sails, and armed it with the demi-culverins. And then they took it to sea. Strangely, it sailed well.

Thereafter, Oxenham made a sailing voyage to the Perlas Islands, being those strategic islands located in the Gulf of Panama that are covered with tropical vegetation. He first had to find a site for his operations. And once he had made his choice, then he transported the Cimarons and their camp followers to his base. They built lean-to houses, as they did not expect to be there for long. It proved to be a fruitful location. Plundering was easy. They first robbed some Indian fishermen of a valuable collection of pearls. Days later they met up with a small Spanish ship from which they obtained 60,000 pesos of gold. A few days later, the English and Cimarons overtook a second Spanish barque which was carrying a rich cargo of silver, being valued at 100,000 pesos. It also had aboard it several passengers. One of these was a beautiful Spanish woman by the name of Maria, who was the wife of an important Spaniard by the name of Don Francisco Xarte. Oxenham boarded this ship with drawn sword, shouting orders to his motley crew who appeared to be a band of cutthroats. Oxenham discovered its cargo of silver, and he became very excited, for he just knew that his fortune was made. But his goal would soon be thwarted by love—for minutes later his eyes fell on the beautiful Spanish woman, Maria, and there they lingered. She had brown hair that fell to her shoulders that had a burgundy sheen when the sun touched it. She had a Castillian face with a sharp, decisive nose; she was of medium height with full breasts that now labored because of fear. Oxenham immediately fell in love with her. And so his plans to become rich were quickly aborted by his new love.

"¡Abajo perros!" Down dogs! Oxenham shouted to the Spaniards on the deck, as he momentarily regained control of his thoughts.

"¡No hagas!" Not you! he politely said to the woman, and he condescendingly smiled at her. It was a smile of love and caring. She knew it, and she gave him a tiny smile in return.

And when all the Spaniards were lying on the deck except for the beautiful woman and the small children traveling with her, Oxenham walked over to her and momentarily studied her. She was dressed in a sea blue dress and a matching hat. Her eyes were wet, while her lips were puckered as she was restraining herself from crying.

"¿Como se llama, señora?" What is your name? he asked in a voice that was full of care and passion.

"Maria." Mary, she replied in a choked voice with her eyes focused on this handsome pirate, who she knew was tendering sexual overtures toward her. She knew that it was wrong to recognize them—worse, to give into them—but she did not make an effort to fight them.

"¡Me llamo Juan!" My name is John, he stated as if he felt that it were important that each know the name of the other. And then there was an expression in his eyes that indicated immediate love for her.

"¡Juan!" she repeated. Her eyes were wide open and filled with light. Her face formed an expression of receptiveness, indicating that she was interested. And it was not that she was a harlot; rather she was a respectable housewife. It was just one of those fortuitous things—there was an emptiness. For she had recently decided that she was married to a man that she no longer loved. They had fussed and quarreled; the words of each to the other had become filled with hate. There was an age difference—it had been enlarged by words directed to it. And then the manner of this pirate was so captivating that she foolishly set aside all the cautions that she knew were proper in such a case.

And when the vast treasure of silver bars had been counted and safely interred, Oxenham anchored the Spanish ship near his island hideaway. Then instead of putting distance between himself and the scene, he took the woman inland, found himself a tropical garden of bananas and coconuts, and there he built himself a lean-to. And he foolishly honeymooned with her as though he were the king of the island, not wanted by anyone, and he had all the idle time that he desired.

And on Oxenham's return to his troops, he found that he had serious dissension amongst his men.

"Why be angry?" he boyishly said to them, as though his decision to honeymoon had been a wise one. They were seated or standing in bunches near the shore. "We are rich. Look at the treasure!" he said. And he was correct—the treasure was immense. They had tons of gold and silver piled up on the shore. The silver was in fifty-pound bars; it totaled 350 bars.

"But you have wasted time—" Thomas Sherwell, his master, sternly said. "We should have left three days ago."

"We will leave right away!" Oxenham replied. "It will take several trips in the pinnace."

"We are ready to abandon the silver. It is too heavy to carry across the mountains," said John Butler, the pilot. And he made sense. They now had almost nine tons of silver piled in a heap, while beside it was a half ton of gold. It was a king's fortune. Why, the gold would have made all of them rich!

"The Cimarons will carry it for us," Oxenham replied, as if they would do his bidding.

"That will help," Sherwell said.

But Oxenham's problems did not end with the confrontation by the crew, for he now had to face Pedro, the Cimaron leader. He had been standing at the water's edge waiting his turn to speak to Oxenham:

"I have come for the prisoners," Pedro said, referring to the 40 Spaniards that Oxenham had captured. They were prisoners on the barque, being guarded by Oxenham's men.

"Do you mean all?" Oxenham asked, as though it were not possible. The Cimaron had to know that Oxenham was a man who had had many amours. And so how could Oxenham explain to Pedro that this relationship with the Spanish woman was serious, and that he had even promised to marry her? But this love affair presented many problems, for she was accompanied by her five-year-old daughter and her 16-year-old stepson. She as well had several friends amongst the other passengers. She and Oxenham had had several heated discussions about the passengers. She had emphatically stated to him that if she were to marry him, all had to be freed.

"All—that includes your mistress," Pedro said. "For she is a Spaniard, too!"

"And what do you intend to do with them?"

"Enslave them as they have enslaved our people!" Pedro stated, frowning. He was deeply troubled at Oxenham's recent behavior in cavorting with the Spanish woman. Had he forgotten that he had made an agreement with him about the slaves!

"I cannot do that," Oxenham said, frowning. His eyelids nervously flicked, indicating the worry that he was suffering, while trying to think himself out of this predicament.

"But you agreed—we helped you to cross the land; we helped you to build your ships; we helped you to capture these treasure ships. And all that we asked in exchange was the prisoners. And now you refuse!"

"But I now love this Spanish woman—"

"But the others?"

"No," Oxenham replied on thinking. He had concluded that such an agreement would make him appear to be a monster to his new love.

"Then we shall return to our villages," Pedro said, frowning, then shaking his head on concluding that further talk would be futile. Then he turned his back and signaled his people.

And Oxenham silently watched the Cimaron leader return to his people, who were waiting for him on the shore. He briefly spoke to them; then they silently began to load their small boats, being those that the pinnace had towed to the Perlas. Within an hour they would sail them back to the mainland.

And thereafter, Oxenham foolishly compounded his problem, for he freed the prisoners; and they sailed back to the mainland in their ship. And then Oxenham and the Englishmen boarded the pinnace with Maria and her children—they previously had put aboard it all the gold and half of the silver. And with the added weight of the people, the pinnace dangerously settled into the water. But Oxenham refused to remove any of the silver. Then they slowly sailed to the mainland. But escape with the treasure was an illusion; for in order to do so, they had to cross the isthmus, which meant that they had to climb mountains and hack their way through wild jungles while lugging tons of treasure. For they could not travel the Camino Real, being a state highway. And even though the silver was a weight about Oxenham's neck, he refused to abandon it. And thus, the Spaniards soon captured them. And with the party of Spaniards who captured them was Don Francisco Xarte, the husband of Maria. And when he saw her, he became insanely angry at her.

"Slut!" the old man shouted on seeing her, raising one hand while angrily twisting his mustache with the other. He already had been told that she had taken up with the pirate Oxenham.

"Snake!" she retorted while attempting to free herself from a soldier and return to the seeming safety of Oxenham's arms.

"But now you shall return to the house of the snake; and then you shall hear his hisses! For I shall use my belt on you!" he shouted.

"Never!" she shouted. She broke loose, grabbed a dagger from the belt of the soldier beside her, and quickly plunged it into her heart. And she died before his eyes!

"My love requires me to do the same!" Oxenham exclaimed on seeing the dying woman fall to the ground. But his wishes were thwarted. For the two soldiers holding him were joined by another, and they quickly manacled him. Then they bound him so that it would be impossible for him to escape.

Four of the Englishmen were killed in the capture, while all of the others were taken as prisoners and shipped to Lima where they were placed in the Inquisition prison. The Inquisition soon thereafter sentenced all of them to life as galley slaves with the exception of Oxenham, the Butler brothers, and Xerses (Thomas Sherwell), being the ship's master. The Inquisitors placed these four men in the calabozo, which was the dungeon of the Inquisition prison in central Lima.

The Inquisition then was an old papal court, as it had been in existence in Spain for many centuries. Thus on the discovery of the New World, it readily became a part of its church court system. This was especially so of Peru. Its avowed purpose was to combat heresy, witchcraft, alchemy and the like. Yet its power was so great that it encompassed most breaches of the law; for no court dared to question its intrusion, since it had the right to question any aspect of immorality.

The dungeon cell of the Englishmen was an abysmal hole, as no sunlight entered it except that which came from the street; and this came through a street-level barred window, which each of the prisoners got to use during a day. Then each took a turn in extending a hand through it so as to beg from persons passing by. And this was an important privilege because money bought food, which was a necessity since the prison food was almost inedible. The room was otherwise a hell hole, as it was dark and damp. The plastered walls were stained from moisture and decay. It smelled of feces and urine.

Silverfish and roaches boldly crawled about the walls. Rats noisily ran across its damp floor.

The prison was populated with many thieves, who were the underworld of Spanish society. Many of these had the run of the prison. And strangely, some had keys to the Englishmen's prison cell and visited it at their leisure, though the English were prohibited from leaving their cell under the penalty of death. One of the most clever prisoners with a free run of the calabozo was a man named Pedro Sanchez, who had been imprisoned for counterfeiting coins; but Pedro was also a confidence man. And from time to time he played the confidence game of entiero, being a game where the principal feigns to some greedy person that he knows of hidden treasure. And on the English arriving in the prison, he had decided that John Oxenham would be an excellent subject for the basis of an entiero, but he first had to gain Oxenham's confidence. "¿Frutas, senor?" Would you like fruit, sir? Pedro asked John Oxenham on entering his dungeon cell; and before Oxenham could answer, Pedro presented him with a huge basket of oranges, lemons, limes, grapes, papayas and granadillas, being passion fruit.

"Gracias—our food is nothing but slop!"

"And tobacco with pipes," Sanchez said, handing him four pipes and a cotton bag filled with leaf tobacco, while being joined by the other Englishmen.

"Oh, how I have craved it!" Oxenham said, and he greedily accepted the pipes and bags of tobacco.

And thereafter, almost daily, Pedro Sanchez, the forger, brought John Oxenham meat, fruit and tobacco. And the two men soon became friends enough so they could converse about Oxenham's adventures on the isthmus.

"Tell me of your adventures, senor," Pedro begged. "I would like to hear your stories." His manner was curious as if Oxenham was a hero of his.

And Oxenham told Pedro of his adventures on the Spanish Main with Drake; he also told of his adventures on the Perlas Islands. He described the amount of gold, silver and pearls that he had taken, pointing out that it was tons, being more than the coffers of the English treasury. He even hinted that he knew of hidden caches of treasure that were still on the Spanish Main. This would be treasure from the Perlas Islands as well as from adventures with Drake. The relationship continued for many weeks; then one day, Pedro wrote secret letters to two wealthy citizens of Lima, whereby he stated to them as follows:

" . . . I am a prisoner sharing a cell with the celebrated prisoner, Captain John Oxenham. Since his arrival here in Lima, he has often confided in me, giving me much information as to his adventures with the pirate Francis Drake, which took place on the coast of Darien. He has also confided in me as to the location of several large caches of treasure. I am willing to share this information with you providing you obtain my release from prison . . . "

The two letters resulted in Pedro Sanchez obtaining his freedom; and on obtaining it, he informed a fellow prisoner that he was soon leaving for Panama with his patron, who was a rich merchant. The second merchant who received a letter was not so cooperative, for he gave it to an officer who worked for the Inquisition. The comments about the hidden treasure resulted in John Oxenham being taken by the prison alcalde before the Grand Inquisitor. This official was a secular priest, who had a hawk-like face with beak nose, which Oxenham actually did not see, because the official always wore a black hood over his head. He sat at a long table; behind him was an alter upon which was a giant crucifix. Oxenham sat 15 feet away, being at the opposite end of the table on which was a lighted candle.

"What is your name?"

"Captain John Oxenham."

"Do you know Captain Francis Drake?"

"Yes."

"When did you last see him?"

"1572." (It was actually 1573.)

"Did you two steal treasure from the Spaniards?"

"Yes."

"Did you hide any treasure in Darien?"

"No—"

"You lie!" the Grand Inquisitor said, searching Oxenham for a weakness. He found none; then he spoke to the alcalde who was standing behind Oxenham, who was well guarded, as a guard was standing on either side of him. Each held a club in his hand. "Take him to the rack!" the Inquisitor ordered.

"Yes, Your Highness."

And then the alcalde led Oxenham to an adjacent room, being the official torture room, which was mainly utilized to obtain confessions. Oxenham then was ordered to mount the rack, being a stretching device. He was strapped to it. Then his foot was attached to a trampozo, being a rope attached to a winch. The operator tightened it.

"Will you now speak the truth?" the alcalde asked.

"I spoke the truth!" Oxenham replied, flinching.

"Attach the trampozo to the other foot!" the alcalde ordered; and the operator quickly did it. Then he turned his wheel, which tightened a rope. Oxenham screamed.

"Will you tell the truth?" the alcalde asked the Englishman.

"I spoke the truth!"

"Place the trampozos to the arms!" the alcalde ordered the operator. The operator did it; then he slowly turned his winch. Oxenham screamed; then he fainted.

"The garrote!" the alcalde ordered.

And the operators quickly put cords around the prisoner, which was done in order to revive him.

"He is conscious!"

"Will you speak the truth?"

"I have spoken the truth," the Englishman weakly replied.

"Inflict the mercuerda!" the alcalde ordered. And the operator turned a winch which was connected to each of the cords; thus he was being stretched from all directions. If the pressure continued, his limbs would be pulled from his body.

"Oh, God!" Oxenham cried.

"Will you tell us the truth!" the alcalde demanded.

"He is unconscious!"

And thereafter John Oxenham was put to the winch on three other occasions; and finally he confessed, giving answers to many of the questions that had been directed at him; and he made many admissions. Yet he refused to reveal the location of any buried treasure. Even though he answered many questions about Drake, the Inquisitors were still not satisfied. And in doing so, the Inquisitors revealed their fear of Drake, as if they knew he were a danger to them; for strangely, they wanted to know more and more about Drake:

"Did Drake sail for the Queen?"

"No—"

"Did Drake leave treasure in the jungles of Pànama?"

"I don't know—"

"Has the Queen authorized Drake to sail to the South Sea?"

"I don't know—"

"Do you know the location of any treasure that you have robbed from the Spaniards and is still hidden in Las Perlas?"

"No!"

"In Darien?"

"No!"

"You lie!"

"Alcalde," the Grand Inquisitor said to the prison chieftain. "Give him the water cure!"

"Yes, sir!"

And thereafter Oxenham was tightly bound to a potro or ladder-like rack. Its rungs had sharp edges so as to prevent movement. Then the ladder was adjusted so that Oxenham's head was much lower than his body. A prong was then put in his mouth so that it would remain open. Then an operator put a piece of linen on his chest that extended to his open mouth.

"Pour the water!"

And the operator took a jar of water and poured it on the linen; it ran down his throat.

"Will you confess!"

Oxenham did not move his head. He now knew that if he moved or swallowed, he would drown.

"Pour!" the alcalde ordered. And more water ran down Oxenham's throat and out his mouth.

"Gurgle! Gurgle!" sounded the water in his throat. For the weight of it had forced him to move. And he now was frantically moving his head.

"He has had enough!" the alcalde said, adding, "Raise his head!"

"Oh, oh!" Oxenham cried.

"Do you confess to your crimes?"

"Yes—"

"And will you confess as to the location of the treasure?"

"Yes."

"Now?"

"Yes!"

"And do you wish to become a member of the Catholic Church?"

300

"I do!" Oxenham said, though he hated it. But his punishment had been so cruel that it had made him want to live. And in doing so, he was willing to confess to anything.

"Release him from the potro!"

But thereafter when John Oxenham signed his statement, it was strangely bereft of any information concerning the treasure that he had taken from the Spaniards. And so on the afternoon of February 13, 1579, being hours after his confession, Oxenham lay on the floor of his dungeon, shaking from his ordeal before the court of the Inquisition.

"Cap'n!" John Butler said on shaking Oxenham.

"Yes, John," Oxenham replied, half awakening.

"The Captain is here!"

"The Captain—where?" he asked, fully awakening at the mention of the Captain. To him and to the others, there was only one Captain—Drake.

"Callao!"

"Callao," he said, his voice indicating real interest. Callao, being six miles away, was the port for Lima.

"He will save us," Oxenham said, as if praying.

"Let us hope so!" Butler replied.

CHAPTER 33

LIMA

Drake was embarrassed by his defeat at Chule. This was not totally because of the great loss of treasure, as he had been close to it before, but the defeat had been given to him by a dozen women—all housewives. He spoke only a few words on the return trip to the *Hind*. Then on boarding her, he refused the eyes of the men lining the rails, though all were silently staring down at him. He ate alone; he even ordered the viol players to play on the main deck, as he did not want them to be too near his cabin, doing it as if he were punishing himself. Then he went to bed, but not for a sound sleep, for his mind raced with thoughts about his loss. He finally decided that his early release of the prisoners had been the single reason for the loss, and he decided to take precautions against it happening again.

Drake rose from his bunk at the break of dawn, filled a wash basin with water; he washed his face, dressed, and stepped out onto the portico deck. He looked down on the main deck and studied it. It was literally covered with sleeping men. Most lay on a single blanket, having another on top, as the air was cool and damp, though the sun was warm. Drake leaned against the cabin, put his hands on it, and pushed against it again and again, as he began his exercise regimen. His shoulders and arms were larger than most men, exemplifying the power that he had in his upper torso. He did 100 presses; then he did 50 pushups. He next looked up to the mainmast. He eyed a rope that stretched from the deck to the top. He grasped it and climbed like a monkey forty feet to the lookout's turret.

"Good mornin', General!" said the lookout seated in the turret, wiping sleep from his eyes, for the noise from Drake had jarred him wide awake.

"It is—and because of it, find me a ship!" Drake demanded, then he quickly descended the rope.

"Aye," the lookout replied, looking down, watching Drake descend the rope in the fashion that he had ascended it.

On Drake landing on the deck, he said to John Drake, his page, who was standing at the door to his cabin:

"Ask Hurd to come to my cabin and join me for breakfast; then raise the flag for Moone—Tom Drake. Then you'd best ask the carpenter to join us for breakfast—well, the cooper, too." He was referring to Simon Woods, the cooper, who was practically a shadow of Marks.

"Aye, General," the lad replied, descending a ladder. Hurd occupied a small cabin, being one of four that was located directly beneath Drake's cabin. He shared it with the sailmaker.

And soon thereafter, Hurd, Marks, Woods, Tom Drake and Moone met with Drake in his cabin, where all dined on stewed prunes, freshly fried fish and newly-baked bread that had been sliced and topped with grape jelly. Drake hungrily ate while talking to the two men.

"We must not let this happen again!" Drake said.

"What can we do, General?" Hurd asked. He knew that the loss of the Chule gold was bothering Drake.

"Prisoners must not be released in ships so they can travel ahead of us!"

"I agree—"

"I want all the cargo that we can use removed from the captured ships. I want it moved onto the *Hind*—the prisoners, too!"

"Tom," Drake said, speaking to Marks, the carpenter. "Can you convert one of the holds to a jail cell?"

"Yes, yes—of course!"

Nuno, the pilot, inconspicuously sat at the end of the table, eyeing and listening, half smiling, seemingly enthralled, as if this scheming mattered to him.

"The sails on the captured ships that are empty need to be set and abandoned—their helms lashed so that they will sail seaward; then the recovery of the ships by the Spaniards will be so far in the future that they will not interfere with our plans."

"Aye!"

"That's it!" Moone said, grinning.

On February 15, 1579, Drake's fleet was about 20 miles from Callao, being the port that services Lima, which was a great seat of power from which the viceroy reigned. Drake's nearness to it brought a change in Drake's luck. For late that morning the *Hind* captured an offshore bark, being a small three-masted sailing vessel with square rigging. It was carrying a valuable cargo of linen clothes, which Drake on boarding had the seamen transfer to the *Golden Hind*. Its captain was Gaspar Martin, a man of medium height and build, having olive complexion and dark, thick beard. Once Drake had the cargo of linen stowed on the *Hind*, he began to interrogate Gaspar Martin:

"I do not plan to harm you, providing that you cooperate with me," Drake said. Drake was sportingly dressed, being almost vaudevillian, which gave him a pirate appearance. He wore bright red pants, a gold shirt, knee-length leather boots, and a heavy gold chain around his neck. He had a short sword attached to his side. Gaspar Martin was guarded by two soldiers, being John Brewer and Tom Drake. One held a pike, while the other held a long sword in his hand. They gave the appearance that they were well-disciplined, for they behaved as though they were professional military. Each had saluted Drake on their stepping onto the main deck. This was in contrast to the appearance of little Willie Fortescue, who was roaming the deck. Willie was a born clown and a continual source of amusement for the men. He was short, verging on being a midget, though he was very strong and agile, having powerful arms and shoulders which enabled him to swing through the rigging like a monkey. He was now dressed in attire similar to that of Drake. John Dean, the cobbler, had made him a pair of knee-length boots for such occasions, while the sailmaker had made him pants and a shirt that matched Drake's. Drake enjoyed Willie and liked his antics at times such as these, but he would not otherwise let him roam the poop deck—that was for officers and those others with the special privilege to appear. Willie wore a short sword on his side. He did a series of cartwheels across the deck and landed on his feet with the sword in his hand. The men on deck smiled. Martin was not amused.

"What do you want of me—I am just an insignificant merchant—and a poor one at that, for I no longer have merchandise," Martin said while sadly wringing his hands and screwing his face.

"Have you just sailed from Lima?"

"Yes—"

"I want to know about the recent arrival or departure of treasure ships from Lima."

"I know nothing of treasure ships—"

"You will tell me of their movements, or you shall swing by your neck!" Drake emphatically said.

"Oh!"

"Get a rope!" Drake said to his brother, Tom Drake. And on Tom Drake producing a rope, Drake said in a harsh voice, "Let him feel it, Tom!"

"You must not identify me as your source!" Gaspar Martin said on refusing to touch the rope. Apprehension was on his face. He had been torn between creating problems with Spanish officials for having conspired with an English pirate and swinging by his neck. He had decided to resolve the neck problem first.

"Señor, I will tell you what I know. I have heard it said that there are two silver ships due to arrive soon in Lima; but, sir, the great prize has already departed Lima. For the *Nuestra Senora de la Concepcion* sailed from Lima two days previously!"

"Where was she bound?" Drake asked. His voice indicated surprise.

"Panama—"

"And what was her cargo?"

"She carried much treasure," he softly said and furtively looked from left to right, as if wondering who had heard him.

"How fast does she sail?" Drake asked, being carefully watched by the pilot, Nuno da Silva.

"She is not fast, and she will make many stops. She will pick up flour—and some gold!"

"Pilot me to Callao!" Drake ordered Martin. He was ordering him to con the *Hind* to Callao, the port city for Lima, being located six miles from it.

"I will!" he said, yet anguish was on his face.

The *Golden Hind* sailed into the Callao channel at 10:00 p.m. on February 15, 1579. Her longboat was in the water trailing; the pinnace was behind it, being manned by Tom Moone and fourteen armed men. All lay on her deck except Tom Moone, who was standing. He had one hand on the tiller. A ship was following the pinnace. When it breasted the *Hind*, Drake said to Gaspar Martin, "Hail her!"

"¿Que barco es este?" Who are you? the captain cried out in Spanish.

306

"*San Cristobal*. We have come from Panama with a cargo of Castillian goods," a sailor said. "We are ready for a glass of wine." Then the same person asked, "And who are you?"

"*Nuestra Senora de Valle*."

"¿De donde?" Where from?

"We are from Chile—we have come for cargo."

"¡Mucho suerte!" Good luck!

"¡Gracias!"

"Left sharp rudder!" Drake said, directing the helmsman and the boatswain to steer the *Hind* to a cluster of small ships. Most did not have lights, which probably indicated that there was no one aboard.

"I can count thirty ships," Hurd said, looking down on the Hind's main deck which was covered with stretched-out sailors who were trying to be inconspicuous. "But most are small." Many were 10 tons or less.

"Over there!" Drake said, pointing to the largest nearby ship. It had a lighted lantern hanging from its stern. "Ask it to tell us where the silver ship is," Drake said. Drake was going right into the nest of ships in search of the treasure ship.

"¿Senor, donde es el barco de la plata?" Sir, where is the silver ship? Martin asked.

"It is there," a voice replied; it came from a man, who appeared to be a mere outline because of the dark of the night. "It is the large one; yet it has not loaded its silver—it is still in the warehouse!"

"¡Gracias!"

"Tom," Drake said, speaking to Tom Hurd, while studying the dark outline of one ship, being one of a dozen ships which now practically surrounded the *Hind*. For Drake had maneuvered the *Hind* so that she was in the midst of many ships.

"Yes, General?"

"I need six men for the dinghy!"

"Well—" Hurd said in a questioning voice, as if wondering what was to be Drake's next move. Drake had the English in a position where they were surrounded by Spanish ships. And Hurd silently wondered: Did the General not understand their precarious position, especially if they were discovered? This was so, even though six of the culverins were manned and loaded and a small fire was nearby.

"General?" Hurd whispered.

"Yes—"

"We're surrounded!"

"I know—I intend to cut the anchor ropes to each of these ships. The offshore breeze will then carry them out to sea. And once that is done, we can capture them, keep them together. I will then send a messenger to the viceroy—advising him that he may have his ships if he releases Oxenham and the other three men. "

"Well, so long as I know," Hurd nervously said. Then he spoke to men who were standing nearby, "You, you, you, join the General in the dinghy. Bring your arquebuses!"

"Aye!"

"Quiet with you, too!" Hurd cautioned them.

Drake entered the dinghy and directed it to the pinnace. Then on reaching it, he spoke to Moone who now appeared to be the only person aboard:

"Tom, I want to cut the cables to the anchored ships. The offshore breeze will then take them out to sea. We can then collect them tomorrow—use them to ransom our mates imprisoned in Lima!"

"Most seem to be without sails, General," Moone said, pointing out that the sails might make a difference.

"They're probably at the sailmaker's being refurbished," Drake whispered. Drake had been told that this was the custom of ships that visited the harbor. As well, many of the ships were not manned. The first anchor cable that Drake cut was to a large bark; but surprisingly it did not move, for the wind had stopped.

"The wind has stopped!" Drake whispered to the pinnace.

"We will cut its mast, General!" Moone said; then his boarding crew boldly threw up their grappling hooks, took hold of the gunwale and boarded. Two men quickly began to cut at the mast with their sharp axes; and the mast fell.

"¡Pare! ¡Pare!" Stop! Stop! the night watch shouted, exiting from a doorway of the ship with a lantern in his hand.

"¡Abajo perro!" Down, dog! Moone shouted, standing and pointing an arquebus at the man's face. The Spaniard quickly lay on the deck. Then Moone tied his feet and hands with a rope. And a sailor quickly put a gag in the man's mouth.

But an unanticipated problem then confronted the ships in the harbor; for a customs officer who had seen the two large ships enter the harbor had now decided to investigate. He rowed out to the nearest, being the Panamanian ship *San Cristobal*. He decided that in order to ascertain its cargo, it would require him to do too much checking that night. So he informed its captain that he would do it the next day; then he rowed over to the *Hind*.

"¿Que barco esta?" What ship is this? the customs official shouted.

"¡*Nuestra Senora de Valle!*" a Spanish-speaking voice answered, giving the name of the ship that he had been instructed to give.

"¿Que?" What? the official asked, and he cautiously took hold of the *Hind's* sea ladder in order to climb the side of the *Hind*. For the answer had aroused his suspicions. He recalled that the *Nuestra Senora de Valle* had arrived from Chile two days before. He had even inspected it. Then when he looked up so as to start his climb, he had to look directly into the barrel of one of the culverins, which was exposed and ready for use. He stopped, as he immediately knew that this was a pirate ship. It had to be, for he knew that there were no Spanish ships with such armament operating on the Peruvian coast.

"Frenchmen! Frenchmen!" he shouted, hurriedly descending the stairs. He had instinctively concluded that the crew was French, as he knew that they had many pirate ships operating in the Caribbean. Thus, they would be the likely ones to be operating here also. Then he jumped into his boat, and his crew frantically rowed for shore. The crew of the *San Cristobal* heard the cry; they became aroused. And they responded by cutting their anchor cable so the *San Cristobal* would drift for shore.

Drake boarded the pinnace and he ordered Moone and his crew to row hard for the drifting *San Cristobal*.

"Surrender!" Drake shouted up to the bridge of the ship.

"Never!"

"Board her!" Drake ordered.

"For Spain!" a voice shouted from the *San Cristobal*.

"For England and the Queen!" Drake angrily retorted.

"Boom!" an arquebus was noisily fired from the *San Cristobal*.

"Thomas is hit in the head, General!" Moone shouted over the din of voices in the pinnace. Thomas, a seaman soldier, had been badly wounded. Some men were firing their bows; others were firing their arquebuses.

"Return me to the *Hind*!" Drake ordered.

"You don't want to board?" Moone asked.

"It's too risky," Drake replied. "We'll stop her with the culverins."

And once Drake was aboard the *Hind*, he ordered Clark, his master gunner, to train out a culverin and aim it at the *San Cristobal*. He did. Then he put fire to its touch hole. The priming powder caught fire.

"Boom!" the gun bellowed.

The shot crossed the water, struck the *San Cristobal*, and then went straight through the ship, leaving a hole almost two feet in diameter. The Spaniards aboard the *San Cristobal* became so upset by this shot that they thereafter lost all interest in fighting. They quickly lowered their boat, got into it, and hurriedly rowed for shore. Drake returned to the pinnace and gave chase. The pinnace was overtaking the Spanish boat until a Spanish crewman fell from the boat. His shipmates kept rowing as though he was not of any importance.

"Save him, General?" Moone asked.

"Yes, but hurry!"

But the stop was fatal, for the thirty-second stop was long enough to enable the Spaniards to continue their lead. And they used it to reach the shore ahead of Drake. They stepped on land shouting:

"Pirates! Pirates!"

"Dong! Dong! Dong!" church bells sounded; their sound dinned the harbor.

"What shall we do with the *San Cristobal*?" Moone asked.

"We'll board her, make a search of her!"

When Drake boarded the abandoned ship, he discovered that it only had one treasure chest of silver. He put the treasure chest under his arm and placed Moone in charge of the prize. Drake then assigned twelve men to Moone's command, and they hoisted sails; thereafter, Drake returned to the *Hind* with the box of silver. Drake ordered the *Hind*'s sails hoisted so that they could sail out of the harbor, being followed by the *San Cristobal*. Then Drake stationed a one-half gunnery watch on the *Hind* so that part of the culverins were manned; the rest of the crew went to sleep. Many slept on deck on a blanket. Some few slept in hammocks. And on dawn breaking, Drake called his crew to quarters in order to bury William Thomas, the seaman, who earlier had been shot in the head; and once a proper funeral had been conducted for him, and his canvas-wrapped body with rocks inside had been dropped into the water, Drake addressed his men as follows:

"As you must have heard, we have been discovered," Drake said. He had heard the sound of bugles and drums coming from the

310

shore. "I had hoped that we would be able to obtain considerable treasure here," Drake said, little realizing that the next silver ship would carry 400,000 pesos of silver and gold. "I had as well hoped to rescue my old comrades who are in the prison in Lima. But we do not have enough men to land and storm their prison. If only the *Elizabeth* had been with us, we might have moved on the prison," he said; then he added, "Preacher, would you say a prayer for them!"

"Yes, I will, General," Fletcher replied; then he raised his hand high and said, "Dear God, not two leagues from here, there are four of your beloved in the prison of the Inquisition. It has to be a hell hole, as those idolaters would not have it any other way. Do what you can to make the lives of our men easier. And save them from the hell on earth that they are suffering and the death that the Spaniards will bestow upon them . . . "

But Preacher Fletcher's prayers would be in vain—for on October 29, 1580, the Inquisition would enter a judgment of *auto fe*, whereby from the Lima cathedral, the Englishmen would be sentenced to serve the rest of their lives as galley slaves; thereafter, a civilian court would override the *auto fe* and enter a judgment of death by hanging. All would be hung except the younger Butler.

"General," John Drake said on Drake entering his cabin.

"Yes—"

"I'm sorry about us having to leave Captain Oxenham—"

"Well, me, too," Drake sadly said.

"I would like to have marched on Lima," John Drake said, as if he would not get to see it again. Yet in three years he would be back in Lima as a prisoner of the Spanish, for in 1582, he, Blackcollar and Master Hurd would join Edward Fenton in an attempt to duplicate Drake's voyage. John Drake would command a forty-ton bark, which would run aground in Argentina where he would be captured by the Spanish. He would spend the rest of his life in Peru.

While Drake and his men were inventorying the goods on the *San Cristobal*, much of it being fine hardware, three hundred armed men were assembling on the shore. Their leader was General Diego de Frias Trejo. He quickly commandeered two ships; then the three hundred men armed with arquebuses hurriedly boarded the two ships. Then they gave chase.

"General, we are being chased!" a lookout shouted from the high turret on the mainmast. His eyes had to have been extra good, as the coastline was shrouded in fog that was bringing condensate to the Peruvian coast.

"How many?"

"Two, General!"

"Aye, keep a good lookout—Mr. Hurd," Drake said, speaking to his m ster, looking back to the channel, over which now soared hundreds of large pelicans, who gracefully swooped over the water, taking mouthfuls of tiny fish that were following the Antarctic stream.

"Aye, General!"

"Assemble all the prisoners except Nuno, put them in the pinnace, sail them to the prize, advise Tom Moone that I wish to abandon the prize, let the prisoners take her to Callao!" Drake said, pointing to the *San Cristobal*, which was practically abreast of the *Hind*.

"Aye, sir!"

Thirty minutes later Hurd returned to the *Hind* without Moone.

"Moone wants to talk to you, General! He says that you need to see how much valuable cargo the prize has!"

"But I gave an order to him!"

"I know, General—" Hurd replied, holding out his hands in a show of despair.

"Let's go!" Drake ordered, hobbling to the sea ladder. For this was another one of those days when the ball in his leg was causing him considerable pain. And on Drake boarding the *San Cristobal*, his face and hair were distorted and askew. For his face was strawberry red, while the hair in his auburn-colored beard was wiry straight. But this was not totally from the pain in his leg.

"Why have you disobeyed me, Tom!" Drake demanded of Moone as soon as he was on deck.

"I just knew that you did not understand about all this valuable hardware. Why, there are hundreds of things more in the holds. Why, there are nails, pikes, clinches, plates—"

"And there is your freedom, too!"

"But why leave her until we get some of this hardware?"

"Because I said so!" Drake declared as if there were no alternative.

"But—"

"No more—you, all of you men, get in the pinnace. Else!" Drake said and put his hand on his short sword. "Enough!"

"Aye!" Moone snapped, then he reluctantly reached for the handrail to the sea ladder.

CHAPTER 34

THE *CAGA FUEGO*

The Spanish General Trejo was not prepared to make a long and protracted chase against the English; nor were his men prepared for rough seas. For on their leaving Callao, the seas soon became very choppy. Their ships began to bob and roll, and so most of the soldiers soon became seasick. They heaved their breakfast into the sea and onto the deck. Their sickness turned into anger. For soon thereafter, a majority huddled on deck and they voted to return to Callao. Trejo acquiesced. On the Spaniards' returning to Callao, they were met by an angry Viceroy, who placed Trejo and his senior officers under arrest. The Viceroy then organized a second pursuit force; it consisted of two ships and 120 soldiers. But by the time that these ships departed, they were 15 days behind Drake, who no longer was giving much thought to pursuit, as he was proceeding north in pursuit of the treasure ship, *Nuestra Senora de la Concepcion*. However, it was known on the Peruvian coast as the *Caga Fuego*, which translates into English as the "Shit Fire."

But Drake was not letting his pursuit of the treasure ship interfere with his plunder of the coast. For he alternated with Moone in manning the pinnace; each took turns in sailing the small ship near land, and by such means, they investigated each bay and harbor. The pinnace was much faster than the *Hind*; thus, its searches did not slow down the chase in the slightest. It was done with difficulty in the mornings, as then a fog or haze blanketed the coast. But toward noon, the coast cleared; then those in the pinnace had an excellent view of the snow-capped mountains in the background. They were majestic in appearance, as they towered above all and gave the appearance that they were alive though mute, being sentinels, having been stationed there to guard the Incas' secrets. But if it were so, it had been a useless act, for on the Spaniards' discovering Peru, they had quickly learned all the Incas' secrets as to where their gold was hidden; for they found it and confiscated it, even though it was a part of the Incas' religion. For the Incas strangely believed that they were descendants of the sun, which was symbolized by gold. And so they had built their religion about the sun and gold, as they believed that gold was a part of the sun. The Incas had even covered the roof of their great sun temple at Cuzco with plates of gold. The temple even had a garden of golden flowers and shrubs. Some of the dwellings of the priests even had a thin sheet of gold running about the exterior doors. But these now were all gone—for they had been looted by the Spaniards shortly after they saw them. The Spaniards had melted down these beautiful artifacts and made the bullion into coins, which the Spaniards had used to pay mercenary soldiers in the Lowlands.

The men sailing in the pinnace met many small coastal ships sailing near the water's edge. Each ship was stopped and searched for treasure. Then its captain was questioned as to his knowledge of the silver ship, for all now knew that it stopped at each coastal village in order to pick up gold, silver and flour.

"Have you seen the *Caga Fuego*?"

"It is two days that way!"

On February 28, 1579, Drake stopped a small bark sailing in the same direction as the pinnace. Drake and 10 of his men boarded her. The bark had a crew of six men and four passengers. One of these passengers was a Mezclata, being a person of racial mixture of Indian and Negro. Drake ordered all to lie on the floor. He momentarily studied the Mezclata.

"Are you a Cimaron?" Drake asked, speaking to a bare-chested Mezclata, who was lying on the floor, looking up at him with fear in his face. Drake had detected something familiar about his face.

"Yes—"

"Your name?" Drake asked, noticing the way that he moved his head—he now seemed to be more familiar.

"Juan—"

"Do you know me?"

"Yes, you are Captain Drake—and some years ago my cousin, Diego, became your servant—he returned to England with you."

"Diego is dead—died fighting!" Drake sadly said and momentarily paused, as if recalling. "It happened south of here—"

"Oh—"

316

"Would you like to join us?" Drake asked, without bothering to question him further. His fondness for the Cimaron was well-known by his crew. This was because of the enthusiastic support that the Cimarons had given to him during his forays in Panama.

"Yes."

"Well, up and over here," Drake said, motioning him to join him, doing it without doubting that the Cimaron would be loyal to him. "Where is the treasure?" Drake asked.

"It is in a chest in the captain's cabin!"

"Where is the key?"

"The captain has it; it is attached to his waist."

"Take it!" Drake ordered.

"I have it," the Cimaron said on taking a ring of keys from the belt of the captain who was lying on the floor.

"Come!" Drake said, motioning to him. Then he beckoned to two soldiers to follow him to a small cabin where Juan, the Cimaron, used a key to open a large chest. It was filled with 80 pounds of gold, many gold rings and a foot-long crucifix of solid gold which was decorated with emeralds that were as large as strawberries.

"They are absolutely beautiful!" Drake exclaimed, smiling, and then he laughed as if gloating.

"You like?" the Cimaron asked.

"Yes, is there more?" Drake asked, still smiling, his eyes shining.

"Yes—the clerk Francisco knows its whereabouts," the Cimaron answered, maintaining a truthful stance, though in truth, there was only an insignificant amount of gold left in the ship, and it was personal. But Juan had been ill-treated by the clerk; and he had decided that now was the time to punish him.

"Bring him to me!" Drake ordered. And in the shortest of time, the clerk stood before Drake. He was half-white half-Negro. He was dressed in a dirty, white shirt, knee-length pants and was barefoot. Tears filled his eyes, while pain was on his face.

"¿Donde esta el oro o la plata?" Where is the gold or silver? Drake asked.

"¡No mas!" There is no more, the clerk tearfully stated.

"Take him to the *Hind*! I will deal with him there!" Drake said.

And once Drake and the clerk were on the *Hind*, Drake ordered a soldier to put a noose around the clerk's neck. Then he said to him, "Will you tell me where the gold is located?"

"I do not know the whereabouts of any more gold!" the clerk said. Then he fitfully sobbed.

"String him up!" Drake ordered Boatswain Fowler, who tightened the knot about the clerk's neck, doing it in a prearranged fashion so that the clerk's neck would not break; then he hauled him up to an upper yardarm so as to frighten him.

"Eh!" the clerk screamed.

"Now drop him!" Drake ordered.

"Splash!"

And the clerk fell to the water.

"Will you tell me where the gold is!" Drake shouted to the clerk who was bobbing in the water.

"There is no more gold!" he answered, frantically splashing the water.

"Take him back to his bark!" Drake said, frowning, wondering which was the liar, Juan or the clerk.

Thereafter, Drake had a conversation with Juan the Cimaron concerning the whereabouts of the treasure ship.

"Did you meet the treasure ship?" Drake asked.

"The *Caga Fuego*?"

"Yes—when?"

"Two days ago—"

"Two days apart!" Drake thoughtfully said. Then he half-smiled as if he already had the treasure aboard the *Hind*. Thereafter, Drake had his men wrap the Spaniards' sails around its anchor. Then they tossed the anchor into the water and let the small bark go free, as it now could not sail ahead of them and abort the mission. And Drake then sailed away from the bark.

Drake now wore a very valuable gold chain about his neck, which was so long that it touched his belt. It had been formed by many links; each was a quarter inch long and as large around as a pencil. This type of chain was known as a "dinero cadena," or a money chain, because when the wearer was short of money he could easily remove a link and exchange it for goods or money.

Drake now stood on the poop deck; the wind was softly blowing in his face. Nuno da Silva was on one side; and on the other was Thomas Hurd. All were searching. They had the pinnace in view near the shore, though there was a slight haze over it.

"I don't want to miss that treasure ship!" Drake declared.

318

"But even sharp eyes may miss a ship on the ocean," Nuno correctly replied. And he put his right hand above his eyes to shield them from the glare of the morning sun. He, too, was now a part of the search, though he held back from appearing to be an enthusiastic member as he knew that would make him an accomplice. The pinnace was traveling within a half mile of land, while the *Hind* was four miles out to sea. It was apparent that a ship sailing at a considerable distance from land and west of the *Hind* could easily be missed.

"Then, I shall make it worthwhile to keep the lookouts alert!" Drake said, fingering his necklace.

"How, General?" Hurd asked.

"I will give this necklace to the lookout who first sights the treasure ship!" Drake said while fingering the gold links.

"Do you wish to announce it?" Hurd asked.

"Yes," Drake replied; then he raised his voice and spoke to the lookouts on the yards and in their turrets and the men on deck. "You lookouts—you men on the yards!" he shouted. All stared at him. "The first man who sights the treasure ship shall receive as a prize this necklace!" And he held it up so all could see it.

"Hurrah!" shouted the men in the turrets, yards and on deck. And they began to talk aggressively amongst themselves. It was a beautiful chain. And thereafter, during the morning, a dozen men were in the topmost part of the ship searching for the ship. And near noon that same day, being March 1, 1579, there was a cry from the fighting top:

"The treasure ship, sir!"

"Where?" Drake shouted on exiting from his cabin. He stood on the portico deck and put his right hand above his eyes so as to shield them from the glare of the midday sun.

"It's almost on our larboard beam, General!" John Drake replied.

"You're right, and I believe that you've won this chain," Drake replied, while possessively touching it. Then he said to Tom Hurd, "She is not making much headway. So with our present sail, we will leave her behind before nightfall."

"Do you wish for me to take in sail?" Hurd asked.

"No, that would arouse her suspicions—and I do not want to attack her or go near her until dark," Drake said. He knew that if he got in close the Spaniard would see the *Hind*'s guns and the armed men seated on her deck; some were oiling their swords; others were cleaning their arquebuses; a few were hand-wrestling. The sight of them and their activity would surely alarm the Spaniard. She might have guns; then she might be able to outsail the *Hind*.

"What do you suggest?"

"Bring top side a dozen or so *botijas*, and I will show you," Drake said, referring to the large, open-mouthed, earthen jars that were filled with olive oil which Horsewill, the cook, had been using to fry his fish.

"Pour the oil over the side," Drake said to Hurd on the jars being brought top side.

"Aye!"

"Now tie a rope to each; we will tie them to our stern. They will fill and act as a brake," Drake explained. The reader will recall that this would be the second time on this venture that Drake would use this pirate trick that he had learned in the Caribbean. The *Hind*'s sail would make it appear that she was making knots, while in truth she was not.

"I understand, General!"

And so throughout the humid afternoon, the *Hind* continued to lag the Spaniard, while the pinnace was being screened by the *Hind*. Thus, the English ship was not being given much thought by San Juan de Anton, the master and owner of the *Nuestra Senora de la Concepcion*. But Anton should have acted with more caution since his ship was carrying a treasury of more than 400,000 pesos in gold, silver and jewels.

Then at sunset, the Spaniards slowly turned about as if she wished to speak to the *Hind*.

"General, she is turning about!"

"I see her!"

"What now?" Hurd asked.

"She may be surrendering and not knowing it!" Drake said, smiling at the thought. Then he added, "Tell the soldiers to stay down; we will not board her until we shoot down her mainmast."

"Ask Master Gunner Clark to report to me!"

"Aye!"

Minutes later Master Gunner Clark joined Drake on the poop deck. Anticipation was on his face.

"Clark, I want to lay her mast on her deck! what kind of shot do you recommend?"

"Chain!" the master gunner quickly replied. A lengthy iron chain would be fired from a culverin. On it being propelled at the ship's mast, it would become an awesome projectile, as it would hurtle through the air at the speed of a ball but it would do much more damage than a ball, as its chain would increase its devastation. It could easily cut down a mast and all the men near it.

Shortly after nine, Drake had the earthen jars released, and the two ships began to converge; Drake pointed the *Hind*'s bow directly for the *Caga Fuego*. This apparently alarmed Anton, who was standing on the bridge deck.

"¿Que barco son ustedes?" What ship are you? he shouted.

"¡*Nuestra Senora de Valle* de Chile!"

"You can't be!" Anton shouted. Then he quickly added, "She was in Callao empty when we sailed!" The Spaniard immediately pondered reasons why the ship would give such an answer. He thought first that possibly the Chileans were having some kind of civil disturbance. And so, he imagined that the persons on her could be insurrectionists. But he did not have long to think on the problem. For a voice soon thereafter cried out from the *Hind*:

"Strike your sails or we shall send you to the bottom!"

"Who are you to give such an order to me?" Anton asked, adding, "If you are so brave, come aboard and try it!" Anton had said this in a strong voice, though he was bluffing, for he did not have a strong fighting force.

"Whe! Whe!" A whistle sounded. Voices activated on the *Hind*.

The voices stilled; the whistle was quickly followed by the peal of a trumpet. This was then followed by the noise from the firing of the arquebuses, then the whining of arrows from the longbows. Then there came a thunderous noise from a culverin, whose barrel had been loaded with chain shot. And it was fired at point blank range. It struck the mizzen mast, which immediately fell, collapsing its sail and lateen yard.

"Board!" Drake ordered.

The soldiers on the deck of the *Hind* threw their grapples; some landed in sails or rigging; ropes quickly stretched from the *Hind* to the *Caga Fuego*; and once a grapple was securely caught, the soldier used it as a swing in order to get from the deck of the *Hind* to the deck of the *Caga Fuego*. Others tossed their grapples, which caught on the Spaniards' gunwales. Then they tied their ropes to the *Hind*'s gunwales, and they quickly climbed onto the Spaniard. And Moone and the pinnace were also active; for the pinnace had quietly tied to the other side of the Spaniards. Then Moone and his men tossed up their grapples and attached them to the gunwales. The men quickly scaled the side of the Spaniard, which now was noisily grinding against the side of the *Hind*, while boarders were climbing over her.

"I submit!" Anton shouted on being surrounded by 40 soldiers with drawn bows, swords and arquebuses. His crew had already deserted him by going below deck. The attack had been so sudden and ferocious that Anton had falsely formed the opinion that there were 100 men involved rather than just 40.

Drake, with steel helmet in his hand, approached the wounded Anton. For an arrow had struck him in the arm. He had put his handkerchief to it. Drake genteelly embraced him; then he said to him:

"Such is the luck of war!" Drake said, now smiling the smile of victory.

"Why my ship?" Anton asked, speaking in Spanish.

"It has treasure!" Drake replied, grinning.

"But it is the King's!" the Spaniard replied.

"I will give you a receipt; you may give it to the King. The King is heavily indebted to me for the treachery of Don Martin Enriquez, which was done in his name at San Juan de Ulua. It was there that I lost 7,000 pesos due to his treachery."

"That has nothing to do with me!" the Spaniard angrily replied. His face was tight from worry.

"Oh, yes, it does; and so I will take part of the treasure for myself—the rest shall go to the Queen!"

"The Queen?" Anton asked, without really believing the statement. He suspiciously paused, thinking. He concluded that the Queen would not dare engage in such an act against Philip!

"Secure the ship!" Drake said to Moone. Put guards on the men below—station three guards over the treasure. I will inventory it in the morning."

The next morning Drake had Anton brought to his cabin on the *Hind* for breakfast. The plate before him was special silver—the knife and fork were also silver. All had been engraved with Drake's crest. Drake was dressed in gold pants and shirt. He wore his floppy burgundy hat. His fingers were regally garnished. He wore large, heavy gold rings on each of his ring fingers. Willie Fortescue was standing beside Drake—he was attired similar to Drake. He even wore over his curls a floppy burgundy hat which Meeks, the sailmaker, had made for him. The viols were being softly played when Anton entered Drake's cabin. The Spaniard's left arm hung limply in a sling at his side.

"I hope that you slept well," Drake said, politely standing.

"I did not—" Anton curtly replied, taking a seat. He sadly looked down, showing a pout on his face.

"Cooperate with me, and I shall release you shortly," Drake sharply said, as if giving Anton a warning.

"You cannot get away with this!" Anton said, snorting to hold back tears. Then he noticed Willie Fortescue, and a look of puzzlement came over his face as if he were wondering what role this boy was to play. He had the appearance of a jester, since he was dressed identically to Drake. Yet he had a serious face and a military stance, as if he were to play an important role in the breakfast.

"Oh, but I can," Drake retorted.

"But the Queen will not condone it!"

"But she is my partner!" Drake tersely said. "I can show you my papers!" And he withdrew from his bosom a leather case which held many papers, being the same papers that he had shown Doughty's jury at Julian Bay. He then placed the case on a silver tray that Willie had taken from the table, and Willie, while standing with a stiff back, offered the leather case to Anton, who shook his head.

"But this will cause a war!" the Spaniard said. Tear drops fell on his cheeks.

"Let it come!" Drake declared with a show of indifference, as though he were the ruler of England and had a superior force to Spain. And the men in the room widely grinned, showing their admiration, indicating that Drake was now speaking for them as well. They had overcome too many obstacles not to enjoy this moment.

"But the Spaniards will not let you escape—the treasure on my ship is worth more than 400,000 pesos."

"How can they stop me?" Drake asked, continuing to smile.

"But you must have come by way of the Magellan Strait?"

"I did—"

"And you must return the same way!" Anton argued, as if it had to be obvious to Drake that Spanish ships would be waiting for him on his return. And Drake let him continue to argue in the same vein, as though it were serving a purpose.

"Not necessarily," Drake replied, eating. "There are other routes that I can use to return to England."

"Oh?"

"I can return by way of the Spice Islands. I could even return by way of Norway," Drake said, as if he knew of some secret way across the top of the world. Then he craftily added, "There is a fourth way, which I will not reveal to you." Drake had cannily said this, knowing that Anton would be interrogated by officials when he arrived in Panama. For Drake wanted to create doubt in their minds on how he would return. "But enough of that. Since you will not eat my food, let me show you the *Golden Hind*. It should be of interest to you."

"Thanks," Anton replied, sipping wine from a silver goblet. He had hardly touched his food.

Drake then led Anton through the *Hind*. He showed him its guns, ammunition and armor which were being used by his soldiers. He even showed him the hold that he was using as a prison cell.

"This ship is actually a man of war," Drake lightly said, obviously enjoying himself. "I furbished it, designed it—"

"And your men are well-disciplined," Anton said. He had noted how the men had stepped aside wherever Drake walked, as though he were a regent; and he was always escorted by two armed soldiers, who stood militarily as though their lives depended on it. He as well was trailed by Willie Fortescue, attired like Drake, who carried the silver tray which held a decanter of wine, with which Drake used to refill their goblets. Anton also had noted something that Drake would rather he had not seen. For he had observed long grass growing from the *Hind*'s hull. And so he knew that shortly Drake's ship would have to be careened. He would report that he thought the *Hind* soon would have to make a two-week stop.

"It did not come easy; I only gained discipline on this ship after I severed the head of one of my officers," Drake casually said, referring to Doughty. "That is a story about which I shall tell you later," Drake said, thinking, frowning, adding, "Would you deliver a message for me?"

"Yes, but to whom?"

"It is to Don Francisco de Toledo, the Viceroy of Peru—"

"Yes, but what?"

"He holds as prisoners four men who are former soldiers of mine. He plans to have them executed. Advise him that he must not execute them, for if he does do it, I shall in turn kill 2,000 Spaniards!"

Drake said, maliciously grinning, showing his teeth. They were irregular and stained yellow.

"But they are prisoners of war!"

"If he does it, I shall have the 2,000 heads!" Drake warned.

"I believe it—"

"You must excuse me, for I must return to your ship to count the treasure."

"I can't bear the thought!" Anton exclaimed. Tears again had begun to water his eyes.

And Anton's remarks correctly expressed his feelings. For the *Caga Fuego* was a tremendous prize as she carried 13 large chests full of silver coins and 26 tons of uncoined silver. She as well carried a dozen smaller chests that held gold, jewels and precious stones. It would take five trips by the pinnace to transfer it all to the *Hind*. Then the stones that the *Hind* had been using as ballast would have to be thrown over the side. Her ballast now would consist of silver. And as the last of the silver was being removed from the *Caga Fuego*, one of the Spanish sailors standing on her deck said to a soldier from the *Hind*:

"¡Este es ahora el *Caga Plata* (Shit Silver)!"

"What did you say?" the soldier asked, not fully understanding the Spanish.

"¡No importa!" It does not matter, the sailor sadly replied, meaning that the title was too lacking in humor to repeat.

CHAPTER 35

CAREENING AT CANO

The *Golden Hind* and its pinnace boldly sailed north. The *Hind* was heavy in the water while the pinnace was light. Even so, the Englishmen continued to search the coast for prizes, doing it even though Drake suspected that the *Hind* was being pursued. However, he did not know any of the particulars of the pursuit. Yet it was being done by two ships from Lima. They were under the command of Don Louis de Toledo, a human bloodhound. The two ships carried 120 soldiers in addition to their crews. The advantage was with Drake for he had a 15-day lead when Toledo sailed. This would lengthen, due to Toledo having elected to search the coast for the English ships; however, instead of Toledo finding the English ships, he would find many Spaniards who had been victims of Drake. This was particularly true of March 17, 1579, when Toledo entered Manta, being a port city which is located in Ecuador. Once Toledo was there, he visited the office of the alcalde to interview a shipowner by the name of Barco.

"And you have also been attacked by this pirate Drake?" Toledo asked a bearded man, who was seated in a chair across from him. The man's appearance indicated that he was suffering from extreme fatigue; his eyes were bloodshot while his face was gaunt and tired. And his clothes were so disheveled that they appeared not to have been changed since he met Drake.

"Seventeen days ago I was robbed by this English pirate whose name is Captain Francis Drake," he said, while looking at the floor. "I swear to you that he is a low-life—I believe that his father was a shoemaker," he said, looking down at his hands, fabricating a low trade for Drake so as to place him in as degrading a position as possible. "But for a low-life, he speaks bodaciously," he said, frowning scornfully.

"What did he take?"

"He took 80 pounds of gold; then he robbed me of my cargo of linens. And so I am a ruined man. And he humiliated my clerk by attempting to hang him by his neck. The poor man was so frightened, that on our landing here at Manta, he fled!"

"Did the pirate say where he was going?"

"Why, yes; he is a boastful louse; he stated that he was in pursuit of the treasure ship, *Caga Fuego*. He said that nothing could stop him from taking her."

Toledo would not learn that Drake actually had captured the *Caga Fuego* until March 30, 1579, when he reached the Perlas Islands.

"And where did he say that he was going?"

"I understood him to say that he was going to the top of the world, then he was going to cross it by the Anian Strait," he said, extending his empty hands and frowning quizzically so as to show that he did not know anything of the strait.

"Anian Strait!" Toledo repeated, trying to place the name.

"Yes, and sir, he does not fear God nor man—he has 100 armed men, all are seasoned fighters; they are well-disciplined. And his large ship carries 20 or more cannon. He made many threats—"

"Like what?"

"He said that England now is the master of the South Sea—that next year he would return to these seas with a dozen ships!"

"Bah!" the Spanish General exclaimed, as if to show that he would not be intimidated. "Now he has 17 days lead!" he said, as if concluding it were practically impossible for him to overtake the English. "But he will have to sail for the Bay of Panama so as to refit!" Toledo added on unrolling a map and pointing to it. Then he put his finger on the Perlas Isles, being near where he had captured Oxenham. "He will sail for here!" he confidently said as if he would bet money on the truth of it.

On Drake capturing the *Caga Fuego*, he took her 20 miles out to sea where he transferred her treasure to the *Golden Hind*; once this was done, he conducted himself as though he were a wealthy host, for he gave a valuable present to San Juan Anton and to each member of his crew.

"Adios, Capitaine!" Goodbye, Captain! Drake said to Anton, continuing the role of a gracious host.

328

"Adios, General," the Spaniard said, descending the sea ladder. Then he stopped and looked up to the deck, looking straight into the gray eyes of Drake, which were intently staring at him. "You will not get away with it!"

"But I will!" Drake replied. "And I will return for more!" he surely added, squinting his eyes from the sun.

"And which way will you travel?"

"North so long as it suits me!" Drake surely replied. And then he watched the longboat until it had pulled away from the *Hind*. Thereafter, Drake motioned for da Silva to follow him to his cabin, where they joined John Drake, who was standing at the chart desk sketching the unloading of the treasure from the *Caga Fuego* by the use of booms and nets.

"We must careen as soon as possible," Drake said, unrolling a map of the coast of Ecuador, Panama and Costa Rica, which he had taken from the *Caga Fuego*. "We must clean our bottom; else we will lose it!" Drake said, referring to the hull of the ship, which was two layers of planking. He knew that unless it were kept clean of barnacles and the like, and then regularly doctored with tar and grease, the teredo, being a ship worm, would eat through it. It could now be a fat, puffy worm, eight to nine inches long, getting fatter as it ate its way through the hull. The crew members would not know how much damage had been done to the hull until the *Hind*'s bilges began to fill with water.

"I suggest that we do it here," Nuno said, pointing to the Perlas Islands. And this was the logical choice. They were not only near the islands, but the islands were so numerous that it would require an extensive search by the Spaniards and some luck in order to find them.

"No," Drake replied, thinking, then adding, "there are ships following us; they will be expecting us to go there. I believe that that is where John Oxenham was captured."

"Where, then?"

"Here!" Drake said, pointing to Cano, being an island located six miles off the coast of present day Costa Rica.

"Cano!" da Silva said. Then he added, "But you discussed it at length with Anton." It had been Anton who had suggested to Drake that it would be a good place for him to careen his ship. Da Silva continued, "You of course know that he will notify the Spanish authorities in Panama that you will be there for several weeks!"

329

"I know," Drake replied. Then he explained, "But we have a start on them. Then we will have to be ready to defend ourselves, as I plan to be there only a week!"

"And then?" Nuno asked, curiously thinking. He had to wonder as to how Drake intended to return to England with his treasure. For he suspected that the time was drawing near for him to make such a decision. Nuno had not mentioned it, but he was also curious as to his future on the *Hind*. He suspected that the length of time that he had already spent on the *Hind* would not be in his favor when he had to confront Spanish authorities. And that was with good reason. For he had been put in a position to where he had become a conspirator to Drake's crimes, was even helping him plot them. Then, on the other hand, if Nuno returned to England with Drake, such would foreclose the possibility of his returning to Spain or Portugal.

"We will sail north!" Drake replied without revealing his ultimate plans. Da Silva had been aboard the *Hind* for more than a year. He had shared Drake's cabin with him during the whole time; yet he did not really understand him. How could he? Drake was garrulous with prisoners, speaking to them as if he were willing to reveal all of his plans. Yet in truth, he did not do it, as he was very close-mouthed with his plans, for he had not revealed to anyone as to how he intended to return to England.

On March 16, 1579, the *Hind* reached Cano, which is a tropical island off the coast of Costa Rica. On their reaching it, the men in the pinnace began to look for a good place to careen. This would be a difficult decision, as it would depend as much on the shore bottom as it did on the tide. And on March 18, Drake found what he thought was a good place to careen the *Hind*. Drake then held a conference in his cabin with Moone, Hurd, Master Gunner Clark, Thomas Marks, the carpenter, Simon Woods, the cooper, Thomas Meeks, the sailmaker, and Tom Drake. The cabin was stifling hot as the men seated themselves in the cabin. All had their glasses filled with red wine, though it was not good wine-drinking weather. The main deck was covered with bare-chested men who were studying the shore where there was a small beach and then jungle.

"Is this the place?" Moone asked, meaning where they would careen.

"Yes—"

"We'll use the longboat and the pinnace to tow her into shore," Drake said, pointing to the nearby beach.

"We'll have to remove her guns. Then we'll be defenseless," Hurd said, pointing out what all knew.

"We will mount six of the guns on shore, charge them, have men stationed by them," Drake said. "Richard, you will handle that!"

"Aye," Clark replied. "I will put plenty of shot, wadding, powder and the like beside them."

"Tom," Drake said, speaking to his brother. "You will be in charge of shore defenses. I want a 24-hour day guard of the treasure."

"Aye!"

"And Richard, I want those culverins ready for firing as soon as we put them ashore!"

"Right, General!"

"And you, Master Hurd, you have the job of careening the *Hind*—"

"And the treasure?" Hurd asked.

"It must be removed, stacked in an orderly fashion; then Tom, you will guard it. Anyone who attempts to pilfer it is to be shot!"

"Who will work on the hull?" Hurd asked.

"All men not otherwise excused," Drake replied. "Time is of the essence!"

"Right—"

"And you two," Drake said, speaking to the carpenter, Thomas Marks, and Simon Woods, the cooper. "You will make whatever repairs are necessary to the hull."

"We will—" Woods said, nodding.

"And you, Moone, I want you to man the pinnace—utilize twenty to twenty-five men—you must patrol the coast—"

"Day and night?" Moone asked, fanning himself, not only from the heat but the mosquitos. The cabin was stifling hot from the morning sun. It was made more uncomfortable by swarms of mosquitos that were entering the open windows.

"Use your best judgment!" Drake said. Then he slapped at a mosquito on his face that had begun to suck blood.

"And prizes?"

"Capture them—bring them to our camp," Drake said, rubbing his face. "We will erect tents for sleeping, cooking—"

"I understand," Moone replied, smiling with resoluteness while exhibiting his snaggle teeth. The writer has mentioned Moone's snag teeth on several occasions. Others had them also, as sailors seldom had dental care. But Moone's missing teeth were most prominent. Then he had a ridiculous, boyish smile, which at times made him appear to be dim-witted—yet no one attempted to force that role on Moone.

And while many of the crew were busy careening the *Hind*, Moone was actively patrolling the waters near Cano. And Moone's alertness resulted in success, for on the afternoon of March 20, 1579, he sighted a 15-ton bark. It was proceeding southward. He would learn later that this small ship was en route from Esparaza, Costa Rica, to Panama. Its owner and captain was Rodrigo Telo.

"Row hard!" Moone shouted. Rowing was necessary since there was very little wind. The sailors responded to the urgency of the moment, though because of the heat, it required great effort. They grunted and sweated while rowing so hard that at times the pinnace acted as if it wanted to leap out of the water.

"¡Alli! ¡Alli!" There! There! a voice from the bark shouted. Numerous persons were manning the rails and fearfully pointing at the approaching pinnace.

"Fire!" Moone shouted.

"Bang!" A half-dozen men fired their arquebuses as one. The shots were deliberately high. The danger was obvious to the Spaniards. Even so, the bark refused to stop.

"Fire for the bark!" Moone ordered.

"Bang!" A shot hit the bark. An injured passenger cried out.

"¡Nos rendimos!" We surrender! cried another voice from the bark. Then a white flag was raised from the bark's mainmast. The English pulled alongside the bark, boarded it, and discovered that there were 14 passengers and crewmen on the small ship. It was not carrying any treasure, while its cargo was not valuable, as it was mostly foodstuff. But it was transporting two passengers who could be of importance to Drake, as they were two navigators named Cochero and Aguirre. Moone brought the bark into the creek where the *Hind* was being careened; then he landed the prisoners on the beach near the encampment site. And on the prisoners' first landing, they were startled to see the many tons of silver that the Englishmen had carelessly deposited on the beach, which now was being baked by the sun. They were also able to see a dozen large Spanish chests that were neatly stacked under a tent. Beside these chests there were a dozen smaller chests. The prisoners would be told that the large chests held silver coins, while the smaller chests were filled with gold and jewels. The treasure in the tent was being guarded by two soldiers. The protection being rendered them was in contrast with the seeming disregard which Drake's soldiers were exercising for the bars of silver, being nearly 2,000 bars. For they were loosely piled on the beach like refuse and were unguarded.

"She is not carrying treasure, General!" Moone said on answering Drake's question as to whether the bark was carrying any.

"That is strange; I wonder if the silver from Zacates is being sent to the other sea," Drake said, referring to a mountainous city in Mexico which he had been told was the location of several very valuable silver mines. He also had been told that these mines were extremely important to the Spaniards, as they produced one-fifth of the silver being mined in the New World. Had he been told wrong?

"Line them up and search them! As soon as that is done, I will go aboard the bark and review her navigational equipment."

"Aye."

And on Moone searching the passengers and crewmen, he confiscated two leather cases that contained documents belonging to the two navigators. He gave these to Nuno da Silva to translate and study.

"General, two of these men are navigators," Nuno reported. He was seated at a temporary table under a tent. His brown beard was bereft of any gray. He now was able to keep his hair and his beard near the same color by washing each weekly in a basin of warm water in which was soaked a piece of panke root that he had obtained in Chile. He presently had a priestly appearance. He was thin, having small arms and a bony chest. He wore black pants, a singlet and a black tam. His face showed very little animation.

"Where?" Drake anxiously asked, meaning the place where they worked. The Spanish used the word "navigator" interchangeably with that of "pilot." Drake knew that Spanish navigators were licensed according to their knowledge of particular waters; such licenses could be further restricted as to particular harbors or areas of the Spanish world.

"The Philippines—China coast!" Nuno replied.

"Well—well—" Drake gleefully replied.

"And better still," Nuno said, "I have before me two maps of the South Sea. The Spaniards now call it the Pacific Ocean. As well, I have a half-dozen maps of the Chinese coast."

"This is better treasure than a trunk of gold coins!" Drake happily said, taking the top map from the table and examining it.

And thereafter, Drake had the two pilots brought to his tent.

"I am in need of a pilot for China; I will pay much silver to the one who volunteers to sail with me," Drake said, eyeing the two men. Both had fallen onto their knees and taken prayerful positions. Drake could of course navigate the open seas; but he wanted a pilot, one who knew the shores and harbors of Asia and America, and he especially wanted someone who had some knowledge as to the location of fresh water.

"Sir, I know nothing of navigation," Cochero stupidly said, looking up at Drake with open mouth and anxious eyes. Cochero was ordinarily not handsome, but his present stance made him appear much worse. The navigator had a sallow complexion; his face was partially covered by a scraggly beard. His head was partially bald. He held a wide-brimmed hat in his hands which he was nervously squeezing like a wet rag.

"And sir, I do not know latitude from longitude. For I am stupid," Aguirre said, frowning as if he would cry. "I would lose you." He now was in such a stooped position that he appeared dwarfish, though in reality he was tall and lean with a turkey neck.

"Liars! Lock them up!" Drake said to his brother, Tom Drake.

And on March 24, 1579, the sailors and soldiers completed their careening of the *Golden Hind*. They had hurriedly cleaned and patched her hull, and then they had doctored it with tar and grease. And on the sea reaching high tide, they put a rope from the pinnace to the *Hind*; then a dozen sailors took their places in the pinnace and rowed hard, beginning to tow the *Hind* into deep water. Once they were there, Gunner Clark and his crew put her guns in place. Hurd and his seamen stowed the more valuable treasure in the treasure hold, being the room on which Marks had installed a very sturdy door and lock; Drake was given the key. Then they laid the silver bars on the bottom deck near the keel so as to stabilize and trim the ship. And thereafter, the *Hind* got under way, continuing its northern course. It now was trailed by the pinnace and the bark, which was commanded by Tom Drake with a 10-man crew.

And on March 29, 1579, the small fleet reached a point near Esparaza, being the starting point of the voyage of the bark. Drake then called Rodrigo Telo to his cabin.

"Señor," Drake said, speaking to the cowed man who at times kneeled before him as if he were Drake's slave. Telo had bushy brown hair, stooped shoulders and brown beard; his face showed his perplexity while he apprehensively stared at Drake. "We are now near Esperanza; therefore, I am going to set you free," Drake said, licking his lips, while studying the cowed man.

"¡Gracias!" Thanks!

"However, I must keep your bark; I have need of it. You can take my pinnace. There are provisions in it. As well," Drake then devilishly added, "I have written a letter of safe conduct for you; it is directed to three English ships of my fleet; they are expected here in a few days," he said, speaking with a straight face, holding the letter, as if reluctant to part with it. "So if you are stopped by one of my ships, you are to show this letter; the Captain will give you safe passage!" And then he presented the letter to Telo.

"¡Gracias!" Thanks! "And, Captain, are my passengers and my crew permitted to leave?" the man asked after bowing to Drake as though he were a king.

"All but Cochero," Drake said, referring to the senior pilot. "I have need of him."

"But he has a wife and children!" the Captain said, contorting his face sadly so as to show his dismay.

"Even so, he stays on my ship!" Drake firmly said.

"I need him—his wife needs him! Please let him go with me!"

"No, he stays!"

And so Telo, his crew and his passengers, with the exception of Cochero, were permitted to depart by way of the pinnace. But Cochero refused to cooperate with Drake. He even refused to pilot Drake into Realejo, being a nearby port from which many ships sailed to China.

On April 4, 1579, near dawn, the *Hind* sighted a poorly lit frigate. He soon would learn that its captain was a merchant whose name was Don Francisco de Zarate. Drake stood on the poop deck eyeing the frigate, noting that it would soon parallel the *Hind*, being then just 100 yards from it.

"Bring me the navigator Cochero," Drake said to Hurd.

"Aye—"

And in minutes the Spanish navigator was standing beside Drake, who now had a pistol in his belt.

"I want you to speak to that ship!" Drake said. He was concerned that his accent would foil his game.

"No!" Cochero declared.

"Do it or lose your head!" Drake declared and put his pistol to Cochero's head. Drake was being watched by many men who were squatting on deck.

"What must I say?"

"Ask him what ship she is!"

"What ship are you?" Cochero shouted at the ship.

"¿*Espirito Santo*—y usted?" And you?

"¡Un barco de Miguel de Peru!" A ship of Miguel of Peru! Cochero said. Drake had whispered the reply. He had learned that on this coast of South America, in many cases, the name of the owner was more important than the name of the ship. But when the ships were 150 feet apart, Drake changed his stance, for he shouted:

"Strike sail!"

"¡Que!" What!

And before Zarate had time to ask another question, the *La Bella Noche* was being boarded by *Hind* soldiers who were scaling her by the use of grappling hooks and ropes.

"Do you yield?" Tom Moone asked on putting his sword to Zarate's throat, who opened wide his mouth in a show of fear that verged on panic.

"I surrender!" Zarate said, trembling from the shock of the attack.

Minutes later Zarate stood before Francis Drake, who carefully studied him as if debating whether to take his head or not. Then Zarate dropped to his knees and crawled to Drake, groveling. He then took Drake's right hand and kissed it.

"Please do not kill me, sir. I am a married man!"

"What is your name?" Drake asked, instinctively sensing that the man kneeling before him was an aristocrat. He had detected it by a momentary study of his clothes, listening to his speech and studying his fine facial features.

"My name is Don Francisco de Zarate. I am a cousin of the Duke of Medina-Sidonia," the man said, saying it in a soft voice, as if he were reluctant to confess his lineage, for he truly was a Spanish aristocrat. Then he stood, wiped tears from his eyes, and bowed as if doing it to show his heritage. Drake knew enough about the name Medina to know that it was the name of one of the great families of

Spain. It would increase in stature as Philip would place the Duke in charge of the Armada in 1588.

"You must tell me the truth or you shall lose your life!" Drake warned. Two armed soldiers stood beside Drake; they looked fiercely at Zarate, as if they were the ones who would take his life.

"I will," the Spaniard meekly answered.

"How much silver and gold does your ship carry?"

"None—we have used it to buy goods!"

"Dogs!" Drake exclaimed in disgust. And then he asked, "What is your cargo?"

"We have come from Acapulco, where we bought goods that had been shipped from China." Acapulco was a great juncture for the Manilla galleons. For on the Spaniards learning the North Pacific winds, they had developed a trade route from Acapulco to Manilla. The Chinese, of course, brought their porcelains, linens and silks to Manilla. Then the Spanish galleons brought these goods to Acapulco, and then most of it was transported by mule across Mexico to Veracruz. These goods were then sent by ship from Juan de Ulua to Spain. The trade had been greatly enlarged by Spaniards who were illegally siphoning silver away from the crown and investing it in this trade. It was a method of laundering their silver, which they shipped to Manilla and exchanged for Chinese goods. Even though the Spaniards had been sailing this route for twenty years, it was still fraught with danger. The Spanish galleons still arrived with many of their crew members and passengers having died from starvation or disease.

"I will inspect it later!"

"Sir, please do not break my porcelain!"

"I will inspect it myself—do you know the Viceroy?"

"Yes—" Zarate haltingly answered. His face had become very troubled.

"Do you have any relatives of his on your ship?" Drake asked, referring to the Viceroy.

"No—"

"Then you must take a message to him—"

"I will gladly do that—" Zarate eagerly replied, as if he could not wait to do so, saying it like a sycophant.

"Tell him that if I ever catch him, I will burn him alive for his villainy!" Drake said, while hatefully frowning.

"What villainy is that, sir?" the Spaniard curiously asked. He was not used to hearing such talk about such a great man. For he knew that the Viceroy was the ruler of the great province of Mexico.

"It is for the villainy that he practiced on us English at San Juan de Ulua!" Drake said in a voice filled with feigned anger.

"The battle—and you were there?" Zarate curiously asked. He had heard about the important battle that had taken place in 1568. It had occurred soon after the new Viceroy Enriquez had agreed to give the slavery fleet of John Hawkins refuge in the Mexican harbor of San Juan de Ulua; then Enriquez's soldiers had treacherously attacked individual sailors and then their ships. The English losses had been heavy. Drake and John Hawkins had barely escaped, each doing it in separate ships. Many of the Englishmen were still prisoners of the Spanish.

"I fortunately escaped, but he must pay for those who did not return!" Drake emphatically said while Zarate quizzically stared at him.

On Sunday after the crew had been fed breakfast, Drake ordered Hurd to dress out the *Hind* and the newly-acquired bark, which he now called the *Christopher*. Drake enjoyed pomp, and when he could, he liked to exaggerate his strength before the Spaniards. He often had his soldiers parade themselves on deck in their military helmets and chest plates; then they would go below and give the equipment to others who would then parade on deck. And by doing this, they would exaggerate their numbers and their equipment. And the dressing out was a further exaggeration. For Hurd had had members of the crew to bedeck the two ships with 100 or more flags and banners. Most of these had been obtained from captured ships. Drake then used the longboat to cross over to the Spaniard to examine its cargo.

The cargo was not exactly treasure; yet it was quite valuable, as it had come from China by way of Manila to Acapulco. It consisted of many bolts of fine linen and silk, and numerous chests of fine porcelain dishes. There was also a wardrobe of fine clothes which belonged to Zarate, which Drake had warned his men not to touch.

"It would look good on you, General," Moone said.

"I promised him that I would not touch it, Tom."

"A promise, a promise," Moone lightly said, taking the end of a chest in order to help carry it topside. "If it fits, wear it, General!"

Moone shouted back over his shoulder and deviously grinned at Drake, as if daring him to take the clothes.

"Put this cargo on the *Hind*; in the meantime, I shall return to the *Hind* and muster the Spaniards!"

"Aye!"

And on Drake boarding the *Hind*, he sent for Zarate who minutes later entered Drake's cabin. Fear was on his face.

"Did you spare my wardrobe, General?"

"I did—"

"Thank you, oh kind sir!" the Spaniard said. And then he withdrew from his bosom a gold falcon that was the size of a man's fist; it had been made to appear more magnificent by having an emerald set in its breast. He presented it to Drake.

"Thank you," Drake replied, thoughtfully smiling on viewing it. Then he asked, "Do you have a pilot?"

"Yes. His name is Pascual."

"And does he know the Mexican coast?"

"That he does," the Spaniard replied.

"I want a look at him—the others, too!"

"Most of them are on the ship's bow," Zarate said. There was an awning there under which they had congregated so as to be out of the hot sun.

"Get them!" Drake ordered his cousin, John Drake.

And minutes later a dozen persons filed into Drake's cabin. One of these was an attractive black woman who was wearing a taffeta dress. She had a madras kerchief about her head. She had a grass-woven handbag on one arm, a parasol was on the other. Her face was well-formed, while her color was a chocolate brown; she had a small waist, a rumble-seat bottom and breasts the size of cantaloupes which were held in place by a Chinese undergarment made of silk that kept them from moving. She eyed Drake as if her future was soon to depend on him.

"¿Como te llamas?" What is your name? Drake asked her in Spanish.

"Maria."

"Are you married?"

"No."

"Do you have things on the *La Bella Noche*?" Drake quickly asked.

"Yes—" she demurely answered, while flirtatiously smiling.

"Where are they?"

"Well—"

"Tell my page," Drake said, nodding to John Drake. "He will gather them for you."

"Why, sir?" Zarate said. He had been attentively listening to Drake. Deep concern showed on his face, and he began to breathe heavily, further showing his apprehension.

"She stays!" Drake said. Then he said to his young cousin, "Put her things in my cabin!"

"But, sir, she is my wife's maid!"

"Where is your wife?"

"Panama—" he said, embarrassingly half smiling at the acknowledgment.

"She stays with me! Your wife can get another!" Drake declared. Then he turned to the others and asked, "Who is the pilot?"

"It is I," said a young man with a cleanly-shaven face, taking a step toward Drake.

"You will stay on this ship, pilot it—"

"But, sir, I know nothing of latitude or longitude—I am stupid—"

"You stay, even though you are stupid," Drake said. "To those of you who are leaving, I wish to give you a present for being aboard the *Golden Hind*." Then he took a bag from the chart table, opened it, and withdrew a handful of silver coins, being pieces of eight. And he gave six coins to each of them. And while they were admiring their coins, Drake respectfully spoke to Don Zarate, "I give this sword to you." And Drake presented to him a beautiful ceremonial sword. Then Drake added in a pious voice as if he were going to do a saintly duty, "I will be as kind to your wife's maid as you were." And he swiftly changed the subject and spoke to the prisoners about something that they knew nothing about.

"And tell the Viceroy that I think every day of John Oxenham languishing in prison in Lima. Tell him that one day I plan to return with an armada of ships and I will free him." He then warned, "And if in the meantime the Viceroy has harmed him, tell him that I shall have his head!"

340

CHAPTER 36

THE SACKING OF GUATALCO

Drake's fleet continued to put distance between itself and its pursuers by sailing north. The bark that had been Telo's and now being manned by Moone hugged the coast, while the *Hind* as usual stayed out to sea three miles or more. And so an observer on shore would not have suspected that the two ships were together. Drake was continuing to search for prizes, though his present sailing objective was the small town of Guatalco, a port located between Tehuantepec and Acapulco. It was here that Drake anticipated that he would be able to fill the fleet's empty water barrels. He and Moone were still taking turns manning the bark. Each had made numerous shoreline searches for water, as the water on the *Hind* had gone stale, but the searches had been futile. The shoreline now consisted of mostly barren wasteland. Drake had tried to get water information from Pascual, the new pilot. But he had refused to cooperate until Drake had put a rope around his neck and threatened to hang him from a yardarm; then he had become very cooperative. He had then informed Drake that there was plenty of water in Guatalco.

"Sir, I guarantee water is in Guatalco."

"And if there is no water?"

"I guarantee—"

"And if there is no water, I guarantee that you will lose your head!" Drake said as though he meant it, being complimented by the stern faces of those men on the poop deck.

And so Drake's fleet was sailing for Guatalco in order to take on fresh water. Those crewmen standing the morning watch were nervously anticipating sighting it. Then shortly after four on the morning of April 13, 1579, a lookout in a turret sighted a tiny light on the horizon. It had to be coming from Guatalco.

"General!" the voice of the boatswain of the watch cried from outside Drake's cabin door.

"Yes!" Drake replied in a half-asleep voice.

"We have a tiny light off our starboard bow."

"Guatalco?" Drake asked, referring to the name of the Mexican city. Drake crawled out of the bed of his mistress and hurriedly exited onto the poop deck. He was dressed only in cutaway pantaloons as he was shirtless. This was because of the heat, for even though it was early morning, the heat had not completely subsided. Strangely, the evening before the pilot Pascual had attempted to deter Drake from entering Guatalco by arguing to him that it was a poor port city.

"General, a rat must bring his own grain to Guatalco!"

"But I must have a look!" Drake had replied.

"What fortification does the town have?" Drake now asked the pilot, Pascual, who was standing beside Thomas Blackcollar, whose hand was on the whipstaff and who was staring directly at the light. Blackcollar would soon go below to cook bread, a chore that was now his, which he was doing daily. Drake was still rubbing sleep from his eyes. Minutes before he had pushed aside his black mistress. He had been pleased to discover that she was an excellent sleeping partner. She pleasantly fitted into the curvature of his body, as Drake liked to sleep on his side. She had lazily rolled over onto her stomach so as to make way for her new master, doing it though she was still asleep. She had easily accepted her new master, doing it as though one master was as good as another.

"It has none," replied Pascual, the pilot, saying it as though he were sorry that it was so.

"How many houses would the port have?" Drake asked.

"Maybe seventeen—a church, a store, and a factory—no more," Pascual reluctantly said, shrugging his shoulders and frowning to show that the town was not important.

"Tom, sail for it!"

"Aye!"

And thereafter, when dawn had clearly broken, Horsewill called the crew to early breakfast. Once all sections had eaten, Drake rang the ship's bell so as to call the men not on watch to morning worship. More than fifty men seated themselves on the after deck. Many wore straw hats in expectancy of the hot morning sun. They reverently removed them as Drake and Reverend Fletcher stepped on

342

the deck. Each carried the end of a table. They set it in place. Two books were set on it. One was the Holy Bible. The other was a larger book, being the Book of Martyrs by John Fox. This book was utilized as much during the *Hind*'s daily church service as was the Bible. But it was a very inflammatory text, being rebellious, as it contained many illustrations which portrayed English Protestants being burned at the stake by English Catholics or Spaniards. And actually it did not differentiate between the two. It as well held a dozen additional illustrations of atrocities that Drake and this young cousin had drawn on separate paper.

"Let us bow our heads in prayer!" Fletcher said. And once there was absolute quiet on the *Hind*, with the exception of normal sea noises that included the flapping of windless sails, the creaking of the ship, and the lap of the sea against the *Hind*, Fletcher began his prayer, speaking in his nasal tone:

"Beloved, we are gathered here to worship our God. We have elected to do it voluntarily and directly and not through wicked idols; for we are true believers in you, our God. Now bless our General, who is our leader; look over him. And keep him free from harm. And bless the words that he is going to read from the Book of Martyrs. Amen!"

"Amen!"

Drake stood and raised his head, as if looking toward the heavens which could be identified by white bags of morning clouds with a background of silky blue sky. The sunlight shone on his beard, accentuating its streaks of gold that were spersed with gray. He then looked toward his cabin, saw the prisoners staring at the service, and angrily said to them, as though they were intruders at a private meeting:

"You idolaters may go to the bow! There," Drake said, pointing to the bow of the ship. He stood near the table until they were out of hearing range of his words. He then looked down at the open book, and then he momentarily studied the words. "I will now read to you a chapter from the Book of the Martyrs. It explains how the Spaniards took up idols and worshipped them in place of the true God . . ."

Thereafter, for thirty minutes Drake read propaganda by Fox alleging that the Spaniards did not worship God and that they worshiped idols instead. When Drake tired of reading, he asked Tom Moone to read; and Tom stepped forth and deliberately read, having at times to skip words for his lack of ability to pronounce them, while lisping and stopping occasionally because words would not come forth due to his emotions. He claimed that when he was a boy, he had witnessed the burning of a preacher, and it had had a lasting effect on him.

The hatred that was being engendered by this religious service was quite common to England just then, and it had been daily fare with the crew, though its members had not had any contact with England since they sailed on December 13, 1577. This hatred for the Catholic church had arisen out of the Protestant revolt which had been brewing for decades. It had finally come to a head when Henry VIII broke with the church over his right to marry. This break had been a popular move with the common man. For he saw the church as being too rich and too powerful. And then many of the rich and political saw it as a chance to acquire the valuable lands of the church. And so Henry had a majority of the English people behind him when he created the Church of England, being a Protestant church. He later was succeeded by his son, Edward VI, who attempted to use Protestantism to avoid the natural right of succession. He tried to make it so that on his death, his sister Mary, daughter of Catherine of Aragon, being a strong Catholic, could not succeed him. But in spite of his efforts, succession was the winner. And Catholic Mary was crowned as Queen in 1553. She thereafter married Philip, son of Charles V of Spain, who was eleven years her junior. He would eventually become Philip II of Spain.

Shortly after Mary took power, she had Parliament reenact the ancient heresy laws. They were met by tremendous dissent. The principal leaders of these dissenters occupied the pulpits of England. Mary turned on them with a vengeance; she had hundreds of Protestant ministers burned at the stake. She banished others from England. One of these was Edmond Drake, father of Francis Drake, about whose banishment the writer has previously written. Mary, of course, was succeeded by the Protestant Elizabeth. Even though Elizabeth was strongly committed to the Protestant Church, she attempted to govern so as to safeguard the rights of all the English whether Protestant or Catholic. But Francis Drake was not a moderate; he had been raised in the house of a Protestant zealot, who hated Catholics; and so Drake carried within his powerful chest the burning fire of a zealot. He saw an evil in the Catholic church that superseded his hatred for the Spanish. During the twice-a-day services on the *Hind*, he usually read from the Book of Martyrs, which had inculcated the same fervor in all of his men. One of these converts was Nuno da Silva, as he now regularly attended these twice-a-day services. The prisoner, Pascual, took note of this; and he would subsequently do Nuno much harm by informing the Inquisition that Nuno da Silva was a Protestant convert.

It was eight in the morning when Drake's two ships stood up the channel that would take them to Guatalco.

"Are the culverins manned?" Drake asked Hurd. Both were standing on the poop deck. The principal man with his hand on the whipstaff was Black Halder, a twenty-two-year-old seaman from Plymouth. Drake had to know they were manned, as he had told Clark to do it. And Clark was extremely obedient.

"Yes, General! Clark has his crews in place," Hurd replied.

"That is the harbor," Pascual said, pointing. The two ships were now near the mouth; they were just minutes from a point where the channel narrowed so that they could not easily turn back.

"What is that ship?" Drake asked Pascual, while pointing.

"A freighter that belongs to Juan de Madrid," Pascual replied, pointing to a small ship anchored in the harbor.

"Would it be armed?" Drake asked.

"No—"

"I will board that ship!" Drake said, cupping his hands to his mouth. He was speaking to Moone, who was steering the nearby *Christopher*. Moone nodded his head to show understanding.

"And the town?" Moone asked. He glanced from the ship to the town.

"We will inspect it together!" Drake replied while showing his teeth.

"Aye!" Moone replied, wiping sweat from his face, as the morning sun was already very hot.

"Tom," Drake said, speaking to his brother, who was dressed out in his armor. "Lower the longboat—we'll board that freighter, check it; then we will make our landing on the town!"

"Right!"

"My armor!" Drake said to his cousin, John, who he noted was developing a sparse chin beard. He was no longer a boy. The *Hind* had had six boys assigned to her. All were growing toward manhood—each was apprenticed to a craft. John had been apprenticed to Drake to learn navigation. But the others were permitted to learn as

345

much navigation as their interest and ability allowed. Most had older brothers aboard. Willie Fortescue and Joey Kidd had been under twelve years old when they came aboard. Drake had permitted them to sail on the voyage because they had older brothers serving in the *Pelican*, which of course he later renamed the *Golden Hind*.

"It is here, General!"

Drake boarded the longboat with twenty armed men; they rowed for the freighter, where two of its crew manned its rails while anxiously studying the boats. Then they turned and shouted warnings to their captain. But Drake and a dozen men were soon on the ship, boarding it by the use of its sea ladder. Then they easily took the ship, and Drake began to make a hurried inspection of it. He discovered that it carried a cargo of grain, which did not interest him, as he was more interested in treasure. But he did not find any. Drake entered the navigator's cabin, and he hurriedly gathered up the master's charts and astrolabe and put them in a leather satchel; he then put it under his arm and returned to the longboat.

"Let's take the town!" Drake cried out to the crew on returning to the boat and taking his place at the tiller.

"Cheers!"

Then at his beckoning, his crew began to row hard for the shore. They were followed by the *Christopher*, whose crew had put out oars; now all were rowing hard for shore. The hard rowing from these two boats aroused concern from those persons standing at the boat landing. These were mostly crewmen and passengers who were preparing to board a small boat that would take them to the ship of Juan de Madrid.

"¡Son ingleses!" They are English! a sailor shouted to some of the townspeople who had assembled in the town square, which also faced the harbor. He had correctly guessed the identity of the men in the boats. This excited the townspeople and they shouted at persons nearby. Confusion reigned.

"¡Armense!" Arm yourselves! the sailor cried.

Then those persons that had been standing in the square ran to their houses and stores. All soon returned with weapons. Some had arquebuses; others had swords. The man in the lead was Gaspar de Vargas, alcalde of the small town. He frantically beckoned to the townspeople to assemble in the square with him and join him in fighting the English.

"Bang! Bang!" the English soldiers in Drake's boat fired their arquebuses toward the square, which was an easy target as it was more than a block square. The arquebus fire did not scatter the townspeople, though they could now see that Drake and his men were landing. The arquebus was an inaccurate weapon at a distance; this was not so of the deck gun located on the bow of *Christopher*. For on Moone firing this gun, called the murderer, chain shot went whistling through the air; it hit a tree and cut down its top which fell near the armed townspeople. This round of fire was terribly demoralizing, as it caused panic among the townspeople, and they ran until they reached a patch of woods on a hill behind the town.

"Tom, you secure that side; I will secure this side," Drake said to Moone, while walking at a cautious trot. He pointed to the church, being on the side that Moone was to search.

"Aye. Whistle if you need me!"

"You, you, follow me!" Drake said, speaking to a group of soldiers. He entered a warehouse and studied its goods, which he immediately knew were valuable and which included linens, cottons, silks, foods, hardware and the like. Its owner was not in sight.

"Over there, Tom!" Drake said to his brother, Tom Drake, pointing to a door which led to a house where Francisco Gomez Rengifo resided, who was the factor of the warehouse.

"It's locked, General!"

"Knock it down!"

A soldier found an ax and struck the door twice. "Whack! Whack!" and the door opened.

"¡Abajo, perro!" Down, dog! Drake shouted to the proprietor who was crouched in a corner of the sitting room. His wife and two children would soon be discovered; they were attempting to hide in an adjacent bedroom.

"¿Donde esta su oro o plata?" Where is your gold and silver? Drake demanded, speaking in an urgent voice.

"¡Aqui!" Here! the Spaniard said. Panic showed on his face. He pointed to a corner where there were two chests and a pot. The latter held almost a bushel of silver coins. The chests held a bag of gold coins and many valuable silks and linens.

"You are my prisoner!" Drake said. "Obey me and you will not be harmed. Your factory is now my property! And this is idolatry!" Drake said on spying a foot-long crucifix. Irritancy was in his voice,

347

as he took the foot-long porcelain crucifix by its feet and struck it against the wall, causing it to break into many pieces.

"What have I done to you to merit this!" Rengifo sadly asked, extending his empty hands in a begging expression.

"This is retribution for the many wrongs that you have done to the English!" Drake haughtily answered without bothering to explain what the wrongs were.

"Me?" the Spaniard doubtfully asked.

"Guard him and the treasure!" Drake said to a soldier; then he added, "Let us move to the next house!"

Tom Moone led a dozen soldiers into the town church. "Destroy those idols!" he shouted to his men, pointing at the life-size images of Christ and Virgin Mary. "Use your axes!" he shouted to soldiers who were pulling them down. Two soldiers then came forward; they took their axes and mutilated them. Thereafter, they took the gold and silver vessels that had been used in the church services. Then one of the soldiers threw the ceremonial wafers to the floor.

"Do you want the bell?" Thomas Grige shouted. Grige was a sailor-swabber with a hunchback. He was pointing to the bell that was in the belfry. He would later make a fitful decision and become one of the first white men to settle in California.

"Yes—get it; we can use it to call the watch!" Moone replied, while momentarily eyeing the hunchback agilely climb to the belfry.

Drake entered a building which was more ornate than any of the previous, and he entered a room with several heavy, highly-embellished chairs and a decorated dais, which Drake correctly surmised was a courtroom; two Spaniards and three obviously poor Negroes were crouched together in a corner.

"¡Que es!" Drake demanded to know.

"¡Corte!" Court! one of the cringing Spaniards replied.

"¿Porque?" Why? Drake asked in an official way. His back was now ramrod straight. He haughtily looked down at them, as if he had the authority to demand to know why there was a trial.

All five nervously talked at once, explaining that a trial had been taking place when Drake attacked the town. The three Blacks were slaves; they were being tried for the serious offense of attempting to burn down the town.

"You are my prisoners!" Drake said to the Spanish officials as if he intended to try them. "And you," he said to the Negroes. "You are free; you may sail with me on my ship if you want!"

"Huh!"

"Do you want to go?"

Two of the blacks immediately raised their hands, having made quick elections to sail with Drake on the *Golden Hind*.

"¡Voy! ¡Voy!" I go! I go!

"Take these prisoners to the longboat," Drake said to a soldier.

Three hours after Drake and his men landed at Guatalco, Drake returned to the *Hind* with his prisoners. He ordered the boatswain to place the prisoners in the *Hind*'s jail; then he spoke to his Master:

"Tom, we must now board water; put together a working party; take your barrels to the town. I have learned that there is plenty of water in the forest behind the town. Be careful, as there are some armed citizens in the woods!"

"When will we be sailing?" Hurd asked.

"We will confer about that after you board your water," Drake deviously said, as if he did not like to answer such questions.

"I'll do it right away!"

The loading of water usually required a strong effort by many men; it was more so on this occasion, since Drake wanted every barrel filled. He even confiscated some barrels from the factory. And he also had them filled. And so the loading of water took several days. On April 16, 1579, the principal officials of the town and state, including the governor, became so concerned about the prisoners that Drake had taken and placed in confinement on the *Hind*, that they held a meeting in the town hall. Thereafter, Governor Lopez, a short man with straight black hair and a dark complexion, boarded the *Hind* on his own volition and he spoke to Drake:

"General, I beseech you to release your prisoners!" the Governor said. Worry was on his face. His chin nervously twitched.

"We will."

"When?" the governor asked. His black eyes anxiously stared.

"In due time," Drake politely said. Then he attempted to change the subject. "Would you like to see my ship? You might find it interesting. I have five more just like it," Drake said as though he were the leader of a great fleet, which was set to converge on the town.

"In due course, we may. But the purpose of our visit is to obtain a release of our people," the Governor said. "General, you must realize our concern! You have robbed us of our goods, our silver and gold—made us poor. What need do you have of our townspeople? Please release them!" the Governor pleaded.

349

"When I am ready, I will do so—however, now I am waiting for the other five ships in my fleet. We were separated by a great storm off the coast of Peru," Drake said, saying it because he knew that such a report would be repeated to the Spanish officials. "Once they are here, I will release them. I will repeat my offer—would you like to inspect my ship, see how an English man-of-war operates?"

"Well—" the Governor reluctantly said, frowning.

"And then we shall have dinner and wine," Drake politely said, speaking as though he wished to be friends.

By noon of April 16, 1579, numerous changes had taken place on the *Hind*. Her water barrels had been filled and stowed. Some were even being used as ballast. Her guns were being dismounted and secured to keep them from moving in a rough sea. The gunport lids were now slammed shut. Sailors were caulking them tight. And shortly after noon, all the prisoners were brought top side; Drake gave each a gift, then he ordered them to be taken ashore. The only prisoners that now remained were his mistress, the two refugees, and Nuno da Silva. Drake called a meeting under a canvas awning that was located on the bow of the ship. Those persons present were Drake, Tom Moone, Tom Hurd and Tom Drake.

"We sail on the morning breeze!" Drake said.

"To where?" Hurd asked.

"North—we must find ourselves a nice cove and refit the *Hind*."

"And then?" Moone asked, half smiling.

"Explore a bit—we may get a chance to trade those petticoats," Drake said, referring to the hundred colorful Indian petticoats that they had taken from the warehouse; then he added, "We will then return to England."

"How?"

"I am not yet certain. It may be through the Strait," meaning the Anian Strait. "But we will be leaving New Spain," Drake replied, sweating. He wore a fancy linen shirt. It now was soaked in perspiration.

"The black woman?" Moone asked.

"She stays," Drake said, frowning as if thinking, trying not to indicate his feelings about her. But in truth he was enjoying her—yet it was sex and nothing else. And how could it be otherwise, for her interests were sex and her toilet. And this was a bother—she was lazy and untidy—her oils and perfumes lay on the floor. John Drake

350

picked up after her; else her petticoats and undergarments would have collected on the floor.

"The blacks from Guatalco?" Moone asked.

"They stay!"

"And Nuno?" Tom Drake asked. He like the others had become attached to the tiny, inoffensive man who Drake had kidnapped more than a year earlier. Nuno had greatly helped the venture. But all knew that they no longer needed him. He did not know this coast. Then, Drake was a splendid navigator, who learned easily, and they had captured many maps. They now would probably be doing more exploring—Nuno certainly did not know the Northern waters.

"This is his last day on the *Hind!*" Drake said in a decisive way, exhibiting an important leadership trait. For Drake had the ability to cut ties when it was to his advantage; however, his doing so was lacking in charity, for Nuno had given much to Drake and he had received little in return. He certainly had taught Drake how to navigate by the use of rhumblines.

"We no longer need him!" Moone said, saying it in spite of the thinking to the contrary by many of the Spaniards who had been prisoners on the *Hind*. For all thought that Nuno was the navigator. Many of the ex-prisoners would subsequently give statements to the effect that Nuno da Silva did all of the navigating. This was possibly because Drake had spent so much time in the pinnace searching for prizes; yet Moone was convinced that whatever knowledge Nuno had, Drake now had also, as he was a quick learner. He was further convinced that Drake was a much better navigator, maybe the best navigator alive.

"I will give him fifteen minutes to gather his personal things; then I shall give him some objects of gold; and then you may take him ashore," Drake decisively said to his brother Tom.

"It will not be easy to leave him," Tom Drake said, speaking for all. He had become attached to the inoffensive man who had sensed when he was wanted and when he was not; and when there was the latter, he would leave Drake's cabin and join the steersman.

"The venture comes first!" Drake said; then he bowed his head and solemnly said, "Let us pray!"

After the prayer, Drake adjourned the meeting. He then returned to his cabin. He entered, ignoring his black mistress who was seated on the bed with her hands clasping her knees. She touched his leg, commenced to rub it softly, and smiled coyly. He pushed her hand away. He eyed Nuno da Silva who was seated at the chart table. John Drake was standing beside him. He was sketching the harbor of Guatalco. Nuno's brown eyes glistened. His tongue apprehensively licked the hair surrounding his lips. Da Silva was suspicious that the meeting that had just taken place on the bow of the *Hind* concerned him.

"What is it, General?" he asked. His voice trembled.

"I am freeing you, allowing you to return to your people," Drake said; then he crossed to the man, reached down and embraced him.

"But you can't! The Inquisition will imprison me!" Nuno hurtfully cried. Then tears flowed from his eyes.

"But you have been my prisoner," Drake argued.

"No—I do not want to go!" Nuno emphatically said. He had not revealed it, but he secretly believed that Drake could not do without him. And then he wanted to help Drake navigate the *Hind* back to England, even claim credit for having navigated the *Hind* on its voyage, which he had decided would become a historic one.

"You must—get your things. You must leave within fifteen minutes!"

"No, General—oh, oh!" Nuno wailed, recalling that he had become a Protestant in his thinking. More so, he had been seen taking part in Protestant services. He did not fully understand the English readings from the *Book of Martyrs*, but he had known that the book was being read. He had even seen the book on the table before the services began. And he did know the thoughts that it expressed. He knew that the Inquisition would punish him. "They will kill me!"

"I will give you some gold—" Drake said in a conciliatory voice.

"That would make it worse!" Nuno said, weeping like a child, taking hold of Drake's hand.

"Use it to bribe them!" Drake said, withdrawing his hand, indicating that he was refusing to change his plans. "You need to return to Portugal, join your family, and this is your last chance!"

"But I want to stay, General!"

"Hurry, man! But first embrace me, and God be with you!" Drake said in a stressful voice.

"God—God, help me!" Nuno wailed, exiting from the room with his ditty bag of possessions that included his diary that he had dutifully kept throughout the voyage.

"Maintain your belief in God and all will be well!" Drake piously said, glancing up at the pilot. Then he dropped his eyes to the chart desk and kept them there as if deep in thought. He would not raise them until Nuno had left the *Hind*.

CHAPTER 37

THE STRAIT OF ANIAN

"And what course shall I steer, General?" Hurd asked Drake. Both men had their hands on the whipstaff. Drake had just stepped from his cabin. The *Hind* was now ten miles at sea; she was sailing due west on a calm sea; the shore was just a line on the horizon at the stern of the *Hind*. The *Christopher* was off her starboard beam. The two ships were only making three knots, though they had a fairly fresh westerly breeze. This poor speed was not only because their bottoms were covered with sea growth, but due to the *Hind* being heavily laden with treasure.

"I would say that we're making three knots," Drake said without answering the question.

"You are right, General. I checked it 30 minutes ago," Hurd replied.

"Take the whip," Drake said to his boatswain. And on Fowler joining the pair on the poop deck, Drake then said to Hurd, "Come!" Then Drake turned and motioned for Hurd to follow him to his cabin. And once they were inside, Drake then said, "We'll sail northwest for about 500 leagues. And by doing that, we will sail clear of the coast," Drake said, pointing to North America on the map, which the mapmaker had drawn so that it extended much further west than in fact it actually does. And once again Drake would accept the map as true, though it was greatly in error, as North America did not extend as far west as shown by the Mercator map.

"And then?" Hurd asked. Expectancy was on his face.

"We'll sail northeast," Drake said, taking a piece of chalk from a box on the table. He took a brass sphere from a shelf and set it on the chart table. This sphere had been a part of the navigational equipment of the *Caga Fuego*. Then he drew a chalk line on the brass sphere. The newly drawn line extended outward in a northwesterly direction so that it stayed clear of the supposed land mass. Then Drake drew another line that extended northeasterly so that it met the land mass at 50 degrees latitude. "We will coast to the strait," he said, meaning that they would follow the coast; and he pointed to his route which he expected to follow, which would have led him into present-day Alaska.

"You intend to seek passage through the Anian Strait?" Hurd asked, though doing so in a manner of accord. He was referring to the mythical passage that many map makers thought existed near the top of the world; they believed that this Anian Strait was an open body of water through which a ship during the summer could sail, doing it much like Drake had done when he sailed the Magellan Strait. If such a passage existed, it would permit the *Hind* to cross the top of the world through the Anian Strait and then exit directly to England; this would save the *Hind* thousands of miles of travel. And this of course would be an additional star for Drake's crown, as he would not only be its discoverer but also the first to traverse it.

"Yes—" Drake indecisively said, while his eyes lingered on the sphere, as if sure that the strait existed.

"Do you know that it exists?"

"Well, that map says that it does," Drake said, referring to the Mercator map on the chart desk which showed that a clear passage existed at 66 degrees latitude. "In my meeting with Dr. Dee, the Queen's geographer, he told me that it existed; and he practically charged me to find it!"

"Dee says it exists?" Hurd asked, thinking of the authority that he commanded. He, too, had heard of Dee. He knew that he was a mathematician who had written much on navigation. He also had prepared many navigation tables. Hurd had even used some of his navigation tables.

"It is the same latitude as Norway or Iceland; and I know many seamen who have sailed to these countries in the summer," Drake said, attempting to explain the possibilities. "But now I must speak to Moone," Drake said, breaking away. He crossed to the open door and exited onto the portico deck. Then he cupped his hands to his mouth and shouted to the bark which was two hundred yards off the *Hind*'s port beam, "Tom—Tom!"

"Yes, General!" Moone replied, standing and putting a hand to his ear.

"Keep within hailing distance; but if for some reason we separate, seek land at forty-eight degrees latitude. We will find you!"

"Not fifty, General?" Hurd asked, quizzically staring at Drake as he had joined him at the door.

"I would look for him at forty-eight!" Drake deviously declared without explaining his incongruous statements.

"Aye! I presume that we'll be needing foul weather clothing, General!"

"Yes—"

"Like the Strait of Magellan?"

"I hope that the weather is not as bad as that which we experienced on leaving the strait," Drake replied, recalling the terrible hardships that they had experienced after the *Hind* had cleared the Magellan Strait. "But it will be summer—for it will probably be July before we reach that point."

"I agree."

"I will tell the men to get out their canvas jackets and re-tar them."

"Aye!"

And thereafter, the *Hind* slowly sailed out to sea; Drake had plotted the course thinking that at all times the *Hind* was keeping within 100 miles of land. Yet that was not so, for the *Hind* was sailing further and further out to sea. This was because the land space on the map was incorrect, for the geographer had drawn North America to be twice its actual size.

"Will there be ice in the strait?" Hurd asked Drake, who was seated at the chart table. He was busily sketching Maria, his Black mistress. He had drawn her astride a finback whale, being one of many that they had seen. He was enjoying Maria. She had easily adjusted to Drake and seemingly had not objected to her capture. She spent most of her time lounging in his cabin, as she was very lazy; she most always sat or lay on his bunk. Much of this time was spent eating. And she had feasted so on Horsewill's cooking until she had become quite plump. This was partially because Willie Fortescue, Horsewill's apprentice, was so fond of her. He showed it by bringing her extra helpings at mealtime. Then he brought her cookies that Blackcollar had made. And then she was learning to play backgammon from Drake. The dice often noisily clicked in Drake's cabin, and their voices would rise from the feverish intensity of their play.

It was now May 15, 1579; the *Hind* had been to sea for almost thirty days. The air had become cool; the men frolicking on the main deck now wore shirts.

"There will soon be ice," Drake replied, raising his eyes and looking out the open door. "Stop that skylarking!" Drake shouted at a sailor on the main deck who was chasing another. There was little room for running. They immediately stopped. A small group of men were huddled with Boatswain Fowler on the deck beneath Drake's cabin; they were tying knots. And to their right was seated another small group of men. They were making rope yarn from some pieces of old rope. This would be used to make chafing gear for serving ropes, bending sails and many other purposes.

"Ice," Hurd said, indicating that he was not quite satisfied with Drake's answer.

"But it will still be summer," Drake explained, dropping his pencil and walking to the door. He stepped outside and took an interesting ornament from his pocket; it was a gold skull the size of a large marble, which he had lifted from the *Caga Fuego*. It was attached to a chain that was linked together by five smaller skulls. All had been made of gold. Drake pried open the skull's jaws; and it became a tiny sundial. He held it to the sun.

"Almost time for a sun sight!" Drake declared on obtaining the time.

"When do we change our course?" Hurd asked, looking at the chart on the table.

"Tomorrow. The bearings that I took of the midday sun yesterday indicated that we were at forty-eight degrees," Drake said.

"And mine put us at forty-nine," Hurd said, now conversing with Drake much like Nuno had done, but doing it in English.

"You were close—the astrolabe is best used on land," Drake said, referring to the instrument that Hurd had used in determining the angle of the sun. This in turn had given him the ship's latitude. Drake had accepted his figure over Hurd's; yet Drake still did not know his position for sure, because he did not have a time piece accurate enough to figure his longitude.

"Tomorrow we will make our cut," meaning toward North America; then you will steer northeast by east," Drake added.

"And how far do you estimate that we are from land, General?" Hurd asked while still studying the chart. Its border had many sketches on it. One of its most unusual was a Spanish ship which had been stopped by a wall of fog.

"I would say ninety to one hundred miles," Drake replied. It had been his plan on sailing northwest to keep a sufficient distance from the shore so that the *Hind* would not be detected by coasting vessels. Yet he had wanted to stay close enough to land so that he could coast whenever he decided that there was no longer any danger from coastal vessels. This would enable him to explore and map the coastline. Then Drake added, "That is providing this map is somewhere near correct."

But Drake's estimate would be wrong, for he had relied on a map that was not only incorrect as to the passage, but the land space that the map maker had given to North America was greatly exaggerated. It would now be weeks before they sighted land. And in order to do so, Drake would need to steer due east.

"I am baffled!" Drake said, staring at the map. It was now May 22, 1579, and they had not yet sighted land. More so, there had not been any sighting of land birds. The reader will recall that Drake knew that the sighting of some birds, like frigates, was a sure sign of nearby land, as such birds do not land on the water. Others, like boobies, always returned to land at nightfall. None of these had been sighted. And then there were other possible signs that indicated land. These included breaks and swells; then there were black, thick clouds that indicated land; as well, there could be motionless clouds that could be caught up in mountains; and then there was the reflection of sand in the mountains.

"General," Master Hurd said to Drake, "the men are tired; the water is bad; we need to touch land." And he pointed to the main deck. Many of the men were feeling the chill; they huddled in groups and occasionally turned to stare at the poop deck. Yet many of the sailors still worked in the rigging, and the sailmaker and his helpers still patched sails. But because the *Hind* had an abundance of manpower, some men did not have jobs. Drake was permitting these men to engage in games, such as backgammon. Yet they had tired of it. Even Mary no longer wanted to toss the dice.

"I know—it's the map," Drake said, glancing out on deck. Most of the men now wore canvas or woolen jackets. A few of the men walked the tiny deck like prisoners in jail. This was in sharp contrast to the many activities that they had pursued at the start of the voyage from Guatalco when many had been engaged in regular shipboard chores. But still, Drake had allotted time for games. He offered prizes of small bags of silver to the winners of backgammon tournaments and arm and leg wrestling jousts. One sailor even produced a deck of cards and had begun a game of trump, which in truth was a gambling game. Drake had stopped it as he was opposed to gambling of any sort. But he was not opposed to jackstones, played with bones, which was ordinarily a gambling game, though the men had agreed not to gamble when playing it. Some played it over and over. And still others had spent time darning or making jackets in expectancy of the cold weather that they knew they would soon experience. Their mood had been jovial; all had thought that they were bound for home—England. But now they were glum. Many were suspicious of Drake's navigational ability. They wondered but that it had been a mistake for him to let Nuno da Silva leave the ship.

"Punch the fire, John!" Drake sharply said to his young cousin on returning to the cabin; he was referring to the fire in the grate. "I feel the cold! Look at Mary! Why, she is freezing!" She was wrapped in a blanket.

"Aye, General!"

"It is the map!" Drake said, repeating his earlier statement.

"And the strait?" Hurd asked. His face was solemn and thoughtful.

"Well, if the map is bad as to one aspect, would it not be bad as to all?" Drake asked. "The geographer certainly has not visited this part of the world, nor has he talked to anyone who has been here." Drake was arguing with himself as much as he was with Hurd.

"I would reason that," the Master replied. "Yet you know much more than I!"

"Let's steer due east!" Drake said.

"Aye!"

The *Hind* sailed due east for fourteen days. It was a trying time for the crew; the weather had turned cold, as the winds from the North Pole were blowing frigid air, and so one norther followed another. The weather had now become so much like an early English spring that many of the sailors in the rigging were thinking about England. Most had not seriously thought of England for some time until this change in the weather.

"Land ho!" a lookout cried on the morning of June 4, 1579.

"America!" Drake said on looking out from his cabin door. The air was still cold but bearable. Drake thoughtfully eyed the distant mountain peaks peeping out from the haze. What was the land like? Was there gold, silver or precious stones in that land? Was the land fit to grow grain? Would it be a fit place for Englishmen to settle?

"How much is the map off, General?" Hurd asked on Drake returning to the chart table. John Drake was once again seated at the chart table. He had had a good view of the mountain peaks of North America, and he was now sketching them.

"A thousand miles at least," Drake replied.

"Incredible!" Hurd declared.

"And what course shall we steer on reaching land?" Hurd asked.

"Well," Drake said, thinking, recalling Dr. John Dee. He could visualize him pacing the floor of his huge library; he now pictured him dressed in his tiny black cap and his long black gown. He seemingly lived in a sea of thousands of books, and the number of those books had overwhelmed Drake. He thought on himself sailing from England with his tiny library consisting of Nicolas de Nicolais' translation of Pedro de Medini's manual, "The Art of Navigation," 1554; Eden's translation of Cortes' "The Art of Navigation," 1561; and Bourne's "Regiment for the Sea," 1574. He as well carried Pigafetta's account of Magellan's voyage. Thus, he had come this far with a library that he could have held in his hands. He recalled Dee saying to him, "You must explore Terra Australius once you have passed through the Magellan Strait!" But there was no Terra Australius, for he had discovered that Tierra del Fuego was an island, which was part of a chain of islands that were not a part of a southern continent. So Dee had been wrong about that. Now he was wrong about North America; his map had included thousands of miles of land space that did not exist. This had caused Drake to sail more than a thousand miles east where land should have been. He recalled Dee's words, "The Strait of Anian has to exist; the world has to have balances. For if a strait exists in the southern hemisphere, then there has to be one in the northern hemisphere!" But Dee had not voyaged, and Drake now knew that voyaging was the only way that the world could be charted. Drake surmised that Dee had read too many books by men with a limited knowledge like himself. And so, Drake concluded that Dee had not experienced the vagaries of traveling the world, which is the only way that one man can really know for sure whether straits exist or not. Drake made his decision:

"The map is bad!" Drake declared, now being expectantly watched also by Mary and John Drake.

"I agree, General. But what course are we to follow?"

"If it is wrong as to land space, then it would be wrong as to the strait!" Drake declared, reasoning with himself. He knew that Dee had asked him to explore the coast, find the strait, traverse it and exit unto England. He also knew that a request from Dee was the same as an order from Elizabeth.

"We shall sail south and search for a place to rest and career the *Hind*!" Drake said, stroking his beard, eyeing his black mistress who was seated on his bunk. She had a blanket about her legs and was eating cookies from a tin that Willie had brought her. Her dress had been so careless that her voluptuous breasts appeared ready to burst from her chemise, which she had to realize was distracting to the men. Even so, she was attempting to understand Drake's explanation.

"And the Queen?" Hurd asked, recalling that Drake had told him that Dee's order was the same as if it had come from the Queen.

"I will handle that—"

Thereafter, Drake took up his pen and wrote into the *Hind*'s log:

"We arrived on the coast of America on June 4, 1579, at a latitude of 48 degrees. We thereafter coasted northward until 50 degrees latitude; then it became very cold; the deck became coated with ice; all ropes froze solid; we began to see huge piles of ice. I have made the decision to seek warm weather and shelter where I can make repairs and rest my men; then once that is done, I shall decide our future course. F. Drake."

CHAPTER 38

NEW ALBION

Drake sailed the *Hind* south along the coast of what is present-day Washington and Oregon closely followed by Moone in the *Christopher*. He was searching for a safe cove where he could sail the *Hind* and careen her, then clean her bottom and make repairs. But that would not be easy to find because of the precipitous, rocky nature of the coast. He as well wanted a site with warmth. But this, too, would be difficult to find because they had been experiencing a norther since they had first sighted land. The cold air was unduly bothersome to the men. This was more due to their having spent so much time in warmer climates than the actual cold. Drake was hindered from finding a cove by the fog, which at times blanketed the coast. This kept him from sending Moone in close. Each time there was a break in the fog and Moone did go in close, he would sight a rocky shore. And that spelled danger!

The *Hind* was having problems with her crew. It had been caused by many things—the cold, the cramped quarters, and the expectancy of home. Even so, the *Hind* had had two serious fist fights between seamen and soldiers. There were threats of more. A soldier had drawn his knife on a sailor. Drake had stopped the games; he had ordered Boatswain Fowler to work all of the men topside and below decks. He had had to put two of the *Hind*'s soldiers aboard the *Christopher*. And so Drake had become so fretful about the weather that he spent much of his time anxiously pacing the poop deck. Then without a warning there was a change.

"The sun is out, General!" Hurd said. This was the first time that the sun had been out in several days. Hurd noted Drake's face. It was lined from strain, but it seemingly began to relax as he eagerly searched the eastern shore for an opening.

"And a beautiful one, too!" Drake exclaimed, beginning to move his arms so as to exercise them.

"I will not be needing this jacket," Hurd said, removing his canvas jacket which was lined with a sheep skin. Hurd's hair was long. It was greased and tied in the back with a strip of leather like Fletcher did his hair.

"Let us enter that bay," Drake said, pointing to an opening on his port bow, which had the appearance of a large bay. The date was June 17, 1579. The two ships were now at 38.5 latitude. The air was rapidly warming; Drake had begun to feel it, and so he removed his jacket. He hung it on a post in the helmsman's shelter. The sun was beginning to burn the fog from the coast, and lift the veil that was clouding it, which also continued to raise Drake's spirits. His voice now had its usual zest.

"Right full rudder!" Hurd said to the helmsman, who then turned his whip staff to the right; this of course would turn the *Hind* left and into the bay. This was because the rudder answered opposite to the movement of the helm. The *Hind* answered nicely; she swung her bow toward the bay. Her sails were bagged with wind; and she quickly reacted, though she was making only two-and-one-half knots. The *Hind* now was sailing directly for the mouth of the bay, which was about six miles across.

"Center your helm!" Hurd said to the helmsman. The *Hind* answered nicely as if she knew that she soon would reach a stopping point and then she would be able to rest.

"There appears to be a pass!" Drake said, pointing to an opening in the bay. The *Hind*'s bow was pointed directly for it.

"Have you noticed those cliffs?" Hurd said, pointing to the port beam. The cliffs were a chalky, pinkish-white color and tall like those at Dover. A colony of murres was nesting there; dozens of them dove from the cliffs and into the water. Flocks of gulls fretfully flew before the cliffs.

"Yes, they remind me of home," Drake replied. "The wind is from the port beam," he added. He was ever conscious of the movement of the wind and the sea current.

"Yet she sails well," Hurd added. Then he asked, "Do you think that it is a safe harbor, General?" Hurd was pointing to the cove to which they were proceeding.

"We will see. Use your lead and line!" Drake shouted to two seamen standing on the bow. Each held a tubular-appearing piece of lead in one hand which was attached to a rope that was held in the other hand. The rope had symbolic markings on it. Each sailor tossed his lead and line in front and to the side of the *Hind*'s bow.

"Six fathoms, General!"

"Aye!" Drake replied, nodding his head, knowing that there was thirty-six feet of water.

"Six fathoms, General!" the other cried.

"Aye!"

"We need a place with a fairly sandy shore," Hurd said. Then he pointed to the shoreline of the bay, which had a crescent shape to it. "That will not do!" Hurd said. He knew that it was too exposed to the wind. Drake already knew it, for he had the *Hind* sailing directly for what appeared to be a pass in the middle of the crescent-shaped bay. This appeared to lead into yet another bay.

"Tom!" Drake shouted to the *Christopher*, which was off the *Hind*'s port beam.

"Aye, General!"

"We need to investigate that passage," Drake said, pointing to the opening between two sand spits. "It may be a strait into a safe harbor."

"Do you want me to do it?"

"I want Tom Drake to traverse it first with the longboat!"

"Right—"

"And you follow—"

"Aye!"

"Take plenty of soundings—we will need fifteen feet to enter!" The *Hind* was drawing thirteen feet due to her heavy load of silver. The extra two feet would be for safety's sake.

"Aye!"

"Reef your sails!" Drake shouted. "I want to drag anchor!"

"Reef 'em!" Boatswain Fowler answered and then he began to speak to sailors in the rigging concerning the reefing of sails.

"Drop anchor!" Drake ordered his brother. He intended to use the anchor to inch the *Hind* toward the passage though he would still have the ability to stop her when he wished.

Drake now had his eye on the longboat. She was moving at a nice speed. She was using rowers, though they were not needed, as Tom Drake had rigged a lateen sail that was bagging wind. Two soldiers aboard her were taking soundings. Tom Drake had his hand on the tiller. His head moved left and right, paying little heed to the hundreds of gulls that were soaring overhead, for he was intently eyeing the water and the sand bars on either side. He passed between the bars and made a small circle of the inner bay while sounding; then he returned to the *Christopher* where he conferred with Tom Moone. Thereafter, Moone piloted the *Christopher* into the harbor. The longboat then returned to the *Hind*.

"How is it, Tom?" Drake asked his brother.

"We're on the flood!" Tom replied. "The passage is not bad at all. There is sixteen to eighteen feet of water between the sand bars. It is much deeper in the harbor," he said, pointing.

"Is there a place to careen?"

"A beautiful place!" Tom Drake said, smiling, showing his happiness in finding a stopping place.

"Then take me in!"

"Aye!"

"Master Hurd," Drake said, "give me some sail!"

"Aye—"

"But make it short!"

"Short sail. Aye!"

The *Hind* thereafter sailed into the harbor that would subsequently carry Drake's name.

"Where do we careen?" Drake asked Tom Drake who was in the longboat which was now alongside.

"There," Tom Drake replied, pointing to a sheltered cove that was now on the *Hind*'s port beam.

"Right full rudder!" Hurd ordered. Then while the *Hind* was slowly answering the rudder, he looked up to the top of the hillside. He saw what appeared to be a cluster of conical huts. "Indians, General!"

"You're right—"

"You still want to locate here?"

"Yes—we will just have to build a fort!"

"On the hill?" Hurd asked, pointing to what appeared to be a natural site.

"No—it would create too much work. We'll build it near the water!"

"Right rudder, helmsman!" Drake said. He of course wished to go left.

"It's going to be a nice day!" Drake said, rolling his sleeves on feeling the new warmth. He looked down on the deck. It was

366

crowded with men. All were talking and pointing, while eyeing the rolling brown hills. Willie Fortescue and Joey Kidd crossed the deck carrying a pail of dishwater which they tossed over the side. Then they joined the others in the pointing. "The warm weather will make careening easier," Drake said. He knew that some members of his crew would have to spend some time in the water in order to careen the *Hind*. He also knew that the *Hind* had to have long weeds and barnacles growing from her hull; thus, her bottom would have to have a good cleaning. But worse, she had a serious leak, which was requiring almost constant pumping. Drake would soon discover that it had been caused by teredo worms.

"There!" Hurd said, pointing at the Indian houses. A dozen near-naked Indians were now standing in front of their skin-covered houses. All were pointing at the ships. They had the right to do so out of curiosity, for these were possibly the first ships that they had ever seen.

"I see them—we will just have to build a strong fort!" Drake said, feeling his face, running his hand over the jagged scar under his left eye, reflecting. These Indians brought to his mind La Mocha, being the place on the coast of Chile where his shore party had been ambushed by hostile Indians.

"There is a boat, General!"

"You're right," Drake said, pointing.

"There's an Indian in it—"

"Keep an eye on it!"

"Shall we put a couple of culverins in the fort?" Hurd asked.

"Yes, and point one up the hill," Drake replied, watching the *Hind* draw near the land. Then he shouted down to his brother, "Tom Drake!"

"Yes, General!"

"Survey the shore. Find me the best site to careen the *Hind*. Then you're going to need to give us a tow!" The *Hind* was now in shallow water.

"Right!"

"You'll need eighteen men!"

"I agree. Do you see that boat, General?" Tom Drake was now referring to the Indian canoe, while Drake was speaking in regards to the longboat. It now carried only twelve men. The additional men would stretch its seating space, but it would take the additional manpower in order to give the *Hind* a good tow in the shallow water. This would be especially so when her bottom began to drag.

"Yes, I see it," Drake replied, eyeing a strange canoe. This canoe, carrying a solitary Indian, had been constructed out of woven reeds; it kept its distance from Drake's fleet. Yet on the following day, a near-naked Indian in a canoe would approach the *Hind*, and the Indian in it would deliver an oration to the men on the *Hind*; then he would pass to Drake a handful of tobacco leaves. Drake would attempt to give him some trinkets. The Indian would refuse them.

The first two days that the two ships were in the harbor most of the men worked building a fort as if their lives depended on it. They dug out an entrenchment about eight feet above the shore, being at the foot of a hill. They utilized the soil that they excavated in order to build a bulwark, which they faced with stone. Then they erected tents inside it for cooking, sleeping and workshops. Drake posted soldiers at four strategic points. All were armed with arquebuses, and they manned their stations both night and day. During the second day, twenty-five or more Indians came to the top of the hill. The soldiers pointed their guns at them in a meaningful fashion. And the Indians withdrew, pointing their heads curiously and babbling at the men in the fort and at the *Hind*, which had been drawn up to shore so that its bottom was resting on small pebbles. All hands would participate in unloading her on the following day so she could be careened.

"Keep clear of the ship!" a sailor shouted to an Indian who was approaching in a canoe. The Indian wore leather pants, though he was shirtless. His long hair was braided. A feather was attached to each braid.

"Baba blah!" the Indian shouted in his native tongue, doing it as if he were arguing; he seemed to be vexed because he was not able to make himself understood.

"He apparently wants to make a gift!" Drake said, looking down at the canoe. Drake was torn between his natural instincts. He had long believed that he could bridge the gap between himself and any primitive person; yet the experiences that he had had at St. Julian Bay and La Mocha now were causing him to be very suspicious of the Indians.

"Baba blah!" the Indian repeated. And he held up a bundle of dried tobacco for Drake to see.

"It's tobacco!" Drake exclaimed. He had used it while he was in Panama. He had even been addicted to it, but he had lost his addiction when he returned to England. He had not used it again until he was coasting Chile.

"Tobah!" the Indian replied, continuing to hold up the tobacco. Its juice dribbled from the corners of his mouth.

"I will take it!" Drake said, descending to the lower deck, where he took the bundle of tobacco and thoughtfully smelled it. Its odor brought back memories of Panama. He anticipated smoking it in one of the pipes that he had confiscated from the Spaniards; however, he would not be the first to do it, for minutes after he put it in his cabin, Maria found one of his pipes, filled it, and began to smoke it. For this tobacco was dry, while the tobacco that Drake had received earlier had been green.

The following day one hundred or more Indians approached the fort. The local Indians had been joined by Indians that lived in distant places. The arrival of the two ships had been big news among the Indians. Most that lived within ten miles of the bay now knew that the white men had arrived. Many of the inland Indians were now visiting with the locals so as to see the English. And strangely most of these Indians were women. All were topless. Their only cover was a skin which they wore about their waists. Drake would soon discover that his fears about these Indians being hostile were for naught, as they were coastal Miwoks, being fairly docile Indians.

"They are unarmed!" Tom Drake said to his older brother. He had approached the Indians and studied them while they babbled at him. Then he had returned to the side of Drake, who was inside the fort.

"Do they appear to want to trade?" Drake asked.

"I think so, General."

Then Drake said, "Send a couple of men to the *Hind*. Get the petticoats!"

"Aye!" Tom Drake replied, grinning. He had wondered what Drake was going to do with the hundred or more petticoats that were in wooden boxes aboard the *Hind*.

Thereafter, a woman's colorful petticoat was given to each sailor and soldier for bartering purposes with the women. On a man giving a petticoat to a woman, she took it and put it under an arm. Then she removed the skin that was shielding her modesty and she handed it to the Englishman. Almost simultaneously all the women stood stark naked with the exception of the moccasins on their feet, while each proudly studied her petticoat. The sailors admiringly studied the women, noting their well-formed bodies and their skin, which was brown with an interesting red tint. Then the women laughed as one while they slipped on the petticoats; and seemingly the color of the landscape changed, though the grassy hills did have color as they were dotted with many colorful spring flowers.

"Let us sing to them some songs that we customarily do at our church services!" Drake declared on noting that many of the women had put their arms about the Englishmen and were becoming amorous with them. Some had even taken the hands of young Englishmen and put them to their bare breasts.

"Let us sing!" Reverend Fletcher shouted as if it were an emergency that required singing to resolve the problem. His face showed that he was appalled at their movements. Then he began to sing, "God is our savior; God is our benefactor; God is the way—" He was soon joined by many of the other men. This momentarily broke up the budding romances. Yet the eyes of the individual women did not leave those of the men that they had selected.

Then the Indian men took the women by the hand and attempted to lead them away from the fort. But they refused to go. The Indian men became angry and pulled at the women. This upset the women, for they commenced to shriek as if they were being beaten; then they used their finger nails to tear at their faces and breasts. Many of the women had blood streaming from their breasts before the Indian men were able to drag them away.

Then on June 26, 1579, a tall Indian who appeared to be a chief approached the fort. He wore a headdress of bird's feathers. He had four short lines painted on either side of his face. A deerskin lay across one shoulder, while he wore buckskin trousers and moccasins. He was followed by a hundred Indians. These were loosely dressed in skins that only covered their privates. They were followed by a hundred women and children. The women were dressed in the colorful petticoats.

"What do you suggest, General?" Tom Drake asked.

"Well, I do not know. What do you think, Tom?" Drake asked his younger brother who was in charge of security. He had a dozen men standing by in loose formation with arquebuses and pikes. But he knew that if the Indians got too close, because of their number, it would be difficult to defend the fort against them.

"I fear the worst, General, but we are prepared," Tom Drake stated.

"I believe that they are friendly because I am convinced that the Spanish have not been here!" Drake replied. And he was correct, as these Englishmen were possibly the first white men that these Indians had ever seen.

"Why is that?" Tom Drake questioned, while anxiously eyeing the Indians.

"The Indians have not shown any hostility—the women want our men. And I believe the Indian men also want their women to have our men!" Drake answered. And this was true. The Indian men now wanted their women to lie with the white men, for they apparently had become convinced that they were gods. Their thinking was that by the women lying with the white men, some of their godliness would rub off on them.

"What does he have in his hand?" Tom Drake asked, pointing, dropping his arquebus to a more usable position; then he slowly shouldered it. He was referring to the Indian chief.

"It is dirt!" Drake replied.

On the Indian chief approaching Drake, the contingency of Indian men who were escorting him set their bows and arrows on the ground to show their peaceful intentions; then the chief approached Drake. On his coming within five feet of Drake who was standing inside the fort, the chief began a long speech which he delivered without ever smiling. Drake listened intently, though he was not able to understand a word that the Indian said. The chief ended it with:

"Hioh!" And he pointed his finger at Drake. All the other Indians repeated, "Hioh!" Then the chief offered Drake a piece of the sod. Drake stepped outside of the fort, took the sod, and nodded his thanks. Then the Indian chief removed his headdress and placed it on Drake's head.

"He is giving you this country!" Fletcher explained. He was standing next to Drake, eyeing in awe the Indian spectacle. For the chief was obviously asking Drake to take charge of their land and become their king.

Then the Indian chief clasped Drake's right hand with his right and used their two hands to point to the Indian men, women and children, most of whom were still standing on the hill.

"He is making you their king!" Fletcher continued to explain, as if Drake did not understand.

Drake nodded his acceptance. Then he said, "Well, I will take this land for England, and I will name it New Albion," Drake added, referring to England's ancient name. Then he explained, "Its cool mornings, its cliffs with their pink-white banks do remind me so much of England."

And seemingly the formalities were over, for the women came racing down the hill. They again were shrieking and wailing like spoiled children, and strangely each singled out the Englishman who previously had given her a petticoat; and she put her arm about him, as if claiming him. Then the Englishmen led the women to their tent lodgings. The Indian men respectfully stepped back to the top of the hill, and they waited there as if the amorous relationships taking place between the women and the visitors had been pre-planned. Thereafter the Indians camped near the English fort so as to be near these white men. For it was now obvious that they were all overawed by the white men's dress, their weaponry, their tools and their great ships. And so all of the Indians had concluded that the white men were gods! And so the Indian men had given their women to the white men as a token to appease them.

Drake tried to stop the Indian adoration out of practical reasoning; for he knew that the men had quit hunting and fishing so they could be near the Englishmen, as if they were gaining something from doing it. He worried about this, for he suspected that if the Englishmen did not soon leave, the Indians would be near starvation, as they were hunters and fishermen.

"What progress are you making on the repairs?" Drake asked Master Hurd. Drake knew that the larboard (port) side had been careened. The ship now lay on that larboard side; Thomas Marks, the carpenter, and Simon Woods, the cooper, were busy working with the planking on the starboard side, as on this side the teredos had eaten through both hulls. They were having to cut out and splice several feet of planking. As well, Thomas Meeks, the sailmaker, had made a new set of sails.

"We will need to work on the *Hind* two or three more days; then it will take three to four days to load and stow our gear and treasure," Hurd said.

"Are the men getting sufficient leisure?"

"Yes; the work day is not all that long. Many fish, hunt seals or deer; they also collect mussels, which we are storing to take to sea with us—"

"You must share the foodstuff with the Indians—"

372

"But they refuse to work, General!" Hurd said, putting an emphasis on work, which Drake knew was a part of their Protestant ethic.

"But it has been caused by our presence—they think that we are gods!"

"I know—and the women—they are with sin. If I would let them, many would stay day and night in the tents with the men—"

"But it has been a long time since the men have had women—and it will be over shortly!" Drake wisely said.

"Then you do not object?"

"I cannot cast a stone!" Drake solemnly replied, referring to the fact that he had taken on a black mistress. He knew that many of the men had made remarks to each other about Drake and his black mistress when Drake had elected to keep her, but that was as far as it had gone. Then Drake abruptly changed the subject. "I would like to go on a hunting expedition, explore the interior—"

"Today?"

"Yes—as soon as possible—"

"You would need two soldiers with long bows—two soldiers with arquebuses—and food?" Hurd asked.

"I would only be gone for one night—"

Drake soon departed on what proved to be a pleasant outing. He led his hunting party over the hills to Olema. He discovered many new Indian villages; all of the Indians that they met were friendly. Many closely followed Drake and his party until they fired their guns. Then the noise caused them to flee; thereafter, they returned but kept at a distance. The Olema area was more wooded and the vegetation was much different than that along the coast. It had many more trees, which included oaks, pines and redwoods. And on the following day, shortly after noon, Drake and the other members of his hunting party returned to their campsite. It had been a most fruitful hunt. They carried two dressed deer. Each hunter had hanging from his neck a half dozen or more of ground squirrels that had been tied together.

"I see that your hunting trip was a success, General," Hurd said, smiling at Drake after greeting him.

"You're right—" Drake replied, also smiling. He added, "The hunting as you can see is magnificent—over those hills, there is much land that would be valuable for a settlement. We found great herds of deer and ground squirrels there. All graze on the brown grass, which seems to be dead, though it is seemingly enjoyed by the animals. There is a plentiful supply of water. There are many valuable herbs. This is a lettuce," he said, taking from a shoulder bag some fresh leaves. "The soil appears to be sweet and fit for raising any kind of crop. Further inland, there are a great variety of trees. Many of these are fit for lumber. I think that this would make an excellent place to settle Englishmen."

"Will you propose that to the Queen?"

"I will—where is Preacher Fletcher?"

"General, he is tending sick Indians—many suffer from ulcers—he has been putting grease and herbs on them!"

"Send for him!"

"Aye!"

Drake removed the bedroll which he had on his back; then while he was removing his hunting jacket, Reverend Fletcher appeared.

"You need me, General?"

"Yes—we will be leaving here shortly—"

"I hope so—the men are—"

"None of that—we will be leaving because we must return to England!" Drake said.

"And by what way shall we return?" the Preacher asked.

"I have not decided," Drake deviously replied, as though he did not consider Fletcher of sufficient rank to know; yet it was not that— Drake was reluctant to share such an important secret with anyone. Yet both Moone and Hurd had already surmised that they would sail for the Spice Islands. Then Drake asked, "You still have your tools for making plaques?"

"Yes, General—"

"I wish to leave a plaque that all may see—I want it to say that on this date, I claim this land for Queen Elizabeth—for England. I want it to say that this land is reserved for English settlers."

"I can do that, General."

"We need something of Elizabeth to put on it!"

"A six pence, General—it has her portrait on it."

"And do it on a brass plate—and set the six pence in it!"

And thereafter, on July 23, 1579, when the *Hind* had been fully loaded and ballasted, Drake instructed Hurd to have the men take down the tents and put them on the *Hind*; this was practically the last gear to be boarded. The Indians who had been standing or sitting on the hill were so surprised to see the tents being taken down that hundreds of them came down the hill and approached Drake. They humbly kneeled down before him and assumed begging positions. Nothing happened. Then they stood, and they became very agitated. The men beat on their chests, while the women mournfully wailed.

"We must go!" Drake firmly said, which of course the Indians did not understand. He eyed the women. Many were attractive, as they had well-formed breasts and narrow waists. Many sailors had gathered there also; they looked from the women to Drake; they were reluctant to express their feelings. Yet Drake understood the wrenching that was taking place in the minds of many of them, because he knew that some few had established special relationships with the women.

"Hioh! Baba blah babu!" the Indian chief said on stepping forth. He now wore a headdress of feathers, a sailor's shirt and pants.

"We leave you these tools," Drake said, pointing to a pile of hoes, rakes and mattocks. "We also leave you these seeds. If you plant them, you can grow many vegetables!" Drake said, making eating signs with his hands and mouth.

"Ha baba!" a woman cried out and rushed to Drake; then she exhibited her stomach, as if wishing to reveal to him that she was pregnant, though he wondered if there had been sufficient time for such. And she pointed to a young sailor who was loading a tent in the longboat to indicate that he had done it. She made signs with her hands so as to indicate that she wished for him to stay with her; then she ran to the pile of tools and picked up a hoe and dug with it. Her motions as much as said that she would work for her man if Drake would only allow him to remain.

"What do you say, John?" Drake asked, speaking to John Audley, who had joined him. Audley was a sailor with blond hair and very fair skin. He wistfully studied the wailing woman. She had bare breasts that were full, though they now were marred by scratch marks; her eyes were wet with tears. She touched him and then pulled him to her. He tightly squeezed her.

"May I stay, General?" Audley asked.

"But—" Drake said, wanting to argue against it.

"I am tired of the *Hind*, General!" Audley said in a final tone of voice, which caused Drake to open wide his eyes, as if he could not believe him.

"Are there others?" Drake asked.

The new Californians!

"Would you like to stay, Thomas?" Audley asked Thomas Grige, a sailor of 20 who was afflicted with a hump back which did not bother him in the slightest. And now it was an asset, for the Indians greatly admired the hump, as though it gave him special powers. Grige was now holding the hand of a pretty Indian girl. He as well was a close friend of Audley. Both were from Plymouth.

"Yes, I would like to stay," he readily confessed.

"Well, are there any others?" Drake asked, carefully eyeing the two sailors. Both were swabbers; each had come aboard the *Hind* not knowing much about seamanship. Both had learned much about seamanship since they boarded the *Hind* in Plymouth. For both had attended Hurd's schools on navigation. He had taught them how to figure the latitude with the use of the astrolabe. Both had served as soldiers with Tom Drake; yet neither possessed such skill that his services would be missed. And Drake knew that the *Hind* was too crowded. It would be more so when Moone's crew boarded it. Thus, he could easily spare the two men.

The sailors and soldiers looked from the women to Drake and then to the *Hind*. All waited for him to speak.

"Well, John and Thomas, we wish you well. And to show that we part on good terms, I will make you a present," Drake said. He pointed to the *Christopher*, being the Spanish bark, which was anchored within a few feet of the shore. "She is yours!"

"Really! Thanks, General! We can use it," Audley said, smiling, pondering its use.

"And to you, Chief," Drake said, speaking to the Indian chief. "We thank you for your hospitality." And the countenance on the chief's face changed to a show of sadness. He, like the others, knew that this was farewell.

"Wa-wa!" the Indian women wailed. Many lay on the ground and scratched their breasts while the last of the tents were put on the longboat. But the two women who had won their sailors tightly clutched their hands as if frightened that they might board the longboat. The two sailors joined the Indians. Thereafter, the Indians and the two English sailors stood on a tall hill and waved continuously until the *Hind* was out of sight.

CHAPTER 39

THE ISLE OF THIEVES

On July 23, 1579, the *Hind*'s yardarms were lined with men as she sailed out of the sheltered North American bay where she had spent almost six weeks. Drake's fleet had narrowed to one ship, being the *Hind*, and it was now the most crowded that it had been since shortly before Drake's men captured the *La Capitaine*. At times her decks, even her yards and shrouds, would be lined with sailors. Drake maneuvered the *Hind* out to sea, and then he set her on a southwesterly course. And soon the *Hind* was sailing directly for two small islands, being the Farallones on which there were numerous seals sunning on the rocks. Drake, on sighting the seals, looked about for his master.

"Tom," Drake said, speaking to Thomas Hurd. "Lower the longboat—I'll need a working party of 40 men!"

"Aye—for the seals?"

"Yes, we must harvest as many as we can!"

Drake and his working party landed on these islands, and they proceeded to harvest the seals, slaughtering hundreds of them. Horsewill then supervised the dressing, salting and storing of them. Once the seals were boarded and stored, Drake again set the *Hind* on a southwesterly course. The sea was modest, while the wind was sufficiently strong so as to bag the sails.

"We will sail for the line," Drake said, referring to the equator. It was now late evening; the sun had already set. Drake was pointing to a chart on the cabin table. The chart had belonged to the pilot, Cochero. Drake was explaining his sailing intentions to Tom Drake, Tom Moone and Tom Hurd. Each was seated while thoughtfully listening. Neither had known for sure Drake's plans until then. John Drake was seated at the end of the table sketching, giving the appearance that he was not listening. Yet he was. Drake now had his finger on the equator. His voice was filled with confidence, while he surely pointed, "Once we get close to this line, then we will pick up a westerly wind that will take us to the Moluccas."

"Is there any danger of great storms?" Moone asked while thoughtfully frowning, accepting their route of departure from America with this question. He had suspected that they were going to sail for the Moluccas, but he had not known for sure until then.

"No. Cochero told me that the worst storms are in April and May. He said that July was a good month to cross."

"I should have known it," Moone said, nodding and now smiling. It had suddenly dawned on him that possibly Drake in sailing north had never intended to search for the Anian Strait; that he had taken this northerly route just to put in time until he could make a July crossing. But he also knew that Drake would never have admitted it. Moone was often taken back by the devious side of Drake. For even though he was close to Drake, he knew that Drake did not completely trust him. But he did not have less regard for Drake because of it, as he surmised that it was a deceptive side of Drake that enabled him to maintain his leadership position with all of the men.

"And we probably will find our proper wind at eight degrees above the line," Drake said, continuing to point, ignoring Moone's remarks. "Then we will follow this course till we reach the Moluccas!"

"It is that easy?" Hurd asked, skeptically eyeing Drake.

"That is what Cochero confessed to me after I put the rope around his neck," Drake said, which brought forth a burst of laughter from the other men. Even John Drake raised from his sketching pad and grinned. And Maria curiously smiled, showing very white teeth, though she did not understand the English. Then Drake added, "The maps agree with that, too."

"Do we have enough food?" Moone asked, recalling the plight which had befallen their predecessor, Magellan when he attempted to cross the Pacific. It had been a terrible voyage. Many of his men had died in attempting it—those men who had survived were eating rats and leather straps when they reached the Philippines. Even then, the Spanish galleons which sailed the short route to Manilla often arrived with their crews and passengers in a famished condition or depleted because of disease.

"Well, our larder is full. And we know our way where Magellan did not!" And he could have added that they had the benefit of Horsewill's and Fletcher's knowledge of herbs. And they had collected armloads. Horsewill had been particularly interested in herbs such as grand thyme, fennel, basil and mints for seasoning, while Fletcher had been more interested in medicinal herbs such as figworts, which were drying. He soon would mix them with seal grease, which he would give to seaman when needed so as to reduce the swelling of piles or the healing of open sores. He as well had collected licorice roots, which he planned to pulverize and use for laxatives. Then he had collected marigolds, which he had learned would heal stubborn sores—however, he was distressed, because he had not been able to find the marvelous sporous herb that Felipe, the Indian chief, had used to treat the men that had been wounded at La Mocha.

The *Hind* continued to sail southwest, sailing south of the Hawaiian Islands where she then found herself in warm waters. Horsewill had his stove, oven and pots moved to the main deck, and he began to cook all of the meals from there. He served freshly fried fish at almost every meal; catching them was easy. This was especially so of the flying fish, for on it being chased by its nemesis, the bonito, it would spread its wings and leap out of the water. Many flew into a net that had been knitted by the boatswain, John Fowler. It now hung across the main deck. The boy mess cooks, Willie Fortescue and Joey Kidd, periodically removed and cleaned them. Then Horsewill cooked them in his hot skillet. There was usually plenty of bread as Blackcollar baked a batch almost every day.

Many of the men in the forecastle stayed busy. For when they were not hauling and pulling on halyards, sheets and braces so as to set the sails incidental to working the ship, they brought their crafts topside. They knitted, sewed and crocheted. A few made baskets and straw hats from grasses that they had brought with them from New Albion. But the old shell backs began to tie knots. The best knotter on the *Hind*, of course, was John Fowler, the toothless boatswain. Many of the seamen called him "Pop," but doing it affectionately, for he was not a man to be trifled with as he had a temper; then he had tremendous strength in his arms and torso and was very agile, as he could move through the rigging like a monkey. And also he had great power of balance, as he often sat on a yard arm in rolling seas without holding to anything. He had made many long voyages to many different parts of the world. And in doing so, while passing time, he had learned many complicated knots. He enjoyed having sailors watch him. But he would not reveal the secrets to his fancy knots to a sailor until he had first sworn him to secrecy. He tied with ease the lanyard knot and the slarth knot for the bottom of a splint basket; he made crow's feet which he had used to make the net that was catching the flying fish. He now had a small school of sailors seated around him. They included William Hawkins and John Brewer. The latter two would subsequently dress much of the *Hind*'s railing with shroud knots. Others who were not so craft-minded had resumed playing games such as backgammon and jackstones. Then at the approach of sundown, the musicians assembled on the main deck and played for an hour; then Preacher Fletcher came forth and preached to the assembled crew. He often preached on subjects that were close to the men, such as "Toss a life line to a drowning mate!" Then he spoke on how the English must stand together against the Spanish.

Drake now spent most of his free time in his cabin sketching. He and his young cousin were now sketching a map of the bay and harbor in New Albion, where they had spent a part of June and most of July. They had already drawn the faces of some of the Indians that they had met. All had oval faces and large, alert eyes. Two of the women wore basket hats; one wore a hat made of an arrow quiver. Drake would next sketch the animals that he had seen on his hunting expedition. Maria, his black mistress, was seated on his bunk. She was dressed in one of her long dresses that touched the floor. Her knees were drawn up so that they almost touched her chin. She was staring straight into space—a frown was on her face. Drake had just spoken to her in Spanish, saying to her that he wanted her to wash his dirty clothes.

"I do not want to wash your clothes!" she said, answering him in Spanish. She still only understood a few words in English.

"I know you don't want to—but I'm telling you that you must!" Drake was irritated at her because of her laziness.

"I would if you gave me more freedom," she said. They were now quarreling. Thirty minutes before Drake had found her in Tom Moone's tiny cabin, being one of those which was directly beneath Drake's. The two had been playing backgammon. Drake had ordered her to return to his cabin, telling her that she could not roam the ship.

"If it were just Tom, but—"

"What is it to you!"

"I am the General! I know the problems that a loose woman can cause—"

"But I am nothing to you—just a slave!" she argued, pouting as if deeply hurt, while her main problem was boredom.

"You must stay out of his cabin—"

"I like Captain Moone."

"Like him, but no other—" he reluctantly said.

"Do you intend to take me to England?" she asked, continuing to sniffle, feigning injury on realizing that Drake was willing to share her with Tom Moone.

"I don't know—"

"Well, then, where do I go—"

"You ask too many questions!" he said without raising his head, which was an arm's length from that of his cousin's who appeared not to hear this domestic quarrel.

The *Hind* now was able to maintain a plentiful supply of fresh water, for every afternoon shortly after noon, the western sky was covered with many dark rain clouds. Then the boatswain would spread two large sails on deck. Then the western sky would rain heavily for 20 to 30 minutes, leaving sufficient water in the sails to last the crew for several days. Then the sailors gathered the sails together and poured the water into barrels. And so the *Hind* did not have a fresh water problem. Many of the younger seamen frolicked like school boys while standing watches in the rigging for there was little to do; they seldom had to turn the yards. Sometimes they played monkey. This was a game usually led by tiny Willie Fortescue who would swing through the braces by making daring moves. The followers had to repeat them—many could not do so. And occasionally one fell into the sea, though there never was a serious injury.

The wind steadily blew against the *Hind*'s sails, slowly taking her to the Moluccas. Yet all was not happiness in the General's cabin. Drake had refused to give Maria an answer as to what was her future, and she had begun to cavort about the ship. She now slept in Moone's cabin. Drake brooded about it. But he was not only committed to the law of the Spanish Main, but his instincts as well. The law of the Spanish Main was a loose set of rules. One of these was that it was a woman's choice as to whom she wished to sleep with. It was no *Hind* rule, even though it had been part of Drake's thinking while on the Main that it was foolish to fight over a woman; this was especially so when there were more women elsewhere; yet there were no more on the *Hind*. But even so, Drake supported the rule—and the woman had made her choice. Furthermore, his instincts told him that he must not let this black woman disrupt the venture. Otherwise, he would end up like John Oxenham.

"Land ho!" a lookout cried on the morning of September 30, 1579.

"Land!" Drake exclaimed with a show of surprise. He studied the horizon just above the bow. He noted that it was either a cloud or land. "We cannot have reached Mindanao!" Drake exclaimed; then he hurriedly returned to his cabin and studied the chart which was spread on the table. He had marked the chart with the mileage that they had sailed each day. This of course was an estimate. But he felt that it was fairly correct, as he knew that he was good at such estimations. Drake had at his disposal the magnetic compass, but it had a pole problem. Drake knew about this. But he did not know about secular variation. This variation of the magnetic compass results from the location of the earth's poles; thus, there is a variation for the different locations where one may be. Variation is measured by the angle between the local magnetic meridian and the true north. It may be east or (+) when the magnetic north is to the right of true north. And when the magnetic lies to the left, the variation is called west or (−).

Drake's principal instrument for ascertaining how far he was north or south of the line was the cross staff. He could have used this in conjunction with tables of the sun's declination. But it did not work well when a ship was sailing within 20 degrees of the line; thus, he had been using the astrolabe; it was an Arabic invention. It was used to ascertain the correct altitude of celestial bodies. It was a flat metal disk whose circumference was graduated in degrees from 0—360. It had a revolving arm that pivoted at the center. Drake would usually hang the astrolabe onto his left thumb; then he would manipulate the arm until a beam of sunlight passed through slits in the vanes at either end of the pointer; thus, in such fashion, he obtained the angle of the sun; thereafter, he made the corrections for the declination. And thus, he ascertained his latitude.

However, Drake did not have any instrument that he could use in order to ascertain the *Hind*'s longitude. The correct way to have done this would have been by the use of a good clock. Drake of course knew that the earth rotated 360 degrees each 24 hours; thus, the earth rotated 15 degrees each hour. And so he really needed to know the exact local time and the time of departure in order to figure the longitude. He did not have such a clock, as none existed; thus, he did his figuring by estimation.

"Is it land?" Hurd asked, carefully studying the horizon. He had learned that in these latitudes there are many cloud formations that look like land.

"It appears to be," Drake replied.

And it was. They now had in view Babeithoup, being the largest of the Palau Islands. It is about 23 miles in length and 5 miles in width at its greatest part. It is located at 7.29 N latitude. Drake had been sailing a bit south of his planned course because he had not taken into account the secular variation. Thus, his navigation was slightly off because of the variance that he had not been able to figure.

"We shall sail for it," Drake said. "There may be natives there who have foodstuff to trade."

"Shall I break out the articles of trade, General?" Hurd asked. He was referring to knives, hatchets, beads, cloth and the like. These items usually were apportioned among the men when there was trade time.

"Yes—" Drake said. "Put down the sea ladders!"

"Aye. And we could use some fresh fruit," Hurd said. And he added, "Some of the men have mushy gums and sore legs!" These were signs of scurvy, which was unavoidable, even though the crew had been well fed.

"Maybe this stop will change that," Drake said, thinking of the fresh fruit.

And soon after the afternoon rain, the island came into full view. It appeared to be of volcanic origin. It had several two hundred foot peaks. The top decks of the *Hind* were now lined with crewmen as the *Hind* slowly sailed for the island. For the wind had practically stopped on their nearing it. Most of the men had ditty bags of trinkets setting on the deck beside them, which they intended to trade.

"There!" Hurd exclaimed, pointing toward the island.

"Yes! Reef your sails!" Drake said. He wanted to slow the *Hind* down to a creep.

"Reef 'em!" Hurd said to Boatswain Fowler.

Drake now cautiously eyed the many canoes coming toward the *Hind*. All were beautiful red-lacquered dugouts. Some were being propelled by paddles; others had sails. All had two booms on one side that were part of an outrigger complex that included a wooden float. White cowries hung from the boats and glistened as the light struck them. Drake estimated that there were more than 800 men and women in the boats. All were naked. They carried in their boats fish, coconuts, fruits and potatoes. On the Paluan boats approaching the *Hind*, many of the naked men and women took hold of the sea ladders and climbed to the *Hind*'s deck. And strangely, they boarded empty handed. Contrariwise, the Englishmen now had their wares displayed on deck. A pretty brown woman took a handful of beads from a sailor and she put them to her breasts, indicating to the vendor that she wanted him to touch them, which should have been a delight, since they were very attractive, being conical and firm. He did. She laughed while pointing to the island, as if to say, "The beads are mine; my side of the bargain will be completed when you come to the island."

"No—return my beads!"

She angrily shook her head; she opened her mouth and displayed her teeth. They were black. She had colored them by mixing some strange herbs with lime and then pasted the mixture on her teeth.

"Look at those teeth!" the sailor said, while pointing.

"And this one!" a soldier said, pointing to the man before him, who was examining his hatchet. He had red spittle at the sides of his mouth. This would be the Englishmen's first experience with betel nut-chewing natives; however, they would soon discover that in Asia such use was quite common. This native had taken the red seed of the areca palm and broken it into bits. He had wrapped it in a leaf from the betel pepper; then he had mixed it with lime which he then carried in a cane holder attached to a string that was tied about his waist. He like the others had ears that hung down almost to his shoulders. A three-inch shell was in each lobe.

"Give me my hatchet!" the Englishman said.

"Na-na!" the naked man hatefully cried. He spat red spittle at the Englishman, who then became so angry that he pushed the native into the water.

"General," Tom Moone cried.

"Yes, Tom!"

"They're stealing the longboat!"

"I see!" Drake said on seeing a dozen natives now in the longboat, which they had cut from its mooring at the stern. They were now trying to remove two oars which were the only ones in the boat. They were secured to the gunwales.

"Shall I lower the dinghy?"

"No—"

"Man your arquebuses!" Drake said.

The natives were undaunted by Drake's warning shouts. They hurriedly grabbed goods and tools that had been lying on the deck. And they quickly crossed to the sea ladder. The Englishmen now knew that the natives had not come to trade. They were thieves. They had come to steal and entice the Englishmen to the island; once they were there, they probably would have killed them.

"Get 'em off!" Hurd shouted.

"Push 'em!"

"Throw 'em!"

But it was not easy to rid the decks of the natives. One had taken a hatchet and he was trying to remove an iron bolt. Moone took a belaying pin from a rack; and he hit the man with it, knocking him into the water. The Englishmen thereafter threw or knocked dozens of them from the ship. The rest dove into the water.

"Get that boat!" Drake ordered.

"My God!" Hurd exclaimed. The natives on returning to their boats had taken up slings and then rocks that were in the bottoms of their canoes. And they were now throwing their rocks at the *Hind*. Many rained onto it. Some of the men were hit.

"Oh! Oh!"

"Fire your arquebuses!" Drake shouted to his brother, Tom, who now was standing on deck with a dozen men. All held these heavy, clumsy guns.

"Boom! Boom!"

"Use the bows on those natives in the longboat!" Drake ordered. He did not want to destroy the boat by the use of the powerful guns. Many were loaded with chain.

"That's it!" Drake said. He was now on the poop deck where he had a good view of the scene. The bowmen fired. Their first arrows struck two natives. One was killed immediately. The other was attempting to withdraw an arrow that had pierced his shoulder. Another had jumped from the boat. Yet others were attempting to push it while under water.

"Sink those boats!" Drake shouted, pointing to nearby canoes.

"Boom!" the arquebuses fired; they killed or maimed eight natives in one boat and four in another.

"They're leaving, Cap'n!" Hurd shouted.

"But the longboat?"

"They've got to come up for air!"

"Shoot them when they do!" Drake ordered the six soldiers with long bows in their hands with arrows ready to fire. It was an awesome weapon in the hands of a skilled user.

"There!" Tom Drake said, pointing to a place 200 feet from the boat where three heads were bobbing.

And the six bowmen fired!

"You hit one!" Drake said, pointing. The other two had submerged and would subsequently surface at a safe distance from the *Hind* where they would board canoes that were waiting for them.

"Tom," Drake said to Tom Moone. "Put over the dinghy. Get the longboat. Protect him," he said to the bowmen.

"I'll get it," Moone said.

"An island of thieves!" Drake said on descending the ladder to his cabin.

"Do you want to try another island?" Hurd asked, pointing to an island to the south.

"No," Drake replied. "Spread your sails. Let's continue on. We shall stop at Mindanao!"

"Aye!"

CHAPTER 40

MINDANAO

On the *Hind* leaving the Palau Islands, a sudden change came over her crew. Most of the men ceased their work at crafts and stopped their games; most appeared to be tired and fractious. A day or so later many became weak. Some began to bleed from their gums, while others began to suffer so badly from leg pain that they could not climb the rigging. And so by the time the *Hind* was near the southernmost Philippine Isles, twenty men had become too weak to stand their watches.

"My calculations place us near Mindanao," Drake said. He was seated at his table studying a hand-drawn map. He was pointing to a cluster of islands labeled the "Mindanao Islands."

"The map may be wrong," Hurd said.

"What is the food situation?" Drake asked.

"It's not good, but we still have some dried food."

"And the men?"

"All are suffering from scurvy—twenty-two are too ill to stand watches."

The condition of the men continued to deteriorate. Then on October 16, 1579, a lookout on the *Hind* sighted a large ship, which created considerable activity. The ship was almost as large as the *Hind*, though it was much different in shape, as it had a high stern while its bow was not so high. The two ships were sailing on a meeting course. The *Hind* approached the ship with all her culverins manned. The meeting ship seemingly saw the *Hind*'s guns, and she veered away.

"¡Senores!" Drake shouted at the ship, which was now off the *Hind*'s port bow and sailing in a westerly direction.

"¿Quien esta usted?" Who are you? a voice from the ship answered.

"English!" Drake answered. "We wish to trade for food." Food now had become very important, for the *Hind* was practically out of food of all types. She was completely out of flour. Two days before, Blackcollar had scraped the bottom of a weevil-ridden barrel in order to get the last flour so as to make hoe cakes.

"Land, General!"

"Where?"

"There!" the lookout said, pointing to the west. A massive island now faced them.

"¿Son Catolicas o Lutheraneos?" Are you Catholics or Lutherans (meaning Protestants)? a man standing on the Spanish ship's high stern shouted. Religion apparently was more important to the person than nationality. Drake looked at Moone, then at Mary, who was standing beside Moone. Both had bloody lips. Mary appeared to be sickly; gray circles were under her eyes. Her color was mottled like spoiled pork—and worse, she now was five months pregnant. She held on to Moone's arm as if to brace herself from falling. Drake was thinking; he knew that starvation could depend on his answer. Drake looked about quickly at his weakened crew standing on deck and in the braces. Their appearance was worse than that of the officers. He knew that all were eagerly awaiting his answer. He suffered, too, for his gums were bleeding and he was suffering severely from painful leg cramps. He decided, however, that he would not be intimidated.

"We are Protestants—we are willing to pay for food!" Drake answered. Drake was now willing to pay a premium for fresh food. He knew that scurvy was beginning to take its toll. He now had many men who were unable to stand. These men lay on hammocks or blankets on the hot orlop deck, as the sun hurt their eyes too badly for them to remain topside.

"¡No vendimos con Lutheraneos!" We do not sell to Lutherans! the same voice shouted back, as if he would fight about it.

"If you won't sell to us, then we will take it!" Drake forcefully replied. His hands were on his hips; defiance was in his voice. His bearded face had become bright red.

"Cheers!" shouted the Englishmen on deck.

"She's sailing for land, General." The Spanish ship had bent on sail and was sailing for land, which was much nearer than the

Englishmen had thought. Rain clouds had been obscuring part of the island; this had made it appear to be much further away than in truth it was.

"Ready the culverins?" Hurd asked. He was looking down at Clark, who was standing on the orlop stairway. The orlop ceiling was only five-and-one-half feet from the floor, which made it difficult for a tall man such as Clark to maneuver. He now had his hand raised with expectancy. He could observe the men manning the culverins. As well, he could see and hear Drake.

"Ready 'em!" Drake said.

"We are ready," Clark, the gunner, replied.

"Give them a shot across the bow!" Drake ordered, and Clark dropped his arm.

"Boom!" a culverin fired. The ball splashed one hundred feet behind the ship which had turned away from the *Hind* and had bent on sail, sailing for shore. She was much faster than the *Hind*, as her bottom was not overgrown with moss and seaweed. Even so, the *Hind* gave chase; the Spaniard continued to sail for shore, which was a poor move and would be its undoing. For on it nearing the shore, surprisingly it ran aground on a reef.

Drake cagily eyed the grounded ship, wondering whether he should engage the Spaniards. But if he did, would he not be making the same mistake as had his predecessor, Magellan? The reader will recall that Magellan, on crossing the Pacific Ocean to the Philippines, had engaged himself in diversions that were far removed from his goal of reaching the Spice Islands. Firstly, he spent considerable time in converting the natives to Christianity. Then he took sides in native feuds, and so on Maltain Island, he got himself killed in a fight with the natives. Consequently, Magellan never reached the coveted Spice Islands.

"Shall I take the longboat—go in and capture it?" Moone asked. He was standing three feet away from Drake. Maria had gone inside Drake's cabin. Moone's hand shaded his eyes while he studied the grounded ship. The sun was hot and high, and it scorched the deck.

"She has a cannon on her bow and another on her stern. It would be too risky!" Drake replied, squinting his eyes from the sun while he, too, studied the grounded ship. Drake could see that the cannon on the stern was now aimed at the *Hind*. As well, he suspiciously eyed the water, studying it for reefs, noting the possibility of the *Hind*'s running aground. He decided to choose caution over valor.

"Bring me about!" Drake ordered. And so the *Hind* abandoned her chase of the Spaniards. The land in view was the southern part of the large island of Mindanao, being six degrees north of the equator. It appeared to be a strange and inhospitable island. Tall mountains towered over it, while in places the Englishmen could see smoking volcanos. And then the English had difficulty in finding anchorage. And thereafter, the *Hind* coasted southern Mindanao, searching for a good anchorage, but there did not appear to be any. Then on October 21, 1579, Drake finally found a suitable anchorage, and the *Hind* anchored. The tired, sick Englishmen landed hoping to find food to alleviate their starvation, but instead they found several dilapidated villages of huts that were on stilts. The inhabitants were mostly emaciated native women who were not only suffering from disease but also from a lack of food. They stared at the Englishmen with hate in their eyes.

"Do you have food to sell?" Drake asked.

"No!" said their facial expressions. "Leave!" expressed the snarls on their faces.

"Let us gather firewood and water!" Drake said to his men, ignoring the unfriendly natives. And so their stay at the villages was a short one. But those crew members who remained on the *Hind* fared much better, for some friendly Filipinos in banca canoes did visit the *Hind*. However, these natives were almost as poor, as trading with them only produced a few coconuts and a bushel of potatoes. And such produce did not do much to abate the hunger of the men on the *Hind*.

CHAPTER 41

TERNATE

On the men boarding water, wood, and a scanty supply of produce, Drake set sail south for the Moluccas, which were commonly known as the Spice Islands. The principle islands in this group were Ternate, Tidmore, Amboyna and the Bandas. These islands then were famous for their spice trade; for they not only grew pepper and ginger but also grew the more expensive spices, such as cloves and nutmeg. The resident natives of these islands had been trading in spices for centuries, doing it mostly with the Arabs and Chinese. The Arabs then took their spices to places like Cairo, where they traded them to the Venetians. Many of the Spice traders were rich, for their prices were always extremely high. Sometimes the Arabs demanded a pound of gold for a pound of spices. Then the Venetians traded the spices with other nationalities, such as the Portuguese. By the end of the 14th century, the Portuguese were beginning to question the Venetian middleman.

"Why is the price of nutmeg so high?"

"Sir, it comes from a distant land where there are great dangers in harvesting it!"

"Where is that land?"

"It is in the east. Sir, those nutmeg trees are guarded by large snakes—"

"And the clove?"

"Its trees are found at the end of the earth. There are many dangers in harvesting it. For if one is not careful, he will fall into a void!"

"All of these islands are probably controlled by the Portuguese," Drake said, having his head bent, intently studying the pencilled map lying on the table, being one of those hand-drawn maps that he had obtained from Cochero.

"Will they trade with us?" Hurd asked, looking over Drake's shoulder. Tom Moone was standing to his left, drumming the table with his fingers, while intently studying the small map, searching it as if he were trying to find something on it that should be there.

"They most likely will since we have plenty of gold and silver to spend. And so we will try trading first. If that fails, then we'll fight for it!" Drake said, showing his teeth. They were stained with blood. Scurvy was having its effect—dried blood covered his lips. Drake spat—determination showed in his eyes. He then said, "One way or the other, we shall have food!"

"But we have less than 40 men who are well enough to fight!" Hurd countered. He, too, had blood on his lips, being caused by anemia from vitamin shortage.

"We will just have to do it with those that are able!"

"Which island?" Hurd asked, meaning which island would they first visit.

"Tidore," Drake said, studying the chart, pointing at it. Cochero finally had revealed to Drake that he had visited this island. He had informed Drake that it was one of the richest of the Spice Islands. He had also warned Drake that he would have to make his peace with the Portuguese in order to trade, as they controlled most of these islands. In turn, they controlled the sale and price of all the spices from the Moluccas. This was because it was only in these islands that the nutmeg, mace and clove spices could be found. Mace was made from the dried external covering of a nutmeg. The clove was the most valuable spice, since it was believed to have magical powers, probably because it is the spice of all seasons, being enjoyed in drinks, food and with betel. At this time only a few men knew for sure that all of the spices were grown in the Moluccas. But since Drake's conversations with Cochero about the Spice Islands had been limited to Tidore, Drake decided to commit the *Hind* for Tidore, which was one of the many small islands that composed the Moluccas. He set a southerly course, finding Sangi Isle, avoiding it, while keeping it off his starboard side; then the *Hind* entered the Molucca passage. She now had land in sight.

"Sail!" a lookout shouted.

"Sail, aye!" Drake answered, pondering whether he should approach it. For on looking out a window on the port side, Drake could see a distant banca canoe. Then Drake said to Hurd, "Let us proceed for it!"

"Aye—left rudder; steer for the sail!" Hurd shouted to men in the rigging. And the foretop men turned the yards so as to permit the *Hind* to sail for the canoe.

Thirty minutes later when the sun was directly overhead, the *Hind* was alongside a banca canoe, being much like those that the English had seen in Palau, although this one was less ornate. It was occupied by two men; both were thin with brown skin, yet they appeared to be quite healthy. One had European features, as well as lighter skin than the other. Both wore straw hats and loin cloths. Sweat and coconut oil covered their torsos.

"¿Hablas espanol?" Do you speak Spanish? Drake asked.

"Si." Yes, the native with the light skin answered.

"Do you know the waters to the Moluccas Islands?" Drake asked, looking down at the men in the boat.

"Oh, yes," the native answered without admitting that all were now in the Moluccas.

"We have silver—we will pay you to guide us to Tidore," Drake said.

"And our banca?" the man asked, now standing, frowning apprehensively, not wanting to go, sensing that they were going to be made to go, then wondering what would happen to their canoe.

"We will tow it!"

"Well—" the speaker said, showing his indecisiveness. Yet he was not ready to challenge Drake, as he sensed that his request was a command.

"Get aboard!" Drake firmly ordered, as if saying to him that time was of the essence.

After the two natives were aboard the *Hind* and their canoe had been secured to the longboat, Drake led the two men to his cabin. Then in a friendly way he began to interrogate the spokesman for the two.

"What is your name?"

"Juan—Juan Gomez!" the man replied, while curiously eyeing Drake's bloody lips.

"Hunger—long voyage at sea!" Drake explained.

"Long voyage—very bad!"

"But we'll get well—we need fruit!"

"We get plenty—"

"Are you Spanish?" Drake asked.

"Half—my father was Spanish. Are you Spanish?" the native asked Drake. Drake now noticed that the man wore a heavy gold chain around his neck. It had attached to it an impressive gold adornment, being a small bird of paradise, which was the Sultan of Ternate's seal. Drake on studying it knew that the man was someone of importance. And really, Drake was in luck, for this man was the Sultan of Ternate's messenger.

"No—we are English," Drake replied, making a serious effort to grin, trying to indicate that he would like to be friends, especially since he now was in need of information.

"You go to Tidore to trade?"

"Yes—"

"My name is Gomez," he repeated.

"And my name is Drake."

"Captain Drake, the island of Tidore is Portuguese," the messenger said, wrying his face, as if the other islands were not. This was a surprise to Drake, for in Mexico Drake had been told that the Portugese controlled all of the Spice Islands. Then the messenger explained to Drake his personal history and then some important events in the recent history of the Moluccas. The messenger related to Drake that his father was a Spaniard, and because of that, he had been raised at a Spanish mission on the island of Mindanoa where he had learned Spanish. He had left the mission at the age of 14 to become a fisherman; then he had become a sailor, which had enabled him to voyage to the Spice Islands. There he had learned to trade, doing it with most of the islands; he had finally settled on the tiny island of Ternate, which was peopled by Malays, Arabs, Chinese, Portuguese and some Spanish. While he was there, he had developed an intense dislike for the Portugese; this had caused him to participate in a revolt that had been led by a member of the royal family named Baber, who on winning it had become Sultan; and he had made Gomez his messenger. And when Drake met Gomez and his friend just hours before, they were returning from the delivery of a message to the Sultan of the island of Morotai, being north of their present position and just north of the equator.

"Are not all the Spice Islands Portuguese?" Drake asked. He had shown considerable surprise on being told that the Portuguese only controlled Tidore. He had been expecting to deal with a Portuguese governor.

"No—Ternate is controlled by Sultan Baber—and I am his messenger. There are no Portuguese on Ternate!" Gomez emphatically said. A frown was on his face, as if he did not like to think of the possibility.

"None there?" Drake asked, and he smiled.

"It is ruled by Sultan Baber!"

"Well, I am surprised!" Drake said, as if he could not believe that the Portuguese no longer controlled the Spice Islands. That was with reason, for it was they who had won them. The Portuguese during the previous two hundred years had been an adventurous people with a fondness for the sea; they had had an extraordinary passion for finding a southern route to the Indies. They had been greatly helped by Henry the Navigator, a member of the ruling family, who founded a navigator's school and supported many adventurous seamen. The southern search had really begun in 1418 when two of Henry's sea captains rediscovered the Madeiras. Thereafter, the Portuguese kept inching their way down the African coast. Finally, in 1497, Vasco da Gama rounded the Cape of Good Hope and set sail for India, reaching it in 1498. They continued their search for the Spice Islands, finally reaching the Moluccas in 1511, arriving there almost one hundred years after they began their search for them. They, of course, were the first Europeans to establish themselves in the Spice Islands. They thereafter expended much effort in an attempt to entrench themselves. They built trading posts, forts and missions on most of these islands. They brought with them the Christian church. And by 1542, they had many Catholic missionaries stationed there. But the Christian church did not make much of an impression, as most of the people refused to convert from their Muslim religion. The Portugese even intermarried with the native women. However, this did little to entrench them, for the natives strongly resented the Portuguese selfishness, as shortly after they arrived, they were in control all of the spice trade. They also resented the many outrages that the Portuguese practiced from time to time against the old ruling class. One of the worst outrages against them had occurred just a few years before at a dinner at the house of the Portuguese governor on the island of Ternate. The Portuguese Governor had enticed the ruling rajah, Hairun, and other members of his family to attend a state dinner; then while the rajah was eating, a soldier had come up behind the rajah and had slit his throat. The other members had miraculously escaped. They then hurriedly joined the rajah's son, Baber, in the mountains. And they helped him raise an army. This was the undoing of the Portuguese, as they had relied more on craft and pomp than numbers in their ruling, and so they did not have enough soldiers in order to fight a war. And in 1574 Baber's army was able to drive the Portuguese out of Ternate. Soon thereafter, they drove the Portuguese out of all the other islands with the exception of Tidore, which was their last stronghold.

"Sir, do you now wish to go to Tidore?"

"Well, no. But will the Sultan of Ternate sell me food?"

"Sir—you will be welcome on Ternate. Do you see that mountain? That is Ternate," Gomez proudly said, pointing to a nearby island with a cone-shaped mountain with three peaks that was rising above it. "Please excuse me, for I must leave. I will go find the Rajah, speak to him—tell him that you are English; that you speak for a great Queen and have come to trade for spices. He will be happy to learn of this. I will ask him to send food and fruit for your sick men."

"And the *Hind*?" Drake asked, pointing to the ship.

"Follow me!"

"Well, you are free to go; and when you return, I will pay you!" Drake craftily said, knowing that he who pays early is a poor payer.

The two Malays set sail in their banca canoe followed by the *Hind*. The two men were good sailors, so they soon out-distanced the slow ship. Those on the *Hind* now could see the cone-shaped isles of Ternate, Tidmore, Motir and Makyan, which are some of the principal Spice Islands. They are so unique that they just as well could be islands of another planet.

"Are you concerned, General?" Hurd asked, wondering as to their safety. The master had his hand on the whipstaff. Moone was on his left, and Drake was on his right. His lips, too, were bloody. All suspiciously eyed these strange islands. Each wondered as to the truthfulness of the messenger and whether they would have to fight for food, and if they did, whether the men had the strength to make such a fight. Those who were on deck did not give a good impression, as they were thin, haggard and bearded.

"Yes—I am always suspicious," Drake truthfully replied. "But the problems of the Portuguese may be in our favor," Drake said, thinking. Juan had explained to Drake that the Sultan would not sell spices to the Portuguese.

"Right rudder—follow that canoe!" Drake said. The distant canoe had entered the mouth of a harbor. And when the *Hind* arrived at the mouth, Drake was surprised to find that the *Hind* was being greeted by four very large warlike canoes. Each was manned by 50 or more rowers that rowed to the beat of a drum. The bow of each was painted with curious designs, while above the deck there was a canvas awning. Beneath it were a dozen soldiers; all were attired in white. In the foremost boat was a richly dressed man wearing a yellow blouse, red pants and a brown turban on his head. Standing beside him was the messenger, Juan. Both were standing as if they were poised to board the *Hind*. Drake would soon learn that the man with the turban on his head was the viceroy.

"Get 'em in some sort of order!" Drake said to his brother, Tom Drake. He was referring to the soldiers.

"Many are too ill to do anything regimental, General!"

"But we've got to make an appearance!"

"Fall in ranks—look alive!" Hurd demanded.

"John," Drake said, speaking to Brewer, the bugler, who had joined him on the poop deck.

"Yes, General."

"Get the musicians together—take positions on the bow—play some music."

"We only have one viol player able to play!"

"What's that?"

"Mincy is too sick!" Mincy played the bass viol and was quite accomplished, too, as he could play a variation of complex viol pieces.

"Well, play!"

"What songs?"

"Something lively!" Drake said. He knew that the musicians could play a complete repertoire of music. They had several books of music. They had been giving afternoon recitals on the main deck until the viol player had become too ill to perform. But, of course, they would miss Mincy since he was the best of the musicians.

"Aye!"

"Tom," Drake said, speaking to Hurd. "I think that the boat following the first four may have the Sultan aboard it. Tell Clark to man the culverins. I want to give the Sultan a twenty-one-gun salute!"

"When?"

"I'll give you the signal!"

Drake offers the Sultan a key to trade.

400

And shortly thereafter, being on November 4, 1579, the four war canoes took in tow the *Hind* while it was still firing its culverins. The viceroy and Juan Gomez boarded the *Hind* as if undaunted by the noise of the guns. They were followed by a dozen men who carried baskets of coconuts, lemons, cucumbers, bananas and sago. They also carried baskets of rice cakes, being a tasty cookie, that they set on the deck. Then the messenger began a conversation that would prepare Drake for a meeting with the Sultan. "Oh, yes, the Sultan would be glad to receive them. Oh, yes, they would soon have plenty of food. Oh, yes, the Sultan wanted to establish trade with England. Oh, yes, the Sultan would exchange spices for cloth and iron goods." And by the time the messenger had finished, the Sultan boarded the *Hind*, being accompanied by two of his brothers. All were resplendently dressed in gold trousers and red shirts. Each wore an Arabic sword whose hilt was adorned with rubies. In addition, the Sultan had pinned to his shirt a beautiful gold badge of a bursting sun. Drake was also resplendently dressed for the occasion. He, too, wore gold pants, a royal blue shirt, and a gold chain about his neck, being the one with the gold skulls linked to it. He wore an impressive ring on the ring finger of each hand. One had an emerald setting; the other had a large amethyst. He wore a cutlass to his left side. Willie Fortescue was acting as his page. He was dressed identically to Drake. He wore a short sword on his left side. He walked behind Drake, carrying before him a silk pillow on which lay Drake's gold key. This special key symbolized trade. All of the men that were able to stand and did not have important stations were now standing at attention on the main deck. Drake and Willie walked between them so as to greet their guests.

"Welcome aboard, Your Highness!" Drake said, turning and presenting the Sultan with the gold key.

"Thank you!" the Sultan said, examining it.

"It is a token from our Queen!"

"Welcome to Ternate, General!" the Sultan replied, speaking through his interpreter, Juan Gomez.

"The Queen's General is honored!" Drake said.

Then the Sultan took Drake's extended hand.

"Thank you," Drake said, bowing.

"We are favored to have in our country the Queen's General!" the Sultan said, eyeing Drake's blood-stained lips.

"Thank you, Your Highness!"

"You have had a long voyage?"

"Very—many of my men are ill—we thank you for the food, fruit and herbs. We will pay for them!" Drake said, eyeing the deck which was now covered with baskets.

"Eat! Eat! There is plenty more!"

"Thank you—would you follow me to my cabin," Drake said, being followed by Willie Fortescue, who now carried a basket of fruit. Thereafter, on the two leaders taking their seats, Drake began to eat a banana, sometimes doing it ravenously, while the Sultan talked of power. The Sultan boastfully explained to Drake that he was now the ruler of 500 islands.

"My Queen is the ruler of a huge island—it has many people— many ships, many soldiers," Drake said, handing a banana peel to Willie Fortescue. Then he continued, "She is a Queen of much trade! And that key," he said, pointing to the cushion on the table with a key on it. "It is the symbol to trade with our island!" Drake said, pointing to the key which the Sultan had taken and now held in his hand.

"Does she do business with Portugal?" the Sultan asked, forcing a half smile.

"No—it is too much like Spain, which we do not like—so we do not like the Portuguese!"

"Would your Queen like to do business with us—trade for our spices?" the Sultan asked.

"Yes."

"Would your Queen send ships like this to protect us from the Portuguese?"

"Yes—"

"It is yours—we must do business," the Sultan said on gleefully clapping his hands. Then he quickly added, "We shall begin with a feast tonight." Then spittle drooled from his mouth which was red and appeared to be spontaneous like new blood.

"That is fine," Drake said. Then he took a bite from a lemon, and he frowned at its taste.

"This is the Ramadan period in Ternate," the Sultan said in an apologetic voice, speaking of the Muslim sacred days of fasting which followed the moon. "We are a strict Muslim people. But, even so, tonight I will give your officers a dinner—you will come?"

"Yes, I will come," Drake replied.

After the *Hind* had safely anchored in Ternate harbor, many more banca canoes came alongside her. Their occupants were very orderly. They filed aboard the *Hind* carrying staple goods, such as rice, hens, sugar, plantains, more coconuts and sago, which Horsewill took charge of.

Later that afternoon, being October 22, 1579, Drake began to have second thoughts about the Sultan's dinner, which befitted Drake's character. For the reader now knows that Drake was a very suspicious person. And so he called a meeting of his senior officers. Drake was dressed only in his underdrawers when he received Hurd, Moone and Tom Drake in his cabin. "It is too hot for pants!" Drake explained.

"I agree," Moone said, fanning himself with a newly acquired hand fan. He then took an orange from a basket on the table and began to peel it.

"I have called you men together so I might confer with you about the dinner tonight," Drake said.

"Are you concerned?" Moone asked. Lack of understanding was on his face. He had not developed the slightest suspicion about these people. More so, he was looking forward to the reception with anticipation.

"Yes—Juan Gomez informed me earlier that dinner assassinations are common in the Spice Islands."

"Why would they assassinate you?" Moone curiously asked while studying Drake, not being able to reason why they would make such an attempt. And he awaited Drake's reply with interest, as he knew that Drake was much wiser than he.

"To get the *Hind*—they may have knowledge of our treasure," Drake suspiciously explained.

"But what if the Sultan is merely making a friendly gesture?" Hurd argued, pointing out that the failure to attend could be a serious affront to the Sultan. This would be especially so since the Sultan had so warmly received them.

"Well—ah," Drake said.

"I understand," Moone said, pondering whether Drake's suspicions were well-founded or not. "It may be a wise move. I will go— take Tom Drake and a couple of soldiers—I will tell the Sultan that you are ill—that you are still suffering from the voyage," Moone said. Then he added, "He would not dare attack us when you are still aboard the *Hind*!"

403

"Right," Drake replied. "I think that is best," he added, nodding, as if agreeing with his own reasoning.

But there was no deceit attached to the reception, as it was a very official dinner. It was held in a large, open hall that seated a thousand people. The four Englishmen were given seats of honor. The Sultan entered seated on a golden chair which was carried by eight bearers. They set his chair on a stage where the four Englishmen were seated. The Sultan greeted them with a wave of his hand. Then at his signal, waiters began to bring forth many bowls of food, which they placed before the diners. The Englishmen ate as though they were near-starved, though they had been eating since they arrived.

The Sultan was so eager to establish trading relations with England that four days after the first visit he again visited Drake on the *Hind*. The Sultan was beaming with interest, while fanning, when he entered Drake's cabin.

"General, please tell your Queen that I am very eager to trade with your country. Tell her that I am willing to give all trade rights to her," the Sultan said in a begging voice, as if he doubted that Drake was willing to do it.

"I will tell that to her—she will be glad."

"Would you like to take some spices to England?"

"Yes—I would like to trade for them—"

"What do you have to trade?"

"I have silks and linens—"

"May I see them?"

"Bring them forth!" Drake said to John Drake.

Sailors soon entered the cabin carrying boxes of valuable linens and silks, being loot that Drake had taken from Spanish ships. They quickly opened the boxes and spread samples of the contents before the Sultan. He carefully examined the materials, as though he was used to seeing such. He smiled, indicating that he was impressed.

"For those," he said, pointing, "I will give you pepper, cloves, mace and nutmeg that could fill one quarter of this room!" the Sultan said, grinning and drooling red saliva.

"Well, I will agree," Drake said. He would later discover when the spices were aboard that they totaled almost 10 tons, which he knew would bring a fortune in England. And so his fortune was to grow, as he now was much richer than when he arrived!

"I will give you that much more spices if you will attack the Portuguese fort at Tidore," the Sultan said, being interpreted by Gomez. He now was apprehensively studying Drake with his brown eyes that had interesting black specks in them. Red spittle oozed from the corners of his mouth; he wiped it with the back of his hand. Beads of perspiration lined the edge of his golden turban. He anxiously awaited Drake's reply.

"Your Highness, many of my men are sick; we are not prepared for war; thus, I will have to decline your offer—" Drake said, in an apologetic voice.

"But if you did it, I would give you more spices; you would be a rich man when you returned to England!" the Sultan said, not knowing that the *Hind* had aboard her enough treasure to change the course of English history. And Drake's part of the treasure would make him the richest man in England once he arrived there. And the Sultan little suspected that Drake on arriving in the Moluccas had decided that he was not going to jeopardize the *Hind's* treasure by fighting an unnecessary battle or war.

"But I cannot—I will trade all my silks and linens for your spices if you will accept some of my sick men—they need a few weeks or a month or two on land so as to recover their strength after our long voyage."

"We will trade—what skills do your men have?"

"All are fighters—many understand guns. Each will have money to buy goods. I am sure most will want to return to Europe when the occasion arises."

"How many of your men are in such condition?"

"Ten—maybe fifteen. They would of course need quarters where they could rest."

"It is agreed."

Thereafter, Drake met on the main deck with all the men who could walk. And he spoke to the men:

"Men, as you know we are now in the Spice Islands; the Sultan, as you have seen, likes Englishmen." This was evident to all. He had brought many gifts of spices, fruits and vegetables, even cloth, to the ship. Baskets of fruit set on deck at all times, being there for anyone who desired fruit. "It has been a long trip from New Albion. Many of you need a good rest—we still have a long way to go to reach England. In a few days I plan to sail the *Hind* west and search for an island where we can careen her. So I am ready to make this offer to

405

any of you who would like to stop here. You may leave the ship. And I will pay you for the services that you have rendered to date. The Sultan has agreed to provide you with food and lodging during your recuperation—"

"And how will you pay us?" asked Nicholas Anthony, a gunner. He had a gaunt face that was covered with a thick beard while his hair was so long that it hung down to his shoulders.

"I will pay you in gold and silver—give you a bonus as well!"

"Well—"

"The Sultan is in need of gunners," Drake added.

"Could a man trade?" asked John Dean, a cobbler who was also a skilled trader whom Drake had utilized in trading with the Indians.

"Yes, he has agreed to that."

"Let Hurd know within two days—I will make arrangements with the Sultan for your lodging and your food. The Sultan also will provide nursing care for the men who are unable to walk."

"Aye."

Subsequently Master Hurd reported to Drake on those men desiring to remain on Ternate.

"There are fourteen men who have decided to stay," Hurd said. He was holding a sheet of paper with their names on it. Drake took it, studied it, and then he said:

"All are good men—but we can make it without them. As well, their leaving will give us a bit of room for spreading out. I will pay them tomorrow!"

CHAPTER 42

CRAB ISLAND

On November 9, 1579, the *Golden Hind* was towed out of Ternate harbor by the four war canoes that days before had towed her into the harbor. The day was hot and muggy. Even so, the *Hind*'s musicians were playing much more enthusiastically than when they entered. The Sultan was enjoying the music; he was seated on a sedan chair that was beneath an umbrella on the lead war canoe. He clapped his hands so as to keep time to the music.

"It shall be good to find a breeze," Hurd said, fanning himself with a Molucca hand fan. His gums had stopped bleeding; seemingly the fresh fruit had performed a miracle on him.

"And I hope that we shall soon find it," Drake said, meaning the breeze, nodding his head, attempting to keep time to the music. The drummer had taken the lead in the band's playing of a stirring military march. The band was still short a member because Edward Mincy was too ill to be topside.

"And what shall be our course?"

"We shall sail southwest," Drake said while unrolling a roughly drawn map and studying it. The Sultan had presented Drake with several hand-drawn maps on his last visit to the *Hind*. The map that Drake was studying was a map of the Moluccas which included the Celebes. "We shall follow this course," Drake added, pointing to the Molucca passage. This passage skirts the large island of the Celebes, which is an island with an octopus-like appearance, possibly symbolizing the entangling problems that would happen to the men of the *Hind* if they were not careful. A landing there could be very dangerous, as Celebes then was populated by many very primitive peoples.

"And then?" Hurd asked, eying the sails bagging wind and the foretop men seated on the yards. All were barefoot and deeply tanned. They sat on the yards as if they were a part of them. The Sultan's canoes had released their tow. All were now waving their farewells. Then the guns on the *Hind* began to fire their salutes. Their thunderous noise muffled the sound of the music, and so the musicians ceased their playing.

"We shall sail this way, parallel with the Celebes," Drake said to the men near him. Then he raised his head, eyed the canoes, and waved a salute to the nearest one which was turning about. Then he dropped his eyes and focused them so as to study the poorly-drawn map that he held in his hand. He knew without being told that there were many islands that should have been on it, but were not. And he also knew that there were some islands on it that were out of position. But he also knew that he had to use it since it was the only map that was available.

"We need to careen ship!" Hurd reminded Drake. This was not just because the *Hind*'s bottom was covered with grass and barnacles, but her bilges stank dreadfully. Their odor could be smelled from the poop deck. The *Hind* had two heads, one being forward and the other aft. Each was on a grating near the water, which exposed the user to the sea. Thus, using the head often meant that a person doing it received a good dousing. This was not an inconvenience in these warm waters except that many men were still too ill to venture to the heads. Thus, the bilges had been an easy alternative.

"I know—we will begin right away to look for an island where we can do it—and once we are there, we will give the crew a rest," Drake said, biting into an orange that he had taken from a basket of fruit sitting on his cabin table.

The *Hind* soon began to make contact with small islands. Moone had the job of surveying each island that appeared to be a likely prospect. It was a full-time job since each time he made a check of one of the islands, he had to report to Drake that the island was not exactly what they needed. It was populated; its shore did not have a sandy bottom; it was treeless; its water's edge was grown over with mangrove thickets with exposed supporting roots; it lacked water; or it had no shelter from the sea. And so it continued until November 14, 1579, when Moone inspected a small, low-lying island. He returned to the *Hind* with happiness on his face.

"General," Moone happily shouted as he climbed the sea ladder, pausing to wipe the sweat from his face. He smiled while squinting from the sun's glare. He was dressed solely in pants that just barely covered his knees and was barefoot. The writer has previously written that Moone was shorter than most members of the crew. Yet his size had not cost him any respect. He was strong; his arms were muscular, while his chin was demanding. And if that were not sufficient to intimidate, he was usually armed. When he was away from his ship, he carried a sword that was attached to his belt. He moved with a swagger as he climbed the ladder to the poop deck. His quick movements indicated that he had recovered from the scurvy. "This is our island," he said, following Drake into his cabin. Hurd and Tom Drake were steps behind the two men. "It is a beaut—"

"Really? Explain."

"It has what we need—it has a lagoon," Moone said, pointing out a window to an opening to the island, which could give it some protection from small storms. "It is a secure harbor—the *Hind* can safely enter it. Then it has a sandy shore where we can easily careen the *Hind*.

"Is there fresh water?" Drake asked.

"Yes, it has a small lake which is two to three hundred yards from the lagoon." He added, "Its water is brackish but potable."

"Well, lead us into it," Drake tiredly said. He was in need of a rest though he would not have admitted it. The stop at Ternate had been too brief.

"Gladly," Moone replied.

Thereafter, the *Golden Hind* followed the longboat into the lagoon which was barely a quarter of a mile across. And it was not much more than a half mile the other way. And because of the location of the lagoon's entrance, it was very sheltered, being a splendid place to careen as there was plenty of sandy bottom that tapered to nothing. It as well appeared to be an idyllic spot to rest the crew. For it was a sunny isle with a beautiful beach, while it had plenty of vegetation growing on its interior. Hundreds of slender coconut trees lined the shore. Many were eighty feet tall. All leaned seaward. Each was laden with coconuts. The *Hind* anchored in fifteen feet of water.

"I'll take the longboat and sail around the island, General," Moone said. The longboat was rigged for a deep sea sailing, as it had a mast and a lateen sail. "I'll find out what is on the other side!"

"Right, and we'll begin moving gear top side," Drake said.

Several hours later, Moone returned to the *Hind*.

"What did you learn, Tom?" Drake asked, referring to the island.

"I did not discover anything to change my mind. The island is about four miles long and about two miles deep. I am now positive that it is uninhabited. There is a reef on the opposite side, which probably would be a good place to fish—"

"And that island?" Drake cautiously asked, pointing to the outline of an island that was probably fifteen miles distant.

"I don't know—we probably ought to build a fort!" Moone replied, softly biting his lower lip, indicating that he was thinking.

"Get me Marks!" Drake said to John Drake. He was referring to his carpenter, Thomas Marks. Seconds later Marks arrived. He was now so stooped that it appeared as if he had a hump on his back . He wore a sleeveless shirt and pants that barely covered his knees. His iron-gray hair was shoulder length while his beard was long and streaked with gray. He was followed by Simon Woods, the cooper. Woods, too, was bearded; his hair was long and more unsightly, as his pate was bald.

"We're goin' to get the *Hind* near the beach; then we'll careen her," Drake said while pointing.

"Aye, General—" Marks said. He was a man of few words. Woods said nothing.

"It may be easy doin' it this time," Drake said, shading his eyes with his hand as he studied the beautiful beach.

Marks thoughtfully nodded.

"What is the big need in your department?" Drake asked.

"Well, I am in good shape, but Simon, the cooper, has water casks that need cooperage," Marks said, referring to the tight barrels. Their staves had been made of white oak, which normally maintained their tightness.

"The staves have shrunk—we'll need to reduce slightly the size of the metal hoops for the bilge and quarter hoops—"

"What will you need?" Drake asked, speaking to Marks who Drake knew spoke for both, as Woods was a man of less words than Marks.

"We will need to set up the blacksmith shop on the beach—and we will need coal—"

"That we don't have!" Drake said, shaking his head while pondering.

"We can use charcoal," Marks replied.

"You will have to make it!" Drake said, realizing that in order for Marks and Woods to make the needed adjustments on the metal hoops of the water barrels, they would have to have a fire with heat of a very high temperature. In this case, it would have to come from activated charcoal.

"We can make it," the carpenter replied.

"Can you use those trees?" Drake asked, referring to the island trees.

"Oh, yes," the carpenter confidently replied. He and Woods would subsequently take some of the coconut trees, and some screw pines, build a fire with them, and partially cover them with sand so as to limit the access of air; and on the fire subsiding, they would gather up the carbonized remainder, which they would use as charcoal.

"We shall build a fort," Drake said, speaking to Hurd. "This will require us to erect tents; put a gun with balls and packing on shore as all sleeping will be done on the beach."

"How soon do you want to get this work done, General?" Hurd asked.

"I am not in a big hurry—I know that many of the men are sick; I know that most are tired. Let us do it this way—those that are able will work a half day, play and rest the remainder. Those that are not able will just lie around and get well!"

"I will report that to the men—that will probably make them happy!" Hurd said. And it did. The men unloaded the *Hind* in four-hour shifts. And on a man completing his shift, he was free to relax as he pleased until his next shift. Many harvested hundreds of coconuts that were encrusted with thick covers of husk. They placed the husks in a huge pile which Horsewill later would use as cooking fuel; they drank the coconut juice and ate the snow-white copra. And they fished. They soon discovered that not only was the fishing excellent, but that there were many land crabs on the reef side of the island; these were a form of king crab which hid by digging caves under the roots of trees. And once the men began to pursue them in their ground hiding places, the crabs began to climb the trees. And the sailors climbed the tree after them, as they were exceedingly good to eat. Some of these crabs were large enough to feed several men. And they were so plentiful and the men liked them so well that they named the island, "Crab Island." The fishermen also discovered that the waters abounded with crayfish. Some of the fishermen built pots and baited them with coconut meat. The bait worked, for they were soon catching crayfish that weighed ten to twelve pounds. Soon the

Englishmen were dining on delicious meals of crabs and crayfish as well as succulent fish. The meals of fish had a healing effect on the sick—but that was not all. The water was so warm that in the late evening Preacher Fletcher, the acting physician, helped bring the sick to the water's edge where they sat for long periods of time in the warm water. It had a healing effect, for those who had been unable to walk were soon walking. Within two weeks most were able to return to their old jobs.

The deck hands cleaned the outside of the *Hind*'s bottom; then Marks and Woods repaired the wood work to that side; then they did the other; then Woods began to make adjustments to the hoops for the water casks. One day while Marks was pumping air to his tiny forge, Drake approached him:

"Thomas," Drake said to Marks. There was feeling in his voice. This was partially because the carpenter was from Plymouth. And so for years Drake had known of Marks and his carpentry skills. Even so, Drake had not sailed with Marks until this voyage. So in planning the voyage, Drake had been especially pleased when Marks had agreed to sail with him.

"Yes, General—"

"You look much better—"

"I am," the carpenter said, attempting to straighten his back, though it fully refused to straighten. "This is a lovely place. We have a breeze most of the day. There is a better one at night. Sleeping is easy. I seldom awake." He and Woods slept on hammocks that they had hung between coconut trees. "Neither the fireflies nor the bats bother me," he said. There were tens of thousands of fireflies which nightly lit up the island; and as well, there were thousands of bats that roosted in the trees around him. "And the fishing is delightful. If I don't back away from my eating, I shall soon be rolling out of my hammock—"

"I am glad that you are rested—"

"What can I do for you, General?" Marks asked, as if he knew that Drake wanted him to do something different.

"I want you and Simon to build me a house—"

"A house—won't we soon be leaving?"

"Yes, we will. But could you build it for me anyway?"

"Out of the trees on this island?"

"Yes—"

"We ought to be able to do that."

412

Thereafter, the carpenter and the cooper went into the interior of the island where there was a small forest of pandanus trees, being a sort of a screw pine. They cut six of these strange trees, which they used to form the house. Two of these were four feet longer than the others. They used these to form a gable roof. They then made some rafters from the trunks of the pandanus trees; these interesting trees were ideal for that since they put down numerous exposed roots which uniquely serve as props for the main trunk, which is quite different from the other parts of the tree. Then the two men tied numerous broken or warped barrel staves onto the props; then they used pandanus leaves to form a roof; some of these leaves were six feet long and four feet wide. And while they were forming the roof, they were joined by Fowler, the toothless boatswain.

"Need a hand?" Fowler asked, shielding his eyes. The sun was still high. The sky was shrouded with baggy rain clouds. The island soon would receive an afternoon rainstorm.

"What knot would you use on them?" the carpenter asked, nodding his head toward the pandanus leaves.

"Let me show you," the boatswain said. He then unraveled some throngs from the same leaves and began to lash them to the roof. His moves were so deft that Marks little understood the knot that he used.

"I could weave you some privacy walls, if you like," Fowler said; then he spoke to John Brewer, the bugler, who had joined him. "John, would you help me by fetching an armload of these leaves from yonder woods. And then would you help me weave a wall for the carpenter?"

"No fishing?" the bugler asked. He was very close to the boatswain. He and the boatswain had planned to line fish for rock bass.

"We will do it after the rain and when the sun is setting!"

"Aye."

"And why this house?" the boatswain asked. He had been so engrossed in making new rope from coconut husks that he had not noticed the carpenter building the house. And once he had taken notice of it, he could not resist joining in the effort.

"It is for the General," Marks replied.

"But we will soon be leaving!" the boatswain said, speaking while his fingers busily weaved; he nodded to the *Hind* which was afloat in twenty feet of clear water. Her bottom had been cleaned,

413

patched and painted. Her water casks had been rebound—they were now being filled with water and stowed on the *Hind*.

"I fear somebody is not going with us!" the carpenter said while frowning, showing several missing teeth.

"I wonder who?" the boatswain curiously asked, though he half-smiled as if he knew.

On the day of tent folding, being the day when all the tents were folded and stowed on the *Hind*, it was apparent that Maria was one of those to be left. For the chest that held her clothes and jewelry had been put in the house. She was now big with child. She had been sleeping in a tent to herself. Moone no longer shared her tent, though he did supply her with food; it was just as well that he did, because she was more interested in her toilet than work, which included cooking. Moone was very kind to her, as each day he brought to her fresh-cooked fish, crabs, crayfish and sago biscuits.

"Let us praise God for his blessings!" Fletcher declared, speaking to the men who were assembled on the sandy beach. He, too, was bearded, while his hair was long and unkempt. It was streaked with gray. It now gave him a saintly appearance. Then he added, "Dear God, we have suffered like Jonah . . . " And he thereafter enumerated the many trials that the venturers had recently suffered. "We have crossed the South Sea, and we have not had to eat rats; but we have had our misfortunes, for we have been attacked by thieving natives; and many of us have become sick and lame, but you brought us to this Crab Island—this tranquil island of beauty. We came sick and tired. And you have healed us, made us strong and healthy, so we can continue on our voyage home to England . . . "

Thereafter, Drake spoke to the assembly:

"Dear God, I thank you for your blessings—it has been a bountiful, restful month and we thank you for it. And we ask you to direct us so that we will live as you would want us to while we resume our voyage . . . "

Thereafter, the men fell out of their disorderly ranks; many waded to the longboat to be the first to board the *Hind*. Drake walked over to Maria, who was standing to herself, and he took her arm. She clumsily moved as she was large with child. He led her to the newly constructed house. She apprehensively stared at him. Tears were in her eyes. She was unsure of the future. She wondered what this thatched hut had to do with her future. Then she looked down and saw her trunk.

414

"Oh!" she cried. "It can't be so!"

"This is your new home, Maria," Drake said, half smiling, speaking in Spanish, as her English still had not improved.

"No—no!" she screamed.

"What is wrong?" he asked, speaking to her in a caring voice, as if there were still a bond between them. The English crew members turned, stared, and pointed. Some whispered.

"I don't want to stay here; I want to go to England!"

"But England is not your home—and we are short of space!" Drake said. Drake had become concerned about space when he no longer needed personnel. This was especially so of fighting men since he had filled the *Hind* with treasure and was no longer desirous of making war in order to gain more.

"Tom! Tom!" she cried to Moone, who was standing ankle-deep in the warm water. He stared at her as if he did not know her. And he did not speak. Nor did he answer her beckon. Drake had already told Moone of his intentions. Moone had only nodded his head. Drake had then said:

"We can't very well take her to England—it would embarrass the Queen."

"Well—"

"And who is the father?" he argued further. "Taking her home with us would jeopardize the homecoming for both of us!"

Moone as well as Drake had a wife. And he was looking forward to seeing her. More so, Tom Moone would not have crossed Drake. It was not just because he feared Drake. Moone would not do it because he instinctively believed that Drake's decisions had to be obeyed. Had he not brought them this far?

"Master Hurd!" Drake shouted.

"Yes, General?"

"Bring the tools—the seeds—"

"Aye," Hurd answered, picking up a small wooden chest that held seeds. Another seaman picked up a pair of hoes and an ax, which they then carried to the hut.

"Francesco—Pedro!" Drake shouted to the two blacks, who were standing to themselves. They were the two blacks that Drake had rescued from the court of law in Guatalco when Drake plundered the town. The two had not become a part of the *Hind*; it was not due to their color, for Drake was partial to blacks, though he only had one black crew member. This was Juan, who he had taken from the pinnace that the *Hind* had captured on February 28, 1579. But these two blacks were unduly surly. They were inclined to be rogues—they had kept to themselves and had refused to join in the ship board work like the Cimaron.

"Come here!" Drake ordered.

"¿Que esta?" What is it? Francesco asked.

"You two will remain on this island—"

"No, General!" Francesco said. Defiance was in his voice. "We will not!"

"Yes, we must lighten ship!" Drake said, not raising his voice, acting as though he had not noticed the defiance.

"No, General!" Maria shouted. "I do not want to stay with these men. They are criminals!"

"But they are men!" Drake sarcastically replied.

"Why them?" she shouted and stomped her feet.

"Does it matter?" Drake asked.

"Oh, I hate you!"

"But I give you two men, not one!" he said with a sneer. Then he shouted to his master, "Tom, let's load her!" He of course was referring to the *Golden Hind*. And then Drake strode across the sand in the direction of the longboat.

"English pirates!" Maria screamed at the men boarding the longboat, while Francesco and Pedro swore vilely. But no one answered them.

CHAPTER 43

AGROUND

The *Hind* departed Crab Island on December 12, 1579, and after doing so, Drake was tired, as it had been a day of decisions. His first big decision had been the matter of leaving Maria and the two blacks. Then he had had to decide which way he would sail. The choice of his route had involved the toughest decision. Drake had spent much of the day pondering which route he should take. During the morning he had committed himself to sailing north, then proceeding westerly across the Celebes Sea. But that evening, after much deliberation, he had decided against it. He had become suspicious that he might meet a Portugese man-of-war. He recalled that at Ternate he had learned that the Portuguese most always followed the Northern route to reach the Spice Islands. So moments before leaving Crab Island, Drake had decided to sail the seldom-used southern route through the Molucca Sea and then the Banda Sea. It had not been done without trepidation, for Drake had been forewarned about the southern route; yet he little imagined the skill and luck that it would take to navigate these waters since they were spersed with dangerous shoals. This route would continue to be hazardous sailing until the *Hind* was able to enter the Indian Ocean; this entry would have to be made by the *Hind*'s traversing a difficult strait which is located just north of Timor. The Sultan's navigator had explained to Drake:

"You must be very careful with your ship."

"Tell me why?"

"Your ship is deep in the water; and there are many shoals."

"How are we to know them?"

"The water coloring will tell you—so night will be your most difficult time—then if you sail, you must be lucky!"

"And when I reach Timor?"

"You will then pass through the Ombai Strait into the Great Sea."

"Then?"

"Your worries will be few—I am told that you then may sail west to the land of the white man. But his land is very far away!"

Drake's chart was a poor navigational instrument; for as the writer stated in the previous chapter, it only depicted the largest islands, and many of these were out of place, as the chart was poorly drawn. And so Drake knew when he turned the *Hind* southward that this aspect of his voyage would be very dangerous. And he took this into account, as he stationed two men on the bow whose job it was to inform the bridge of any change in the color of the water which would clue Drake that the *Hind* was entering shallow water. Then Drake paid particular attention to the *Hind*'s sails.

"Water is changing!"

"Where away?"

"To larboard!"

"Left rudder!" the helmsman shouted. But the reader will recall that the whipstaff could only be turned five degrees either way; thus, the boatswain of the watch and the seamen had to be on their toes and turn the yards quickly so as to make the *Hind* turn in time.

On the night of January 9, 1580, being shortly after 8:00 p.m., the *Hind* was sailing south, being just west of the Lower Celebes. The air was moist and sultry. The night sky was lit up by hundreds of glittering stars. The Southern Cross was directly overhead, as if attempting to outline the English ship. Some men on deck aimlessly walked about; others lay on deck attempting to sleep. Those men on watch eyed their sails, for they were filling with air, as the *Hind* was feeling the tail end of a monsoon.

"Thump!"

"What is it!" Drake cried, falling from his bunk to the deck. He got himself up and he raced to the open door. The *Hind* had stopped, though her sails were still bagged with wind. All hands were now on their feet. All now looked up at Drake, who was exiting from his cabin.

"Hurd!" Drake shouted.

"Aye!"

"Aground, General!" Boatswain Fowler interjected from the main deck. Concern was in his voice.

"Oh!" Drake cried. Anguish was on his face. "Furl those sails!" Drake said. He knew that he must now keep the wind from blowing them further aground. The deck was now filled with whispering men. Those men not working with ropes and sails focused their eyes on Drake.

"Aye!"

"Boatswain, sound me!" Drake cried, asking Fuller to give him the depth of the water.

"Aye!" the boatswain answered. He was quickly joined by two sailors who had their sounding gear in hand. Then they began to cast out their sounders, each being a leaded weight that was attached to a heaving line, which was marked in fathoms so to indicate the depth of the water.

"Six feet to starboard!"

"Deep to larboard (port)!" This meant that he could not find bottom.

"Six feet to starboard!"

"Deep to larboard!"

And thus the soundings continued, while Drake surveyed the ship for damage until the soundings were the same on each side of the ship from bow to stern.

"Aground, General," Hurd stated on joining Drake, whose face reflected the worry of both.

"Yes—we apparently are on the edge of a shoal!"

"How's that?" the master asked. He did not quite understand Drake's surmise that the *Hind* was half on and half off a reef.

"We have deep water to larboard—six feet to starboard!"

"What do you suggest?"

"Tom Moone! Tom!" Drake cried, seeking the help of the man who in many ways had been his right arm during much of the voyage. For usually he had been the man that Drake had turned to when he had had a difficult problem.

"Yes, General!" Moone said. He was now bare-chested and standing beside Hurd. Worry was on his face.

"Take the longboat; survey the water; find out for me if there is some way we can use the anchor so as to get the *Hind* off this shoal!"

"Shall I use the sheet?" Moone asked, referring to the *Hind's* largest anchor, which was kept in a hold amidship. It was carried just for such a purpose.

"Yes—hurry!"

419

They quickly agreed on a plan whereby a long, heavy rope would be attached to the sheet anchor, and then it would be hooked to a place on the bottom where it could get a very good grip. The rope in turn would be brought back to the *Hind* and put about its capstan. A dozen men would then turn the capstan and hopefully pull the *Hind* off the reef.

"Aye—you men, give me a hand; let's get the longboat, hurry! You men, get the sheet anchor. Put it in the longboat!" Moone shouted.

"Aye!"

Moone thoroughly surveyed the water surrounding the *Hind*, and then he returned to the *Hind*.

"General," Moone said, while climbing the sea ladder. "We've made a good survey—"

"What did you find?" Drake eagerly asked. He was barefoot and dressed only in his underdrawers as the night air was warm and humid.

"It's like you said; we've run aground onto a shoal—"

"I know. Is there any bottom that we can get a bite on so we can use the anchor?"

"It will have to be done from the larboard side—and the water is very deep to our larboard. I could not find bottom—"

"And to our starboard?"

"It is six feet constant!"

"We are on the edge of a shoal!"

"I agree—has it damaged her keel?"

"We do not have any leaks—we have just finished pumping her dry!" Drake said. He had been to the bilges where he had helped the men pump the *Hind*'s bilges. He had been pleased to learn that she was not taking aboard any new water.

"Is this high water?" Moone asked.

"It would take seven feet or more of additional water to float her!" Drake replied, thinking, knowing that she was 13 feet in the water.

"What do we do next?" Hurd asked.

"Well," Drake said, adding, "It is dawn. Reverend," he said, speaking to Fletcher who was standing on the main deck with his Bible in his hand.

"Yes, General?" Fletcher solemnly questioned. His face was one of dejection as if he were thinking the worst.

420

"Get the men to quarters—let us have prayer service—I want you to call on the Lord. Ask Him to help us get the *Hind* off this shoal!"

"I agree. It must be done, General," Fletcher answered in a pious voice, as though readying himself by setting a tone for communication.

And while the men were assembling, those men on deck began to get themselves in prayerful positions; some had merely bowed their heads, while others had fallen on their knees. Drake, too, bowed his head, and he thought on his plight. He had come such a long way since he first started to going to sea at the age of twelve. It had been a long, hard trek. For from the beginning, while just a boy, he had done the manly, dangerous work of a seaman. Then at twenty, he had sold his bark and gone on a slaving expedition as an investor as well as a member. He had made two difficult slaving expeditions; all had exposed him to extreme dangers, and at Ulua in Mexico, he had almost been annihilated while he was adjusting to his first command. Thereafter, he had become a privateer pirate, plundering and adventuring on the Spanish Main. From these forays he had acquired considerable wealth. Then he had aided Essex in Ireland, and for the first time, he had made a connection with the ruling class, which had led him to a commission from the Queen. He may not have done exactly what she had wished, but he had robbed and stolen until he had filled his ship with treasure which he was taking to England. So far he had eluded the Spaniards. Much of his thoughts of late had been in making it back to England, for he knew that once he got there, irrespective of his misdeeds, the Queen would have to accept him. Money equalized. But he had overlooked luck. It apparently had ended for him. Now the *Hind* was on top of a shoal—it soon would break in two. The wind would see to that, and the treasure would be covered with water. There was the peak of a nearby island in sight, but he surmised that it was eighteen miles away. The longboat would not carry more than twenty men. The dinghy might carry four to six. What could he do to save his ship and treasure?

"Dearly beloved, shall we sing . . . God is our refuge . . . " the men sang. Then Fletcher extended communion to all the men. They sipped wine from a glass, ate a bit of biscuit, and passed the plate and glass to the next man, each tasting the symbolic blood and body of Jesus. When it was completed, the sun began to rise and the deck of the *Hind* began to warm.

421

"Dear God, please forgive us of our sins—and we have sinned. And our sins are many. Forgive us of them . . . " And Fletcher continued, preaching and railing of their sins, naming many of the transgressions that had been made by crew members; then he burst forth in a voice of exaltation, "Hallelujah, dear God, I know why you have done this to us. It is because of the transgressions of our General—yes, our General!" he exclaimed. His face had abruptly changed. It now wore a frown that showed his bitterness. And he pointed a finger at Drake, saying, "He cut off the head of his partner, Doughty, which you know was a horrible crime. And dear God, you punished us by driving our ship into strange, cold seas—"

"Eh!" Drake softly exclaimed, eyeing the tall, hatchet-faced, stoop-shouldered man with an ugly nose. Drake's mouth became dry as he listened to the rasping voice of the preacher.

"He chucked to the Spanish, our little Portuguese navigator, like he was chaff for the wind; and then he impregnated his black mistress. And if that were not bad enough, he then exiled her and her unborn offspring onto a strange island with criminals. And now you are punishing all of us for his crimes. And so I know why you are doing it to us! Dear God, when you call us home, remember that such a decision was his and not ours!" Fletcher cried out, trying to separate the crew from Drake.

"Enough!" Drake exclaimed.

"But not until I have finished my sermon!" Fletcher shouted.

"But you have told enough lies, you blackguard!" Drake shouted.

"But let me pray for you, General; your wickedness has brought us to this end!" Fletcher shouted, as though they would soon perish.

"Enough!" Drake shouted and stood and pulled the preacher's arm, as if he were trying to jerk some sense into his head, and Fletcher did not say anything further. But he had said enough. For he had laid the blame of their plight on Drake for having beheaded Doughty and for having put Nuno da Silva ashore at Guatalco and for having exiled his Black mistress onto Crab Island. But on the service ending, Drake indicated that he was not ready to follow the course outlined by Fletcher and to concede victory to the sea.

"Master Hurd, let's cast into the sea half of the cloves!"

"Aye!" the master said. His eyes nervously blinked at the thought. Cloves were extremely valuable—for they were thought to be a magical spice. Alexander of Trallee, a famous physician, had

422

claimed that cloves stimulated the appetite, prevented seasickness and cured the gout. Thus, Hurd slowly walked away so as to carry out Drake's order, knowing that in doing so, they would be casting a fortune of spices into the water.

Drake frowned as the bails of cloves fell into the water and floated like flotsam on the surface.

"Dump two of the culverins—dump the beans—the meal!"

"Aye!" Hurd answered, directing sailors to respond to the order.

"Have I gained anything, boatswain?" Drake asked Fowler on his orders having been fulfilled.

"Nothing, General!"

"Well—Tom—Tom Moone!" Drake cried. He was not giving up, as if he knew that perseverance was the mother of accomplishment.

"Aye, General!"

"Rig your sail on the longboat—you'll need 14 rowers."

"Yes—"

"Tie your rope to the larboard beam!"

"Aye!" And Moone did.

"Master Hurd, have all the men run from starboard to larboard!" Drake said. He was referring to the *Hind*.

"Aye!"

"Now you men in the boat, row hard!" Drake shouted. He was trying to force the *Hind* to fall from the shoal, for it was apparent to him that she was only half aground.

"Row hard!"

"Aye!" Hurd replied. Sweat soaked his chest. The sun was bearing down on the *Hind*. Its deck was sizzling from the heat.

The men in the boat rowed hard. And the men on the *Hind* ran back and forth and they stomped their feet, but the *Hind* did not move.

"The wind may change, General!" Hurd condescendingly said on eyeing Drake's face which showed his worry.

"Ready your sails!" Drake said to the boatswain.

"How's that, General?"

"Train your yards so that they face starboard!"

"Aye!"

"When the wind blows from the starboard, release your sails!" Drake said. He would attempt to use the *Hind*'s sails to pull her off the reef.

"Aye!"

And late that evening, when the sun was setting, the wind began to change. Uneasiness permeated the *Hind*, though there was little talk concerning her plight.

"The wind is changing, General!"

"I feel it—when it blows directly from the starboard, hoist that sail!" Drake said, pointing to the foresail.

"It blows, General!"

"I know—" Drake said. All eyes were on him. He was waiting for the right moment.

"It blows strong, General!"

"Hoist it!" Drake shouted, knowing now that the wind could move the *Hind*, but in doing so, he was gambling that she would not capsize when she slid from the reef. And the *Hind* then leaned to the larboard as if she would capsize, seemingly doing it intentionally, being a part of her refusal to leave the reef.

"Furl it—move!" Drake shouted. He was withdrawing the sail.

"Plop!" The *Hind* fell from the reef, freeing herself; then she straightened.

"She's free!"

"Hurrah!"

"Cheers for the General!"

"Tom!" Drake shouted to Moone in the longboat. "Tow us clear of this shoal!"

"Aye!" Moone replied. And then on the line from the longboat to the *Hind* becoming taut, the larger ship was towed free of the reef.

The morning following the freeing of the *Hind*, just as the sun had begun to break the horizon, Marks, the carpenter, came on the main deck with a hammer and large staple. He was stooped and slow moving. He drove the staple into the foot of the main mast. He took from his apron a set of leg irons which he then attached to the staple. He then looked up to the portico deck; and he eyed Drake who was stepping from his cabin onto the tiny deck. Drake was resplendently dressed in a gold vest and red pantaloons; he wore his baggy burgundy hat, which was shaped like a crushed stovepipe. He held a navigator's ruler in his right hand, which he waved as though it were a wand. Then onto the main deck stepped the sailmaker, Meeks, and

Willie Fortescue, who always tried to emulate Drake, and so at dress-ups he attempted to dress as much like him as possible. This time was no exception. The sailmaker grinned with pleasure at the boy in his attire, which he had just completed by adding the red pantaloons. Willie did a dozen cartwheels on deck and then he joined Drake on the portico deck.

"Assemble the men, Mr. Hurd!"

"Aye! Hear ye—hear ye! All hands on deck!" Breakfast had not been served. Horsewill was cooking oatmeal in a huge pot. A second pot was filled with pease and leeks, while Blackcollar was baking biscuits made from sago, being a starchy meal that was made from the pith of the sago palm.

Because of the early morning heat, most of the men were already on deck. The viol players, John Martyn and Edward Mincy, stood to themselves on the poop deck. They began softly to play a dirge. Fletcher stood by himself on the larboard side of the main deck. He screwed up his mouth and then his nose, while he suspiciously eyed the carpenter, Marks, who was finishing his work.

"Bring forth the knave!" Drake said, speaking to his brother, Tom Drake, who was standing beside another soldier near the mainmast. Each was armed with a short pike. They marched to Preacher Fletcher, took hold of his arms, and marched him back to the mainmast where Drake and Willie Fortescue now were standing.

"Preacher Fletcher, you have a false tongue!" Drake said, carelessly pointing his ruler at him. There was a frivolity in his voice and in the manner that he moved, which the assembled crew sensed. They sensed it more because Willie Fortescue was participating in the ceremony. Drake only liked levity when he dressed for it. And then he often shared it with Willie who was a natural comic. He could make faces to suit the occasion. Then he was also a natural acrobatic. And being the youngest person aboard, he was encouraged to act the part of a young clown. Most smiled at his antics. All had been greatly relieved on their being saved from foundering—the treasure was saved. All had gained new respect for Drake. All were once again convinced that he was the greatest sailor in the world.

"But God delivered us!" Fletcher answered, as if advising that his prayer had played a part.

"Manacle him!" Drake ordered.

And after Tom Drake had manacled Fletcher's legs to the main mast, Drake waved his wand, then he ceremonially waved it over Fletcher, doing it as though he were a high priest.

"You are a foul-mouthed knave—you preach lies; you have caused dissent amongst the crew. And because of that, I do hereby excommunicate you from the Christian church!" Drake said, pretending that he was the Pope.

"You do not have the power, General!" Fletcher obstinately replied; yet he anxiously studied Drake, as he sensed that he was in serious trouble, wondering but what Drake would have his head.

"But if you are a preacher, I am your pope," Drake sarcastically said, pointing to his costume. "And the Pope does have the power to excommunicate a false priest!" Drake argued, smiling.

"But you are not a pope!" Fletcher argued, sniffing, showing his nervousness.

"And you are not a priest! Even so, I am going to sentence you to wear this sign on your sleeve," he said, holding up a paper with a pin attached to it.

"What does it say?" Fletcher asked, looking perplexed, beginning to feel some humiliation at the scene. Many of the men were smiling. All were seeing a humorous side to the hearing before the mast, though they had held back their laughter as they did not quite know how to receive the hearing. Were they to laugh? Was Drake going to do more? Would he decapitate Fletcher? He had done it to Doughty.

"It says, 'Francis Fletcher is a liar!'"

"But I am not a liar!"

"And I answer that you are—and I say further to you, Francis Fletcher, that if you come before me again charged with having told lies, I shall hang you to the yard arm—and that will end your telling of lies!" Drake said without smiling.

"Well—" Fletcher stammered, blanching, sensing seriousness in Drake's voice, which caused him to be at a loss for words.

"Do you understand?"

"I do—General," Fletcher said, humbling himself, and then falling on his knees, recognizing that the law of the *Hind* was Drake— and the law decreed that he must not speak ill of Drake.

CHAPTER 44

THE SULTAN OF BANTAM

The *Hind* was sailing due south toward Ombai Strait; however, Drake was not yet giving much thought to the strait, though he knew that its passage would be a difficult one, being the passage between the islands of Wetta and Ombai, and then Ombai and Timor. The *Hind* was only carrying half sail as she was carefully sailing the Banda Sea, being dangerous waters since they were largely uncharted. And in many cases charts would not have helped, since just beneath the water in some places there were dangerous shoals that could only be identified by the color of the water. Drake was using extra precautions in order to avoid running aground a second time. He now required the *Hind* to lay to at night, and he was taking more precautions during the day.

"What is it like, Tom?" Drake shouted for the tenth time that hour to Tom Moone, who was in the longboat, which was now 100 yards ahead of the *Hind*. It carried a small sail so as to keep it from sailing away from the *Hind*.

"Safe, General!" Moone replied while pouring a coconut shell of water on his head. The sun's rays were fiercely searing Moone as well as the other men in the boat, though most had become as brown as a Malay. The heat was to be expected since the sun was high as it was almost noon. In just a few more minutes Tom Moone and his crew would be relieved by Tom Drake and his crew.

"Thank you!" Drake replied. He was standing on the *Hind*'s bow, being outside the *Hind*'s awning. He wore a wet rag on his head. He was dressed only in his underdrawers.

"A canoe, General!" a topmast lookout shouted.

"Where?" Drake asked, looking through the haze.

"The starboard bow."

The *Hind* shortly thereafter came alongside the newly-sighted banca canoe with lateen sail. It was carrying two men who were dressed in loin cloths and straw hats. Each had golden brown skin, which had been heavily oiled. Their hair was black and long. Their eyes, as well, were black as charcoal, while each was slender as bamboo. One of the men spoke sufficient Portuguese-Spanish in order for Drake to communicate with him.

"I am a sailor from Java—my home is in Bantam, West Java."

"For whom have you sailed?"

"My last ship was a Portuguese trader—"

"And where is your ship?"

"We ran aground in the Banda Sea—it sank."

"And where do you wish to go?"

"Baratiua."

"And where is it?"

"South—"

"And do you know these waters?"

"Yes—"

"If you will pilot us, we will take you there," Drake said.

"Oh, sir, we can do that!" the Javanese sailor eagerly replied as if eager to leave the cramped quarters of the canoe. Then both men began to paddle hard, directing their canoe toward the *Hind*.

"Then tie your canoe to the stern and come aboard," Drake said, pointing. And once the two sailors were aboard the *Hind*, Drake led them into his cabin, and he continued his conversation with the sailor with whom he had been speaking earlier.

"What is your name?"

"My name is Kapang," the spokesman said, smiling. "His name is Longa," he said, pointing to his friend.

"What is your business?"

"Sailor—trader," said the spokesman for the two.

"And where have you come from?" Drake suspiciously asked. He had noted that the banca canoe was practically empty of trade goods.

"We began in Tidore. I bought this canoe after our ship sank!"

"What did you do there?"

"We traded—worked for the Portuguese!" he said, while curiously smiling.

"And did they pay you?"

"Oh, yes," the man said, pointing his head toward the bag in his hands.

"And where are you going?" Drake asked.

"The island of Baratiua."

"And then?"

"Java."

"And do you know the Ombai Strait?" Drake asked, referring to the strait previously mentioned, being the strait which separates the small island of Wetta from Ombai and the large island of Timor. Drake had been told in Ternate that it would be difficult to traverse it in a ship the size of the *Hind* without the aid of a pilot.

"Oh, yes—"

"And would you pilot us? We would pay you."

"We would, providing you first take us to Baratiua," Kapang replied, smiling.

"Why there?"

"Food—diversion!" he said, smiling.

"And where is Baratiua?"

"It is a small island three days sailing from here—it is on the way to Ombai—you will like it," he said, smiling and confidently nodding his head, as if he wished to say more, but he was reluctant to do so.

"And from those people can we purchase fresh water, food, fruit and herbs?"

"And much more," Kapang replied, smiling mischievously and showing blackened teeth.

"Is there a place to careen my ship?"

"Very good place—"

"And do the winds blow to Java?" Drake asked, meaning once they had passed through the strait and they were in the Indian Ocean, would the winds blow westerly? The *Hind* was a square-rigged ship, which would make her easy to sail westerly with a following wind. But without such a wind, she would be a difficult ship to tack.

"Oh, yes—there is good wind to Java," Kapang said. He would subsequently explain that at other times of the year, such as July, there was a strong easterly wind which then would make it difficult to sail to Java.

Thereafter, Drake permitted Kapang to pilot the *Hind* to the island of Baratiua, where on February 11, 1580, the *Hind* anchored in a beautiful lagoon amidst dozens of banca canoes. Many were large enough to haul cargo. At that time Baratiua was ruled by a pleasant-appearing rajah. He was a tall, brown man with a round face and gray hair. His limbs were muscular and well-formed. He was dressed only in a sarong. He received Drake warmly, bowing to him as if he were the head of a country. He smiled felicitously while boarding the *Hind*; then he respectfully bowed once again to Drake while the *Hind's* culverins were firing their salute. "General, welcome to Baratiua. My country is your country," the Rajah said, speaking through Kapang. "How may I help you?"

"Many thanks. My men need to rest," said Drake.

"You may do that. I hope that you will stay for a long time," the Rajah respectfully said, while once again bowing. Then he added, "You like to trade, we trade—no like trade, rest—no problem!"

"We will stay at least two or three weeks," Drake said, not quite knowing the unusual temptations that soon would face his men.

The people of the island were Buddhist Hindus. However, their religion did not present a problem—but there would be other distractions. Firstly, the women as a rule were well-formed, which they displayed for all to see, as the women, like the men, did not wear any clothes on the upper part of their bodies. And then they were lacking in modesty. This would especially be so when they removed their sarongs to swim, as they swam in the nude, and they often swam. The first night the Englishmen were on the island, the Rajah gave a reception for them. It was a gala affair. Torches were lighted and placed in the midst of a grove of coconut trees. A feast of fruit and vegetables was spread on the ground before the guests, as the island was a bountiful place, being blessed with a diversity of vegetables and fruits. Coconut shells filled with toddy were passed from man to man. Toddy was an alcoholic drink that had been made from the sap of young coconut trees. The sap had been allowed to ferment until the juice tasted like a sweet beer. And once the men had had their fill of food and drink, dozens of young girls came forth and danced the legong, being a sensuous but artistic dance. And on each concluding her part of the dance, she took a seat beside an Englishman and coquettishly smiled at him. And then she began to entertain her man by the artful use of her hands, which she moved about her body, even motioning for her new friend to do the same. And the Rajah kept encouraging new dancers to come forth until each man had a beautiful girl seated beside him, who then entertained him as though she were his lover. Many of the girls followed the men onto the *Hind*; others lay with them on the beach, as they apparently did not have any mores against doing so. And those girls that followed the men onto the *Hind* remained—the next morning they walked about the deck, laughing and flirting with the Englishmen. And soon they were joined by many other young women who boarded the *Hind*, carrying trays of food on their heads. The trays were so well-balanced that they stayed in place without the women's hands touching them. The men soon were so enamored with the women that they were reluctant to leave their sides. And on the afternoon of the second day, when the decks of the *Hind* were blanketed with pretty women entwined with sailors, Kapang quietly entered Drake's cabin and stopped.

Drake was seated at his table—he was dressed in white linen trousers and shirt. He had his left hand to his left cheek; he was obviously deep in thought. Hurd was seated opposite to him. Drake turned and eyed Kapang, the Malay, who was standing obeisantly at the door.

"General, the Rajah invites you and your men to another party—"

"Thanks," Drake said with a nonchalance as if he only half-heard him. His thoughts were apparently elsewhere. He took a hand fan from the table and fanned himself.

"You may clean your ship here—"

"Thanks, but we sail tomorrow," Drake curtly replied.

"Tomorrow?" Kapang said. Surprise was on his face.

"Tomorrow!" Hurd said. Surprise was also on his face. "I thought that you intended to career the ship here—give the men a vacation!"

"There are problems on this island that only a general in charge of a ship would understand—" Drake deviously said, standing and looking out a window at the line of coconut trees jutting forth from the island. Between the *Hind* and the island were dozens of banca canoes that were coming and going to the English ship. Several were tied alongside—women with baskets of fruit were climbing onto the *Hind*. Their laughter rang from the deck; it was mixed with the happy shouts of the sailors.

"And what time do we sail?"

"At dawn—" Drake replied, as if it were important that they leave the next day before daybreak.

431

"Dawn—so we will careen on Java?" Hurd asked.

"Yes—I will need you to pilot us to Java—" Drake said, speaking to Kapang.

"I do not want to leave—" Kapang said. His face was a picture of dejection. He adamantly shook his head.

"I will pay you well!"

"But only if you sail to Bantam," Kapang reluctantly said. It was one of the principal cities on the island of Java.

"Well—"

"The others are very bad, General," Kapang cleverly argued, referring to the other cities.

"Why?"

"Too much bad religion," Kapang said, pointing out to Drake that all of Java was now Muslim with the exception of the city/state of Bantam, which was located on the extreme northwestern tip of Java. It still had some vestige of Indo-Javanese culture, though it was beginning to crumble due to the powerful influence of the Muslim religion, which was driving out the weaker Buddhist-Hindu culture, which Drake and his men were presently experiencing and whose lenient sex mores had really frightened Drake. Its beautiful half-naked women had caused him to imagine the worst. He had become suspicious that many of his men might jump ship and leave him without enough men to sail the *Hind* back to England. Then his treasure would be easy plunder for pirates.

"I must sail tomorrow!"

"And I will pilot you—but I must be paid in advance!"

"I will do that—"

But Drake was not able to sail at dawn, for when dawn broke, more than half of his men were still on the beach. He did not get all of his men aboard the *Hind* until mid-afternoon. Then his brother Tom Drake and three of his soldiers had to use force to bring the last three of the men aboard ship. Thereafter, on February 13, 1580, the *Hind* departed Baratiua, while fifty or more tearful girls waved their farewells at the sad sailors on the *Hind* as it was being towed from the lagoon by the longboat. The sailors then climbed high in the braces and waved their farewells until the girls were out of sight.

The *Hind* sailed west. It made an uneventful passage through the Ombai Strait due to the excellent piloting of Kapang. The *Hind* soon was in the Timor Sea, which was much deeper water, while having on her right the Soenda Islands, which are located in an

432

unstable zone of island arcs, undersea ridges and active volcanoes. Drake did not have a decent map of this area. The maps that he did have of the region were so poorly drawn that they only gave him a general idea of Southeast Asia. Drake attempted to learn something of this region by questioning Kapang. Yet he knew very little about the inhabitants of these islands, for he would shake his head and frown when Drake questioned him about them. He repeatedly explained to Drake that these islands were unimportant because there was no trade with them, saying it as though trade were the primary reason for importance. The port that Drake now was sailing for was Bantam, which was located on the island of Java. Kapang had explained to Drake that Bantam was the most important city in Java because the Bantamese were traders who did much of their trading in spices. Kapang said again and again that Drake would get a fine reception because he was a trader. But Drake did not fully believe this talk, because he was suspicious that Kapang was saying this only because it was the home of the two Malays, and he had agreed to take them there. Even so, Drake's present goal was Bantam, being a place where Kapang had promised Drake that he could careen his ship and rest his crew without them becoming captives of beautiful sirens. But in order to do it, the *Hind* first had to reach the Sunda Strait. On March 11, 1580, the *Hind* finally reached the strait, being a narrow passage that separates the islands of Java on the right and Sumatra on the left.

"And how will we be received?" Drake asked his pilot who had just completed a lengthy conversation with two men who were seated in an ornately painted banca canoe. These Malays had begun their conversation first by partaking of the betel nut. One had handed Kapang a severed piece of cane that was filled with crushed betel nut, cloves and lime. Kapang bowed, then he partook of it. Then he passed it to his fellow traveler, who partook of it and then handed it back to the Malay in the boat. And then they had a highly animated conversation, doing it with frowns, grimaces and smiles, while dramatically using their hands.

"General, I can assure you that you will be well received. I have told these messengers to report to the Sultan of Bantam that you are a trader and your ship is English and that you will soon arrive in Bantam. I also told them that you are its General and that you represent a great Queen. And that you would like an audience with the Sultan concerning trade between the two countries."

"What was their response?" Drake asked, wiping his sweaty hands on his shirt, while looking out at the canoe which was turning about without the messengers having even boarded the *Hind*. It soon began to gain momentum as its sails filled with wind.

"Very good—the messenger said that the Sultan is a man who seeks trade. The messenger wanted to know if you were Portuguese. I told him that you were not. If you had been, that would have been bad, for the Sultan does not like the Portuguese. The messengers were pleased that you are English," Kapang said to Drake, who was eyeing the strange shape of a volcanic island in the middle of the strait.

"With what countries does Bantam now trade?" Drake asked.

"Trading is now done only with the Arabs and Chinese."

"And what does the Sultan have to trade?"

"Spices—much pepper. See, that is Java," Kapang said, pointing to land jutting forth on the right. They were now proceeding due north in the Sunda Strait, being trailed by the *Hind*'s longboat and Kapang's banca canoe.

"What is the smoke?" Drake asked, pointing to his starboard beam, being perturbed at this active volcano which was one of many.

"Fire—Java is hot inside," Kapang explained. "It oftentimes belches ash, which at first does much harm, though it is good for the land, for it makes it grow much rice. We go that way," Kapang said, pointing to the right, being a four-mile wide channel. The low-lying island of Sangiang had split the strait.

"Left rudder, Hurd!"

"Aye!"

"Deep water?" Drake cautiously asked his pilot.

"Plenty deep," Kapang said, grinning, showing his red gums which was due to the earlier meeting with the messenger. It was then that he had fully charged his mouth with betel nut, cloves and lime. His spittle was so red that it appeared to be pure blood.

Late that afternoon the *Hind* anchored in Bantam harbor. It was soon surrounded by dozens of banca canoes. Most were occupied by traders whose canoes were filled with rice, onions, beans, peppers, oil palms, fish, fruit and brightly colored cloth; many were vending an ornately decorated dagger. All were shouting to sailors who lined the *Hind*'s decks. The sailors right away became very interested in the daggers, strangely trading for them first, though it had been weeks since they had had fresh fruit. Then a very large canoe approached the *Hind*. It was unique in other ways, as its sides had been painted with many incongruous pictures, which included pictures of the Sultan, his palace, an ancient temple, and an exploding volcano. The other canoes drew away from the *Hind* as this gaily painted canoe came alongside.

"That is a rajah," Kapang explained with a slight bow, pointing out the man's importance, though in truth he was minor royalty.

"And?" Drake asked, standing near the sea ladder so as to greet the Rajah.

"He is a prince—"

"Oh, yes."

"Welcome aboard," Drake said to the Rajah, who was standing on the canoe, being screened from the sun by a soldier holding an umbrella. Drake's words were being interpreted by Kapang.

"Welcome to Bantam. We now salute you!" the Rajah said, taking Drake's hand to be pulled aboard the *Hind*. He stepped on the deck of the *Hind* and then he respectfully bowed.

"Boom! Boom! Boom! . . . " a large gun sounded from the shore. It continued to fire until it had fired 21 volleys.

"And now England salutes the Sultan of Bantam!" Drake said. And on turning, he said to his gunner, "Gunner Clark, fire your guns!"

"Aye, General—"

"Boom! Boom! Boom!" The *Hind*'s guns sounded until they, too, had fired 21 shots.

"The Sultan has arranged a reception for you at the palace at six. Is that agreeable with you?" the Rajah asked. Then he unashamedly used the back of his hand to wipe the red spittle oozing from his lips. Then he wiped his hand on his trouser leg.

"We're honored—who is invited?"

"You and your officers."

"What are we to expect?" Drake asked Kapang, meaning ceremonially. Then the messenger spoke to the prince, asking him what might be expected of the Englishmen at such a reception. And on the Rajah giving his lengthy reply, Kapang said to Drake in a boastful manner, as he was now feeling unduly important because of his linguistic ability:

"The Sultan will give a great banquet. He will have musicians and soldiers to perform. He would like as well for your men to entertain the Sultan. Otherwise, the party will be casual; the Sultan will discuss with you your plans to rest your crew, your length of stay, the careening of your ship and the provisioning of it for your next voyage."

"I understand," Drake said. "Tell him that my men will be glad to perform."

The Sultan's entertainment palace was a low, ornate building with many carvings, which was open on four sides; there was a long raised table on a dias on the east end, being the table of honor. Drake sat on the dias beside the Sultan who was dressed in a white silk robe that was gaily decorated with embroidered pictures of birds. A dozen senior princes sat at the table with them. The lesser Rajahs sat at ten tables on the main floor with members of Drake's crew. All were dressed in white shirts and pantaloons. The food was brought forth without notice. The first course was a highly seasoned soup of fish, rice and spices, which was very tasty.

"And you have a Queen?" the Sultan curiously asked Drake, and he expectantly raised his eyebrows while waiting for Kapang to translate.

"Yes, she is a magnificent ruler—"

"And is England rich?"

"Quite!"

"And does it have many soldiers?"

"Yes, many!"

"And would you like to bring your ships to Bantam and buy our spices?"

"Yes—do you do business with the Portuguese?" Drake cleverly asked, saying it as if the Sultan did, then that would block any possibility of trade.

"No—we do not trust the Portuguese—" the Sultan said, frowning and shaking his head as if he would not consider it.

"Good—and with whom do you trade?" Drake asked.

"The Arabs—the Chinese—but we need more trade—"

"Could we have it all?" Drake greedily asked, little knowing that his visit would result in the founding of the great East India Company, which would become an empire within an empire, as it would rule much of Asia. One of its first leaders would be the youthful William Hawkins now sailing on the *Hind*. He would establish a trading post at Bantam in 1602.

"Yes—if you treat us fairly. It is time for music," the Sultan said and spoke to a servant that was standing behind him. Thereafter, two

Javanese servants brought a table into the dining room on which set what appeared to be an xylophone, then they placed it directly in front of the Sultan. Thereafter, an elderly man appeared before the Sultan and played the instrument. But the music was discordant and ill-sounding on Drake's ears, though he did not breach any rules of etiquette and evidence it. Yet once the recital was completed, Drake, along with the others, politely applauded.

"You like?" the Sultan asked.

"Very much!" Drake said. "But you must hear my musicians," Drake added, raising his hand to John Brewer, who was seated in the front row. He and the other musicians stood; then they took their instruments from the floor. They were the two viol players, Martyn and Mincy, one trumpeter, John Brewer, and the drummer, John Drake. They played a march which was well-done, as the musicians heavily accented the first beats easily pointing out that it was marching music. And when they were done, they received an enthusiastic response. They played again; and once more they received a nice response. And then they played a third march and returned to their seats. The Sultan then raised his hand and a man dressed in baggy burgundy shirt and burgundy trousers stepped forth. He held in his right hand a parang, being a native sword. Its handle was richly decorated with numerous semi-precious jewels. He expertly threw it into the air, caught it, slashed the air, utilizing it so expertly that he was heavily applauded. Drake raised his hand and his brother Tom Drake stood and took from beside him his helmet and breast plate and donned them. He took up his pike and sword; then he was joined by a dozen of his soldiers. They expertly marched before the Sultan, exhibiting their pikes and swords, then they demonstrated their use in a uniform manner.

"Excellent!" the Sultan spontaneously said. "And are they good fighters?"

"Very—" Drake replied.

"Would you lend them to me for a year?" the Sultan craftily said.

"I cannot; I have promised to return them to England."

"Would you send me some like them?"

"I will—"

"And what can I do for you while you're in Bantam—"

"My men have been at sea for a long time; they need some housing—rest—"

"And how long will you visit us?" the Sultan asked.

"For two or three weeks—"

"Ah—that is not enough time. Your men should see our city—our island. It is old but changing. Many of our people are Muslims. Others like myself are mixed," referring to the fact that part of his belief was Buddhist, while the other part was Hindu. Because of such a mixture of mystical beliefs, he surely had the right to pick the best from each. These religions were exemplified by the 10th century temple at Prambanan and the 9th century Buddhist temple, which was an ornate building at Barobudur. His religion, unlike the Muslims, had long before made its adjustment with death, the great fear of man, as his co-religionists considered it to be just a cycle of life. So the Sultan thoroughly enjoyed life and the worldly pleasures, such as those of the flesh. He was greatly vexed by the widespread interest in the rigid Muslim religion, which was a fervor that had been brought there by the Arab traders.

"We would like a beach where my men can careen our ship—clean and repair it."

"We have it—and we can furnish you labor."

"But my men will do it!"

"My people work cheap—they would otherwise be offended!" the Sultan said, frowning.

"But my men must clean our ship—it is the custom!" Drake said.

"Oh, well—"

"Agreed. And I will need five tons of spices—"

"I will sell them to you."

"Good."

"For gold or exchange?"

"Exchange—"

"And once we have careened and repaired our ship, we will need to revictual it—"

"With food?"

"Yes, rice, chickens, goats, beans, fruit and the like."

"We can furnish that to you."

"Good."

"And General, our women are beautiful—may I send some dancers to your quarters and the quarters of your crew. They are very good dancers—all are lovely!"

"Do they wear clothes?" Drake curiously asked, as he was still greatly bothered by the experience that his men had received at Baratiua. It was not so much a moral matter with Drake, but rather a fear that the women would entice away his crew. But now that they were getting closer to England—

"Yes—they wear sarongs and kabayas (blouses)," the Sultan said, grinning at Kapang, who on explaining the Sultan's remarks to Drake, had to put his hand on his mouth to hold back the laughter.

CHAPTER 45

HOMEWARD BOUND

The *Hind* sailed from Java on March 26, 1580. Drake's plan on leaving was to sail non-stop to Plymouth. Before the *Hind* sailed, Drake's concern for the treasure had intensified. It became so much so that he did not attend the last banquet at Bantam. He had become too suspicious of the Sultan; he had even convinced himself that the Sultan had learned that the *Hind* was carrying treasure. And on the *Hind* leaving Bantam, Drake was more concerned than ever about the treasure. He had decided that there was not a friendly stop between Java and England. So he set a course for the *Hind* that took her south of the sea lanes that were usually traveled by the most adventurous Portuguese, though most still coasted when possible.

The weather was now cooler; yet it was not so cold that it kept most of the men from sleeping top side. Horsewill, the cook, still did his cooking on the main deck, doing it on the cumbersome iron cage that held the fire that was kept by Joey Kidd and Willie Fortescue. Piles of wood set beside the stove, which had an iron bar spanning it that held hooks from which hung three iron pots. An iron lid could be set on top, which served as a grill for cooking fish; onto this Blackcollar set a metal box which he used as an oven for cooking bread. He now was baking bread made from sago. Even so, the fire at times was a problem because of the wind.

"General," Hurd said on entering Drake's cabin.

"Yes," Drake replied. He was leaning over the chart table where he was intently sketching in a book the undulating surface of the sea. He would next sketch the noses of a school of porpoises that were presently leading the *Hind*, as if they had been trained to do so.

"We've got a man dead!"

"Dead?"

"Yes, dead!"

"Who?" exclaimed Drake, turning and facing his master.

"William Charles!"

"The seaman?" Drake asked, thoughtfully frowning, as if he were working a problem and not concerned, though he was.

"Yes—he had been ill with the ague!"

"I know—did he have a rash or sores?" Drake curiously asked, raising from his sketch and thinking. Like many men before and after him, he was overly interested in death and those ailments that caused it. His curiosity had reached an apex in 1572 when he helped perform an autopsy on the body of his brother, Joseph, who had died of fever in Panama. He had carefully removed Joseph's heart, liver and stomach; then he had curiously studied them, noting their anomalies, as if he had the scientific knowledge to judge them.

"No, General. He just quit breathing," Hurd said, cocking his head, then nodding it while frowning. "He died like an old man!"

"Gave out," Drake sympathetically commented. He knew that it had been a long, hard voyage. Many of the men had had several bouts with scurvy, and then they had had bouts with fevers. These had unduly taxed their systems. Most were stooped before their time. "Prepare the body for burial. Then speak to Preacher Fletcher about a service. Let us do it at two. We should then be off the Cape."

"Do you plan to stop?"

"No—I do not plan to stop until we reach Plymouth."

"But we must—the water is very bad, General!" Hurd said. Warning was in his voice. "It will get worse," he added.

"We must depend on the rain water," Drake said. He now had returned to his sketch. His head was down; his eyes were focused on his sketch pad, doing it as if that took his focus from their plight. And it appeared that Drake would not change his plans, though he was daily confronted by Hurd voicing concerns while the *Hind* slowly sailed north. The confrontations by Hurd were wisely made for the *Hind*'s water supply had worsened, as she was not now receiving the rains, while her food was fast being depleted. And Hurd repeatedly pointed this out to Drake.

"We will soon get some rain water—catch some fish," Drake argued.

"It is not sufficient—we've got 58 men!" Hurd argued.

"We must make do—"

442

"How about stopping at Sierra Leone?" Hurd urged, referring to the small country that was located on the west coast of Africa. He was not willing to concede that they could sail to Plymouth without making a stop.

"We," Drake said, meaning the English, "we do not have a settlement there. We could meet hostile ships!" Drake unsurely argued. He continued to be overly protective about the treasure. However, he had good reasons for not wanting to stop at the nearby coast. The *Hind* might meet a Spanish war ship, since Spanish ships regularly visited these waters, as they were the principle slavers. They had had an absolute monopoly on the trade until it was broken by Captain John Hawkins. Even so, once Hawkins accumulated a shipload of slaves, he had had to use his guns to force the Spaniards to purchase them. The reader will recall that Drake had made several slaving voyages to the coast; thus, he knew the coast and its perils.

"Neither does anyone else!" Hurd argued. He was pointing something out to Drake that he already knew—that on the slave coast there were numerous black kings. Each presided over a small territory; the principle business of each was the trading of black slaves to European sea captains for cloth and iron goods. Many of these slaves were obtained from warring chiefs; others were bought from blacks. It was a degrading trade. And the blacks played the major role: fathers sold their children; strong brothers sold weak brothers; and strong men even captured and sold their unsuspecting neighbors. These then were chained together and marched to the coast where they were sold to the coastal kings who put the captives in bacaroons, being prison-like barracks where they were kept until slaving ships arrived. The captains of these ships used stocks of cotton and iron goods to trade for the slaves.

"The fevers are bad," Drake argued, thinking of the problem of the coast.

"But we must have water, General!" Hurd said, continuing to argue.

"And the agues?"

"Many men now suffer from it!" Hurd reminded Drake, who was thoughtfully stroking his beard, though still having his eyes on his sketch.

"Let us sail for Taggarin!" Drake said, raising his eyes from his sketch and then studying a chart of the African coast. The place that Drake had named was located in Sierra Leone, being a place with which he was familiar. He knew that English slavers sometimes visited it. Thus, this could work in his favor.

"Man the culverins, General?" Hurd asked.

"Yes—when we near the coast," Drake added, returning his eyes to the sketch.

The day was hot and humid when on June 22, 1580, the *Hind* sighted the coast of Sierra Leone. Drake cautiously conned the *Hind* toward it; the lookouts in their high turrets sounded out reports every few minutes:

"No ships!"

"No ships!"

The *Hind* was out of drinking water when she approached Taggarin, which was the town where Freetown now stands. If she had not arrived when she did, men soon would have been dying of thirst.

"Tom Moone, man your longboat!"

"With water barrels?"

"Yes—you will need to follow the river. We'll need a barrel right away!"

"Aye!"

"Canoes, General!" a lookout shouted, reporting that four canoes were proceeding toward the *Hind*. They had come from a turn in the river.

"Aye!" Drake replied. Then he said to his brother, Tom, who was standing on the main deck:

"Tom, station two men on deck with arquebuses—six below decks with arquebuses, keep those hidden!"

"Aye!"

"Boatswain!" Drake shouted on deck to Fowler.

"Aye!"

"Give me readings on the depth of the river!"

"Aye!"

"Master Hurd, lay on deck some of our silks, linens and spices; lay out some knives and hatchets—those spades—water kettles— trade things—we shall do some trading!"

"For slaves?"

"Nay—for elephant tusks and gold—food, fruit, hens and the like!"

"Hola!" shouted a tall black man with short kinky hair who was standing on the bow of the first canoe. This man was the king of Pow, a tiny country that in truth was just a slaving station. He was dressed in knee-length pants and a half shirt; he wore a short sword. Sweat beaded his neck. A query was on his face.

"Hello!" Drake shouted in return.

"What country?" the man shouted in pidgin English.

"England!" Drake replied.

"Ah, friend?" the Negro asked. Then he raised his hand as if offering a signal. His canoe had stopped. He raised a stalk of bananas indicating that he would like to trade.

"Ah, friend!" Drake replied in almost the same dialect as the Negro, speaking it with a rhythm. Then Drake ceremoniously drew a half-bucket of water from the sea. He put his finger into it and proceeded to put three drops of water on his forehead and another three drops on each of his eyelids, doing what he had seen Hawkins do, which were signifying to the blacks that they were friends. The black, on seeing Drake do this, quickly tied his canoe to the *Hind*; then he climbed the sea ladder up to the main deck where Hurd had laid out the trade goods. He quickly studied them.

"You need slaves?" the black man asked, speaking in Pidgin English. He was large and muscular. His face had a seriousness to it that verged on urgency.

"No—"

"Why no slaves—let's do business—have plenty good slaves in one week!" he said in an argumentative voice, as if it would be an affront to him if Drake did not do it.

"We need food, fruit, hens, animals and water—"

"We trade!" the king quickly said. Then he began to talk to Drake on ways to take slaves as the *Hind* sailed up the river. When the *Hind* reached eight fathoms of water, Drake ordered Fowler to furl the sails and drop anchor. The king left the *Hind* after he had stationed eight Negroes on her. One of these was a Captain Booda, being a tall, muscular, very black Negro who the king had left there to represent his interests. The king would receive a fifth of all goods or money that the Africans received in exchange for their goods. The other seven Negroes were now stationed there in order to maintain order during the trading. Shortly after the sun had begun to set, many canoes approached the *Hind*. These held trading mamas and trade goods. So the *Hind*'s decks were soon covered with seated Negro women who had arranged before them huge baskets that held lemons, oranges, coconuts, plantains and bananas; there were some black men traders who had ivory elephant tusks, beautiful pieces of coral, gold dust, rice and honey. Other women had laid out on the deck sides of freshly killed beef and hogs; and yet others offered for sale live hens, eggs and tethered goats. The hens and goats would be important additions to the *Hind*'s food larder, as they could live for long periods of time while aboard ship.

While Moone and his men loaded the water casks with fresh water, the Englishmen with the best trading skills began to trade with the Negroes for their goods. Once the English had traded for the goods on deck, more women boarded the deck with goods to trade. By noon of the second day, the *Hind*'s provision hold was filled with goods from the trading.

"General, we have about traded out!" Hurd said on studying the deck. There was very little room left for foodstuff. The coops below deck were filled with chickens and ducks—goats filled a newly-built pen on the orlop deck.

"And Tom?" Drake asked Moone. "Are all the water casks filled?"

"All are full, General!"

"And it is sweet water," Drake commented. "Then we will sail on the morning trades."

"Yes—"

"Shall we be stopping at Mordego to careen, General?" Hurd asked. He was referring to a place on the African coast that was often used by English sea captains to careen their ships.

"Not if we can help it," Drake replied, showing his teeth, indicating that he had made his last stop. Then he added, "Our next stop is Plymouth!"

"I would like some of that Plymouth chill today," Hurd said, wiping sweat from his brow. He was referring to the cool air that Plymouth received from the English Channel even in mid-summer.

The *Hind* sailed from Sierra Leone on June 24, 1580. The new provisions did much to change the temperament of the crew. Horsewill's cook pot perfumed the *Hind*—it emitted the odor of lamb, herbs and spices. He even cooked a richly seasoned pease pudding; the second day he baked a pig, and with the normal remainder he cooked a brawn; he mildly salted it in the pot and simmered it in rosemary, fennel and sage until the meat fell from the bones. Then he boiled down the liquor and poured it over the meat. Its effect on the crew was like a good tonic. Those men who had been sickly began to eat and drink as if they had not been ill. It was so much so that on July 1, 1580, Preacher Fletcher approached Drake. Neither man since had mentioned the confrontation that they had had in the Banda Sea.

"What is the condition of the sick?" Drake asked. Preacher Fletcher was still the acting nurse-medical doctor.

"General, I have a good report. You will recall that when we arrived in Sierra Leone, we had fourteen men on the non-work list. Since then I have gotten all of them eating fruit and meat. We now have six men on the sick list. I am feeding the sick beef broth. I also have been squeezing oranges and lemons into a juice which I feed them—all are improving."

"That is a good report—are all still below deck?"

"Yes—the sun hurts their eyes—"

"It is time that they came top side—the salt air and the sun will help heal them."

On July 15, 1580, Fletcher reported to Drake that all the men that previously had been on the sick list were now available to do their regular jobs. But there was not that much work to be done. It now took only a few men to sail the *Hind*, as there was only a little turning of her yards to be done, since there was no wind, being air in horizontal motion. There just was no difference in the atmospheric pressure at sea level—the ocean's surface was sluggish, torpid and oppressive. So without any wind the *Hind* was only making a few miles each day. Her bilges were only taking in a few gallons of water a day, and so her pumps only occasionally had to be manned. But that was to be expected since the *Hind* was on the edge of the doldrums. Her sails just had trouble filling with air—Drake tried pouring water onto them. But that only slightly helped. Finally, he steered for the coast, tacking; but the square sailer handled clumsily, as she did not tack well. But finally the *Hind* broke clear of the doldrums, and once she was clear of them she began to make about two knots an hour, being about 27 miles a day. And so her progress to Plymouth continued, but it was very slow. And so she did not reach the English Channel until September 24, 1580; and by then the men had eaten all of the hens, goats and foodstuffs that they had taken aboard in Sierra Leone.

"Oh, this jacket feels good!" Hurd said, touching his canvas jacket whose seams had been sealed with tar.

"It is Plymouth, Tom," Drake said, smiling. "It is a freshet—" Drake added, while eyeing the bow and studying the faded green swells. Clouds busily moved across the northern sky.

"You'll be seeing your wife shortly, General!" Hurd said, smiling at the thought. "I hope that she has a good report to give you!"

"Hopefully," Drake said, thinking, pondering the problems that his return would bring. And he would soon have to confront them, for he was now just a day from Plymouth. But he now knew that he had almost reached home with the richest shipload of treasure ever taken by any ship. He wondered whether the stories about him capturing the Spanish prizes had been reported to the Queen. And if they had, he wondered how she had received them. He wondered if she would still support him or would she order his arrest. And if there were a warrant for his arrest, what should be his next move— where should he go? He surely could not stay in Plymouth. He had too much gold and silver to submit willingly to prison.

"A sail, General!" a lookout shouted.

"Helmsman, steer for it!" Drake ordered.

"Aye!"

"It's a fisherman," Hurd explained on the *Hind* approaching a smack, which was used for inshore fishing.

"Hello!" Drake shouted.

"Hello," the fisherman answered. "Who are you?" the voice questioned, studying the *Hind*. She appeared ghostly, as she was so worn and haggard. Long grass grew from her water line.

"Drake—Francis Drake of Plymouth!"

"Glory be, Cap'n—and you made it!" the fisherman exclaimed, holding his hand to his eyes to shield them from the bright sun and to enable him to see Drake better. "Praise God, everybody has worried 'bout you! It's been so long since we've heard 'bout you!"

"Around the world we've been!"

"Around the world!" the fisherman said in awe while studying the *Hind*, which was low in the water and paintless.

"Yes, around the world!"

"And how did you fare?" the fisherman asked, leaning forth on the gunwale.

"We have a ship load of treasure!"

"A ship load?" the fisherman asked with a show of awe.

"Of gold, silver, jewels—" Drake said, smiling proudly at the thought.

"My oath!"

"And how is Plymouth?"

"I am sorry to report that it has the plague."

"Plague?" Drake asked. His voice showed his immediate concern.

"Many are dead!"

"And does the Queen still live?" Drake expectantly asked.

"Yes—"

"Thank God!" Drake declared. He knew that the worst thing that could have happened to him while he was gone would have been for her to have died and Parliament to have installed a pro-Spanish regent in her place.

"There would be a great reception for you in Plymouth, Captain, except for the plague!"

"We dare not enter," Drake said, adding, "Who is the mayor of Plymouth?" Drake asked. The mayor served for a one-year term.

"It is Mayor John Blythman—" the fisherman replied. Then he said in awe, "Around the world!"

"Well, would you do me this favor—we are heavy in the water, and our bottom needs scraping—speed we cannot make. Sail to Plymouth and tell John that I have returned with a ship load of treasure. That I dare not bring the *Golden Hind* into Sutton Hole until I have had word from the Queen advising me as to what reception I shall receive! Ask him to visit with me. I shall anchor the *Hind* just south of Nicholas Island—I shall pay you for your bother!"

"That I shall do, Cap'n!"

On September 26, 1580, Drake anchored the *Golden Hind* just south of Nicholas Island which was just a half mile from the hoe, being a level field on a steep cliff that was located at the land's end. It was a favorite gathering place for Plymouth folk, especially the wives who often stood there while searching for a sail, as Plymouth was a great seafaring city for men of trade and prey. It then had more privateers sailing from it than any other port in England. Its cliff was now lined with townsmen attempting to get a glimpse of Drake's ship. Many of these were wives of men now aboard the *Hind*, but Drake was not ready to board them until he had spoken with the mayor. And so the women only occasionally got a glimpse of the *Hind*'s bow as she swung on her anchor.

"There is the mayor's barge!" Drake said, pointing out an approaching small craft. It was propelled by a sail and rowers.

449

"And now?" Moone asked, meaning what shall they do. He was in a group that stood near the whipstaff.

"We must stay together—keep the crew together!" Drake said.

"I understand," Moone said, nodding, realizing that if there was a price on Drake's head, then there possibly was a price on the heads of all the men standing on the poop deck. Their strong suit was the treasure. And if they kept the treasure on the *Hind*, and the ship manned, then on short notice they could sail to Ireland or some other refuge until the climate changed.

"And he has Mary with him!" Drake said, intently staring. His wife was standing beside the mayor. She was fashionably dressed in a farthingale, being a petticoat distended with whale bone hoops that were covered with taffeta. The wind was whipping against her dress, exposing her underclothes, as a freshet was blowing from the sea. She held her hat in her hand.

"Come aboard!" Drake shouted. And he took his wife's hand, pulled her onto the *Hind*; then he hugged and kissed her lips and wet cheeks while she limply fell into his arms.

"Francis, I thought you would never return—but you finally did—you made it. You went around the world! And I love you more and more! But please do not leave me again!"

"But it was a long voyage," he replied, saying it as if he were feeling tired from it for the first time. Yet he was tired from anticipation, as he had not slept the night before.

"Welcome to Plymouth, Francis!" the mayor said on taking Drake's hand; then he put his arms about him and tightly squeezed him. And then he momentarily eyed Drake with deep respect. "I hope that I have not contaminated you, but we have the plague!"

"So we have learned!" Drake said.

"And how did you fare?"

"We have a ship load of treasure—let me show it to you," Drake said, proudly grinning, taking his wife by the waist.

"We would like that."

"And what news have you heard about me, my crew?" Drake asked.

"Much—"

"And is it good or bad?" Drake asked, leading the pair down a stairway to the lower decks. On their reaching the lowest deck, their movement was blocked by stacked bars of silver.

"This is silver—we must have 30 to 40 tons of it," Drake said.

"My God!" the mayor exclaimed at the enormity of it.

"Does the Queen know?"

"She will soon know."

"And what does the Queen say?" Drake reluctantly asked.

"John Hawkins says that he hears different stories."

"And how is John?"

"Fine—I will have him visit you."

"Well," Drake said; then he took a chest that was on top of some other chests. It was so heavy that he could barely lift it. Months before he had filled it and put it there for just such an occasion. "Mary, this chest is yours; it is filled with treasure: jewels, gold—it is very heavy. I will have a couple of men bring it top side, put it in the mayor's boat. You must hide it—and in case something untoward happens to me, it will be of much benefit to you."

"I will help her—" the mayor said.

"And John, I have something for you. It is very rare and quite valuable." Then he took from another chest a hand-carved ivory sun dial, which was a very rare diptych. It was so small that it could be held in one hand. "It is a sun dial. You use it by setting these two leaves. But first you must set it with the aid of your compass."

"A million thanks—I shall always treasure it," the mayor said while proudly smiling, eyeing the gift with anticipation.

Then Drake led the two top side. "I shall now see if I can change the situation in London!"

Drake thereafter sat at his table and he wrote a letter to Walsingham. He outlined his exploits, the treasure that he now had aboard the *Golden Hind*; and he asked for his help in securing for him a favorable response from the Queen.

"John—John Brewer!" Drake shouted to the men standing down on the deck talking to the men from the mayor's barge.

"Yes, General," Brewer replied. He hurriedly climbed the ladder to the portico deck and to Drake's cabin. He had grown four inches and gained 20 pounds since he first came aboard the *Golden Hind*. He had boarded her as a boy and now he was a man.

"This is Mayor Blythman and my wife, Mary; this is John Brewer. Mary, you remember John. He was my bugler at the time we sailed."

"I remember," she said as Brewer politely bowed to both.

"John, I want you to ride to London; visit the Queen's court—you will tell the sentries at the gate that you are a messenger from

451

General Francis Drake; that you must see Secretary Walsingham—give him this letter."

"I will need a horse—"

"I will furnish you horses," the mayor said. "Give you names of people in other towns who will aid you." It would be a long ride, as it was more than 200 miles by road from Plymouth to London.

"We anxiously await your reply," Drake said, smiling solemnly. "We will stay here until you return."

"Aye!"

CHAPTER 46

A DISPATCH FROM ESCORIAL

While Drake's *Hind* was slowly winding its way along the African coast, Drake had been the subject of much discussion and thought by some persons in high places. One of the most important persons devoting thought to Drake was Philip II of Spain.

Philip II was the ruler of one of the greatest empires that the world has seen. He had lived a life of ruling. He had become a ruler at an early age, for he became Regent of Spain in 1543 when he was just 16 years old. He thereafter became absolute ruler of the empire in 1558. But during the interim in 1554, he married Mary, Queen of England, who the writer has referred to as Catholic Mary. And he was a joint ruler of England with Mary until her death in 1558. Mary was succeeded by Elizabeth, being the sister-in-law to Philip. Philip's empire was vast, as it stretched from the southern tip of Chile up to Florida; it included the Philippines; it encompassed much of Europe. His father, Charles V, had obtained part of Europe by inheritance. He had obtained the remainder by conquest. The heart of the empire, of course, was Spain. Ruling the empire was troublesome. For in order for Philip to maintain this vast empire, he had to be constantly at war. One of the most troublesome aspects of Philip's empire was the Netherlands where he had to keep thousands of expensive, hard-to-control mercenary soldiers.

King Philip was actually a handsome man since he did not have many of the ugly Hapsburg features, though he did have the distinctive Hapsburg chin. He was of average height and build, being slightly on the thin side; however, his somber manner of dress caused him to have an austere appearance. He had straw-colored hair and beard, with very pale skin, which gave him an albino-like coloring.

He had dreamy blue eyes, an aquiline nose and because he was quite slender, many thought that he was not very strong. Yet he was.

Philip surprisingly ruled his vast empire in a very autocratic fashion, as he made most of the important decisions himself, though because of distance, he did allow his administrators in the American colonies more power. Yet he carefully reviewed their decisions, doing so by reviewing the paperwork only, as he strongly believed that it was his duty to review the problems of his empire through dispatches without permitting interviews, which he believed were not only time-consuming but practically valueless. Thus, he seldom saw the people to whom he addressed, and so his method of ruling was very sterile. But this did not deter him in the slightest in maintaining an interest in events that were transpiring. He mainly kept abreast of his vast empire by reading dispatches and documents. For during the course of any day, he would read hundreds of important documents upon which he made written comments on a myriad of subjects that established policies for his underlings to follow. It was an arduous existence, as he did all of this reading and writing himself. And as one might expect, the more he wrote, the worse his writing became. It soon became just scribbles. It was not until the latter part of his reign that he would acquire a secretary, being Vasaquez, who then would relieve him of much reading and writing.

Philip was a pious man, being a strict Catholic and very bigoted, as he sincerely believed that any belief to the contrary was heretic. He was absolutely convinced that the Catholic way was the only way to heaven. He was a firm believer in the Inquisition, and during his reign he did much to expand its power. But even so, he was a man of the flesh, as he had had numerous mistresses and wives. One of these wives was Catholic Mary, Queen of England and sister to Elizabeth, which actually made him a part of the English royalty. Though Philip was a lay ruler, he, as well, had monastic tendencies which at times caused him to operate his government in a religious atmosphere. And because of this inclination, in 1563 he began to build one of the largest and most handsome religious establishments in the world. It would be called the Escorial, being a monastery/palace at a village by the same name which was located 33 miles from Madrid. It would not be completed until 1594.

Philip built Escorial with the intent that it would not only be a ruling palace but would also be a pantheon, being a place for Spain to house its royal dead. The body of Philip's father, Charles V, had been re-buried there in 1568. Philip would one day be buried near him. The palace was 675 feet by 525 feet. Its center was a richly ornamented church. Near it was an ornate library, which presently held 14,000 volumes of very valuable books, which was the largest library in all of Western civilization. Many were rare and priceless. Philip spent as much time in this room as possible. For he not only was a great reader of books and manuscripts, but he liked to sit in his library and read and answer official documents. This was so even though its walls and ceilings were bare, though one day they would be enhanced by stucco and paintings by Tibaldi.

Early one evening in the summer of 1580, Philip followed an aide up the stairs to his library. Philip was a dramatic complainer, always wishing that he had a simple existence, for he muttered as he struggled with the stone staircase that led to his library, "Oh, these fifty steps—oh, these steps of my life, they will be my death!"

The aide entered the beautiful library and set two official leather pouches on a richly ornamented table. Then on bowing, he said:

"Buenos tardes, mi majestade—"

"Buenos—" Philip replied in a voice of disinterest, and he deliberately sat on a leather chair.

"¡Seran mi muerte!" They will be my death! he said again as he reached for the documents, doing it like a spider would draw prey to its web. He held before him a huge magnifying glass, looking through it, as he began to study the handwritten documents.

"¡Esta mal!" It is bad! Philip said, now rubbing his right shoulder. He was dressed in a black gown like those worn by the monks. Beneath it was an undershirt made of horsehair, which he was wearing as a penance. "Christ, my Christ! When shall I join you!" he softly said.

These two pouches on the table before Philip had held numerous affidavits and charges from the investigations concerning Captain Francis Drake which had been made by the Viceroys of Peru and Mexico. They included affidavits from John Greco, Nuno da Silva, Franciso de Zarate, and San Juan de Anton, Captain of the *Caga Fuego*.

"¡Estoy quebrado!" I am bankrupt! Philip said, speaking to the documents. For there was no one else in the giant room. Philip was easily depressed. His thoughts now dwelled on the worst scenario. He had just imagined that hundreds of English pirates like Drake had begun to attack his treasure ships. He just knew that if they did, they

Philip II: "I have received dispatches from the Indies!"

456

would destroy his empire. And this would be worse than bankruptcy. His money problems had already forced him to declare bankruptcy as to his debts in 1575 and then again in 1577. In 1575 he had shocked his creditors in the Netherlands by declaring bankruptcy as to his debts. What was surprising was that he had done it even though the treasure from Peru was presently pouring into his treasury; yet it barely paid his bills. His treasury was in a precarious state, as half of all the money that he received as revenue had to be used to pay interest on borrowed money. Even so, he had refused to stop spending money. He continued to purchase paintings and manuscripts for Escorial, though the artists charged him excessive prices. Then he had to pay soldiers, for in order to keep his empire in tact—he had to have soldiers, and they demanded to be paid in gold or silver. In order to get it, he had to depend on the Indies. This was so even though much of its gold was ceremonial. For many of the most beautiful art objects that the Spaniards had found in Mexico and Peru had already been melted down in order to pay the salaries of soldiers.

"¡Hay que pararlo!" It must be stopped!

And then he felt better on taking up his pen. Work was his principal relief from money worries. And they were plentiful. And so to maintain his sanity, he buried himself in the management of his far-flung empire. Consequently, the reading and writing of dispatches eased his mind.

"Mi querido Embasador Don Bernardino de Mendozo." My dear ambassador, he wrote. "I must inform you that I have received dispatches on this date from the Indies—each viceroy has sent me news of more piracies committed by an Englishman by the name of Francis Drake. This is the same Englishman about whom I have previously written you; he is the same person who on numerous previous occasions attacked Nombre Dios. It is he who attacked my treasure caravans on the isthmus. He also has attacked many ships in the sea nearby. I am now informed by the viceroys of Peru and Mexico that he entered the South Sea by way of the Magellan Strait; that he then coasted Peru where he robbed many villages, churches and ships of their treasure. My viceroys have further informed me that he robbed the crown as well as many Spanish citizens, robbing them of possibly a million pesos. And worse, he has told many captives that Queen Elizabeth was an investor in his venture, which I doubt is true. He should be arriving in England shortly . . . "

Organ music filtered into the library, and Philip raised his head and looked into the distance. Then he slightly smiled on hearing singing voices. It was not unusual, as it was the beginning of evening worship in the great church, being the time of vespers. Philip then looked out the window at the Basilica that was across the Courtyard of the Kings; he eyed the site where the statue of King David would set, and he thoughtfully listened. He imaginatively saw the monks seating themselves in the ornately decorated church. He greatly admired them for their dedication to God—if he just had not had the burden of ruling this great empire, he, too, would have been a monk. Instead, he had built this great palace for the monks. They were his solace; they prayed for his government; and they would pray for his soul when his body was entombed in Escorial!

"¡Que Dios los bendiga!" Bless them! he said, thoughtfully listening; and then he returned to his writing:

"You must go directly to my sister-in-law, give her my greetings—" he wrote in his spidery way, abbreviating, which made his writing unintelligible to the recipient unless he were accustomed to reading it. Then he had to read the letter several times. "You must relate to my sister-in-law," referring of course to Queen Elizabeth, for Philip, as previously stated, had been married to Mary, the older sister of Elizabeth. He felt that Elizabeth was indebted to him, as he possibly had saved her from being beheaded by Mary. "You must inform her of the many piracies that have been committed by this Francis Drake; you must frankly state to her that his treasure must be confiscated and then it must be given to you which you must inventory; then you must transmit it to Spain. You must insist that she have this man Drake hung by the neck until he is dead. If this is not done, and if this man goes free, then it will amount to an invitation to all Englishmen to attack my treasure ships. And that will destroy the Spanish empire. It will of course bankrupt us. For we cannot survive without regular supplies of treasure from the West Indies!

"And," he wrote, stopping, raising his head, looking over his glasses. The music had stopped. But even so he could hear the chant of the monks as they prayed in unison. He studied the top of the table where he worked. There was now a huge pile of documents at the far end. He had reviewed them. There was a small pile near him. He vented air to show his exhaustion. He eyed the bound volumes in cases; their buckram-bound spines were against the wall in order to

458

protect them from the light; he wondered as to their contents. Would he ever have time to read them?

"¡Solamente un hora o algo mas!" Only an hour or so more! Then he began to write again:

"If she refuses to give up my treasure or hang this Drake, you must then speak bluntly to her. You must advise her that she then will lose her kingdom. For I will put together a great armada of ships, like we did against the Turks at Lepanto. I will put aboard them my well-seasoned troops that are now stationed in Flanders. And I shall invade her little country; I shall take it; then I shall install a prince of my choosing on the throne in her place; then I shall ask the Court of Inquisition to use its devices to force the English people to return to the true faith . . . I worry about the Empire—everyone is so greedy—it is late—everything is so expensive—the cost of masons—and those painters. They are the greediest of all. It is late. I have other dispatches to write. I enclose with this dispatch the documents that I received from the viceroys of Mexico and Peru. Keep them safe.

"Su majestade, Felipe II, Rey de Espana."

CHAPTER 47

THE QUEEN'S RECEPTION

While Drake waited for news from London, the people of Plymouth apparently ridded themselves of the plague. For just two weeks after Drake's return, the mayor of Plymouth advised his council that he did not have any reports of new cases, while many that had said that they had the plague now reported that they were well or getting well. It was generally espoused by the people that it was a miracle brought by the return of Drake. And thereafter, many more miracles would be attributed to him. He would be considered the real Robin Hood of England. "Beat my drum and I shall come to the aid of England!" would be attributed to him as a saving grace for England.

Each day thousands of townspeople came to the hoe and stood on its cliffside and admiringly eyed the *Hind*. All now knew that it held a fortune in treasure. And just recently, Drake had moved the *Hind* so that it could be observed by the people standing on the hoe. Drake was now permitting wives and girlfriends to visit the *Hind*; many were sleeping aboard ship, though he had refused to let them view the treasure, as it was being carefully guarded by Tom Drake and his soldiers.

"I want you to come home to me," said a tiny woman with a whiskey-hardened face and long, stringy, gray hair, speaking as though it were imperative that he do it. The speaker was Molly Fortescue, mother of Willie. He had refused to take her hand. It was dress ship day, and so the crew had hung out hundreds of flags and banners which now were flying from the *Hind*. Most of the men were dressed in their finery. Willie was dressed up, too, as he wore the same finery that he had worn that day in the Banda Sea when Drake

461

held captain's mast for Preacher Fletcher. He was wearing his gold vest, red pantaloons, knee-length boots and a floppy burgundy hat.

"Naye—I cannot!" he said, frowning, being protectively watched by George Fortescue, Willie's older brother, who stood just a few feet from him. He eyed his mother with cautious disdain.

"But you must! I am your mother!"

"But I'm in the Navy!"

"You are not! You're too young! You were stolen from me when I was in me cups!" she screamed.

"You only want his half share!" George argued, frowning.

"But his share is mine!" Molly said, attempting to take Willie's hand. "I'm here to claim it!"

"Leave him be!" Drake declared, hurrying across the deck.

"But he's only a boy!"

"He's old enough for me!" Drake tersely said. "He stays on the *Hind*. And his half share will be looked after by me and the mayor! We might just invest Willie's share in a nice farm," Drake added, while tightly grasping Willie's arm.

"Then I'll go to court!"

"And I'll ask the judge to put you in jail—now off the *Hind*!"

Many writers of pamphlets had visited the *Hind*; they had talked to Drake and other members of his crew, who had spoken freely of their adventures. And the writers were beginning to write pamphlets, penning interesting reports of the adventures of Drake and his men. And so all Devon and Cornwall were now learning of Drake's adventures. These stories would soon be reprinted in London newspapers and pamphlets. And then Drake would become as well known in England as the Queen.

It was 18 days after Drake sent Brewer to London to deliver his letter to Walsingham that the bugler returned to the *Hind*. He made an impressive appearance when he boarded the *Hind*, as he was dressed in London finery. He was wearing a new woolen suit, a shirt with ruffs, a stovepipe hat and new shoes with shiny buckles.

"Welcome aboard!" Drake said, greeting the bugler, who was climbing the *Hind*'s sea ladder. Drake studied his face for signs.

"Thanks, General," Brewer replied, proudly smiling at his shipmates, who were admiringly eyeing his fine clothes. Brewer walked stiffly as he followed Drake up the ladder to the poop deck. He only turned back once before he entered Drake's cabin.

"Did you see Walsingham?" Drake asked on entering his cabin. Others were already in the cabin. They were Hurd, Fletcher, Moone, Tom Drake and William Horsewill, the cook. The latter had had many visitors from Tavistock. Friends and relatives had brought him baskets of herbs and tubs of carrots, turnips, beets, colewarts, onions, beans and apples. He had begun to use them to cook some interesting dishes.

"Yes—and he sends his best regards," Brewer said.

"Did you get to see the Queen?"

"Oh, no—" he answered, as though it were out of the question.

"What is our position?" Drake asked. All anxiously listened.

"Not good—Walsingham says that Don Mendozo, the Spanish Ambassador, has the ear of Lord Burghley. Mendozo has demanded of Lord Burghley that he order you to turn our treasure over to him so he can send it to Philip of Spain. And he has asked that all of us be punished—"

"And what has Burghley done?"

"Lord Burghley, Crofts and Sussex have agreed to his demands," Brewer carefully said, speaking deliberately, as if realizing the importance of his answers. "Secretary Walsingham says that the ministers have received much pressure from the London merchants, who are on the side of the Spaniards. They are saying that we are pirates!"

"Nonsense—"

"And what has the Queen done?" Drake asked.

"She is wavering—she tends to agree with Burghley—"

"Oh!" Drake exclaimed. His face became white. Surprise showed on his face.

"Walsingham sends this message: 'The future of England depends on what happens with this issue; lie close until the Queen changes her mind!'"

"Lie close until she changes her mind!" Drake repeated. Then he stared into the great distance, thinking on where he would take the *Hind* if the Queen decided against him, as he knew that he would not submit to punishment for his attacks on Spaniards.

Each day that the Queen procrastinated, the public interest in Drake became more intense. For each day that passed they received new information about his exploits. His name now had become a household name in all England. The English people wanted to see him, read more about him, and acclaim him. This acclaim was having an adverse effect on the frail woman who ruled England. She was being bothered by a churning within her. She was being pulled on the one side by Burghley, her treasurer and principal advisor. He was not a Catholic; yet it was thought by many that he had Catholic sympathies. He was siding with Spain because he was a fiscal conservative, as he did not want the expense of a war with Spain, one that he was of the opinion that England could not win. Yet on the other hand, Elizabeth was a Protestant—she did not like Catholics. This was probably because she had been a prisoner of theirs prior to becoming Queen. In 1554 the Catholics had imprisoned Elizabeth in the Tower; and for a while, it appeared that she would lose her head to them. And so she had lived in dreadful fear of them until she was crowned queen.

Elizabeth was a very English queen. She was so much so that she had not married. And how could she? She was married to the realm of England. And it needed heroes! And now there was one— this Drake—this short, cocky man with the West Country accent, who had stood before her and had said, "I am the best seaman in all England—" And apparently he was, as well as being the best seaman in the world. And because of his daring feat of circumnavigating the globe, was he not entitled to a hero's welcome? Magellan did not do it—Cano did it in his stead. And Cano had not been a captain of one of Magellan's ships at the start of the voyage.

But then if she did receive him, would not that be sufficient reason for Philip to invade England. Mendozo had said to her not two days before:

"Philip has stated to me in this letter," Mendozo said, holding up the spidery dispatch from Escorial, speaking to her as though she were a hireling. "That if the treasure is not restored to Spain and this man Drake is not punished, that he will send a great armada to England, invade it and put himself on the throne!"

"Bah!" she had replied, though saying it without deciding what she was going to do.

And she thought and she pondered: This Philip of Spain with his threats, where would it end? It had to end in war. It had to come unless she submitted to Philip! And if war came now, could England defend herself against Spain? That would take ships and men to man them; those ships would require daring sailors from Devon and Cornwall. That would require leaders like Drake who had little fear of Spaniards, while the Spaniards greatly feared him. Why, he had circumnavigated the world! He had done what Magellan could not do. And more so, he had brought back his ship loaded with treasure. Yes, he had stolen it from the Spaniards; yet the Spaniards had stolen it from the Indians. And then the Spaniards claim of owning most of the New World had no basis; it had come about by the selfish proposal of Pope Alexander VI that had resulted in the Treaty of Tordesillas, where in 1494 Spain and Portugal had signed a pact whereby they had drawn a line that divided the lands of the New World. They had done it by simply drawing a line around the globe, giving half of the new lands to each. What rubbish! England was entitled to some of this new land. She as well was entitled to trade with the East—and—

"Your Highness," an aid said on entering the ornately embellished room where Elizabeth was seated at her desk. A pen was in her hand. Paper was on the desk top.

"Yes, Thomas—"

"Your Highness—"

"Yes—"

"Ambassador Mendozo of Spain is in the parlor; he demands to see you. He says that he must have an answer at this moment on this Drake business!"

"Demands?" she asked, looking into a fire in the huge fireplace that was decorated with the heads of Greyhounds. They were so real, that at times she waited for their bark.

"Yes—"

"He wants—" she said, thinking. He wants me to imprison the man who has circumnavigated the globe—the man of England—and give back his treasure that he won for England! Why that treasure is England's! He brought it back for all England. And that it shall be! She greedily thought.

"Your—"

"Thomas—"

"Will you see him?"

"Thomas, tell Ambassador Mendozo that my answer is no. Tell him that I am composing a letter to General Drake, inviting him to London to honor him as is his due. And he may tell Philip that he may do what he pleases about his Armada!"

"Your Highness!"

"Enough—I am an English Queen and not a vassal of Philip!"

465

It would be several days later before the news would reach the *Hind*.

"General," Hurd said. "The Mayor's barge approaches!"

"Aye. He must have news," Drake said, eyeing the approaching boat whose sail was filled with wind.

"Good or bad?" Hurd asked, rubbing his hands. They were feeling the chill.

"I hope that it is good," Drake softly said; apprehension was in his voice. He knew that if it were bad that he would have to make an immediate decision as to where he would take the *Hind*.

"Good afternoon, Francis," the Mayor said on stepping onto the deck of the *Hind*.

"Greetings!" Drake said.

"I have a letter for you, Francis. It is from the Queen."

"Well—"

"I hope it is good news," the Mayor said, handing the envelope to Drake. "Open it!" he added. And then with anticipation he watched Drake's face, which as well was being studied by the men on deck. Many were standing beside their women. Anticipation was on the faces of all!

Drake opened the letter and read—then his face beamed like the sun on the tips of nearby waves.

"What is it?" Tom Drake asked.

"Our place is made!" Drake exclaimed. "She accepts us—"

"Hurrah!" the men assembled on the main deck cheered.

"Bless her!" the Mayor said.

"What does it say?" Hurd asked.

"It says—" and he read:

Dear General Drake:

Welcome to England! I have heard much about your great trip in circumnavigating the globe. This is a great honor to you and your crew; it is also a great honor to England. And I am anxious to hear about your adventures. Please honor me with a visit as soon as it is possible for you to do so. Please bring with you some samples of your labors for me to view; place in safe custody the remainder.

Fear nothing, for I shall protect you,

Elizabeth, Queen of England

"God be praised!" Fletcher said.

"The wind blows with us!" Moone said.

"The treasure?" Tom Drake asked. It was his job to guard it.

"We shall first have prayer service; then we shall hoist anchor and sail for Sutton Hole," Drake said, referring to Plymouth's small harbor which was protected from the sea by a thick wall.

"Then?" Hurd asked.

"All except the treasure guards will go to St. Andrews Church to give thanks!" Drake said. The reader will recall that it was to this church that Drake and his crew had visited in 1573 on their returning from Nombre Dios with much treasure.

"Will you be leaving the treasure on your ship?" the Mayor asked.

"I would rather deposit it with trustees from the city—"

"We can arrange that," the Mayor replied.

On the following day, Drake, his brother Tom, John Brewer and Tom Moone loaded five horses with interesting gold objects and jewels. Then the four men started out for Sion House, which was the Queen's palace at Richmond, where she was presently residing.

It was necessary for the four men to travel slowly because of the loads on the horses. Thus, their progress was slow; it also enabled those persons that Drake and his men met on their way to London to notify other persons of his travels. They then passed the word that Drake, the privateer from Plymouth who had circumnavigated the globe, was in route to see the Queen. Thus, farmers working in paddocks separated by hedgerows or fences of rocks stopped their harvesting and laid down their tools in order to greet and watch Drake pass. Likewise, every town in which Drake passed had hundreds of people waiting to greet him. Women were waiting to be kissed, while others held cups of English ale for the men to taste. And it was more so in London. The streets of Richmond were lined with common folk; however, the merchants kept to their shops. They mumbled and shook their heads, for they were sure that the honoring of Drake for his antics would lead to war, and they knew that war meant burdensome taxes on them.

"Halt!"

"Aye!" Drake replied.

"Who are you?" a yeoman asked. He was standing beneath an archway which led to the entrance court. The yeoman guard was dressed in a royal red tunic with purple facings and stripes with gold lace ornaments. He wore red knee britches and red stockings. He as well wore a black felt hat and black shoes.

"Francis Drake and some of his officers!"

"Oh, yes—oh, yes," the yeoman said. "I must notify my captain immediately." Minutes later the captain appeared, being in truth a vice chamberlain, who was in charge of the security for the Queen. One of his most important symbolic jobs was supervising the making of Elizabeth's bed, which of course pointed out to him daily the importance of his responsibilities. He was dressed in a regular army uniform. He had a serious face. He did not say or do anything to show that he was excited by Drake's visit.

"Cap'n Drake!" he said.

"General Drake!" Drake corrected.

"Oh, yes—General, the Queen will see you in 15 minutes—and the baggage?" he asked, referring to the large sacks that the men were carrying.

"That is treasure—jewels, rubies, pearls, gold filigree, and the like!"

"Really—I will take it to my office—"

"No, it must stay with us!"

"Of course—" he politely said on seeing Drake's face harden. He already had heard much about Drake. He knew that many in the household considered him to be a pirate. Yet others looked on him as a hero. Thus, he was not ready to take sides.

"And there is more!" Drake said.

"Oh—well—oh—Her Highness still wishes to see you!" he said as though he had doubts that she should.

"Very well," Drake said.

"Follow me!" the Captain replied. And he led the four men down a wide corridor whose walls were lined with portraits of members of the royal family. Then they went up a stair then down a corridor whose walls were adorned with tapestries. He stopped at a heavy oak door. "Your Highness," he said on knocking. "It is Captain John Drury!"

"Enter, John!"

"Follow me!" the Captain said.

The four men entered the room. It was a large drawing room that was adjacent to Elizabeth's quarters. This was Elizabeth's state room; it was in this great room that she was accustomed to receiving visits from important guests. The walls of this room were partially covered with rich tapestries that had been made of pure gold and fine silver. They had been garnished with gold, pearls and precious stones. The space between the tapestries was embellished with paintings by Masters; to the left there was a writing table that had been inlaid with mother of pearl; and at the far end there was a magnificent throne that was studded with diamonds, rubies, sapphires and the like. Elizabeth was seated on this magnificent throne. She stood as the seamen approached and then they fell to their knees. The high ceiling above was just as magnificent; it was arranged in octagonal panels that were covered with decorative scroll work. There were balls and leaden leaves at the intersections. These were gilded, being the color of gold. Then Elizabeth stepped down to the main floor, beckoning to the kneeling men to rise. Elizabeth was dressed in a white silk dress which was covered with purple polka dots. Her sleeves were overly full. A ten-inch lace ruff was about her neck. Her face was painted white to cover scarring from smallpox; her hair was henna red. A gold inlaid fan with a mirror attached hung from a chain attached to her waist. She smiled and beckoned for the men to come forward and join her; each carried a bag, except Moone; he carried two.

"Cap'n Drake!" she said.

"He is a General, Your Highness!" the Captain of the guards corrected in a respectful voice, while nodding to Drake, who like the other three men was now on his knees.

"I know—I know. Gentlemen, come closer!" she said, smiling, exhibiting teeth that were almost black. "Give me your hand, General Drake—now buss me—" she said, and Drake gently pulled her to him. And she squeezed him.

"These men are officers of mine who made the voyage with me!" Drake said, pointing to them. Each had dropped his bag. "This is Tom Moone, my right hand. This is my brother, Tom Drake, who was in charge of my soldiers; and this is John Brewer, my bugler, and a brave soldier is he."

"Give me your hand, each of you!" Elizabeth said.

"All are from Devon," Drake explained as Elizabeth took the hand of each and squeezed it.

"I know of Devon bravery," she said, smiling.

"Your grace," Drake said.

"May I call you Captain?" Elizabeth asked, speaking to Drake. Her eyes brightly shined.

"Well, yes," Drake replied.

"That is because you will always be my Captain of the South Seas!" she explained, her eyes watering from emotion. "It is you who made it known to me—I have thought of you so much and wondered about your well being during these last three years!"

"And our thoughts were on you," Drake replied.

"And what do you have in those bags?" Elizabeth asked, her voice changing, as she now was speaking like a small girl.

"Many beautiful things—may we put them on this table?" Drake asked.

"Yes—of course!" she replied.

"We have bags of pearls for our Queen," Drake said, opening a chamois bag. He poured its contents onto the table. There were 20 grape-size pearls. They appeared to be almost identical in size and shape.

"Oh!" she exclaimed.

"And we have ten bags of them—but you may like the rubies better!" Drake said. And he opened a bag and poured a dozen matched rubies onto the table.

"Oh, I love them!" Elizabeth cried. She put several in her hands and rubbed them so as to develop their color. "They are gorgeous!"

"And we have a crown for your head," Drake said, holding a beautiful crown that was studded with stones. "May I?"

"Yes, please do!" she answered. And Drake gently set it on her head.

"And this cross," Drake said, holding up a foot-long gold cross that was covered with emeralds. It was attached to a heavy gold chain. "This is for our Protestant Queen!"

"Magnificent—"

"These are for you!" Drake said, pointing to the many other gold art objects that lay on the table. "They are for our Queen!"

"And you have more?"

"Yes, we have thirty-five to forty tons of silver and gold in Plymouth."

"My God!" she exclaimed, biting her lip.

"For England!" Drake said.

"And it is safely secured?" she asked.

"Yes—"

"Oh, I am so excited!" she rightly exclaimed, for her treasury was empty. "I shall use the treasure to begin an empire."

"And we have brought you the logs of the *Golden Hind*—my cousin, John Drake, and I drew and painted the world as we saw and explored it. Your Highness may find these to be interesting," he said, handing her a log, the Mercator map and two thick sketch books. Many of their sketches had been made on the daily logs; all would subsequently be lost while they were in her custody.

"I cannot wait to review them!"

"Captain Drury," she said to her vice chamberlain.

"Yes, Your Highness?"

"Would you entertain these three men while I discuss with my Captain Drake his great voyage. Some of the things that I wish to discuss with him will involve issues of state."

"Yes, of course," he said, deeply bowing.

Thereafter, when the heavy oak door closed behind the exiting men, Elizabeth said to Drake, pointing to the brass globe of the world, "Now, Captain, tell me about your voyage."

Thereafter, Drake related to the Queen many of the events of his voyage. He often utilized drawings from pages of his logs in order to explain his travels. And when Drake began to relate to Elizabeth about the events leading to the trial and execution of Doughty, Drake sensed that the Queen already knew of its happening; and she did, because she had previously interviewed John Wynter, Captain of the *Elizabeth*. He of course had given a very biased report of the events, relating it as though Drake had murdered Doughty.

"And was his execution necessary, Francis?"

"Well, yes; I could not control him; he was determined to share the command."

"Ah—"

"And that cannot be done at sea, especially on a dangerous voyage," Drake said, shaking his head. "There has to be one man responsible and answerable."

"The same is true of the land," she wistfully said, recalling that she had elected not to have a mate or children because she dared not share the throne with another.

"It may lack some legalities but the expedition would have failed if I had not done it."

"I understand—" she said, passing over it while pondering sketches of the trial and execution.

And thereafter, Drake related to her how the *Golden Hind* had traversed the Strait of Magellan in record time; then he explained

471

how it was shortly thereafter struck by a great storm, which blew his ship south for many days. And then he related to her of his discovery:

"There is no continent beneath the Strait!"

"Are you sure?"

"I saw the sea—it is an open body of water!"

"And so one does not have to use the Strait?"

"That is correct!" Drake replied, raising his head on hearing an aid enter the room.

"Yes?" Elizabeth curiously asked.

"Your Highness, Lord Burghley wishes to see you on a matter of importance."

"I am busy—" she said; her voice had impatience to it. "Tell Cecil—I will speak to him later."

"Yes—"

"And," she added, "Captain Drake and I will have our lunch in here. Bring red wine for me and a tankard of English ale for him!"

"I would like red wine, too, Your Majesty!"

"A man with taste—two glasses of red wine!"

"Yes, Your Majesty!"

And then Drake related to Elizabeth the highlights of many of his adventures on the coast of Chile.

"There is a mountain of silver on that coast, Elizabeth—I am sorry!" Drake, at his first meeting with Elizabeth, had mentioned such a mountain to her, though at the time he had thought that it was fictitious.

"Please, Francis, call me Elizabeth when we are together like this—oh, a mountain of silver!"

"It is the richest site of silver in the world!"

"And would you have done better if you had had the assistance of Wynter's ship?" she curiously asked.

"Greatly—we could have obtained twice the treasure. We possibly could have freed John Oxenham."

"He has been executed!" Elizabeth surely confided, though in truth he had not yet been executed. Yet he soon would die by hanging.

"I suspected it!" Drake replied, momentarily pondering the import of the message. But then he continued to relate his travels, doing it with sketches made by himself or John Drake. And finally he reached the part of his travels to the Far East, which included the Spice Islands and Java.

"And you think that the English can trade in these islands?" she asked.

"Yes, the Sultan of Ternate will trade—Baber hates the Portuguese. They are cruel masters. The Sultan of Ternate is already planning on doing business with England. I have arranged that. I think that our merchants could go there immediately and trade. They would of course need to arm themselves against not only the Portuguese and Spanish but the natives. But the rewards would be worth the risks."

"The crown needs an interest—"

"It possibly should be done as a joint venture," Drake replied, pointing out that it should be done with private and state money, which eventually would be done with the formation of the East India Company.

"Maybe we could form a company—make it a permanent venture!"

"I would invest!" Drake said.

"And Francis," she said. "I would like for you to take 10,000 pounds of the treasure for yourself before you send it to the Tower—how much does your crew deserve?"

"The same."

"And you will fairly divide it according to the service of each?"

"Yes—"

"And Francis, I expect that there will be repercussions from me keeping this treasure. Philip threatens—"

"Your Majesty," he said, being interrupted by an aid entering.

"Yes?"

"Ambassador Mendozo is here. He says that he must see you—"

"Tell him that Philip must remove his troops from Ireland before I will talk to the Ambassador again!"

"He has troops in Ireland?" Drake asked.

"Yes—and Philip threatens to send a great armada and invade England if I do what I am presently doing with you!"

"Well, the danger would still remain if you had elected to do otherwise!"

"I had come to that conclusion," she said smiling, adding, "and what do you suggest?"

"I would say singe Philip's beard—carry the fight to him!"

"And would my Captain of the South Seas like to play a role in doing that?"

"I would enjoy it, my Queen," Drake replied, grinning, indicating that he would relish it.

"I am proud of you, Francis," Elizabeth said, fondly looking onto the red face of the bearded Englishman, seeing in it the strength of England.

"And I of you!" Drake replied, bowing his head; then he raised his head and looked into her eyes. "For I willingly fight for my Queen—and I am glad that I can do homage to my Queen, for my Queen is England!"

POSTSCRIPT

And within the year, Elizabeth knighted Drake, doing it on the *Golden Hind*, which thereafter became a shrine on the Thames until age ended her existence. Drake even purchased a great Devon estate, Buckland Abbey, that was owned by his archrival Sir Richard Greenville, doing it deviously, as he purchased it through an intermediary. Greenville only discovered the name of the true purchaser after the deal was closed. And he was irate. Drake subsequently received many other honors: he became the Mayor of Plymouth; he became a member of Parliament; then he became an Admiral of the English Navy, where he was able to set the standards for all seamen who followed, not only in seamanship but in valor, as he personally led many daring forays against Spain, which kept Philip from attacking England. Then in 1588 Philip finally sent his armada to attack England. Drake was one of the admirals who drove this armada from the sea. And in turn, England became the world's greatest sea power.

Plymou[th]

New Albion

Madeira

Guatalco

Cape Verde
Isles

Cano

Caca
Fuego

Lima

Callao

Arica

Valparaiso

Rio La Plata

La Mocha

San Julian Bay

Magellan Strait

Cape Horn